INSTRUCTOR'S

World Literature

Donna Rosenberg

National Textbook Company
a division of *NTC Publishing Group* • Lincolnwood, Illinois USA

Cover Art: *Icarus*, plate 8 from *Jazz* by Henri Matisse. Paris, Tériade, 1947. Pochoir, printed in color, composition: 16¼ × 10¾″. Collection, The Museum of Modern Art, New York. The Louis E. Stern Collection. Photograph © 1992 The Museum of Modern Art, New York.

Cover Design: Linda Snow Shum

1994 Printing

Published by National Textbook Company, a division of NTC Publishing Group.
©1992 by NTC Publishing Group, 4255 West Touhy Avenue,
Lincolnwood (Chicago), Illinois 60646-1975 U.S.A.

    3 4 5 6 7 8 9 0 VP 9 8 7 6 5 4 3

Contents

Part One: Introduction to *World Literature* and This *Instructor's Manual*

The purpose of this *Instructor's Manual* is to facilitate your use of the *World Literature* student's text. The following section will give you an overview of the contents of this *Manual* and of the philosophy that shapes the instructional format of *World Literature*.

Part One of the *Manual* begins with the criteria for choosing the selections in *World Literature*. It includes teaching objectives and suggestions for using the text in the classroom, and it also includes charts that organize the contents of *World Literature* by genre, by major themes, and by particular literary techniques.

Part One also includes a section that explains how to use the instructional format of *World Literature* and this *Manual* to enhance your students' literary experience. It explains the many elements of the student's text and of the *Instructor's Manual*, and it includes a discussion of the Socratic method of questioning (one that emphasizes open-ended questions and multiple responses).

In addition, Part One includes suggestions for testing and evaluating students' knowledge and skills.

Part Two of this *Manual* is devoted to a detailed treatment of each of the seventy-seven selections in *World Literature*.

Finally, this *Manual* concludes with an up-to-date Selected Bibliography of works related to the selections in *World Literature*.

Choice of Selections in *World Literature*

When selecting works for inclusion in *World Literature*, I applied five important criteria:

1. *Global Scope.* *World Literature* is a truly global anthology in that it contains short stories, poems, and seven plays from around the world. In order to emphasize the global aspect of its contents, I have organized the selections into seven geographical sections: The Mediterranean, Continental Europe, Africa, The Far East, Latin America, North America, and Great Britain. Each geographical section contains many short stories and poems and one play. In addition to their global scope, the selections in *World Literature* include a variety of subjects and themes.

2. *Literary Quality.* Each selection included in *World Literature* is an outstanding work by a world-famous author. As you peruse the contents of the student's text, you will find many old favorites and—equally exciting—you can anticipate making many new friends.

3. *Appeal and Value.* I chose the selections in *World Literature* with three principal goals in mind. First, I wanted to promote the enjoyment and appreciation of great literature from around the world. Until recently, the concept of "world literature" has meant European literature. However, we owe it to ourselves and our students to become aware of the literary treasures that exist in other world cultures as well.

Next, I wanted to choose selections that would reveal how, for all their cultural differences, human beings through time and across space are members of one universal family. The selections in *World Literature* reveal how, for nearly three thousand years, people have asked themselves such questions as: Who am I? How should I lead my life? Is my primary responsibility to my community or to myself? What can sustain me as I face the uncertainties of living and the inevitability of death?

Like all human beings, the characters in these selections experience joy, tragedy, and difficult challenges. For them as for us, life includes the despair of failed dreams and the triumph of perseverance, the frustration of prejudice and the power of friendship, the danger of impulsive behavior and the value of self-discovery, the bondage of outworn tradition and the achievement of self-respect, the devastation of war and the delight in nature's beauty, the loss of loved ones and the joy of love.

Finally, I wanted the experience of reading and discussing fine literature to be fun, to be informative, and to be a stimulating intellectual experience. Therefore, in addition to its literary quality, each selection can provide interesting and enjoyable reading and can provoke stimulating classroom discussion. In the process of discussing the thoughts, feelings, conflicts, and choices of others, students become more sensitive to the human condition, more aware of the quality of their own relationships, and more knowledgeable about themselves.

4. *Complete and Unabridged.*   An important feature of *World Literature* is that each selection appears in its complete form. This approach respects the integrity of the work and also respects the need of readers to consider a work in its entirety in order to form a thoughtful response that is based on a close reading of the text.

5. *Modern Translations.*   Each non-English selection appears in a fine modern translation. Translators always must decide the extent to which they can remain true to the literal word while preserving the intended effect of the original work. They also accommodate their translations to the prevailing literary styles of their age. Modern readers are accustomed to hearing and reading English styles that achieve their power through language that is clear, concise, and direct. Consequently, given a choice of translations of literary classics, I rejected older, more complex and verbose translations in favor of those that translate the spirit of the original in a modern idiom. Because modern translations emphasize the intended, rather than the literal, meaning of a work, I found it more appropriate to analyze these selections in terms of their meaning rather than in terms of the particular writer's use of language. Therefore, when I analyze a writer's literary technique, you will find a greater emphasis on connotative and figurative language in the questions that relate to the selections from North America and Great Britain.

Teaching Objectives for *World Literature*

World Literature meets three primary objectives:

1. *To Foster an Enjoyment of Literature.*   In my opinion, an instructor's primary goal must be to create or foster the love of learning in his or her students. The study of

literature is of little use to those who discard it as soon as they leave the classroom. Something about the experience of reading and sharing through discussion must be enjoyable in itself, either because the process is enjoyable or because the student finds it to be of personal value, or both. Students should be exposed to the best in order to learn to distinguish it from what is ordinary or bad and, in the process, to develop a taste for the best.

The variety of selections in *World Literature* has the potential to provide something of interest and value for every student. I chose these particular selections because of their literary quality and because some aspect of each of them relates to students' own life-experiences. Each selection is interesting to read and stimulating to discuss. Students feel valuable and important when they can express their ideas in an accepting environment. Sharing their ideas with their classmates enables them to enrich their understanding of themselves and others.

2. *To Increase Awareness of Human Values, Attitudes, and Behavior.* Another major goal in the teaching of global literature is to encourage students to recognize a common humanity through time and across space. The selections in *World Literature* reveal that the human needs for love and friendship, for the respect of oneself and others, for a secure and beautiful environment, and for a sense of personal accomplishment know no boundaries. We understand and sympathize with Antigone in ancient Greece, with Jade in eighth-century China, with Rosendo in Argentina, and with Okeke in Nigeria. We are aware of ways in which their cultures differ from our own, but their stories teach us that the human bond that connects us is stronger than the differences that divide us. Armed with this understanding, we no longer view what is foreign as necessarily threatening. Instead, we view variety as stimulating and valuable; and we become interested in what we can learn from others.

3. *To Learn to Analyze Literature.* Finally, the goal of learning to analyze literature is valuable both as a way to appreciate each selection in *World Literature* and as a means of learning to distinguish any fine work of literature from ordinary writing. The questions students study under Analyzing Literary Technique lead them to discover important keys to the artistic quality of each story, poem, and play in *World Literature*. Students become aware of how a writer manipulates plot, narration, structure, and language in order to arouse particular reactions in the reader. As they learn to appreciate the writer's tools, students become more demanding of what they read and more skillful in their own creative writing.

Using *World Literature* in the Curriculum

Because *World Literature* is an anthology of excellent short stories, poems, and plays, it is ideally suited for use as an integral part of the standard English curriculum. Each selection includes the following supporting materials in the student's text:

- *An Introduction* highlights important biographical, historical, and literary information. It is designed to provide students with a framework for appreciating the selection while preserving their ability to discover and experience the work for themselves.

- *Footnotes* explain foreign words and allusions that appear in the selection in order to aid students' comprehension.
- *Interpretive and analytical questions* lead students toward an understanding of both content and style and are designed to stimulate class discussion and thoughtful analysis of important issues.
- *Expository and creative writing assignments* provide students with the opportunity both to analyze the work in depth and to enlarge upon it in an imaginative way. These questions and expository writing assignments are also useful for purposes of testing and evaluating students' knowledge and skills.
- *The Glossary of Literary Terms* at the back of *World Literature* enriches students' appreciation of writing as an artistic pursuit.

Moreover, this *Manual* includes the following supporting materials for each selection:

- *An Introduction* provides an authoritative literary analysis of the work.
- *Questions for students' responses in their Private Literary Journals (PLJ)* are designed to help each student relate in personal terms to an important theme in the selection.
- *A list of appropriate Literary Terms* alerts you to the importance of these techniques in the selection.
- *A group of short-answer questions and answers* test factual knowledge of the particular selection.
- *Complete possible answers to all interpretive and analytical questions* help you prepare for class discussion.
- *Information about expository and creative writing assignments* prepares for students' writing.
- *A list of Further Reading* enables you to guide interested students toward additional works by the same author.

In addition to the materials in this *Manual* that relate to each selection in *World Literature*, this *Manual* provides you with suggestions for discussing the selections, for teaching expository writing, and for evaluating and testing students' knowledge and skills.

In addition to being used within the standard English curriculum, *World Literature* is also ideally suited to be the text for a global literature elective. Moreover, it can be used in an English–social studies core program that focuses on the study of world cultures or as a literature supplement to a course in world history.

In whatever way you choose to use *World Literature* in your curriculum, you may use part or all of the material in the student's text. If you wish, you can choose the selections that you want to use based on a particular type of interrelationship, such as culture, genre, theme, or literary technique. Depending on how much world literature you wish to include in your program, *World Literature* can meet your needs for a week, a term, or a year.

The table of contents in *World Literature* organizes the selections by geographical location. The following three charts organize the selections by genre (Chart A), by theme (Chart B), and by literary technique (Chart C).

Chart A
Selections Organized by Genre
Note: Page numbers refer to student's text.

	Short Story	Play	Poem
The Mediterranean			
Akhenaton (pp. 2–8)			x
David (pp. 8–10)			x
Sappho (pp. 11–13)			x
Sophocles (pp. 14–67)		x	
Dante (pp. 68–70)			x
Pirandello (pp. 71–76)	x		
Agnon (pp. 77–100)	x		
García Lorca (pp. 101–11)			x
Continental Europe			
Schiller (pp. 114–16)			x
Andersen (pp. 117–28)	x		
Dostoyevski (pp. 129–34)	x		
Ibsen (pp. 135–212)		x	
Tolstoy (pp. 213–29)	x		
Lagerlöf (pp. 230–46)	x		
Chekhov (pp. 247–64)	x		
Colette (pp. 265–69)	x		
Rilke (pp. 270–72)			x
Kafka (pp. 273–80)	x		
Sartre (pp. 281–301)	x		
Camus (pp. 302–15)	x		
Africa			
Dahomey Traditional (pp. 318–19)			x
Casely-Hayford (pp. 320–30)	x		
Paton (pp. 331–39)	x		
Senghor (pp. 340–42)			x
Dadié (pp. 343–45)			x
Lessing (pp. 346–55)	x		
Gordimer (pp. 356–69)	x		

Chart A
Selections Organized by Genre *(continued)*
Note: Page numbers refer to student's text.

	Short Story	Play	Poem
Diop (pp. 370–72)			x
Achebe (pp. 373–80)	x		
Ogot (pp. 381–90)	x		
Soyinka (pp. 391–421)		x	
Head (pp. 422–39)	x		
The Far East Li Po (pp. 442–45)			x
Jiang Fang (pp. 445–55)	x		
Zeami (pp. 455–63)		x	
Tagore (pp. 464–68)			x
Tayama (pp. 468–83)	x		
Lu Hsün (pp. 484–501)	x		
Akutagawa (pp. 501–10)	x		
Kawabata (pp. 511–16)	x		
Hayashi (pp. 517–30)	x		
Ting Ling (pp. 531–37)	x		
Narayan (pp. 538–44)	x		
Chandar (pp. 545–55)	x		
Latin America Mistral (pp. 558–60)			x
Borges (pp. 561–68)	x		
Neruda (pp. 569–72)			x
Ocampo (pp. 573–76)	x		
Rosa (pp. 577–83)	x		
Bombal (pp. 584–95)	x		
Paz (pp. 596–98)			x
Solórzano (pp. 599–612)		x	
Donoso (pp. 613–29)	x		
Castellanos (pp. 630–32)			x
García Márquez (pp. 633–41)	x		

Chart A
Selections Organized by Genre *(concluded)*

Note: Page numbers refer to student's text.

	Short Story	Play	Poem
North America			
Zuñi Traditional (pp. 644–46)			x
Poe (pp. 647–56)	x		
Whitman (pp. 657–60)			x
Dickinson (pp. 661–63)			x
O'Neill (pp. 664–81)		x	
Hemingway (pp. 682–87)	x		
Hughes (pp. 687–89)			x
Welty (pp. 690–99)	x		
Jackson (pp. 700–706)	x		
Munro (pp. 707–17)	x		
Walker (pp. 718–23)	x		
Great Britain			
Shakespeare (pp. 726–97)		x	
Milton (pp. 798–800)			x
Wordsworth (pp. 801–3)			x
Barrett Browning (pp. 804–5)			x
Brontë (pp. 806–8)			x
Rossetti (pp. 809–25)			x
Conrad (pp. 826–48)	x		
Yeats (pp. 849–51)			x
Joyce (pp. 852–59)	x		
Eliot (pp. 860–66)			x
Mansfield (pp. 867–73)	x		

Chart B
Selections Organized by Theme

Note: Page numbers refer to student's text.

	fantasy and imagination	friendships	the individual and society	justice and dignity	love and romance	the natural world	roots and origins	self-discovery	values and beliefs	war and peace	youth and age
The Mediterranean											
Akhenaton (pp. 2–8)							x		x		
David (pp. 8–10)									x		
Sappho (pp. 11–13)		x									
Sophocles (pp. 14–67)			x	x				x	x		x
Dante (pp. 68–70)					x						
Pirandello (pp. 71–76)			x					x		x	
Agnon (pp. 77–100)				x	x						
García Lorca (pp. 101–11)		x						x	x		
Continental Europe											
Schiller (pp. 114–16)						x			x		
Andersen (pp. 117–28)	x								x		
Dostoyevski (pp. 129–34)				x					x		
Ibsen (pp. 135–212)			x	x	x			x	x		
Tolstoy (pp. 213–29)			x						x		
Lagerlöf (pp. 230–46)		x				x					
Chekhov (pp. 247–64)			x			x					
Colette (pp. 265–69)						x					
Rilke (pp. 270–72)							x		x		
Kafka (pp. 273–80)	x		x					x			
Sartre (pp. 281–301)									x	x	
Camus (pp. 302–15)		x			x				x		
Africa											
Dahomey Traditional (pp. 318–19)							x		x		
Casely-Hayford (pp. 320–30)							x				x
Paton (pp. 331–39)		x			x				x		

Chart B
Selections Organized by Theme *(continued)*
Note: Page numbers refer to student's text.

	fantasy and imagination	friendships	the individual and society	justice and dignity	love and romance	the natural world	roots and origins	self-discovery	values and beliefs	war and peace	youth and age
Senghor (pp. 340–42)							x		x		
Dadié (pp. 343–45)						x	x		x		
Lessing (pp. 346–55)						x		x			
Gordimer (pp. 356–69)			x					x			
Diop (pp. 370–72)							x		x		
Achebe (pp. 373–80)					x						
Ogot (pp. 381–90)					x				x		x
Soyinka (pp. 391–421)			x					x			
Head (pp. 422–39)			x		x		x				
The Far East											
Li Po (pp. 442–45)			x							x	
Jiang Fang (pp. 445–55)					x				x		
Zeami (pp. 455–63)	x			x	x						
Tagore (pp. 464–68)			x						x		
Tayama (pp. 468–83)			x	x						x	
Lu Hsün (pp. 484–501)			x	x					x		
Akutagawa (pp. 501–10)							x		x		
Kawabata (pp. 511–16)						x			x		
Hayashi (pp. 517–30)				x	x					x	
Ting Ling (pp. 531–37)			x	x						x	
Narayan (pp. 538–44)			x	x							
Chandar (pp. 545–55)		x			x					x	
Latin America											
Mistral (pp. 558–60)						x			x		x
Borges (pp. 561–68)		x						x			x
Neruda (pp. 569–72)							x		x		

Chart B
Selections Organized by Theme *(continued)*

Note: Page numbers refer to student's text.

	fantasy and imagination	friendships	the individual and society	justice and dignity	love and romance	the natural world	roots and origins	self-discovery	values and beliefs	war and peace	youth and age
Ocampo (pp. 573–76)			X								X
Rosa (pp. 577–83)	X		X								X
Bombal (pp. 584–95)					X	X		X			
Paz (pp. 596–98)					X				X		
Solórzano (pp. 599–612)					X		X				
Donoso (pp. 613–29)		X	X								X
Castellanos (p. 630–32)		X			X						
García Márquez (pp. 633–41)	X		X	X					X		
North America Zuñi Traditional (pp. 644–46)							X		X		
Poe (pp. 647–56)		X						X			
Whitman (p. 657–60)			X			X		X			
Dickinson (pp. 661–63)		X							X		
O'Neill (pp. 664–81)			X			X			X		
Hemingway (pp. 682–87)		X			X				X		
Hughes (pp. 687–89)			X	X			X		X		
Welty (pp. 690–99)			X	X							
Jackson (pp. 700–706)			X	X							
Munro (pp. 707–17)		X		X							X
Walker (pp. 718–23)			X	X					X		
Great Britain Shakespeare (pp. 726–97)	X		X		X				X		X
Milton (pp. 798–800)			X						X		
Wordsworth (pp. 801–3)						X					X
Barrett Browning (pp. 804–5)					X			X			

Chart B

Selections Organized by Theme *(concluded)*

Note: Page numbers refer to student's text.

	fantasy and imagination	friendships	the individual and society	justice and dignity	love and romance	the natural world	roots and origins	self-discovery	values and beliefs	war and peace	youth and age
Brontë (pp. 806–8)			x						x		
Rossetti (pp. 809–25)	x	x							x		
Conrad (pp. 826–48)			x					x	x		
Yeats (pp. 849–51)						x			x		
Joyce (pp. 852–59)					x			x			x
Eliot (pp. 860–66)			x						x		
Mansfield (pp. 867–73)								x		x	x

Chart C
Selections Organized by Literary Technique

Note: Page numbers refer to student's text.

	allusion	antihero	apostrophe	characterization	comedy	connotative language	dialogue	doppelgänger or Shadow	epiphany	figurative language	foreshadowing	free verse	hero	imagery	irony	leitmotif or motif	lyric	narrative perspective	paradox	reversal	satire	setting	sound devices	symbolism	theme	tone	tragedy
The Mediterranean																											
Akhenaton (pp. 2–8)			X														X		X							X	
David (pp. 8–10)														X			X								X	X	
Sappho (pp. 11–13)	X		X							X							X										
Sophocles (pp. 14–67)	X			X		X	X	X		X	X		X		X		X	X	X	X				X	X	X	X
Dante (pp. 68–70)			X											X			X										
Pirandello (pp. 71–76)				X											X				X		X				X		
Agnon (pp. 77–100)	X		X	X							X				X				X	X					X	X	X
García Lorca (pp. 101–11)										X	X			X	X		X	X	X			X	X	X			
Continental Europe																											
Schiller (pp. 114–16)	X							X		X					X		X		X						X		
Andersen (pp. 117–28)				X							X				X			X	X		X				X	X	
Dostoyevski (pp. 129–34)				X				X							X				X		X				X	X	
Ibsen (pp. 135–212)				X			X	X			X		X		X				X		X				X		X

Chart C
Selections Organized by Literary Technique *(continued)*

Note: Page numbers refer to student's text.

Selection	allusion	antihero	apostrophe	characterization	comedy	connotative language	dialogue	doppelgänger or Shadow	epiphany	figurative language	foreshadowing	free verse	hero	imagery	irony	leitmotif or motif	lyric	narrative perspective	paradox	reversal	satire	setting	sound devices	symbolism	theme	tone	tragedy
Tolstoy (pp. 213–29)				X							X			X	X				X		X			X	X		
Lagerlöf (pp. 230–46)											X		X		X			X						X	X		
Chekhov (pp. 247–64)				X											X	X		X	X		X	X				X	
Colette (pp. 265–69)				X							X				X	X		X	X		X	X				X	
Rilke (pp. 270–72)			X							X							X										
Kafka (pp. 273–80)				X				X						X	X			X	X			X		X	X	X	
Sartre (pp. 281–301)		X		X										X	X			X	X					X	X		
Camus (pp. 302–15)		X								X					X			X				X	X	X	X		X
Africa																											
Dahomey Traditional (pp. 318–19)																	X								X	X	
Casely-Hayford (pp. 320–30)				X											X			X									
Paton (pp. 331–39)				X						X	X				X							X	X	X	X		
Senghor (pp. 340–42)										X	X			X	X								X	X	X		X
Dadié (pp. 343–45)										X				X			X						X	X	X		

Chart C
Selections Organized by Literary Technique (continued)

Note: Page numbers refer to student's text.

	tragedy	tone	theme	symbolism	sound devices	setting	satire	reversal	paradox	narrative perspective	lyric	leitmotif or motif	irony	imagery	hero	free verse	foreshadowing	figurative language	epiphany	doppelgänger or Shadow	dialogue	connotative language	comedy	characterization	apostrophe	antihero	allusion
Lessing (pp. 346–55)			×	×		×				×			×					×	×			×					
Gordimer (pp. 356–69)		×	×	×		×	×			×			×	×										×			
Diop (pp. 370–72)			×						×		×		×					×									
Achebe (pp. 373–80)		×	×			×							×				×							×			
Ogot (pp. 381–90)							×			×			×				×				×		×	×			
Soyinka (pp. 391–421)		×			×		×	×					×											×		×	×
Head (pp. 422–39)			×			×				×			×		×		×	×				×		×		×	×
The Far East																											
Li Po (pp. 442–45)	×		×			×				×			×		×		×							×			
Jiang Fang (pp. 445–55)	×		×								×		×											×			
Zeami (pp. 455–63)			×	×			×		×									×			×						×
Tagore (pp. 464–68)		×	×	×		×							×														
Tayama (pp. 468–83)	×			×	×					×			×				×	×									
Lu Hsün (pp. 484–501)	×		×	×		×			×				×											×			

Chart C
Selections Organized by Literary Technique *(continued)*

Note: Page numbers refer to student's text.

	tragedy	tone	theme	symbolism	sound devices	setting	satire	reversal	paradox	narrative perspective	lyric	leitmotif or motif	irony	imagery	hero	free verse	foreshadowing	figurative language	epiphany	doppelgänger or Shadow	dialogue	connotative language	comedy	characterization	apostrophe	antihero	allusion
Akutagawa (pp. 501–10)			×			×				×			×											×			
Kawabata (pp. 511–16)		×	×	×	×					×			×									×			×		
Hayashi (pp. 517–30)		×	×			×							×		×			×						×			
Ting Ling (pp. 531–37)	×	×	×	×	×																	×					
Narayan (pp. 538–44)	×		×						×	×			×				×							×			
Chandar (pp. 545–55)	×		×			×			×				×		×									×			
Latin America																											
Mistral (pp. 558–60)											×							×				×				×	×
Borges (pp. 561–68)		×	×	×					×	×			×				×			×				×			×
Neruda (pp. 569–72)					×		×				×		×					×									×
Ocampo (pp. 573–76)			×							×			×				×							×			
Rosa (pp. 577–83)			×	×		×				×										×				×		×	

Chart C
Selections Organized by Literary Technique (continued)

Note: Page numbers refer to student's text.

Selection	tragedy	tone	theme	symbolism	sound devices	setting	satire	reversal	paradox	narrative perspective	lyric	leitmotif or motif	irony	imagery	hero	free verse	foreshadowing	figurative language	epiphany	doppelgänger or Shadow	dialogue	connotative language	comedy	characterization	apostrophe	antihero	allusion
Bombal (pp. 584–95)				X		X			X	X		X	X					X				X		X			
Paz (pp. 596–98)				X	X						X			X				X									
Solórzano (pp. 599–612)	X		X	X		X			X				X								X		X	X			
Donoso (pp. 613–29)	X		X	X					X				X				X	X						X			
Castellanos (pp. 630–32)			X	X			X			X	X	X	X	X			X										
García Márquez (pp. 633–41)	X	X	X						X				X										X				X
North America																											
Zuñi Traditional (pp. 644–46)				X						X	X	X		X	X			X							X		
Poe (pp. 647–56)		X			X				X		X		X							X				X		X	
Whitman (pp. 657–60)									X		X					X						X			X		
Dickinson (pp. 661–63)																X						X					
O'Neill (pp. 664–81)		X		X	X	X			X				X				X				X			X			
Hemingway (pp. 682–87)		X			X								X						X			X		X	X		
Hughes (pp. 687–89)	X	X	X	X														X						X	X		
Welty (pp. 690–99)		X	X	X		X				X								X						X			

Chart C
Selections Organized by Literary Technique *(concluded)*

Note: Page numbers refer to student's text.

Selection	allusion	antihero	apostrophe	characterization	comedy	connotative language	dialogue	doppelgänger or Shadow	epiphany	figurative language	foreshadowing	free verse	hero	imagery	irony	leitmotif or motif	lyric	narrative perspective	paradox	reversal	satire	setting	sound devices	symbolism	theme	tone	tragedy
Jackson (pp. 700–706)	X			X									X		X				X		X			X	X	X	
Munro (pp. 707–17)				X						X						X		X	X					X			
Walker (pp. 718–23)	X			X	X					X						X		X						X	X		
Great Britain																											
Shakespeare (pp. 726–97)	X			X			X			X	X		X	X	X		X		X	X		X	X	X	X	X	
Milton (pp. 798–800)										X				X	X		X		X					X	X	X	
Wordsworth (pp. 801–3)										X					X		X		X				X			X	
Barrett Browning (pp. 804–5)										X							X						X				
Brontë (pp. 806–8)						X		X							X								X				
Rossetti (pp. 809–25)				X		X		X	X	X	X		X	X	X	X	X	X	X			X	X	X	X		
Conrad (pp. 826–48)		X		X		X			X	X	X				X							X	X	X		X	X
Yeats (pp. 849–51)	X									X		X															
Joyce (pp. 852–59)	X									X				X				X						X			
Eliot (pp. 860–66)	X			X		X		X		X	X			X			X		X				X	X	X	X	
Mansfield (pp. 867–73)				X				X	X	X	X							X	X					X	X	X	

Techniques for Teaching Selections in *World Literature*

This section of the *Manual* includes specific suggestions for using the many instructional aids that are included in *World Literature*.

Private Literary Journal (PLJ)

The use of a Private Literary Journal (PLJ) permits students to relate in a personal, nonthreatening way to the principal issues and values in each selection while retaining their right to privacy. Consequently, it is imperative that these journals remain the private property of their authors and that these questions do not become the focus of class discussion.

I have designed the PLJ concept to be used after your students have read the introduction in the student's text and before they read the selection itself. The open-ended questions that are listed in connection with the PLJ motivate students to think about and record their own attitudes and experiences before they encounter the protagonist's choices in the selection. Thus, the PLJ functions as an additional framework for understanding and appreciating the selection. In order to preserve your students' opportunity to discover and experience each selection for themselves, do not discuss the relationship that exists between the PLJ questions and issues in the work that they are about to read.

Selection Introductions

Studies in the psychology of learning reveal that just as seeds strewn on cement will not sprout, people cannot understand, remember, and enjoy what they read unless they possess a background or framework that enables them to relate the selection to some aspect of their own experience. This is the purpose of the two introductions to each selection. One precedes the selection in the student's text; the other opens the discussion of the selection in this *Manual*.

Introductions in the *Student's Text*

My goal in writing student's text introductions was to provide you and your students with a framework for understanding and appreciating each selection and its author while permitting your students to discover and experience the work for themselves. Each of these introductions contains information about the author's stature, the author's life, factors in the culture that influenced the author, and aspects of the author's literary focus that relate to the selection that follows. Because of the need to conserve space, most introductions in the student's text are about a page in length. However, wherever necessary, such as in my discussions of *Antigone, The Tempest, The Damask Drum*, and ''The New Year's Sacrifice,'' I have extended the length of the introduction in order to provide additional information that will help students understand and appreciate the work.

Introductions in This *Manual*

My goal in writing the introductions that appear in this *Manual* was to provide you with an authoritative literary analysis of each selection that, in the process, relates the work to human behavior so that you can help your students gain insights into themselves and others. This is not to say that mine is the only possible literary analysis. Any analysis that can be supported with details from the selection and that is consistent with all of the details in that selection may be equally valid. However, these introductions will give you a foundation on which to build; they supply the framework for the possible answers contained in this *Manual* to the questions that you will find under Understanding the Selection and Analyzing Literary Technique in the student's text.

List of Literary Terms

The lists of Literary Terms that follows the PLJ assignments are for your own information and use. They prepare you for stylistic devices that you will find in a particular selection. The questions in Analyzing Literary Technique involve a discussion of how most of these techniques are used in the work, and I usually define each term that I use. I also have defined each term in the Glossary of Literary Terms that is located at the end of the student's text. Often, an expository writing assignment will ask students to analyze what the writer achieves by using one or more of these techniques. Such a question or writing assignment can also be used as part of a test or evaluation of your students' knowledge.

Reading for Understanding and Appreciation

You may wish to advise your students to prepare for a discussion in the following way. Ask them to read the selection twice, first quickly and then slowly. Their superficial reading will acquaint them with the general content of the selection and will provide a framework for integrating the knowledge that they will acquire from their careful reading. Thus, the second reading will build upon the first and will increase your students' ability to understand and appreciate the selection's content, structure, and language.

Following their second reading, ask your students to write down their opinions of the selection, their reasons for their opinions, and any questions that the work has raised in their minds. Tell them that any response will be acceptable as long as they can support it with details in the selection. Explain that you are not interested in a summary of the work, since everyone will have read it. Also explain that they should focus on the selection that is about to be discussed; this is not the time to discuss other works or experiences. Finally, explain that you will call on everyone before beginning an open discussion. This approach gives each student something personal to contribute to the preliminary discussion. It validates each individual's response to the work, before that response is influenced by the opinions of others and before the emphasis of the discussion shifts to an analysis of particular aspects of the work.

Before beginning any discussion of the work, you may wish to use the Comprehension Questions that appear with each selection in this *Manual* after the Literary Terms.

Comprehension Questions

I designed these Comprehension Questions as a way for you to be certain that your students have read the selection and have grasped its obvious points. You may choose to use the questions for discussion, or as a way of testing and evaluating the knowledge of less able students, or, in conjunction with more interpretive questions, as a way of testing and evaluating the knowledge of your more able students.

Discussing Selections

As a teacher, I recommend conducting class discussions by using the Socratic method, a method of shared inquiry. It involves asking open-ended interpretive questions to which more than one correct answer often exists, and it places the burden of the discussion and the answers upon the students rather than upon the instructor. Some answers are better than others in that they are consistent with all of the details in the selection. However, students will often have different opinions that are equally supported by details in the selection, and to close a discussion without resolving all differences of opinion is perfectly acceptable.

It often works best to open a discussion with a preliminary activity in which you call upon each student to read from his or her prepared response. Remind your students that discussion of their points of view will occur later, after everyone has had an initial opportunity to respond. Without being critical, you should question anyone whose response is based on incorrect facts, and you may also question anyone whose opinion needs clarification. However, it is important to give everyone the opportunity to contribute before any discussion occurs.

This approach enhances students' self-esteem and encourages their active involvement in a literature program. Thus, the Socratic method enables students to become active and involved participants in their own education. Many among them will read the selection more than twice in order to contribute to the discussion, and you will find that they will discover many of the issues that you would choose to discuss.

You will probably find it very useful to take notes on your students' responses. These notes will remind you of questions to discuss, and they will enable you to give your students credit for their opinions and ideas. During this preliminary activity, accept all contributions that are based on a reading of the selection that is factually correct. Remember that a response to a work of literature depends as much upon the experiences and attitudes of the reader as upon an accurate reading. When everyone has contributed, you will be ready to discuss the selection. You will have three sources of questions available to you: your students' questions; your own questions; and the questions that follow the particular selection in *World Literature*.

Understanding the Selection: Interpretive Questions and Possible Answers

These questions focus on understanding the content of the work on an interpretive level. They emphasize inferential thinking and open-ended class discussion, and they prepare students for thoughtful expository and creative writing. These questions can engage the attention of your students for an entire class period. Because the questions may have more than one correct answer, this *Manual* provides a variety of possible answers. You and your students may find other answers, and you should accept any answer that is consistent with all of the details in the selection.

You will notice that certain answers in this *Manual* have an asterisk preceding the question number. These asterisks relate to particular writing assignments that you will find listed under Writing About Literature. Once you are aware of the relationship between the question and the writing assignment, you can choose to discuss these questions as preparation for the assignment, or you can choose to ignore these questions in order to test or evaluate your students' knowledge of the selection. For example, the questions that relate to characterization and theme are excellent ways of testing and evaluating your students' knowledge of a particular selection.

Analyzing Literary Technique: Analytical Questions and Possible Answers
These questions focus on understanding the structure and style of the work in order to appreciate it as a work of art. They deal with such aspects as narrative perspective, foreshadowing, irony, symbolism, and figurative language. I usually briefly define the particular literary term as part of the question. I also have defined each term in the Glossary of Literary Terms that is located at the back of the student's text.

Like the questions in Understanding the Selection, these also prepare students for thoughtful expository and creative writing. They, too, can engage the attention of your students for an entire class period. Moreover, they, too, often have more than one correct answer, so that this *Manual* provides a variety of possible answers. Here too, you and your students may find other answers, and you should accept any answer that is supported by specific details in the selection.

Once again, you will notice that certain answers in this *Manual* have an asterisk preceding the question number. As with the Understanding the Selection questions, these asterisks relate to particular writing assignments that you will find listed under Writing About Literature. You can choose to discuss these questions as preparation for the assignment, or you can ignore these questions in order to test or evaluate your students' knowledge of the selection. For example, the questions that relate to narrative perspective and symbolism are excellent for testing and evaluating your students' knowledge of a particular selection.

Glossary of Literary Terms

For the convenience of your students, a Glossary of Literary Terms is located at the back of the student's text. It defines the terms used in *World Literature*, including literary techniques, literary movements, and terms that relate to the relevant psychological aspects of behavior. At the end of each explanation, your students will find a sampling of the selections in *World Literature* that illustrate the use of the particular term. In this way, the Glossary prepares them to analyze the selections more thoughtfully and to write about them with greater understanding and in greater depth.

Writing About Literature

Teaching Expository Writing
Those of you whose students know how to write an expository essay may prefer to move directly to the next section, Writing an Expository Essay, which relates directly to the *World Literature* student's text. However, if your students need help with expository writing, and if you are not obligated to follow a particular method of instruction, the following approach may be useful to you.

I begin the teaching of expository writing with a formal approach because a specific format enables students to understand exactly what to do and how to do it. I use shorter works, such as the short stories and poems in *World Literature*, because they provide enough detail to permit students to learn how to write an introduction that states the subject of their essay and provides background material; at least one core paragraph that states the major point of the essay and discusses two or three examples of this point, using direct quotations from the text that support each of these examples; and a good conclusion. (I discuss these components in greater detail in the section, Evaluating and Grading an Expository Essay.)

Once students are comfortable with the procedure, they feel competent to handle the complexity of longer works, such as novels and plays, which support three or more core paragraphs, each of which is devoted to a discussion of a major point that the student must support with three or more examples from the text. Finally, students who have mastered this approach can discard the rigid structure and write interesting essays that, regardless of length, are both organized and scholarly.

Thinking must precede writing. Consequently, I begin a writing assignment with two concrete prewriting activities that I assign as independent work in class, since I want to supervise and evaluate each student's individual performance. First, I ask my students to brainstorm possible topics related to the assigned subject and to gather and make note of the direct quotations from the text that support each topic. In this way, they learn that some topics do not receive enough support in the text to be suitable for an essay, while other topics can be strengthened by grouping them. My students' close examination of the selection enables them to choose their major points and to be certain of their supporting details before they progress to their next step, which is to create an outline.

In my experience, without proper planning, students' literary essays can be particularly weak in two areas. First, students may not support their examples with direct quotations from the text, and consequently they may make statements about the selection that are wrong. Second, when they use direct quotations, they may not explain how each quotation relates both to the example it supports and to the point of the paragraph, and consequently they may choose quotations that are not appropriate. Their analysis of these quotations is a major aspect of their essays, and it permits you, the instructor, to evaluate their intellectual growth.

Because students are willing to make changes before they have invested themselves in their writing, I use an outline that reveals their problems at the pre-writing stage, a time when it is easy to find and correct them. My outline form reflects the fact that each example that supports the major point of a core paragraph must have two subpoints: first, a direct quotation that supports that example; and second, the student's explanation of how or why the particular quotation supports both the example and the major point of that core paragraph. Consequently, when it is complete, this outline contains all of the ideas that students will include in their first draft of the essay.

Since my students now know exactly what they are going to say, they feel free to concentrate on how well they can express their ideas and create smooth transitions in a first draft. Meanwhile, I have been observing their work in process, answering their questions, asking leading questions, praising their strengths, and evaluating their progress.

Writing an Expository Essay

Each selection in *World Literature* is accompanied by at least one suggestion for an expository essay that emphasizes critical thinking skills. When these assignments involve analyzing the author's use of a particular literary technique or the way in which the work is consistent with the principles of a particular literary movement, I have included a definition of the literary term or information about the movement. However, these terms are also defined in the Glossary of Literary Terms that is located at the back of the student's text. I often include suggestions to help students choose a focus for their essays, and I may include directions for organizing their essays as well.

You will notice that the explanations of these assignments in this *Manual* are followed by such directions as "See **U.P.** or **A.L.T.** question — above." This direction refers you back to the answers with the asterisks that relate to this particular assignment. **U.P.** and **U.S.** refer to Understanding the Poem, the Play, or the Story; **A.L.T.** refers to Analyzing Literary Technique. Once you are aware of the relationship between the questions and the writing assignment, you can choose to discuss these questions as preparation for the assignment, or you can choose to ignore these questions in order to test or evaluate your students' knowledge of the selection.

Writing Creatively

Each selection in *World Literature* is accompanied by at least one suggestion for creative writing that focuses on some aspect of the selection and enlarges upon it in an imaginative way. For example, some assignments involve continuing a story or telling it from the point of view of a different character. I usually include a group of leading questions to help students choose a focus for their creative piece, and I often give them the choice of writing in prose or in poetry.

Students who are uneasy about writing poetry will find it easy to use the following technique. First, they should write their selection in prose, with attention both to detail and to descriptive language. Next, they should remove all but the essential words from each sentence. Then they should arrange these words in a poetic form that pleases them. (Many students will find it easiest to write in free verse, without the constrictions of regular rhythm and rhyme.) Finally, they should work to improve the poetic content and form of their work by sharpening the focus of their ideas and by improving their choice and arrangement of words.

You will notice that the explanations of these assignments in this *Manual* are usually followed by "**(PLJ)**," which refers to the students' Private Literary Journal. Often students' responses to the questions listed under PLJ (located after the Introduction to each selection in this *Manual*) can lead them to imagine how another character might respond to the situation presented in the selection.

Occasionally, I have also included the directions "See **U.P.** or **A.L.T.** question — above." This direction refers you back to the answers with the asterisks that relate to this particular assignment. **U.P.** and **U.S.** refer to Understanding the Poem, the Play, or the Story; **A.L.T.** refers to Analyzing Literary Technique.

Evaluating Students' Knowledge and Skills

Using Tests for the Purpose of Evaluation
The Comprehension Questions and answers that follow the list of Literary Terms for each selection in this *Manual* are a fine way to evaluate whether students have read and understood the facts in each selection. Even less able students can answer these questions.

Many of the questions that you will find under Understanding the Selection, such as those devoted to characterization and theme, and under Analyzing Literary Technique, such as those devoted to narrative perspective, irony, and symbolism, are excellent for testing and evaluating more sophisticated knowledge. Depending on the ability of your students, you can use them as they are, or you can expand upon them.

Using Expository Essays for the Purpose of Evaluation
Expository writing is a superb test of the knowledge and skills that your students have acquired. The writing of an essay demands that students select, organize, analyze, and draw conclusions about some aspect of a work of literature. Many of the expository writing assignments that deal with characterization or with an analysis of a writer's use of a particular literary technique are excellent for this purpose. These are often very similar to the questions under Analyzing Literary Technique that support them, but they are expressed in a more complex form and demand a more complex response to the subject.

It is possible to give one of these expository writing assignments as an essay test to be written in class during one period. If you create a test that has four major points that your students are expected to discuss, such as a brief analysis of why Creon, in *Antigone*, is a traditional Greek hero, you can grade each essay from A to D, depending on how many of these points are stated in the answer. You can use pluses and minuses to reflect skimpy or excellent use of supporting detail and analysis. Permitting students to use their texts for such a test enables them to use direct quotations to support their ideas. However, remind your students that, in order to have enough time to finish their essay, they should outline their points before beginning to write so that they will know what they are going to write and where to look for their documentation.

In a longer and more complex essay, it is possible to test and evaluate students' critical thinking skills and knowledge by having them compare and contrast two appropriate selections that have already been discussed individually in class. While it is possible to write such an essay by discussing first one work and then the other, it is more effective to take one point at a time and to compare or contrast the two selections side by side.

Moreover, if you have exposed your students to a complete analysis of one selection in *World Literature*, it is possible to evaluate their knowledge and skills by assigning them a similar selection in their text to read and analyze independently. In order to feel comfortable with this type of assignment, your students must know how to analyze a particular aspect of a selection, such as characterization, theme, or style, and they must know how to write such an essay.

One approach is to assign the reading of the story for homework and to use the next class period for pre-writing activities under your personal supervision. By observing this stage of the writing process, you can evaluate how each student is progressing, and your students will feel more comfortable knowing that you are present to provide encouragement and support. If writing an outline is part of your procedure, it is valuable for your students and easy for you to make the outline the focal point of the assignment and to evaluate that.

Another approach is to assign the entire project as an independent activity. If your students are familiar with your expectations and have had enough experience in writing about literature, they will perform well without your direct supervision.

The three charts in this *Manual* that organize the selections by genre (Chart A), by theme (Chart B), and by literary technique (Chart C) will guide you to choose appropriately paired selections to compare and contrast. For example, the stories by Alan Paton and Nadine Gordimer both deal with apartheid in South Africa, those by Fyodor Dostoyevski and Lu Hsün both focus on the plight of the outcast in society, those by James Joyce and Doris Lessing both focus on initiation, and those by Fumiko Hayashi and Krishan Chandar both deal with the aftermath of war. The plays by Sophocles and Eugene O'Neill can be paired tragedies, and the stories by Joseph Conrad and Franz Kafka can be paired as night journeys. Moreover, if you wish your students to focus on an analysis of literary technique, the stories by Silvina Ocampo and Ting Ling are both told by an unreliable narrator, and those by Edgar Allan Poe and Alice Walker use interior monologue. In addition, you can pair the story by María Luisa Bombal with the poem by Federico García Lorca for the use of leitmotifs and pair the poem by Friedrich von Schiller with the story by Albert Camus for the use of paradox.

Evaluating and Grading an Expository Essay

If your department has uniform procedures for evaluation and grading, you may wish to proceed to the next section, Encouraging Further Reading, which relates directly to the *World Literature* student's text. However, if you are not obligated to follow a particular method, the following approach may be useful to you.

In order to be able to explain their evaluation to students and parents, some instructors prefer to assign numerical values to components of an essay and to make students aware of this grading system. Then, as the instructor marks each essay, he or she keeps a running tally of the score in the margins and bases the student's grade upon the total score. When instructors use this type of method, both they and their students can see that a good outline makes a valuable contribution to the essay's total score.

You, as the instructor, can create your own point system that reflects your priorities for the essay. The following example sets forth one method that you, as the instructor, can use to evaluate and grade a five-paragraph essay, where a perfect score would be 100 points or an A. You will notice that, in my example, I have allocated the points so as to emphasize and reward the student's analysis of the selection. However, had I preferred to do so, I could have allocated them in a manner that would have emphasized and rewarded the student's use of structure, language, and mechanics. Obviously, you would allocate the 100 points in whatever manner best suits your own objectives for the essay.

In my sample essay, a good introductory paragraph (for a total of 10 points) would contain a thesis sentence that states what the essay is going to be about (1 point), an organizing sentence that lists the three major points that will be discussed in the three core paragraphs (3 points), and some background material on the subject (6 points)—for example, either a brief summary of related aspects of the plot if the focus of the essay is characterization or theme, or else a statement about the general importance of the particular literary technique if that is the focus of the essay. The purpose of the background information would be to interest readers in the subject and to give them a framework for understanding and appreciating the essay. Students would be free to arrange this information in an effective way, usually either beginning or ending with their thesis sentence.

The three core paragraphs would be most important in terms of ideas, supporting details, and analysis (for 25 points each). Each would contain a topic sentence that sets forth the main point of the paragraph and connects it with the thesis idea (1 point). Three examples from the text would follow (1 point each), each with a supporting detail in the form of a direct quotation (2 points each) that, in turn, would be followed by the student's analysis, in a minimum of two sentences, of why this particular quotation supports the topic of the paragraph (5 points each).

A good concluding paragraph (for a total of 10 points) would briefly summarize the subject (5 points) and express the student's evaluation of its importance in the literary work (5 points).

Finally, the essay would be judged for its overall quality of expression (for a total of 5 points), including choice of words (1 point), interesting sentence structure (1 point), the use of transitions (1 point), correct spelling (1 point), and correct punctuation (1 point).

Motivating Students' Responsibility for Their Progress

Nothing is more frustrating for an instructor than to spend an hour correcting an essay only to have the student look at the grade, ignore the instructor's comments, and proceed to make the same mistakes in the next essay. In order to give my students a sense of responsibility for their own progress, I keep an anecdotal record of each student's work that is available to the student and that includes the type of errors the student makes on each assignment. This record tells me what I must teach and the extent to which I am succeeding; it tells my students that I am watching to see if they are learning from their mistakes and that they are responsible for working with me to be sure that this learning occurs. If a student continues to make the same type of errors, we must confront the problem together.

Further Reading

One of the objectives of *World Literature* is to foster an enjoyment of good literature. Consequently, at the end of the discussion of each selection in this *Manual*, you will find a reading list of works, usually by the same author, that will interest you and your students. The selections are available in paperback or from the library. You can enrich your program by having a group of students read and discuss a particular selection, or by having different students read different selections and then share their responses with the class as a whole.

Selected Bibliography

As an additional resource, this *Manual* concludes with a Selected Bibliography of secondary sources. This Bibliography supplements the selections in *World Literature*. In addition to biographical materials and works of literary criticism, I have occasionally included autobiographical materials such as letters and diaries. I have intentionally omitted literary criticism that specifically relates to works that are not included in *World Literature*, such as novels or other plays. I have arranged the Selected Bibliography to correlate with the organization of *World Literature* and the writer to which each reference work relates. Since these works are continually being reissued or reprinted, more recent editions may be available. Moreover, new reference works continue to be published.

The Mediterranean

The Hymn to the Aton

AKHENATON

INTRODUCING THE POEM

"The Hymn to the Aton" praises the beauty, goodness, creative powers, and universal presence of the sun. The Aton's light drives away darkness, with its danger and risk of death. With daybreak, all of nature flourishes and joyfully offers praise to the one god. The Aton creates all life and the reproductive capacities of all life. The Aton also provides what each needs for sustenance. As the son of Aton, only Akhenaton knows the Aton's plans and strength.

Through his use of contrast (day and night, light and darkness, life and death), repetition, and enumeration of examples, the poet creates a paean to the sun's awesome powers in a land of secure political borders and economic well-being.

In addition to its inherent appeal as a work of literature from the fourteenth century B.C., "The Hymn to the Aton" is interesting as it compares, in idea and wording, to Psalm 104 (lines 11–14; 20–26) in the Bible. Some scholars think that the psalmist knew "The Hymn to the Aton" and consciously patterned part of Psalm 104 on the earlier poem.

PLJ: What aspects of nature do you find most powerful? Most worthy of praise? Most frightening? Explain the reasons for each of your choices.

Literary Terms: apostrophe, contrast, lyric, paradox, tone

COMPREHENSION QUESTIONS

1. What is the Aton? (the sun)
2. What type of power does the Aton have? (creates all life and sustenance)
3. What characterizes the Aton's absence? (danger and death)
4. What does Ahkenaton know about the Aton? (the Aton's plans and strength)

UNDERSTANDING THE POEM: POSSIBLE ANSWERS

*1. *Nature of Aton*   The Aton is unique, universal, and beneficent. Functioning as a combined mother and father, the Aton creates and sustains all life, and all of the Aton's creations are good and beautiful. Have students find examples of supporting details.

*2. *How life reacts to Aton*   Every living thing is conscious of its creator, revels in the sustenance and beauty of the Aton's light, and offers praise to it. Have students find examples of supporting details.

3. *What view of Aton reveals about poet's world*   The beneficent nature and accomplishments of the Aton reflect a satisfied and optimistic people living in a fertile, prosperous, peaceful, and secure environment.

ANALYZING LITERARY TECHNIQUE: POSSIBLE ANSWERS

1. *Apostrophe*   The use of apostrophe creates a sense of immediacy and a sense of intimacy between the poet and the Aton. The poet assumes that the Aton is present and that the god is listening to his hymn.
2. *Paradox*   It is paradoxical that the sun is distant, yet its rays are near. It is also paradoxical that its rays are visible, yet its plans and strength are hidden. Both paradoxes reveal the great power of the Aton.
*3. *Contrast*   Examples of contrast include: life/death; light/darkness; day/night. The contrasts reveal the power and beneficence of the sun.
*4. *Tone*   The tone is one of joy and well-being, achieved through numerous positive examples of the Aton's power.
5. *Lyric poem*   This is a lyric poem in that it expresses the personal thoughts and feelings of the speaker and emphasizes descriptive detail.

WRITING ABOUT LITERATURE

1. *Expository theme analyzing use of detail*   Call students' attention to the directions and suggestions in the textbook assignment. Note that stanzas 2, 4, and 5 provide excellent detail. The poet's use of elaborate detail reveals the poet's appreciation of the power and beneficence of the Aton and establishes the tone of joy and prosperity. (See **U.P.** questions 1 and 2, and **A.L.T.** questions 3 and 4 above.)

2. *Creative writing: Hymn to a god of a people who live in an unstable environment* An area with unpredictable weather might have a storm god, who would be angry or temperamental. The tone might be pleading. An area with aggressive neighbors might have a war god, who would support warriors who possess courage, strength, and skill in battle against their country's enemies. The tone would be heroic, a call to provide strength and to reward courage and skill. **(PLJ)**

FURTHER READING

Psalm 104 in the Bible.

Psalm 23

DAVID

INTRODUCING THE POEM

Psalm 23 reflects the relationship between the psalmist and God. The psalmist is confident that he can put complete trust in God and that God will guide and protect him through life.

Because the Israelites originally were a nomadic people who herded sheep, the metaphor of God the shepherd was a concept they understood and valued. The popularity of this psalm rests largely on the lasting appeal of the personification of God as a shepherd, an image that simply and effectively conveys the idea of God as caring, nurturing, guiding, and comforting.

The psalmist's parallel, repetitive phrasing also contributes to the appeal and power of the psalm. The simple cadences are calm and soothing, and they reflect a simple faith.

It is possible that Psalm 23 is a "pilgrim" psalm, describing a pilgrim's thoughts as he or she begins the dangerous journey to the Temple in Jerusalem. The pilgrim trusts that God will provide sustenance, clear direction, and protection, and that God will ensure a safe arrival at the destination. In this interpretation, the "green pastures" and "still waters" signify food and water, or an oasis. The "soul" is the pilgrim's physical vitality. (In Judaism, at the time the psalms were written, a person was considered a totality, with no separation between body and spirit or soul.) The "paths of righteousness" are the correct paths for the journey. God's rod and staff direct or lead the pilgrim, who will be welcomed hospitably and respectfully by having oil poured on his or her head. The overflowing cup of wine symbolizes a blessed life, and the pilgrim will remain near God's presence in the Temple.

The "valley of the shadow of death" is a literal translation of the Hebrew. Other translators translate the phrase as "in the midst of total darkness," "the valley of dark shadows," or "the valley of deep gloom." In the "pilgrim" interpretation, the phrase implies danger from robbers rather than the inevitability of human mortality.

It is also possible that Psalm 23 is a "monarch" psalm, describing the feelings of a new king as he is about to celebrate his coronation. Just as a shepherd cares for the sheep, so God will sustain and protect the king. In this interpretation, the "valley of the shadow of death" implies danger from political enemies who threaten the king's authority and his life. The coronation ceremony involves anointing the new king's head with oil, which is symbolic of investing him with divine approval. The overflowing cup symbolizes his blessed life. With God's guidance, the king will live according to God's precepts.

PLJ: Most people feel that they have some support or guidance in their lives in the form of family, friends, teachers, neighbors, or systems of belief. Think about some of the sources of support in your life. When have you felt especially guided or protected?

Literary Terms: metaphor, parallelism, personification, theme, tone

COMPREHENSION QUESTIONS

1. To what does the psalmist compare God? (shepherd)
2. To what does the psalmist compare himself? (a sheep)
3. What is the psalmist's attitude toward the world? (good, because of God's caring presence)

UNDERSTANDING THE POEM:
POSSIBLE ANSWERS

1. *Attitude toward God*   God nurtures and supports the individual throughout his or her life or journey or reign.
2. *Why expect life filled with goodness and mercy*   Life is filled with goodness and mercy because God possesses these qualities and sees to it that the individual experiences them in his or her own life.
3. *"Pilgrim" psalm*   Note above introductory material. The pilgrim expects God to supply shelter, food, and water during the journey to the Temple (lines 1–3, 5); to provide safe passage along the way (lines 3–4); and to bring the pilgrim safely to the Temple (line 6).
4. *"Monarch" psalm*   Note above introductory material. The king expects God to support him in his role as political leader (line 3); to provide guidance and protect him against his political enemies (lines 4–5); and to provide divine sanction, symbolized by anointing his head with oil as part of the coronation ceremony (line 5).
*5. *Theme*   Life is good, since a caring God watches over a person's life.

ANALYZING LITERARY TECHNIQUE:
POSSIBLE ANSWERS

*1. *Why personify God as shepherd? Attributes of God*   Because the Israelites originally were a nomadic people who herded sheep, the metaphor of God the shepherd was a concept they understood and valued. Like the shepherd, God is caring, nurturing, guiding, and comforting.
2. *Metaphors*   Other metaphors include: (1) "the valley of the shadow of death" (see question 3 below); (2) "cup runneth over": a life of blessings and well-being; and (3) "paths of righteousness": correct, ethical behavior.
3. *The "valley of the shadow of death"*   (1) The "valley of the shadow of death" makes death present and a possibility, but not necessarily an actuality. God's protection will ward off evil. (2) The "valley of deep gloom" is depressing, but not necessarily dangerous. It can make following the correct path difficult. (3) The "valley of dark shadows" suggests a cause for anxiety because shadows can conceal what is dangerous. (4) Being "in the midst of total darkness" makes following the correct path impossible; it also conceals what is dangerous. Translations 2, 3, and 4 omit the idea of mortality that is present in the original Hebrew.
4. *Parallelism*   Parallelism creates rhythm through repetition of phrase and clause patterns. Examples: "He maketh me . . . he leadeth me. . . . He restoreth my . . . he leadeth me. . . ." "thou art . . . Thou preparest . . . thou anointest. . . ." The repetition contributes to the appeal and power of the psalm. The simple cadences are soothing.
5. *Tone*   The tone is one of security and peace. It is achieved by means of personifying God as a shepherd, with the protective and nurturing qualities inherent in that role. It is also achieved through parallelism, the repetition of simple, soothing, cadenced clauses.

WRITING ABOUT LITERATURE

1. *Expository analysis of a function of personification.*   Call students' attention to the directions in the textbook assignment. Possibilities include: government as big brother, and the nation as father, mother, or uncle. (See: **A.L.T.** question 1 above.)
2. *Creative writing: A poem based on personification*   Call students' attention to the directions and suggestions in the textbook assignment. (See: **A.L.T.** question 1 above.)

FURTHER READING

Any of the other Psalms.

To an Army Wife, in Sardis

SAPPHO

INTRODUCING THE POEM

Sappho's poem is a love letter. It may be from Sappho, addressed to a friend who is now married to a soldier, or it may be from a soldier to his wife. Either way, the speaker argues that whatever one loves is the finest sight on earth.

The speaker's argument has a circular structure (a-b-c-b-a). The speaker argues as follows: (a) Others say [stanzas 1 and 2]; (b) I say [stanza 2]; (c) An example from days of old proves my point [stanzas 3–5]; (b) Therefore, I say that I am correct [stanza 6]; and (a) The others are wrong [stanza 7].

The speaker alludes to Helen of Troy, who left her husband, King Menelaus, in Sparta to live in Troy with Paris, son of Priam and Hecuba, the Trojan king and queen. The Trojans fought the Trojan War against the Greek siege of their palace-state rather than return Helen to the Greeks. However, after ten years, the Greeks entered the walled city by hiding inside the Trojan horse. Troy fell in flames, Paris was killed by Achilles' son (Achilles had died earlier), and Menelaus took Helen back to Sparta.

The appealing subject matter, the artful quality of the speaker's reasoning, the appropriate nature of the allusion, the pictorial detail, and the sincerity of the emotional component all contribute to the great charm of the poem.

PLJ: If you want to convince someone that your opinion is correct and well-founded what do you do? Is it enough to state your opinion, or do you make an effort to support it with reasons?

Literary Terms: allusion, apostrophe, contrast, lyric

COMPREHENSION QUESTIONS

1. Who is the speaker of this poem? (probably Sappho, but it may be a soldier)
2. Where is the speaker? (probably back home, but possibly away from home)
3. What is the speaker's argument? (whatever one loves is the finest sight on earth)
4. What event in Greek mythology is alluded to in the poem? (the Trojan War)
5. What emotion is expressed in this poem? (love; longing)

UNDERSTANDING THE POEM: POSSIBLE ANSWERS

1. *Speaker* (*a*) The speaker is probably Sappho. The lines, "although you/being far away forget us" imply that Anactoria has forgotten more than just the speaker. It is possible that Anactoria has left Sappho and her friends to go off with her soldier-husband (as Helen went off with Paris) and that she has made no effort to communicate with those back home who love her.

    (*b*) The major reason for believing the speaker to be the soldier-husband is the striking use of military details. However, Sappho lived through politically tumultuous times and was probably familiar with the sights that she describes. Viewing the speaker as the soldier-husband involves overlooking three problems: (1) the troublesome use of "us" just described; (2) the direct comparison between Anactoria and Helen, both of whom have gone off with a loving male and have left loved ones behind; and (3) the fact that Sappho usually writes about her own experiences and emotions.

    (*c*) Either choice of speaker is legitimate, because the emotion is what is most important in the poem, and the emotion is conveyed either way.
2. *Opinions of others* The technique of contrasting the opinions of others sets the speaker apart and emphasizes the superiority of her or his opinion.
3. *Anactoria's situation* If the speaker is Sappho, it is likely that Anactoria has left her old friends to accompany her husband, and she has not forgotten them; she has simply become very involved in her new life. If the speaker is Anactoria's husband, who is apart from Anactoria, word from her may not have reached the speaker in a while, and he may feel lonely and homesick.

ANALYZING LITERARY TECHNIQUE: POSSIBLE ANSWERS

1. *Appeal to the senses* The poem comes alive with visual military images: cavalry corps on glittering Lydian horses; armored infantry; and the swift, oar-powered naval fleet. The visual appeal is enhanced by the elaborated repetition of the opening descriptions in the concluding lines.
2. *Contrast* Sappho uses contrast to dramatize the speaker's distinctive viewpoint, to emphasize that individuals determine what is most beautiful to them.

3. *Apostrophe*   Apostrophe adds the personal touch of direct address. It creates a sense of immediacy, as though Anactoria were able to hear the speaker's words.

*4. *Allusion to Helen of Troy*   Helen left her husband, King Menelaus, in Sparta in order to live in Troy with Paris. Anactoria is like Helen in that she has gone off with a loving male and has left other loved ones behind. The allusion to Helen also relates to the theme of beauty, since Helen was considered to be the most beautiful woman of her time.

WRITING ABOUT LITERATURE

1. *Expository writing: Helen of Troy*   You will need to direct students to the resource center or to the neighborhood library for books on Greek mythology. If you prefer, you can bring an appropriate selection of books into the classroom. Possible authors include Alfred Church, Padraic Colum, Robert Graves, Roger L. Green, Edith Hamilton, and Rex Warner. The textbook *World Mythology* (National Textbook Co.) presents the *Iliad*, the *Odyssey*, and the *Aeneid* with attention to characterization and language.

2. *Creative writing: Anactoria's response*   Call students' attention to the suggestions in the textbook assignment. Note that background reading will enhance this assignment (**PLJ**).

FURTHER READING

Sappho, *Greek Lyrics*.

Antigone

SOPHOCLES

INTRODUCING THE PLAY

Theater performances in Athens in the fifth century B.C. were given at a religious and civic festival that occurred each spring in honor of the god Dionysus. The open-air theater was located in the area sacred to the god. The actors were all men, who wore robes and large masks that they changed when they changed roles. Actions were stylized, and violence always occurred offstage. In Sophocles' time, tragedy was a developing dramatic form that originated with a Chorus that sang and danced in honor of Dionysus. Thespis added an actor, Aeschylus a second actor, and Sophocles a third. Sophocles also invented painted scenery.

Sophocles wrote his plays to be performed and judged in the dramatic competitions that were part of the festival honoring Dionysus. Each playwright would submit a group of four plays (three of them tragedies), and a committee would choose three groups of plays for performance in each day's competition. In these festivals Sophocles won first prize for twenty-four groups of plays.

Each day during the festival, 17,000 spectators would watch the day-long dramatic competition. They always knew the subject of each tragedy because playwrights were expected to choose their material from the well-loved stories that comprise Greek mythic history (pre-seventh century B.C.). The Theban cycle of myths was so popular that several different versions still exist: *Oedipus the King, Oedipus at Colonus*, and *Antigone* by Sophocles; *Seven Against Thebes* by Aeschylus; and *The Suppliant Women* and *The Phoenician Women* by Euripides.

The existing seven complete plays of Sophocles were found in Byzantine textbook anthologies. In modern times, a large part of an eighth play has been found on papyrus in Egypt, where many Greek plays were imported between 300 and 200 B.C.

Antigone is a play about the conflicting rights of the state and the individual. Creon believes that the law must always be obeyed, whereas Antigone believes that one's religious duties are more important than civil laws. However, *Antigone* is much more than an "idea play." It is a play of conflicting personalities. If ideas were the only issue, it would have been possible to consider an acceptable compromise between the two positions. Instead, the personalities of Creon and Antigone do not permit compromise. As the drama evolves, worthy principles become secondary, both to Creon's pride and his growing hatred of Antigone and to Antigone's belief in the importance of being true to her personal values. No character escapes the tragic consequences of this confrontation.

Antigone is enjoyable because it appeals to the intellect as well as to the emotions. One group of intellectual issues involves questions such as: Is there anything or anyone more important than the good of the state? What takes priority when issues of state directly conflict with religious principles? What does the citizen owe the state? What does the state owe the citizen?

In the fifth century B.C., loyalty to one's city-state was a practical necessity. Wars between city-states were frequent and were a threat to life, freedom, and property. Massacre, pillage, and enslavement accompanied defeat. Thus, the welfare of the individual and the family was dependent upon the welfare of their city-state. The Athenians had seen their great city burned by the Persians, and they could understand Creon's attitude toward the burial of invading warriors.

However, far older values were still honored along with the newer ones. People were reared in a tradition that viewed family relationships as the strongest and most important ties. Proper burial and mourning rites were required, even of enemies. This was primarily the women's domain, except that warriors on foreign soil were responsible for their own dead. People believed that they would live forever with the consequences of their behavior on earth.

Loyalty to the state and to the family clash directly in this play. While Creon eloquently articulates what the citizen owes the city, he ignores what he as king owes the citizens. Antigone is determined to bury Polynices because it is important in her society to honor family ties and religious conventions, and because she believes that these values take precedence over a conflicting royal edict.

A second group of intellectual issues involves questions about the role and value of women in society. Even in a society where a woman's primary roles are rearing children and burying the dead, her responsibilities are important to the welfare of her community. Is it ever right to treat a human being as an object even if that person has a different political, economic, or social status? Creon places the rights and status of women on a par with that of slaves, whom he also treats like objects.

A third group of intellectual issues involves family relationships. What do fathers owe their sons and sisters owe their siblings? Do the living have more of a responsibility to their living siblings or to those who have died? In the fifth century B.C., authority in the family resided with the father, who expected unquestioning obedience from his children. Obligations to the dead simply involved proper funeral rites; then, the family could devote its attention to the living.

While these intellectual issues provide the framework for the play, the characters in *Antigone* are not symbols of principles: they are real people with real strengths and weaknesses. Because they are inherently well-meaning and take positions that make sense, all of the characters elicit some degree of understanding and sympathy.

Sophocles introduces Creon and Antigone at a point where they are at odds with each other and are under great stress. They are both so committed to the principles by which they live that they do not understand the other's point of view, and they ignore advice, even when it is in their own best interests to be flexible. In a masterful way, Sophocles dramatically plays these two characters off each other and off the minor characters who love them. The process gradually reveals what type of people Creon and Antigone are, and how they are responsible for their own tragic fates. Even when they are not likeable, they are heroic. Their principles are admirable, and they stand up to their destinies with dignity.

Creon's actions fit the psychological pattern typical of many great people in Greek myth. Excellence in ruling Thebes after Laius' death (*aretē*) makes Creon excessively proud of his ability as a ruler (*hubris*). His pride leads him into rash behavior, the "blind recklessness" of *atē*. In his legitimate and admirable pursuit of justice, he issues an edict that defies conventional religious practices. In an important sense, this is Creon's fatal step, because respect for the gods reminds mortals of their human limitations. What follows is not surprising. Creon becomes inflexibly attached to the merit of the edict, imposes the death penalty on anyone who defies it, and then repeatedly ignores all suggestions that conflict with his ideas.

At the end of the play, Creon's behavior brings disaster on himself and his family (*nemesis*). Too late he sees that Antigone was partially correct when she criticized him for being motivated by hatred. Under stress, he has seen others only in terms of what they should do for him, and the only person he has respected and loved has been himself. Haemon's death makes Creon realize that although he is king, he is still only a human being. Finally, with dignity, he accepts responsibility for his behavior and his fate.

Antigone is the Sophoclean hero who is willing to die for her convictions. She is as concerned with justice as Creon is, but her concept of what is right differs dramatically. Whereas Creon focuses on the needs of the city-state and the obligation of citizens to obey the law, Antigone is preoccupied with the needs of family and the obligations of religion. Going to her death alone, Antigone suddenly realizes that she does what she has to do, not only because of religious principles, but because of feelings deep within her that go beyond religious duty.

The translation of *Antigone* in the *World Literature* textbook is complete and unabridged. It includes a passage (lines 995–1004) that has been omitted in the translation by Fitts and Fitzgerald on the theory that it is inconsistent with a traditional interpretation of Antigone's character (that she died for her religious principles) and that, therefore, Sophocles did not write it. Although its authenticity is still debated, many leading scholars accept this passage as the work of Sophocles and find it to be consistent with his ability to portray psychologically complex characters. Not only did Aristotle accept the passage in his time (less than a century after Sophocles) and imply that it was well-known, but he used part of it in his treatise on rhetoric.

In the disputed lines, Antigone reveals that her motive is not solely to fulfill her religious duties, but to act in a way that is consistent with her love for her brother and her deepest personal values. This analysis is consistent with the fact that no one in the play indicates that religious law requires Antigone to risk martyrdom, and that Ismene's attitude supports the idea that religious obligations do not require disobedience to civil law.

Sophocles dramatizes the virtues of "the golden mean" in human behavior by revealing the terrible consequences that may result from rigid attitudes and extreme actions. He was aware of the paradox that rigid adherence to an inherently good cause may produce evil results. This is true of both Creon's adherence to his belief that the citizen is obligated to be loyal to the state and Antigone's adherence to her belief that the citizen is obligated to be loyal to religious principles and family needs. Their self-righteous attitudes toward their own principles cause both Creon and Antigone to disregard the reality of conflicting loyalties; in the end, paradoxically, each of them wins a disastrous victory.

Sophocles emphasizes this important psychological lesson by creating Haemon as a foil for Creon and Ismene as a foil for Antigone. Both minor characters exhibit rational thinking and self-control and plead the virtues of these values against the destructive values of passion and inflexibility. Ismene's relationship to Antigone is particularly important because of its psychological dimension. The sisters, whom Creon treats as if they are twins, function as alter ego (literally, "other I") to one another and represent two sides of one human personality. Antigone functions as Ismene's darker, passionate, and unrestrained self (in psychological terms, as Ismene's doppelgänger), and it is Ismene rather than Antigone who represents the values that were prized by the ancient Greeks. Haemon and Ismene are unsuccessful in their efforts with Creon and Antigone, and the audience learns the danger of behavior that is based on uncontrolled passion from the magnitude of the ensuing tragedy.

No discussion of *Antigone* is complete without emphasizing the beauty of the lyric odes that are recited by the Chorus. In connotative and figurative language that no writer has ever surpassed in eloquence, the Chorus speaks about the nature of the human condition.

PLJ: What qualities must a person possess in order to earn your respect? Would you ever disobey the laws of your community and country? If so, under what circumstances?

Literary Terms: allusion, alter ego, antagonist, *aretē, atē,* catastrophe, catharsis, characterization, chorus, climax, conflict, connotative language, contrast, crisis, discovery, doppelgänger, figurative language, foil, foreshadowing, *hubris,* irony, lyric, myth, *nemesis,* ode, paradox, protagonist, resolution, reversal, symbol, theme, tragedy

COMPREHENSION QUESTIONS

1. What edict does Creon issue? (not to bury Polynices)
2. Why does he do this? (He considers Polynices a traitor.)
3. How does Antigone react? (She defies Creon and attempts burial.)
4. How does Ismene react? (helpless; offers to die; afraid to be alone)
5. What advice does Haemon give Creon? (The people sympathize with Antigone, so Polynices should be buried.)
6. How does Creon punish Antigone? (buries her alive)
7. What happens to Haemon? (After finding Antigone dead, he tries to kill Creon, then kills himself.)
8. What does Tiresias do in the play? (prophesies doom for Creon)
9. Why does Creon make the decisions he does? (thinks he knows best)
10. What is Creon's attitude toward women? (no respect; treats them like slaves)

UNDERSTANDING THE PLAY: POSSIBLE ANSWERS

*1. *Antigone   a) Antigone's attitude toward laws of Thebes*   Antigone will not obey political laws that conflict with religious practices. She does not view herself as a traitor because she feels that her cause is just.

b) Why Antigone risks death to bury Polynices   (1) She believes that displeasing the gods is worse than displeasing Creon; (2) she loves Polynices; and (3) she believes that it is essential for people to act on their beliefs.

c) Why Antigone won't let Ismene join her   Antigone wants to be rewarded for her courage by a glorious death. She views Ismene as a coward who doesn't deserve to share her "reward." Antigone also sees no reason for Ismene to die for a cause in which Ismene does not believe. Antigone wants Ismene to publicize her deed because she believes death with glory is better than life or death without it.

d) How Antigone would have fared if she had treated Creon with respect   Based on Creon's response to Haemon, Creon probably would have shown no mercy toward Antigone.

e) Antigone's ambivalence about her sacrifice   On her way to her tomb, Antigone laments that her principles and her love of Polynices force her to give up love, marriage, and children. She is not ambivalent—she regrets her great loss.

f) Antigone's heroic qualities   Antigone's motives are consistent with religious laws and are based on love and loyalty. She recognizes right and wrong, acts in accordance with her convictions, and is willing to die for what she believes.

g) Danger in behavior like Antigone's   Antigone's devotion to her principles and her attitudes toward advice and death make her a fanatic. Religious, political, and social fanatics are a danger to the established order because no prohibition can stop them from attempting to take the law into their own hands.

*2. *Creon*   *a) *Creon's edict as an emergency decree; Creon's right to issue such an edict*   It is very important that Creon's edict is an emergency decree because this reveals the law breaks custom. According to Tiresias, who says that the laws of the gods take precedence over laws of a king, Creon has no right to issue such an edict. Creon later says, "It's best to keep the established laws to the very day we die" (lines 1237–38).

b) Creon's arete (excellence) is that he is a good man who possesses the leadership qualities to be a good king. His *hubris* (excessive pride) is his feeling as king that everything is within his power. His *hubris* leads to *ate* (rash behavior based on his excessive pride, which the Greeks called "blind recklessness"): he enacts his emergency decree that it is against the law to bury those who attacked the city, including his nephew, Polynices. Creon's *nemesis* (retribution) occurs at the end of the play with the suicides of his wife and his son.

c) Possible for Creon to honor Eteocles and still to bury Polynices   It would have been possible to honor Eteocles and still to bury Polynices. Creon could have given Eteocles a different ceremony and could have buried him in a different location. Because everyone is entitled to proper burial, Polynices' burial would have been no injustice to Eteocles.

d) Important that Haemon is sole surviving son of Creon   Creon's behavior toward Haemon shows how harsh Creon is. One would expect that Creon would value Haemon more highly and be more flexible.

e) Creon's attitude toward disobedience   Creon's attitude toward disobedience reveals that he respects neither humans nor gods.

f) Why Creon changes nature of Antigone's sentence   Haemon reveals to Creon the Theban support for Antigone and reminds him of his obligations to be sensitive to the needs and interests of his people. Burying Antigone alive with food permits divine (or other) intervention, and Creon does not have to risk further defiance by forcing the Thebans to stone Antigone to death.

g) Creon's responses to Tiresias show disrespect for gods   Tiresias speaks for the gods and their values. When Creon accuses Tiresias of prophesying for personal profit, he demeans Tiresias, his role, and his message. Creon's statement that he is free to do whatever he chooses because "we can't defile the gods—no mortal has the power" (lines 1156–57) is insulting and irreverent, revealing that Creon no longer recognizes his place in the universe. Creon's responses reflect the psychological pattern of *arete*, *hubris*, and *ate* because it is his overestimation (*hubris*) of his excellent qualities (*arete*) and his feeling of omnipotence as king (*hubris*) that lead him to criticize Tiresias (*ate*) and lose his perspective in terms of his relationship to the gods (*ate*).

h) Why Creon buries Polynices before rescuing Antigone   Creon buries Polynices first because he puts duty to the state before duty to his family. He realizes he has wronged the dead and offended the gods. In addition, Creon has no reason to think that Antigone is in danger.

i) Creon motivated by hatred   Hatred of the enemy, particularly of Polynices as the initiator of the attack, motivates Creon to issue the burial edict. Hatred of anyone who defies his authority causes Creon to impose the death penalty. Only after Haemon's death is Creon able to feel remorse and to question his actions. Thus, Creon's feelings of hatred can be said to have determined his fate. However, these feelings are not the sole determinant. Creon's hatred is empowered by his political position, and it is his excessive pride (*hubris*) that motivates him to create and enforce the edict (*atē*).

j) Creon as a tragic figure   Creon is a tragic figure in that he was a good man and was qualified to be the king of Thebes. Unfortunately, his excessive pride in his ability and power as a ruler (*hubris*) leads to the rash action of his edict (*atē*), which in turn causes disaster for himself (*nemesis*) and his family. Creon is also a tragic figure in that he causes the tragedy within his family, and he recognizes his errors too late to make amends. The fact that he accepts his fate with dignity enhances his tragic stature.

k) Absolute power corrupts absolutely   Creon is a capable leader who, when he becomes king, treats criticism as treason and tramples on the rights of the individual. These facts reveal the truth of Lord Acton's principle as well as the truth of the Greek view that it is risky to be a human being of great stature or power.

3. Ismene: a) Different from Antigone   Ismene and Antigone are very different. Ismene is passive and Antigone is active. Ismene is subservient, accepting the conventional role of women in Greek society and in relation to civil law, while Antigone is defiant of both. Ismene is fearful, while Antigone is courageous. Ismene is flexible, while Antigone is intransigent.

b) Ismene a coward   Those who would defend Ismene from the charge of cowardice would argue that Antigone is foolish. If one obeys the state, perhaps the gods will forgive. Also, Ismene is willing to die with Antigone. She questions Creon about the wisdom of his intent to kill Antigone and its effect on Haemon. Those who would accuse Ismene of being a coward would argue that she lacks both convictions and courage. Ismene is afraid to die, but she is more afraid to be left without Antigone.

4. Haemon: a) Diplomatic elements in Haemon's speech   (1) Haemon accepts Creon's wishes; (2) Haemon says that another view is possible; (3) Haemon reveals the attitudes of the citizens, but not his own; and (4) Haemon shows concern for Creon, not Antigone.

b) Haemon's different concept of kingship   Haemon believes that rulers must consider the needs and attitudes of their people. A king must listen to advice, realize that he is not infallible, and be flexible. Creon believes that the king always knows what is best for himself and for everyone else. Without the king's law, anarchy would occur. Thus the king's laws must be obeyed even if they are wrong.

*5. *Chorus:* *a)* *"For mortal men there is no escape from the doom we must endure."* (lines 1457–58) Students might argue that Creon, Antigone, and Haemon could have chosen to behave differently: Creon and Antigone to be flexible; Haemon to accept Creon's behavior. Only Ismene has no choice, since her fate is determined by the actions of Creon and Antigone. However, given the personality of each, each could only behave as he or she did.

b) *"Love, you wrench the minds of righteous into outrage, swerve them to their ruin."* (lines 887–88) This concept applies to both Antigone and Haemon, who commit suicide because of the death of a loved one. Haemon's suicide is complicated by his feelings about Creon's role in Antigone's suicide and by his own attempt to kill Creon.

c) *"No towering form of greatness enters into the lives of mortals free and clear of ruin."* (lines 687–89) This concept applies to both Antigone and Creon. Antigone is a loving sister who becomes the victim of her loyalty to Polynices. She disregards the loyalty she owes Thebes in favor of her obligation to give Polynices a religious burial. Yet, no one indicates that religious law requires that Antigone become a martyr. On the contrary, Ismene's attitude supports the idea that religious obligations do not require disobedience to civil law. Therefore, Antigone brings her fate upon herself and, in the process, she inadvertently brings about Haemon's death as well.

Creon is a good man and a qualified ruler who becomes the victim of his kingship. Once he sees no limitations to the extent of his power, he is on a slippery slope toward destruction. He creates an unjust edict that defies religious principles and practices, and then he refuses to adapt it to extenuating circumstances or, better yet, to repeal it. As a result, he brings immediate disaster upon his family and himself and future disaster upon Thebes.

*6. *Themes at the end of the play* (lines 1466–70) *a)* "Wisdom is by far the greatest part of joy": One of the primary lessons of the Oedipus myth is that a lack of knowledge—especially self-knowledge—is destructive. In contrast, wisdom creates the possibility for happiness by revealing what in life is a source of happiness.

b) "Reverence toward the gods must be safeguarded": Whether or not they are religious, people still must recognize that they are not free to behave just as they please, without regard for the rights of other human beings and the condition of the environment.

c) "The mighty words of the proud are paid in full with mighty blows of fate": The ancient concepts of *aretē, hubris, atē,* and *nemesis* are still a potential part of the human personality. People who act with too much pride still bring disaster upon themselves. Power still tends to corrupt; absolute power still corrupts absolutely; and human beings still have long memories when it comes to retribution.

d) "At long last those blows will teach us wisdom": People can learn from the experience of others, but it is a hard task to accomplish. The ancient Greeks did not learn from their history, although plays like *Antigone* were designed to try to make the audiences who saw them more sensitive to these issues in their own lives.

ANALYZING LITERARY TECHNIQUE: POSSIBLE ANSWERS

1. *Function of minor characters*   a) Ismene is a foil for Antigone. She supplies the contrast of a sister who reacts in a significantly different manner to a crisis, and she represents the values that were important in ancient Greece. Ismene is the reasonable sister who exhibits rational thinking, self-control, and flexibility. Her attitude toward Antigone and Creon's attitude toward both sisters imply that, psychologically, Antigone and Ismene are alter egos for each other before Creon issues his emergency edict. The issue of Polynices' burial causes them to separate and to function psychologically as two sides of one human personality. Ismene's attitudes and behavior are characteristic of the Greek ideal of "the golden mean," while Antigone represents Ismene's darker, passionate, and unrestrained self that, in psychological terms, is called the double or the doppelgänger.

   b) Haemon is a foil for Creon, revealing Creon's inhumanity. Haemon also reveals that the people support Antigone, and this foreshadows a tragic end for Creon.

   c) Tiresias reveals the value of the gods to Creon and also how the gods view both Creon and Antigone. The Chorus reveals the feelings and concerns of the people of Thebes and, by extension, of the audience. Both characters, therefore, represent forces in the world that are larger and more enduring than the personalities of the play's central characters.

2. *Late introduction of Antigone's engagement*   Sophocles achieves greater dramatic power, since this magnifies the conflict between Creon and Antigone. Also, Antigone's engagement is not important either to Creon or to Antigone, only to Haemon.

*3. *Choice of title: the more important character*   Antigone is the title because Antigone is the Sophoclean type of Greek hero, one who dies for her convictions. Antigone is a more sympathetic character than Creon in that her motivation is more attractive than Creon's. However, Antigone and Creon are equally important. Creon is typical of many Greek tragic heroes, and the play does not end until he learns his lesson about life. However, Antigone's response to Creon creates the lesson. Much of the play's impact results from how Sophocles has interwoven Creon and Antigone so that they cannot be viewed as independent of each other. Students may disagree about which character is the protagonist and which is the antagonist; each character is both, depending on the perspective. Such a relationship between two different kinds of heroes creates a taut, dramatic experience for the audience.

4. *Dramatic irony*   For the informed audience, dramatic irony lends drama and suspense to the play. The audience knows something the character does not know and wonders how and when that character is going to learn it. Creon's certainty that a *man* has buried Polynices (beginning with line 280) reveals Creon's view of women as submissive, obedient creatures, reinforces Ismene's amazement at Antigone's behavior, and reveals how very unusual Antigone's defiance of the edict actually is. Sophocles has Creon refer to a *man's* deed repeatedly, each repetition enhancing the drama of the situation. Because the audience knows the story—knows more than Creon does at the time—the suspense continues to build.

*5. *Paradox* (*a*) Paradox is evident in the nature of the victories that Antigone and Creon win: Both are disastrous. Antigone persists in giving Polynices a symbolic burial despite Creon's decree, and she dies because of her defiance. Creon succeeds in killing Antigone, with the result that Haemon and then the queen commit suicide.

(*b*) Paradox is also evident in the psychological fact that a person's greatest strength is often that person's greatest weakness. Both Antigone and Creon reveal the truth of this paradox. Antigone's devotion to her brother's burial is an admirable trait; however, when she persists despite the circumstances, it becomes a fault of character. Creon's devotion to the state and his determination to enforce its laws are also admirable traits in a political leader; however, when Creon creates an unjust law and then kills anyone who defies it, these traits also become faults of character.

6. *Climax, crisis, and discovery* (*a*) The climax occurs when Antigone goes to her death. This becomes the event that changes Creon's fate.

(*b*) The crisis, or turning point, occurs when Creon finally realizes that his attitudes and behavior toward Polynices and Antigone are contrary to important religious precepts and that, unless he can make amends, the gods will punish him. Dramatic irony makes this a powerful moment because it is too late for Creon to save anyone, including himself.

(*c*) The discovery, or recognition, occurs because of the catastrophe of Haemon's death. Creon realizes that he is a beaten man and that his own errors are responsible for Haemon's suicide. Creon's later acceptance of responsibility for the queen's death is part of the resolution, the projection of the action into a future beyond the play itself.

7. *Function of mythological allusions: Niobe, Persephone, Danaë* Antigone and the Chorus use these allusions to comfort Antigone. Niobe, Persephone, and Danaë all suffered terrible fates, but all were compensated by the gods for their sufferings.

WRITING ABOUT LITERATURE

1. *Expository theme evaluating Creon's leadership* Students may find it helpful to refer back to their answers to **U.P.** questions 2, 4, 5, and 6, and to **A.L.T.** questions 3 and 5. Encourage students to consider the consistencies and inconsistencies between Creon the man—uncle, father, husband—and Creon the ruler of Thebes.

2. *Expository analysis of Creon's character in terms of the concepts of aretē, hubris, atē, and nemesis* You may wish to assign this as an alternate to the first **W.A.L.** assignment, to which it is closely related. This writing assignment challenges students to apply their new knowledge of the personality traits of classical characters. Students who wish a further alternative could apply these characteristics to the other major character in the play, Antigone. (See **U.P.** questions 1, 2, 4, 5, and 6, and **A.L.T.** questions 3 and 5 above.)

3. *Expository analysis of the relationship between the paradox in the "Ode to Man" (lines 376–416) and the dramatic irony of the action in* Antigone Call students' attention to the suggestions in the textbook assignment. Remind them that they

should use direct quotations from the play to support their ideas. Antigone, Creon, and Haemon all behave in ways that reflect with dramatic irony the paradox expressed in this ode. Human beings are both wonderful and terrifying; they "forge on, now to destruction / now again to greatness." It is ironic that for all of their material well-being and strengths of personality, Antigone, Creon, and Haemon are unable to cope flexibly and creatively with the course of their lives.

4. *Creative writing:* Antigone *from Ismene's or Haemon's point of view*   Call students' attention to the suggestions in the textbook assignment.

FURTHER READING

Aeschylus, *Seven Against Thebes.*
Anouilh, Jean, *Antigone.*
Brecht, Bertolt, *Antigone* and *Oedipus Rex.*
Cocteau, Jean, *The Infernal Machine.*
Eliot, T. S., *The Elder Statesman.*
Euripides, *The Suppliant Women* and *The Phoenician Women.*
Seneca, *Oedipus.*
Sophocles, *Oedipus the King* and *Oedipus at Colonus.*
Voltaire, *Oedipus.*

Because you know you're young in beauty yet

Dante Alighieri

INTRODUCING THE POEM

In a poem that spans the ages, Dante expresses a young man's resentment and anger at the young woman who has rejected his offer of love. Because it is told from the young man's point of view, the young woman is presented as being arrogant, proud, cruel, and stonelike in her insensitivity to his feelings. So great is the young man's anguish and anger that he concludes by wishing that she will experience similar pain in love.

It is interesting to put the speaker's feelings into perspective by imagining this relationship from the woman's point of view. The young woman simply may not like the young man and may think that it is best to act honestly. She may view treating him kindly as offering him false hope and thereby postponing or prolonging his pain.

It is also interesting to consider this poem in terms of the tradition of courtly love. Courtly love often involved the idealization of the loved one, the offer of pure love from the safety of distance, and the passionate expression of emotion on the part of the lover. The lover would despair if his loved one were unattainable, and he would be angry at her cruelty if she rejected his offer of love. Dante conveys the speaker's emotions so realistically, however, that the poem is meaningful to anyone who has experienced unrequited love.

PLJ: Have you ever cared about someone who did not reciprocate your feelings? How did the experience make you feel about that person? How did it make you feel about yourself?

Literary Terms: apostrophe, courtly love, image, lyric, stanza

COMPREHENSION QUESTIONS

1. Describe the speaker in the poem. (young man)
2. To whom is the speaker speaking? (young woman)
3. What has happened to the speaker? (woman rejected his love)
4. What does the speaker wish for? (woman will suffer rejection as he has suffered)

UNDERSTANDING THE POEM: POSSIBLE ANSWERS

*1. *Validity of the speaker's analysis*   The speaker is most likely incorrect. He feels that the woman is playing with his affection for her, and that she is enjoying his emotional frustration and hurt. It is more likely that she simply does not like the speaker. It is natural for the speaker to blame the woman rather than to acknowledge his own part in the failure of the relationship.

2. *Speaker's continued love for the woman*   The speaker is letting his passion rather than his reason control him.

3. *Speaker's state of mind*   The speaker is foolish and masochistic to persist in imposing himself on someone who does not like him. His final curse is understandable, but not justified. Uncontrolled passion can cause even intelligent people to behave in a way that hurts others and is contrary to their own best interests.

*4. *The woman's behavior*   The woman is correct to turn down the speaker's love if she has no interest in it. While she could make an effort to put herself into the speaker's position and to be kind to him, she may feel that if she does this, she risks encouraging him.

ANALYZING LITERARY TECHNIQUE: POSSIBLE ANSWERS

1. *Apostrophe*   Dante uses apostrophe in order to achieve immediacy. It appears that the speaker is addressing a woman who is present.

2. *Central image*   The central image of the poem is that of a woman who is made of stone. The image of a stone connotes such qualities as hardness, insensitivity, and the inability to feel emotion. Thus, by describing the woman as stonelike, the

speaker dehumanizes her and implies that she is unnatural because she has rejected him. His closing curse reveals the depth of his anguish and anger. However, in blaming the woman for their lack of relationship, the speaker is denying his own role in the situation. Anyone who ventures to offer love takes on the risk of rejection, for romantic love requires mutuality of regard. Unrequited love is actually infatuation.

3. *Stanzas in poem*   The first, short stanza (lines 1–3) sets up the central image of the poem and sets the scene. The second stanza (lines 4–10) fills out the imagery and provides additional detail. The central image of the stonelike woman, her rejection of the speaker, and Love's "hard" rule connect the two stanzas.

WRITING ABOUT LITERATURE

1. *Expository essay analyzing relationship to courtly love*   Call students' attention to the information about courtly love in the Introduction. If they are familiar with the well-known version of King Arthur by Sir Thomas Malory, remind them that courtly love provides the setting for the Knights of the Round Table. Students may view this poem as a courtly lover's sincere complaint about the hardship of unrequited love. Others may think that the strong emotion in the last lines reflects a courtly lover's hostility to a tradition that encourages women to be arrogant and insensitive to a lover's plight. Most important about the poem may be the universality of the human feelings being expressed. They may be adolescent and excessive, but they represent a common human reaction to rejection. (**PLJ**)

2. *Creative writing: Retell this incident from the woman's point of view*   Call students' attention to the suggestions in the textbook assignment. Encourage the students who choose to write a poem to select a central image that the woman will apply to her lover. (**PLJ**)

FURTHER READING

Dante Alighieri, "Inferno" from the *Divine Comedy; The New Life*.

War
LUIGI PIRANDELLO

INTRODUCING THE STORY

In "War," Pirandello examines war's toll. Soldiers must confront their mortality and the ideal of a heroic death. Their parents must confront the inconsolable loss of a child. The story overflows with the emotions of anger and sorrow, opening with the sorrow of a mother who can only growl wordlessly, like a wild animal that has lost its young, and closing with the sobs of a father, for whom the best intellectual reasons are powerless to stifle the cry from his heart.

Pirandello uses the stylistic device of a debate to elaborate and intensify the nature and extent of a parent's grief. The mother of the son about to leave for the front, the fathers who have sons at the front, and the father whose son was satisfied to die a hero all mourn war's devastating effect upon their children's and their own lives. The sorrowing mother is amazed to find a parent capable of stoically accepting the loss of his child, only to find that his stoicism has been a self-protective sham and that, paradoxically, his emotions are as intolerably painful as her own.

"War" illustrates Pirandello's view that reality differs from person to person. The story's paradoxical theme is that reality may be the opposite of what one perceives it to be. People who feel unbearable emotions may conceal them from themselves and from others. In this story, Pirandello's attention to psychological mechanisms for controlling grief is more important than the obvious theme that war causes grief.

PLJ: How do you deal with a great disappointment or loss?

Literary Terms: characterization, climax, conflict, foreshadowing, irony, paradox, resolution, reversal, satire, theme

COMPREHENSION QUESTIONS

1. Why is the woman in deep mourning? (only son being sent into war)
2. What is the general reaction to her sorrow? (Others believe they have greater reason to complain.)
3. What attitude does the fat man express? (Decent young men die willingly as heroes.)
4. What question does the woman ask the fat man? (Is your son really dead?)
5. How does the fat man react? (realizes fact of his son's death and bursts into tears)

UNDERSTANDING THE STORY: POSSIBLE ANSWERS

*1. *Nameless characters* The characters have no names in order to make them universal.
 2. *Parent's love for child* All children receive their parents' total love, no matter how many siblings there are.
 3. *"We belong to them but they never belong to us."* Parents devote their lives to the development of their children, with the goal of rearing independent, well-functioning adults. Children grow up to become independent of their parents and to lead their own lives.
*4. *Why woman asks if man's son has really died* She cannot believe that a mourning parent can be so stoic about his loss.

*5. *Fat man/old man*   The change in description registers the toll that the realization of his loss has taken on him.

6. *Patriotism and "decent boys"*   Pirandello suggests that patriotism is simply a rationalization, a way of making the devastation of war acceptable. The fat man is serious when he says that "decent boys" are patriotic. However, warlike behavior is anything but "decent," so that the phrase "decent boys" has a satiric and ironic tone. The fat man's eventual rejection of his own intellectual arguments demolishes the charade of rationalization.

*7. *Themes*   Themes include: (*a*) War causes irreconcilable grief; (*b*) reality may be different from, and even the opposite of, what one perceives it to be; (*c*) people who feel unbearable emotions may attempt to conceal them from themselves.

ANALYZING LITERARY TECHNIQUE: POSSIBLE ANSWERS

1. *Hiding one's face*   The description is important because hiding a face comes to symbolize hiding emotion. The woman hides her face to conceal her sorrow. The fat man covers his mouth to hide his missing teeth, just as he hides his inner feelings behind his arguments. The fat man's missing teeth suggest that the substance, or "bite," of his arguments also is missing.

*2. *Characterization*   Characters are distinguished by the particular attitudes and ideas they express and by their physical appearance. The last description of the fat man as "old" adds a new dimension to his characterization; facing reality has sapped his vitality and has aged him.

3. *Conflict and resolution*   The conflict is both external and internal. The external conflict is the debate over the proper attitude of parents when their children go to war. It includes the conflict between an intellectual and an emotional response to the death of a child killed in war. The internal conflict is the fat man's struggle to realize his loss and express his true emotions.

*4. *Climax*   The climax is the woman's question ("is your son really dead?"), when she challenges the intellectual approach to a son's death. The question touches off the plot's reversal and confirms the validity of the woman's emotional response.

*5. *Reversal*   The fat man's sudden switch from intellectual to emotional response gives the story its surprise ending and its tremendous power.

*6. *Irony*   It is ironic that reality may be the opposite of what one perceives it to be. It is a psychological paradox that people who feel unbearable emotions may conceal them or even express the opposite emotions.

WRITING ABOUT LITERATURE

1. *Expository analysis of emotional impact of story*   Call students' attention to the suggestions in the textbook assignment. (See **U.S.** questions 1, 4, 5, and 7, and **A.L.T.** questions 2, 4, 5, and 6 above.)

2. *Creative writing: A poem about war*   Call students' attention to the suggestions and directions in the textbook assignment. Encourage them to choose a focus and then to think in terms of images that will elicit an emotional reaction in the reader. Patriotism and heroism can inspire pride and joy; destruction and carnage arouse disgust and horror; the thought of loved ones arouses longing and love; and the idea of self-sacrifice elicits feelings that depend on the person's personal values and his or her attitudes toward the particular war.

FURTHER READING

Pirandello, Luigi, collections of stories: *Better Think Twice about It, A Character in Distress, Horse in the Moon, The Medals and Other Stories;* plays: *Enrico IV, Six Characters in Search of an Author.*

The Doctor's Divorce
S. Y. AGNON

INTRODUCING THE STORY

"The Doctor's Divorce" is the powerful and disturbing story of a doctor whose self-esteem is so low that he cannot permit himself to accept the love of his wife. Instead, he is compelled to think the worst of her in order to feel worthy of her. He is so alienated from himself that his marriage becomes a paradox: The woman he considers most desirable is a source of continual torment, and he hates the woman he loves. The catalyst for the dissolution of the marriage is a man whom Dinah loved in the past but did not marry. Succumbing to what Edgar Allan Poe calls "the spirit of perverseness," the dark side of his nature, the doctor becomes obsessed with the ex-lover's role in Dinah's life and in his own marriage. His paranoid, masochistic fantasies multiply, culminating in an absurd and terrifying dream.

Meanwhile, Dinah accepts her husband's masochistic and sadistic behavior in the hope that her love will nurse him back to emotional health. However, by not rejecting his accusations, she gives her husband tacit permission to continue indulging his paranoia. Thus, she inadvertently perpetuates and exacerbates her husband's anxieties instead of alleviating them as she intends. Her husband's dream causes her to confront the reality of their marriage, which, in turn, enables the doctor to put aside his denials and manipulations and finally give her a divorce.

The doctor's last words in the story, said in the present (after World War II), proclaim his undying love for Dinah and reveal the continued split in his personality between the man who loves her and the man who feels unworthy of her. This crowning irony infuses the entire story with a tremendous surge of psychological power because the doctor has subtly revealed through his associative thinking that he is telling this story about thirty years after it occurred (shortly after World War I). In his mind, both past and present have merged into one continual torment.

Agnon's decision to tell this story from the doctor's point of view permits the reader to enter the mind of a man who has two personalities, an exterior personality that enables him to be a professionally competent and presumably reasonably attractive doctor and a dark inner personality (his doppelgänger or shadow) that prohibits him from loving himself and, therefore, anyone else. By traveling the tortuous paths of the doctor's mind, readers discover how the doctor succeeds in destroying his own life—they see the power that paranoia and denial of reality can have on human behavior. Moreover, they see how Dinah's own guilt about her past and her love for the doctor combine to fuel and perpetuate her husband's victimization of her.

PLJ: When someone whom you love treats you in a way that you consider to be unjust, do you attempt to communicate your view of the situation, or do you ignore the accusations? If you attempt to communicate, are you successful? If you choose to ignore the situation, what do you hope to achieve, and are you successful?

Literary Terms: characterization, contrast, crisis, doppelgänger, expressionism, first-person limited omniscience, foreshadowing, irony, narrative perspective, paradox, psychological realism, theme, unreliable narrator

COMPREHENSION QUESTIONS

1. What attracts the doctor to Dinah? (her smile and eyes; everyone's love for her)
2. How does the doctor feel about the period of his engagement? (best time in his life)
3. What about Dinah's love begins to bother the doctor? (sadness in it)
4. What does the doctor learn about Dinah's past? (previous love affair)
5. How does the doctor initially feel about Dinah's past? (earlier lover is unworthy of her; Dinah has not yet fallen in doctor's esteem)
6. What is surprising about the wedding? (no relatives or friends invited; the story the doctor remembers)
7. What does the doctor find most disturbing about his honeymoon? (man's footsteps in the next room)
8. What characterizes the first year of marriage? (happiness destroyed by thoughts of Dinah's earlier love)
9. How does the doctor feel about Dinah's relatives? (so admires them that he pretends they're his own)
10. What is unusual about the doctor's patient in the hospital? (Dinah's ex-lover)
11. What dream does the doctor reveal to Dinah? (ex-lover accuses Dinah of rape)
12. What action of Dinah's frightens the doctor? (chooses to lock herself in room)
13. Who wants the divorce? (Dinah)
14. How does Dinah change? (becomes self-assertive and independent; returns to work)
15. How does the doctor feel after the divorce? (still loves Dinah)

UNDERSTANDING THE STORY: POSSIBLE ANSWERS

*1. *Dinah's sadness* (a) The doctor instinctively views something in himself as the cause of Dinah's sadness because subconsciously he is certain that he is not good enough for her; (b) Dinah might be sad to see a problem in his reaction to her and fear a second broken relationship.

*2. *Doctor's thoughts at wedding* (a) The doctor's view of the witnesses reveals his unstable mind. He views them first as greedy paupers who will squander his money and then as poor people who need his money for survival. He is unaware of the juxtaposition and of the inconsistency.

(b) The doctor's liking for the groom in his fantasy reveals his simultaneous needs to remind Dinah of her shame and to punish himself for choosing to marry someone whom he feels is superior to himself.

(c) The doctor has such low self-esteem that he is compelled to use Dinah's past as a way to reduce her worth and thereby make her acceptable to him. When he considers that Dinah is too good for him, her excellence increases his feelings of worthlessness.

*3. *Doctor's view of himself as Dinah's "lord"; Dinah's remark about depravity* The doctor's view of himself as Dinah's lord reveals excessive pride and arrogance. It matches in degree his underlying feelings of worthlessness.

The collapse of her earlier relationship has left Dinah with deep wounds to her own self-esteem. Her extraordinary ability (and need) to appeal to everyone and to be "supernurse" may be her way of dealing with her own feelings of worthlessness.

*4. *Why doctor blames Dinah's ex-lover for destroying happiness* The doctor's self-esteem is so low that sometimes he cannot tolerate faults within himself, while at other times he has the masochistic need to act in a way that destroys the admiration of others. In this instance, in order to remain blameless, he is compelled to blame other people for his problems.

The doctor is manipulating the most likely facts in order to make them emotionally acceptable to him. The only way that he can tolerate the thought of Dinah's having intimately related to another man is to view that man as demanding and to view Dinah as weak.

*5. *Why doctor torments in spite of remorse; Why Dinah ignores doctor's taunts* Both the doctor's torments and his remorse for his behavior reinforce how contemptible he thinks he is, and they reflect the lack of self-esteem that forms the basis of his personality.

Having unsuccessfully tried love and sympathy, Dinah now tries to ignore the doctor's taunts in the hope that lack of attention will cause them to die out. Her behavior infuriates the doctor because he needs to view her as the cause of his problems and under his control.

6. *Why doctor is kind to man he hates* The doctor gains power in that he exercises control over the man, he is able to feel superior to him, and he causes the man to be obligated to him.

(*a*) The doctor is wrong when he blames Dinah's ex-lover for ruining his life; he alone is to blame for that.

(*b*) Dinah is as responsible as her ex-lover for the fact that their broken romance has left her with a low self-image. If she had more self-esteem, she would not tolerate being victimized a second time by the doctor.

7. *Significance of "This is the face that had the power . . . "*   The past tense of the verb (*had*) is significant in that it reveals that Dinah's face no longer has this power for him. Dinah's silence in response to her husband's taunts angers him more than her loving acceptance does.

*8. *Significance in doctor's change from Sec. 4 to Sec. 10; Dinah's embrace*   The doctor's blame of Dinah in his dream leads her to break with him. His change in focus from her ex-lover to herself reveals that his emotional problems are beyond her ability to cure. Both her loving acceptance and her attempt to ignore the situation have failed. She refuses to tolerate any more abuse, and her embrace is one of love and farewell.

*9. *Doctor's efforts to be good; the divorce*   (*a*) The doctor is arrogant and patronizing; he will be good to Dinah out of pity.

(*b*) He views Dinah as forcing him to give her a divorce because it reverses their roles to his advantage, making Dinah the evildoer and himself the victim.

(*c*) He agrees to the divorce when Dinah's behavior finally makes it impossible for him to deny the reality of their relationship, and he must relinquish any hope that he can win her back.

*10. *Doctor's responsibility and guilt about Dinah's possible suicide*   Dinah's locking herself in her room is her first indisputable rejection of her husband, and it forces him to face his true self. Dinah's past acceptance of his behavior has condoned it and encouraged his further victimization of her. In the doctor's warped mind, if Dinah permits him to treat her this way, his accusations must be correct, and she must be to blame. Thus, until this response, Dinah has been an unwitting partner in the doctor's disease.

*11. *Why doctor accuses Dinah of sudden change in behavior*   By keeping her true reactions to herself, Dinah has not prepared her husband to face reality, and his surprise is his way of blaming her for that. He, of course, refused to see reality until it overwhelmed him.

*12. *Doctor's view of Dinah's job*   The doctor sees Dinah's job in terms of what it means to him. Therefore, he sees its negative aspects and, in his mind, finds a way for Dinah still to need him as a caretaker and a source of financial security.

*13. *Doctor's last line*   Thirty years later, the doctor still loves the woman that he felt compelled to torment, and his behavior remains in his mind with an immediacy that is horrifying.

14. *Question of change in the doctor; different marriage without Dinah's past*   (*a*) The doctor probably could not cure such severe emotional problems without professional help. If he had received such help, he would have been able to leave behind his marriage of long ago and move on to new experiences in life.

(*b*) A person who has such severe emotional problems will bring them to any marriage. If Dinah had not had a past that caused the doctor a problem, he would have found other aspects of her life that bothered him, for his need to feel that he was worthy of her would still necessitate that he find sufficient fault with her to make their choice of each other acceptable to him.

ANALYZING LITERARY TECHNIQUE: POSSIBLE ANSWERS

1. *Agnon's choice of doctor and nurse*   (a) It is ironic that a doctor should be sick and unable to heal himself. Similarly, it is ironic that a nurse—someone who is more likely to cater to a sick person and to feel that, with proper care, the person will recover—is unable to cure the doctor.

2. *Paradox*   It is a paradox that the doctor finds the sweetest woman in the world to be an intolerable torment to him and that he hates the woman he loves. The man who considers himself "more fortunate than all others" (Sec. 2) is overwrought with anxiety and suffering from the end of his honeymoon (Sec. 6) until the dream that leads to his divorce (Sec. 10).

3. *Dramatic irony*   (a) The doctor's situation is ironic in that having won the prize, he cannot enjoy it.

   (b) The doctor is happier engaged than he is married.

   (c) The doctor cannot heal himself.

   (d) Dinah is a nurse, but all her care cannot improve the doctor's condition.

4. *Verbal irony*   (a) (Sec. 6) The doctor says, "I knew she was entirely mine," but is tormented by footsteps in the next room that he is certain belong to Dinah's ex-lover.

   (b) (Sec. 7) The doctor tells Dinah, "All your illness comes to you only because of the man who ruined your life," implying that he means her ex-lover when, as he reveals in the preceding sentence, he himself is that man.

   Both examples convey that the doctor is not the master of his own perceptions. The doctor is so certain that anyone as wonderful as Dinah cannot possibly be satisfied with him that virtually anything can threaten his security.

5. *Examples of foreshadowing*   (a) (Sec. 2) "One shouldn't worry about a girl that has gone because others will soon come along": After his divorce, thirty years pass without anyone's replacing Dinah.

   (b) (Sec. 2) "Can one find another girl like Dinah?": The doctor cannot.

   (c) (Sec. 3) "Let's be happy and not disturb our happiness": Dinah accurately senses that her disclosure will destroy their happiness.

   (d) (Sec. 4) ". . . as though she had in no way fallen in esteem. And . . . was as dear to me as always": This statement reveals the doctor's underlying attitude toward Dinah's past.

   (e) (Sec. 10) "This is the face that had the power to . . . dissipate the anger . . .": The doctor has already turned against Dinah before his dream.

*6. *Narrative perspective*   Agnon's use of a first-person limited omniscient narrator puts readers into the doctor's diseased mind so that they know his most intimate thoughts and feelings. Readers first begin to question the doctor's reliability as a narrator in Sec. 3, when he overreacts to Dinah's sadness. His continual questioning of her and his investigation of her relatives is unusual behavior, and it foreshadows his inability to accept any imperfection in her.

The doctor's neurotic behavior continues to escalate. In Sec. 4, he overreacts to Dinah's past and continues his persistent questioning. In Sec. 5, his thoughts during the marriage ceremony reveal that his psychological problem is very serious. Thereafter, the reader is not surprised to find that, in Sec. 6, the doctor is paranoid about the person in the next room, and that he continues to indulge in increasingly grotesque and pernicious thoughts. As the story progresses, the doctor's distorted view of reality becomes a nightmare. The narrative perspective causes readers to be both participants and objective observers as they experience the horror of the doctor's madness.

7. *Contrast*   The contrast between the portrait the doctor paints of Dinah in Sec. 1 and his later view of her is a measure of his psychological disease. The contrast between his perceptions and reality gives the story the tremendous power of a personal tragedy.

8. *Themes*   (a) Reality may be different from what a person perceives it to be; (b) People can bring their happiness or unhappiness upon themselves; (c) Relationships are fragile and cannot always be repaired when they break.

9. *The doctor's personality*   The doctor apparently has a split personality. His public personality is that of a successful doctor who earns Dinah's love and loyalty. His private personality is dark and irrational, a type of personality described as "the spirit of perverseness" by Edgar Allan Poe, "the *doppelgänger*" by G. H. Schubert, and "the shadow" by Carl Jung. Jung writes that only those who acknowledge the existence of their shadow-selves can control its role in their lives. The doctor's denial of his shadow-self is evident in his abdication of responsibility for his attitudes and behavior and in his blame of Dinah. His blindness permits his dark personality to create irreparable damage that eventually causes the woman he loves to divorce him.

WRITING ABOUT LITERATURE

1. *Expository essay analyzing Dinah's character and the three stages of her love for the doctor*   Dinah suffers from low self-esteem from her previous romance, combined with high self-esteem as a nurse. The three stages of her love are (1) delighted; (2) worried—tries to cure doctor with her love; (3) recognizes futility after dream and prepares for divorce. Remind students to use direct quotations from the story to support their ideas. (See **U.P.** questions 1, 5, and 8–11.)

2. *Expository essay analyzing the importance of narrative perspective*   Most students probably will choose option *b*, that the story would be less effective if told by an objective narrator. Reasons might include: (*a*) an objective narrator would elimi-

nate the immediacy of the first-person perspective; (*b*) an objective narrator would eliminate or at least dilute some of the emotional intensity of the story; (*c*) an objective narrator would undercut the dramatic irony produced by the doctor's unreliable narrative. Key examples from the text would be any of the instances where the doctor's words to Dinah are directly contradicted by his actions, such as the passage in Sec. 7 in which he tells Dinah that ''All your illness comes to you only because of the man who ruined your life.'' (See **U.P.** questions 1–5, 8, 10, 12, and 13, and **A.L.T.** question 6 above.)

3. *Creative writing: Tell story from Dinah's point of view*   Students should include Dinah's explanation of why she tolerates such treatment and how she feels after the divorce.

FURTHER READING

Agnon, S. Y., *Twenty-One Stories; A Guest for the Night; The Bridal Canopy.*

Lament for Ignacio Sánchez Mejías
FEDERICO GARCÍA LORCA

INTRODUCING THE POEM

''Lament for Ignacio Sánchez Mejías'' is a modern masterpiece. It speaks to every reader because it is a poem about the inevitability of death and the human need to be immortal. The poem moves on two levels simultaneously. On one level is García Lorca's eulogy to his close friend in which he documents his own gradual acceptance of Ignacio's death. On another level is García Lorca's acceptance of his own mortality. The double focus on this subject is natural because the death of a dear one always becomes, in the mind of the bereaved, both a personal loss and a reminder that death is the unalterable fate of every human being. Moreover, it is the poet's personal identification with the issue of mortality that supplies the tremendous emotional power behind the poetry.

García Lorca divides the poem into four sections. Each reflects a psychological stage in the mourning process. As the poet moves from Part 1 to Part 4, he moves from denial to acceptance of Ignacio's death, and from the inability to contemplate the meaning of death to a way of coping with it (through his writing) that satisfies him. Therefore, García Lorca's acceptance and understanding of his friend's death becomes a type of ''night journey'' in which the poet comes to terms with his own mortality.

Part 1: ''Cogida (Goring) and Death'' depicts García Lorca's attempt to register the fact that a bull has gored Ignacio to death in a bullfight. The fact has taken the poet by surprise: He has had no time to prepare himself psychologically for the event. Thus, Part 1 represents the poet's shock and horror at the news. Over and over, he repeats the chant that swings like a pendulum on a clock, ''at five in the afternoon.'' Life has stopped for both the matador and the poet. The poet expresses no emotion in this section because he feels none. He is numb with shock and disbelief.

Part 2: "The Spilled Blood" depicts García Lorca's denial of reality, his adamant refusal to face Ignacio's death. While he tentatively acknowledges the fact of his dear friend's death, it is only as an abstract phenomenon. He refuses to confront the concrete, physical reality of his friend's death. He refuses to visit Ignacio and watch him wage a futile struggle for life. García Lorca's emotional response reveals the extent to which his friend's death has deeply wounded him. The pain of this raw wound forces him to cry out: "I will not see it!" "I do not want to see it!" "Do not ask me to see it." Ignacio's sudden death also has deep emotional implications for his own life. It reminds him that life is unpredictable and that he, too, cannot predict his own death.

The poet copes with death by remembering the past. He connects Ignacio Sánchez Mejías with the bullfighters in ancient Crete, who sacrificed their lives to the bull, symbol of the god Poseidon, so that Crete would prosper. Like them, Ignacio is a hero. He bravely risked death, not blanching before the bull's horns. Although he could not avoid death, he could control the manner in which he lived and died. Thus, he faced his death with dignity and fortitude.

"There was no prince in Seville who could compare with him," the poet says, by way of introducing a section of eloquent praise that, in fact, will make Ignacio a living memory. García Lorca can handle memory, and even such abstractions about death as "Now the moss and the grass / open with sure fingers / the flower of his skull. / And now his blood comes out singing" Blood both sings and forms "a pool of agony." It connects life and death. However, visualizing what is abstract is emotionally easier for the poet than confronting the corpse of his friend. "I will not see it!" he concludes.

In Part 3: "The Laid Out Body," García Lorca acknowledges the finality of death. It is no longer possible to deny the fact that Ignacio is dead. Everything dies eventually; "even the sea dies." Now, the poet must confront the meaning of death, and his wish to deny death takes a new direction. He wants death to be more than eternal sleep. He contrasts stone, for him a symbol of death, with water, for him a symbol of life.

He repeats the idea that "All is finished," but the emotional issue behind the end of life and the eternity of death is not finished for him. Leave the body to the moss and the grass, but let the soul free itself of straps and fly into a sweet eternity. "I want . . . , I want . . . , I want . . . ," he repeats. For García Lorca, death cannot and must not be the complete end of life. He invokes the greatest of men ("those that break horses and dominate rivers") and the greatest of poets ("men of sonorous skeleton who sing with a mouth full of sun and flint") to tell him how to cope with the fact of mortality, his own as well as that of his friend, and to give him the power to create a fitting elegy for Ignacio.

Finally, in Part 4: "Absent Soul," García Lorca examines the meaning of death for those who are alive. He is concerned about the anonymity that death confers, both for Ignacio and, in the future, for himself. He realizes that those who have died will be remembered by the living if a poet will sing about them. His refrain, "(Nobody) knows you because you have died for ever," gives way to his solution, "But I sing of you / For posterity I sing of your . . . " García Lorca's poetic tribute to Ignacio Sánchez Mejías will become part of his own legacy to the world.

The last two lines of the poem reveal García Lorca's recognition and acceptance of the universal human condition. Ignacio's special qualities make his death a cause of sorrow, but death is part of life. "A sad breeze," for the poet a symbol of the grief in life, blows "through the olive trees," for him a symbol of the sustaining powers in life. Life is beautiful but transitory, and death is the price that each person must pay for all the joys of being human.

The language that García Lorca uses to convey his thoughts and feelings is so striking that, at first, it overwhelms both the intellect and the emotions of the reader and becomes a barrier to understanding and enjoying the poem. Paradoxically, with study, the reader comes to enjoy the poem because of the very phrases that made the initial reading difficult. Part of the difficulty is caused by the fact that most readers have little or no knowledge about bullfights, the treatment of a wounded bullfighter, and related Spanish terminology. Part of the difficulty is caused by a surrealist and symbolist artist's unusual choice and juxtaposition of images and metaphors. Readers must cope with strange comparisons and contrasts. Familiarity and analysis foster appreciation of this important poem.

PLJ: How would you react to the death of a very good friend? What would be your initial reaction? How would your first thoughts and feelings change with the passage of time? How would the death of someone dear to you affect your own life? How would you preserve the memory of that person?

Literary Terms: allusion, apostrophe, contrast, expressionism, figurative language, imagism, irony, metaphor, night journey, personification, repetition, setting, simile, surrealism, symbolism, theme

COMPREHENSION QUESTIONS

1. What event caused García Lorca to write this poem? (His friend Ignacio died.)
2. What time did the event in the poem occur? (5:00 in the afternoon)
3. What was Ignacio doing prior to this event? (fighting a bull)
4. How does García Lorca first react to the event? (horror and denial)
5. What is García Lorca's purpose in writing this poem? (to memorialize Ignacio)

UNDERSTANDING THE POEM: POSSIBLE ANSWERS

*1. *Part 1:* (a) *What happened, where, and when* Ignacio Sánchez Mejías has died in a bullfight (in a bullring) at 5:00 P.M.

(b) *Why speaker isn't more specific* (1) García Lorca's contemporaries know who Ignacio is and what happened. (2) The poem is more about García Lorca's reaction to the event than about the event itself.

(c) *Repetition of "at five in the afternoon"* Repetition reflects García Lorca's shock and horror at Ignacio's death. Life has stopped for García Lorca as well.

(*d*) *Relationship between speaker's attitude and timing*   His shock and lack of emotion reflect the fact that he has just heard the news.

*2. *Part 2:* (*a*) *What speaker doesn't want to see*   He doesn't want to see Ignacio's death, either his body or where it happened. He wants no proof of his friend's death, and he doesn't want to see signs of Ignacio's suffering. He wants to ignore the fact that his friend has died (denial).

(*b*) *Connection between speaker's refusal and his eulogy of Ignacio*   Ignacio was a close friend, a fine poet and dramatist, and an excellent bullfighter who was only thirty-four years old when he was killed. Thus, he was too extraordinary, too dear, and too young to die. García Lorca does not want to think of his friend as being dead (denial). If the poet can remember Ignacio as he was when he was alive, he will remain alive, if only in García Lorca's memory.

(*c*) *Repetition of "I will not see it!"*   Repetition reflects the speaker's denial of his friend's death.

(*d*) *Relationship between speaker's attitude and timing*   The speaker's denial reflects the fact that the news of his friend's death is still very new. References to the moon indicate that Part 2 may concern García Lorca's thoughts later in the evening, after Ignacio's death. Denial is typical of the early stages of grief. One purpose of a funeral (described in the last lines of the section) is to help a bereaved person accept reality.

*3. *Part 3:* (*a*) *Problem speaker confronts*   He confronts the meaning of death for the man who has died. He wants death to be more than nothingness or eternal sleep.

(*b*) *Meaning of "All is finished"*   "All is finished" implies that death is the end of all aspects of life, that death contains nothing.

(*c*) *Repetition of "I want . . ."*   Repetition reflects and emphasizes García Lorca's great need to learn how to cope with the finality of death. He wants the greatest of men to tell him about Ignacio's future. He wants to hear that Ignacio and other great men conquer and dominate death, and that a sweet afterlife exists. In the process, he begins to conceive of how he will deal with his friend's death.

(*d*) *Relationship between speaker's attitude and timing*   More time has passed since Ignacio's death. He is about to be buried, and García Lorca is looking at his corpse. It is no longer possible for him to deny that his friend is dead.

(*e*) *Speaker's role in Ignacio's death*   García Lorca wants the greatest of men to inspire him with a lament for Ignacio that will free Ignacio from the constraints of death.

*4. *Part 4:* (*a*) *Problem speaker examines*   He examines the meaning of death for those who continue to live.

(*b*) *Meaning of "does not know you"*   Death causes the one who has died to be forgotten by those who remain alive, and to be unknown to those who live at a later time. This is an emotional issue for García Lorca because it is going to be his problem when he dies, just as it is now Ignacio's problem.

(*c*) *Speaker's solution*   García Lorca will write an elegy for his friend that will recapture Ignacio's greatness and make his memory immortal. García Lorca must realize that his own poems and dramas will be his form of immortality.

(*d*) *Relationship between speaker's attitude and timing*   Enough time has passed since Ignacio's death that the poet has been able to reconcile himself to his friend's death and his own mortality. García Lorca can now proceed with his own life as a poet.

(*e*) *Attitude toward life at end of poem*   The last two lines reflect García Lorca's acceptance of death as an integral part of the universal human condition. Life can be beautiful, but it is transitory.

5. *Night journey*   The focus of the poem is García Lorca's psychological response to his friend Ignacio's death. The poet moves from denial to acceptance of Ignacio's death, and, in the process, from the inability to contemplate the meaning of death to a satisfying way of coping with it by viewing poetry as a form of immortality. Thus, the development of García Lorca's attitudes toward death is a night journey, an experience through which the poet gains important self-knowledge and the ability to accept his own mortality.

ANALYZING LITERARY TECHNIQUE: POSSIBLE ANSWERS

1. *Apostrophe*   García Lorca's technique of addressing Ignacio at the end of Part 3 and in Part 4 as if he were alive and with the poet makes it appear as if Ignacio is, in fact, present. This technique would be satisfying to the poet, in that it brings his friend closer to him.

*2. *Allusion to Minotaur*   The allusion to the bullfights in ancient Crete, which are believed to have had a connection to the worship of the god Poseidon in the form of a bull, enhances Ignacio's battle with the bull and his death. It gives his death a higher purpose and emphasizes his role as that of a hero.

In Greek mythology, the Minotaur is a monster with a bull's head and a man's body. Archaeologists believe that Minos, the king of Crete, wore the head of a bull on state religious occasions, and that the Minotaur was actually such a king. Theseus, who killed the Minotaur, is a symbol of the Greeks' conquest of Minoan Crete (c. 1450 B.C.).

3. *References to nature*   The poet's juxtaposition of human and natural images conveys the fact that human beings are an integral part of the natural world. Examples: (*a*) "moss and grass open . . . flower of his skull," (*b*) "even the sea dies," and (*c*) "mouth full of sun and flint."

4. *How contrast reinforces emotional content*   Contrast heightens perception because it highlights differences. The poet contrasts life with death, remembering with forgetting, past with present, and reality with denial. Each of these contrasts helps convey the depth of the poet's sense of loss and the poignancy of his search for meaning beyond the finality of death.

5. *Figures of speech*   Choices will vary. Examples: (1) Part 2: "Now the moss and the grass open with sure fingers the flower of his skull"—the personification of nature and the description of Ignacio's skull as a flower. (2) Part 2: "And now his

blood comes out singing''—the vitality and joy of life, even as it gives way to death. (3) Part 3: ''those men of sonorous skeleton who sing with a mouth full of sun and flint''—poets whose words capture heaven and earth, brilliance and darkness, the range of life-experience.

WRITING ABOUT LITERATURE

1. *Expository essay analyzing García Lorca's use of repetition in poem* Call students' attention to the directions in the textbook assignment. Remind them to use direct quotations to support their ideas and that the poem's effect on them is important. (See **U.P.** questions 1–4 above.)
2. *Creative writing: Story of Ignacio Sánchez Mejías' death from bull's point of view* Encourage students who like this assignment to consult an encyclopedia or similar source about bullfights in order to acquire details to which the bull will react. The stories of Ernest Hemingway may also be a good resource for students. (See **A.L.T.** question 2 above.)
3. *Creative writing: Essay or poem eulogizing a person* Call students' attention to the directions in the textbook assignment. Remind them that making lists may help them determine whom to write about and which qualities and details to include. Remind them also that examining their use of language will significantly improve the effect of their writing.

FURTHER READING

García Lorca, Federico, *The Selected Poems of Federico García Lorca.*

Continental Europe

Human Knowledge

FRIEDRICH VON SCHILLER

INTRODUCING THE POEM

In "Human Knowledge," Schiller examines the limitations of human knowledge. He calls attention to the limitations of the subjective interpretation of facts, and he questions the value of deducing the whole by examining only part. He reveals the paradox that even scientists are as ignorant as they are knowledgeable because they emphasize an exclusively rational approach to learning.

The power of the poem comes from its structure, in which the poet concludes with an ironic question that reveals the paradox inherent in his philosophical subject. In addition, the tension between elements of classicism and romanticism adds texture and depth to the poem. Schiller relates his subject objectively, which is consistent with the highly rational content and approach of classicism. At the same time, he is a romantic in that he advocates that people rely upon their intuition and accept the existence of the irrational as an important part of the meaning of the universe.

PLJ: How do you know that what you know is really correct? Do you think that it is possible to know everything that there is to know about something? What factors determine whether or not the acquisition of total knowledge is possible? What factors can change the knowledge that one has acquired?

Literary Terms: allusion, classicism, irony, metaphor, paradox, romanticism, theme, tone

COMPREHENSION QUESTIONS

1. What do human beings read in Nature? (their own ideas)
2. What do human beings do to Nature's wonders? (arrange them into categories)
3. What do human beings do to Nature's expanses? (tie them with cords; in other words, attempt to classify them or arrange them into manageable subunits)
4. How does the astronomer explain the universe? (through reducing it to sets of constellations)
5. What part of the heavens does the astronomer see? (only its surface)

UNDERSTANDING THE POEM: POSSIBLE ANSWERS

*1. *Why people think they understand Nature*   People project systems and ideas on to Nature. Once those projected systems seem to become "natural," people no longer recognize that the systems reflect their own interests, biases, and limited understanding.

*2. *Why astronomer believes he understands the universe*   The astronomer, trained to see the heavens only in terms of constellations, does what he is trained to do and ends up believing that he understands the universe. However, all he really sees are the systems of constellations—the "figures" of the "swan" and the "bull"—that he has projected onto the sky.

*3. *How stanzas relate to each other*   The first stanza is concerned with "Nature"—the natural principles that govern the universe; the second is concerned specifically with the heavens. In addition, the first stanza addresses the reader directly, while the second stanza uses a third-person perspective to describe the actions of the astronomer. The astronomer is just one example of the kind of limited thinking that the poet is criticizing.

*4. *What Schiller is criticizing*   Schiller is criticizing the fact that the astronomer links stars into constellations, though the stars have no real connection with each other. (They are a "Sirius-distance" apart.) Consequently, the astronomer, like the reader in the first stanza, reads into the universe only what he himself has written there.

*5. *Themes*   Some possible themes include: (*a*) A little knowledge is a dangerous thing because it is incomplete and inaccurate; (*b*) People know much less about the universe than they think they know; (*c*) The universe contains two types of elements—those that the human mind can grasp, and those that are beyond the limitations of the human mind.

ANALYZING LITERARY TECHNIQUE: POSSIBLE ANSWERS

*1. *Paradox about knowledge*   The paradox in this poem is that those who think themselves wise are, in fact, ignorant of the true nature of the universe, whether they consider the earth or the heavens.

*2. *Meaning of the "spheres' mystic dance" (line 10)*   Literally, the image means "how the stars move in the sky." In a broader sense, "mystic" in this metaphor refers to the knowledge beyond the ability of the human mind to comprehend, and "dance" implies harmonious relationships and patterns in the universe that cannot be explained by using systems and scientific methods. By using a metaphor, Schiller underscores the fact that much of human understanding of how the universe works is based on analogy—on comparing the large and mysterious with the small and commonplace.

3. *Classicism vs. romanticism*   The form of the poem adheres to principles of classicism in that (*a*) the two stanzas complement and balance each other, and (*b*) the poet stands apart from the poem and presents his ideas objectively.

   On the other hand, the content of the poem is more reflective of romanticism than of classicism. The poet argues against a rational approach to understanding the universe, maintaining that its meaning is mystical, and therefore beyond human comprehension. It would be in keeping with romanticism to value one's emotional instincts and intuition about the nature of the universe, even if one could find no tangible confirmation of this type of knowledge.

The tension between classical and romantic elements adds complexity and interest to the poem.

*4. *Tone of poem*   The tone can be described as the ironic smile of one who is observing a very serious person pursue the wrong path. Schiller achieves this by considering the approach to knowledge of the reader and the astronomer and then asking the question about the "spheres' mystic dance." The question implies that each approach is a blind alley, for neither will lead to true knowledge.

WRITING ABOUT LITERATURE

1. *Expository analysis of Schiller's technique in presenting theme*   Students' responses will vary, depending on which theme they choose. (See **U.P.** questions 1–5, and **A.L.T.** questions 1, 2, and 4.)
2. *Creative writing: Changing human knowledge*   Encourage students to focus on one specific issue or area. Changing ideas about the role of heredity and environment in human development, the ability to cure certain diseases, the role of women in society, or the effects of automobile emissions on the environment are examples of possible topics. Students should try to convey what difference a developing understanding makes in how people perceive the world. (**PLJ**)

FURTHER READING

Schiller, Friedrich, "Ode to Joy"; *The Maid of Orleans; William Tell; Don Carlos.*

The Shadow
HANS CHRISTIAN ANDERSEN

INTRODUCING THE STORY

"The Shadow" appeals to readers of all ages. On the surface, it is a highly imaginative story of a shadow that becomes independent of its master and lives its own kind of life. On this level, the language is informal and often humorous, with details that children love. On a deeper level, "The Shadow" is a serious, satirical commentary on social values and the relationship of art to life, as well as a study of human psychology.

The "learned man" in the story, a dedicated scholar of what is "good and true and beautiful," cannot share his vision because society has no interest in it. Veneer rather than substance counts. The Shadow is the learned man's double, the dark counterpart of his former master. He is the learned man's doppelgänger in that he personifies everything that the learned man cannot permit himself to be, cannot acknowledge in himself, and cannot recognize in others. Thus, the learned man and the Shadow represent one complete personality that is split between them. The learned man personifies the human desire to be good, while the Shadow personifies the human desire to be free to act without controls.

Being interested only in what is evil, false, and ugly, the Shadow easily adapts to the society in which he lives, and it rewards him. Living completely without moral or ethical values, he acquires wealth, social prestige, and power through blackmail. Meanwhile, the "over-sharp-sighted" Princess, who is blind to what is good, true, and beautiful, finds the Shadow to be noble. She is impressed with his appearance of wealth and cleverness but fails to recognize the learned man's true value.

Through the learned man, Andersen attempts to explode one of the guiding principles of romanticism. In his view, goodness cannot destroy evil; if left to its own devices, evil will destroy what is good. The learned man becomes the Shadow's victim because, being unwilling to see what is evil, false, and ugly, he cannot deal with these qualities when they confront him. Hearing the Shadow's tales of blackmail, he says, "Extraordinary!" He makes no value judgment; he voices no condemnation. He accompanies the Shadow with no perception of what the future holds for him. Although the learned man finally takes a stand, refusing to surrender his integrity and to become the Shadow's shadow, he acts too late. The Shadow has him killed. The only ray of light in this dark tale is that the Shadow's evil cannot contaminate the learned man; he dies true to the humane values by which he has lived.

Andersen's theme belongs to a tradition that remains vital to contemporary life. Human beings cannot control their capacity to hurt others unless they recognize that each person's heart is composed of two chambers, a "heart of darkness" and a heart of virtue. From the time of the ancient Greeks, the principle "Know thyself" has demanded a self-knowledge that acknowledges the totality of what it is to be human.

The story also functions as a social satire on society's inability to understand and appreciate learning and art. The landlord, who represents the ordinary person, regards Poetry's music as tiresome. The learned man, who is often called a philosopher and who is a student of aesthetics (the study of the good, the true, and the beautiful), writes about Poetry and yet can find no way to approach her apartment since he is an observer and not an artist. Meanwhile, the Shadow claims that he has entered the antechamber of Poetry's apartment and that he has seen everything and knows everything about her. His inability to be specific reveals that his words have no more substance than he himself possesses. However, society accepts and praises the Shadow because it values his pretensions. It succumbs to his blackmail and makes him a wealthy person without ever realizing that he is a fake. The Princess easily accepts the Shadow's pretensions because they are consistent with her own.

Andersen's symbolic use of light (good) vs. dark (evil) and sight (truth) vs. blindness (fraudulence) enriches both the moral and satiric aspects of the story. The learned man, who is good, functions in sunlight, but not during the hours around noon, when the light is brightest. He sees more clearly than others, but not clearly enough to recognize evil in life. In contrast, the Shadow, who is evil, is composed of darkness and operates when light is low. Society is blind to the reality of what the learned man sees (his knowledge of truth and beauty) and therefore has no interest in his writings. The Princess, who should represent the best in society, takes pride in her "over-sharp" sight and yet cannot see beneath the appearances that she values, such as the Shadow's pretensions.

PLJ: What makes a person human? To what extent, if any, is an evil person human? What makes a person wise? What are the most important goals in life?

Literary Terms: characterization, doppelgänger, irony, satire, theme

COMPREHENSION QUESTIONS

1. What is important to the learned man about being human? (to be able to appreciate what is good, true, and beautiful)
2. What is important to the Shadow about being human? (to be wealthy, powerful, and accepted by high society)
3. How does the Shadow separate from the learned man? (climbs wall across the street and disappears)
4. How does the Shadow gain wealth? (blackmails people he spies on)
5. How does the Shadow gain prestige? (marries the Princess)
6. How does the Shadow gain power? (through blackmail, marriage, travel with learned man)
7. What relationship develops between the learned man and the Shadow? (Shadow becomes the master; learned man becomes shadow)
8. What happens to the Shadow at the end of the story? (marries Princess)
9. What happens to the learned man at the end? (Shadow has learned man killed)

UNDERSTANDING THE STORY: POSSIBLE ANSWERS

1. *Shadow's identity* The Shadow takes on his own identity as an independent person who is a fraud. His responses to the learned man's questions reveal his arrogance and his pretensions because if he really possessed the knowledge of Poetry that he claims, he would be able to provide detailed answers. His inability to get beyond the antechamber reveals that Poetry remained inaccessible to him as well as to the learned man. Andersen may be implying that a true understanding of art is inaccessible to observers (the landlord and the Shadow), to students of art (philosophers like the learned man and critics), and, in fact, to anyone except the artist. The Shadow's replies to the learned man reveal the type of person he is, and his success in society and with the Princess reveals that they share and appreciate his fake values.
2. *Who is more human?* Both learned man and Shadow are human, each representing an opposite side of human nature. It is the weakness of the learned man that he confuses *human* with *humane* and refuses to consider whatever in life is not "the true and the good and the beautiful." This weakness makes him vulnerable to the Shadow, for the learned man cannot deal with qualities that he cannot acknowledge.
3. *Wisdom of learned man and Shadow* Each possesses a different kind of wisdom. The learned man finds his in books and knows much more about ideas and facts.

The Shadow finds his in daily life and knows much more about the values and interests of most people.

4. *Why Shadow visits learned man*   The Shadow first comes in order to brag about his personal success. He wants to show off to his former master. The learned man's reaction, finding him "extraordinary" rather than repulsive, leads the Shadow to sense a tolerance in the learned man that may permit the Shadow to use him, just as he uses other people, for his own personal gain. With the trip to the spa, the Shadow succeeds.

    The learned man continues to allow the Shadow to visit him because his denial of evil makes it impossible for him to deal with it. This blind spot makes the learned man vulnerable to the Shadow. Also, the fact that the learned man is poor and in ill health makes the Shadow's offer very hard to resist.

*5. *Should learned man have accepted Shadow's terms?*   The learned man retains his dignity and integrity by refusing the Shadow's offer. To accept would be to deny the principles by which the learned man has lived his entire life, not just by becoming a shadow, but by becoming the shadow of an amoral being. For the learned man, death is preferable to a life of wealth and comfort with the loss of his integrity.

*6. *Triumphs of learned man and Shadow*   The learned man triumphs in the end in that he dies without sacrificing his integrity and his belief in the principles by which he has lived. He has not demeaned himself. The Shadow has triumphed in that he has acquired the power to put the learned man to death for not agreeing to become his servant. Evil has triumphed to the extent that the Shadow has gained wealth, prestige, and power. That evil behavior, like that of the Shadow, can and does triumph whenever good human beings like the learned man stand by and do nothing, is a significant lesson for all of humanity. People like the learned man, who remain true to their humane principles when confronted with the temptations of evil, are models of heroic behavior.

*7. *Themes*   *(a)* The serious underlying theme is that evil cannot be controlled unless individuals acknowledge its existence. All human beings can better control their behavior if they recognize their capability to be callous and cruel, dishonest and disloyal.

    (b) Another, more obvious theme is that "You cannot judge a book by its cover." The Shadow, the learned man, and the Princess all have trouble both with judging others by their appearances and with being judged by their appearances.

ANALYZING LITERARY TECHNIQUE: POSSIBLE ANSWERS

*1. *Fairy tale effect*   Andersen achieves the fairy tale effect of the story through its informality of tone. The narrator's colloquial expressions ("My word!" "Well,") and asides ("in the hot countries every window has a balcony"; "he made up his mind to say nothing about it, and that was very sensible of him") create the feeling of listening to a storyteller, thus adding immediacy to the story.

The first clear indication that the story has a deeper meaning than a tale told for children comes when the Shadow returns. The Shadow's treatment of the learned man's new shadow reveals the Shadow to be a cruel person and foreshadows that he will also mistreat his former master.

*2. *Relationship between learned man and Shadow*   The Shadow is the learned man's double. He is also the learned man's literal and figurative doppelgänger (dark counterpart). The Shadow personifies everything that the learned man cannot permit himself to be, cannot acknowledge in himself, and cannot recognize in others. The Shadow represents the learned man's unrestrained self, the part of his nature that desires to act without any internal or external controls.

3. *Function of light imagery*   Andersen uses conventional images of light in this story. On a literal level, the sun, moon, and other lights provide the scientific rationale for the Shadow's development and activities: There can be no shadow without a source of light. On a more symbolic level, images of light and dark emphasize the importance of seeing things clearly, as they really are. The Shadow sees most of the world in twilight and moonlight; even the learned man has to retire from the "full blaze of the sun."

*4. *Humor*   Humor adds to the fairy-tale tone of the story. It makes the tale more enjoyable and, therefore, more likely to have an impact on the audience. Some examples of humor in this story are (1) the basic idea of a person's shadow assuming an independent life; (2) the Shadow's repeated comment: "I have seen everything and I know everything" in response to every question about specific details, because it always evades the question. In the end, the Shadow admits that he never even entered Poetry's inner rooms; (3) the Shadow's comments about the need for a beard and the importance of being fat. In addition, many of the narrator's asides are quite funny, as when the learned man says " 'a man's as good as his word' " and the Shadow replies in "the only way possible": " 'And so is a shadow.' "

*5. *Irony*   Irony gives the story power. It keeps the reader alert to the discrepancies between appearances and reality, and it contains the element of surprise. It is the technique Andersen uses to satirize society. Some examples of irony include: (1) The Princess, who suffers from "over-sharp sight" and can "very nearly see right through" the Shadow, cannot see what kind of a person he really is; (2) The Princess's remark that the Shadow has "a noble character," since the Shadow has gained wealth, social prestige, and power through blackmail, and since he instigates the murder of the learned man; (3) The Shadow's remark that his "innermost nature" is that he is a man evades the issue of what type of man he is; (4) The Shadow's remark that he deserves respect because he is independent, well-informed, and has good standing and excellent connections points out false values and superficial qualities valued by the Shadow and society; (5) The good, learned man has no worldly success, while the evil Shadow achieves fortune and fame.

The power of "The Shadow" is in its satirization of society. Each humorous and ironic example is also an example of satire because Andersen is ridiculing the characters who are making the remarks for being socially pretentious and for espousing inferior values. In this story, clothes literally do not make a man.

WRITING ABOUT LITERATURE

1. *Expository theme on Andersen's view of society*   Call students' attention to the directions in the textbook assignment. (See **A.L.T.** questions 2, 5 above.)
2. *Creative writing: a fairy tale*   You may want to make some collections of fairy tales available to the class to spark students' ideas. Encourage independent thinking and creativity. **(PLJ)**

FURTHER READING

Andersen, Hans Christian, ''The Bell''; ''The Drop of Water''; ''The Emperor's New Clothes''; ''The Fir Tree''; ''The Little Match Girl''; ''The Nightingale''; ''The Snow Queen''; ''The Story of a Mother''; ''The Sweethearts''; ''The Ugly Duckling.''

The Heavenly Christmas Tree

FYODOR DOSTOYEVSKI

INTRODUCING THE STORY

''The Heavenly Christmas Tree'' is a small gem that displays one of Dostoyevski's major themes, society's lack of moral responsibility for the poor and downtrodden in its midst. The style is an example of psychological realism. Dostoyevski's respect for the poor, his interest in their plight, his concern with the moral growth of society, and his decision to portray his characters realistically reflect the influence of Nicolai Gogol and Charles Dickens. However, the psychological aspect of his realism is his own creation and his unique focus.

The plot of this story describes, with chilling dramatic irony, how a six-year-old boy becomes orphaned, starves, and freezes to death on Christmas Eve while the wealthy and the middle class turn away in self-conscious discomfort. The subject and setting appeal to readers' hearts, for Christmas is associated with love, family, plentiful food, and gifts. The contrast between this festive, joyous holiday and the poor, starving orphan's isolation and abandonment makes the story a searing indictment of any society that is indifferent to those in need.

In order to convey psychological realism in his characterization of the little boy, Dostoyevski writes in a style that seeks to imitate a young child's thought processes and language, dramatizing his emotional as well as physical experiences. Dostoyevski focuses on what captures the child's attention and how he reacts to what he sees, expressing his thoughts and feelings in language patterns that are appropriately repetitive and rambling.

The last line of the story reminds the educated reader that some of Dostoyevski's writing contains the roots of existentialism. By questioning the existence of heaven (and God), Dostoyevski leaves the fate of such children and mothers as those in this story to the social conscience of his readers. The readers, as members of society, must exert themselves to help the poor and homeless, for the compensation of a better world is not certain after death.

Your students will be interested in hearing the following descriptive passage from the April 1864 issue of *Vremya* (the literary journal that Dostoyevski and his brother founded). It reveals what is probably the source of Dostoyevski's inspiration for this story.

> Once I remember seeing among the crowd of people in the street a little girl who could not have been more than six years old. Her clothes were in tatters. She was dirty, barefoot, and beaten black and blue. Her body, which could be seen through the holes in her clothes, was all bruised. She was walking along aimlessly, hardly knowing where she was, and without apparently being in any hurry to get anywhere. Goodness knows why she was roaming about in the crowd; perhaps she was hungry. No one paid any attention to her. But what struck me most about her was that she looked so wretched and unhappy. Such hopeless despair was written all over her face that to see that little creature already experiencing so much damnation and despair was to the highest degree unnatural and terribly painful. She kept shaking her dishevelled head from side to side, as though debating some highly important question with herself, waving her little hands about and gesticulating wildly, and then, suddenly, clapping them together and pressing them to her bosom. I went back and gave her sixpence. She seized the small silver coin, gave me a wild look of startled surprise, and suddenly began running in the opposite direction as fast as her little legs would carry her, as though terrified that I should take the money away from her.

Juxtaposed with "The Heavenly Christmas Tree," this passage reveals how Dostoyevski transformed a particular life-experience into universal art.

PLJ: To what extent are you responsible for the welfare of other human beings? What are your obligations to others?

Literary Terms: characterization, contrast, fairy tale, folktale, dramatic irony, narrative perspective, naturalism, paradox, protagonist, psychological realism, realism, theme, and tone

COMPREHENSION QUESTIONS

1. What sends the child wandering into the street? (mother's death, hunger)
2. How is he treated? (ignored)
3. What gives him pleasure? (Christmas store windows and parties)
4. What happens to him? (dies of cold and hunger)
5. What does the author question? (heaven)

UNDERSTANDING THE STORY: POSSIBLE ANSWERS

1. *Dostoyevski's purpose in writing this tale*   Dostoyevski has a social purpose: to dramatize the plight of the poor and to motivate others to help.

*2. *Boy's treatment and society*   The boy's treatment reveals that (1) a great gap exists between the rich and the poor (the Christmas parties); (2) those who have the ability to be helpful ignore those in need (the policeman; the woman at the party the boy enters); and (3) the poor are friendless and helpless (the people on the street; the bigger boy).

3. *Effect of Christmas festivities on boy's life*   The Christmas festivities were the highlight of the boy's day, and possibly the highlight of his life. He would have died of starvation whether or not he had seen them, so it can be argued that his life was briefly cheered by his views of Christmas magic.

4. *Importance of Dostoyevski's final comment about Christ's Christmas tree*   Dostoyevski puts the burden of the welfare of the poor and downtrodden on society, rather than on religious beliefs. He does not permit his readers to avoid their moral responsibilities by assuming the existence of heaven and compensation there for misery on earth.

ANALYZING LITERARY TECHNIQUE: POSSIBLE ANSWERS

*1. *Why protagonist is a young child*   The young child is more vulnerable, more helpless, more frightened, more appealing and less threatening to strangers who could help him, and more appealing to readers' sympathies.

*2. *Why a Christmas setting?*   Christmas is the happiest time of year for many children, who receive gifts and enjoy family parties. The holiday contrasts the plight of the poor and downtrodden child with the happiness of those who receive love and care. The story shows that most people do not act upon their religious principles of love and charity.

*3. *Important human traits*   Dostoyevski most values the human traits of love, compassion, and charity. He reveals them by negative inference, in that the reader sees the consequences of their absence for the little boy.

4. *Elements reminiscent of a folktale; their contribution*   The style of the story resembles a folktale in three ways: (1) repetitive sentence structure; (2) a pattern of three episodes that invite the child's attention (two parties and a window display of toys); and (3) the use of colloquial expressions. This style conveys dramatic irony in that the story reads like a tale, but it depicts a harsh and cruel reality.

The story is the opposite of a fairy tale in the following ways: (1) it lacks magic; (2) it has no beneficent adult; (3) it lacks a happy ending. The child dies, and Dostoyevski states that he's not certain that a paradise exists that could compensate the child for his suffering. Nothing redeems the tragic conclusion.

*5. *Psychological realism*   Examples of psychological realism include: (1) the boy's focus on his fear of the dog, his enjoyment of the parties, and his fascination with the toys; (2) the boy's rambling and repetitive sentence patterns; and (3) the boy's childlike imitation of adult expressions. These combine to make the boy a real child with whom the reader can identify. When the boy dies, the reader is profoundly affected by society's role in his fate.

*6. *Irony*   Irony exists in: (*a*) the contrast between the Christmas season, which is the time of "brotherly love," and the starving, poorly clothed boy, whom no one attempts to help; (*b*) the nurse, who has spent her life caring for others but is now left to die alone; and (*c*) the contrast between the style of a folk tale for children and the content that depicts a harsh reality of life.

*7. *Tone*   The tone of the story is heart-wrenching and grim. Dostoyevski achieves it by placing the center of consciousness in a vulnerable six-year-old, whose view of Christmastime is that of the deprived outsider. The technique of psychological realism emphasizes the contrast between the child's devastating situation and the world that fascinates and ignores him.

WRITING ABOUT LITERATURE

1. *Expository essay on realism vs. naturalism*   (a) The story is in the tradition of realism in that it attempts to achieve an accurate depiction of life. The realists focused on ordinary people, ordinary locations, and ordinary occurrences. Specific details about the appearance of objects and people were important.

   (b) The story is in the tradition of naturalism in its focus on "sordid realism" and in its more subjective presentation of the subject. The technique of psychological realism would have been too subjective for the realists. The choice of a helpless, uncomprehending protagonist helps place this story in the naturalist tradition.

2. *Expository analysis of psychological realism*   Call students' attention to the directions in the textbook assignment with regard to content and organization. (See **A.L.T.** questions 1, 2, 3, 5 and 7 above.)

3. *Creative writing: This story from another character's point of view*   Call students' attention to the questions suggested in the textbook assignment. Remind students that some people justify their own behavior and others feel guilty. **(PLJ)**

FURTHER READING

Dostoyevski, Fyodor, "The Double"; "The Gambler"; "A Gentle Spirit"; "An Honest Thief"; "Notes From the Underground"; *Crime and Punishment.*

A Doll's House

HENRIK IBSEN

INTRODUCING THE PLAY

Nora, Torvald's "sweet little song-bird," is an interesting and complex character. She is a woman of her time (the 1880s), but that time lasted well into the 1950s, and, today, women are still fighting for independence and equality. In the late nineteenth century, a middle-class woman's place was in the home, and career opportunities for women who wanted or needed to work were largely limited to those of seamstress, teacher, nurse, or in some instances clerical worker or shop salesperson. A girl was reared to be a good wife and mother. She was not expected to be educated (considered a waste of money) or to have a career (considered unnecessary), but to marry well by attracting a husband who would be a good provider as well as a loving mate. Her husband would earn and manage the family finances, giving her an allowance for household expenses and personal clothing.

As *A Doll's House* opens, Nora is a young woman who, in order to please her husband, must conceal whatever independent actions she takes. Some are trivial, such as eating sweets, but one action is crucial to the development of the plot. Nora has borrowed money in order to finance a year in Italy for Torvald's health, and she must repay the loan. As a woman, she lacks training, experience, and opportunity in financial matters—most importantly, she lacks the legal status to negotiate the loan in her own name. That she develops a secret life to negotiate and conceal the loan reveals strength of character: She possesses the imagination, conviction, and courageous initiative to sail in uncharted waters.

Nora's explanations to Mrs. Linden (Christina) in Act I make it clear that she enjoys the independence and enhanced self-image that her secret life brings her. Working at copying in order to earn money has been wonderfully masculine. However, she also states that she plans to continue to be Torvald's "sweet little song-bird" until "it doesn't amuse him any longer to see me skipping about, and dressing up and acting." As tasty as the fruits of independence are, as Nora sees from Mrs. Linden's experience, the task of supporting herself would be difficult. Nora is content to pretend to be "silly" and a "spendthrift" until Torvald's horrified response to her well-intentioned forgery of her father's guaranty of her loan forces her to choose between her two lives.

At the close of the play, Nora courageously faces public condemnation by leaving her husband and children in order to discover who she really is. The fact that she and Torvald are incompatible and that she no longer loves him are sufficient reasons to leave him. The cost of leaving her children is much higher, but she believes that greater self-knowledge will be worth that cost. In fact, the message of the play is that learning who one is and becoming that person is worth any price.

Nora and Mrs. Linden have an interesting psychological relationship in the play. Mrs. Linden functions as Nora's double or doppelgänger, in that she represents what Nora secretly would like to be, an autonomous woman who is free to take risks and to assume the consequences. It is a form of dramatic irony that whereas Nora wants the freedom that Mrs. Linden has, Mrs. Linden wants the loving husband and family that Nora has.

The plot and style of *A Doll's House* are completely and naturally fused so that the texture of language and action is rich with layered meanings. Ibsen carefully prepares the audience for Nora's final action through his frequent use of foreshadowing and irony. *A Doll's House* is an unusually good vehicle for gaining a fine understanding of these particular literary techniques.

Similarly, both Torvald and Nora provide fine vehicles for the study of characterization. Whereas Nora's actions are premeditated and self-conscious, Torvald's are natural and instinctive. What Torvald says and how he treats Nora and the other characters reveal his consistent selfishness and his inability to tolerate any point of view but his own.

PLJ: Which do you consider more important, your obligation to yourself or your obligation to those you love? Are these obligations equally important? To what extent are you responsible for your own life, and to what extent are others responsible for it?

Literary Terms: characterization, doppelgänger, foreshadowing, irony, naturalism, paradox, theme

COMPREHENSION QUESTIONS

1. (I) What do Nora and Torvald argue about? (Nora spends too much money.)
2. (I) What secret does Nora tell Mrs. Linden? (Nora secretly borrowed money for the trip to Italy and is working hard to repay it.)
3. (I) What does Nora do for Mrs. Linden? (Nora gets her a job at Torvald's bank.)
4. (I)What does Krogstad ask Nora to do for him? (Nora must get Torvald not to fire Krogstad.)
5. (I) What crime has Nora committed? (Nora forged her father's name as guarantor of her loan.)
6. (II) Who is Dr. Rank? (A friend of Torvald's who is in love with Nora; he is dying.)
7. (II) What does Krogstad intend to do with Nora's IOU? (Krogstad will keep it for blackmail.)
8. (II) What does Nora ask Torvald to promise at the end of Act II? (Nora asks Torvald to promise not to open any letters until after the dance.)
9. (III) What is the relationship between Mrs. Linden and Krogstad? (They loved each other before Christina married for financial security; they will now marry.)
10. (III) When Torvald reads Krogstad's letter, how does Nora expect him to react? (Nora expects Torvald to try to save her and to suffer for her sake.)
11. (III) How does Torvald actually react? (Torvald considers Nora a liar and a criminal; she has ruined his happiness and his future and caused him to be blackmailed by Krogstad; she may not rear the children.)
12. (III) What does Krogstad do for Nora? (Krogstad returns her forged IOU.)
13. (III) How does Torvald react? (Saved from disaster, Torvald forgives Nora and returns to his old attitudes.)
14. (III) What miracle failed to happen? (Torvald didn't support Nora against Krogstad.)
15. (III) How does Nora change? (Nora realizes her husband's limitations mean she cannot be happy with him. She decides to leave him and the children to learn about herself and life.)

UNDERSTANDING THE PLAY: POSSIBLE ANSWERS

*1. (I) *Significance of Nora's lies* Torvald is so opinionated and demanding that Nora cannot afford to be truthful. Control over sweets reveals that Torvald attempts to control all aspects of Nora's life and treats her like a child. Thus, the lie reveals that Nora and Torvald's marriage may be in trouble.

*2. (I) *Significance of Torvald's view of Nora as an expensive little bird*   Torvald views himself as being in total charge of his household. Marriage is no partnership; Nora's role is to serve and amuse her husband.

*3. (I) *Significance of Nora's description of her own behavior*   Nora is consciously playing a role in her marriage, appearing to be the type of wife that Torvald wants her to be. If she could, she would be different: more serious, more independent, and more honest about who she really is.

*4. (I) *Irony of Nora's situation at the end of Act I*   The audience knows that Nora is guilty of the same crimes that Krogstad has committed. The audience and Nora both suspect that Torvald will not be any more forgiving of Nora than he is of Krogstad.

*5. (II) *Significance of Nora's comment about giving in to Torvald*   Nora wants to feel that she makes her own decisions.

*6. (II) *Torvald's image if Nora or others influenced him*   Torvald claims that he would become a "laughing-stock" and would be regarded as ineffectual. However, Torvald need not publicize Nora's influence, and consulting with others could enable him to make better decisions. Acting hastily and with poor judgment on his own should be a more serious worry for Torvald.

 7. *Nora's miracle*   Nora realizes it is inevitable that Torvald will find out about the money she borrowed from Krogstad. The "miracle" is her belief that Torvald will take all the responsibility for the forgery upon himself—that he will try to "bear the whole burden" of her disgrace. However, the fact that Nora describes this act as a "miracle" shows that subconsciously she knows how unlikely it is to happen: She recognizes and fears Torvald's selfishness, inflexibility, and quickness to condemn moral flaws in others.

 8. (III) *Incredible things; why Krogstad should leave his letter*   Mrs. Linden is worried about Nora's talk of going out of her mind, of not being there any longer, and of a "miracle." She feels that if Torvald were to know the truth, Nora no longer would have to lie and could relax. Mrs. Linden expects that Nora and Torvald would reach an understanding that would be satisfying to both of them, and that Torvald would understand Nora's motivation and appreciate her later generous efforts on his behalf.

*9. (III) *Why Nora is not pleased to be Torvald's dearest treasure*   Nora has been forced to leave the dance before she was ready to go, and she is annoyed at Torvald as well as worried about how soon he will read Krogstad's letter. Additionally, Nora resents Torvald's objectification of her and his appropriation of her as something belonging to him. All of these emotions mean that she is not receptive to Torvald's ill-timed attempts at romance.

At the same time, Nora still believes that the "miracle" is possible—that Torvald is capable of taking responsibility for the loan and for the forgery. Therefore, she is concerned about Torvald's misperception of her: Although he idealizes her, she knows that she is flawed.

*10. (III) *Torvald's reactions to Dr. Rank's suffering*   Torvald's reactions reveal him to be a narcissistic person, someone who sees others as objects that have interest only to the extent that they reflect favorably upon himself. He has no sympathy for Dr. Rank, merely finding Dr. Rank's death a horrible intrusion into his own romantic plans.

*11. (III) *Nora tells Torvald that she's never understood him*   Nora has been blind to the type of man that Torvald is because she herself has been playing a role. Because she knew herself to be more than a doll, she assumed that he did, too. Torvald has often professed his great love for Nora and his interest in proving his devotion, giving her reason to believe in his love.

A further reason that Nora has been blind to Torvald's true nature is the very unpleasant emotional and economic consequences of facing up to an unsatisfactory marriage.

*12. (III) *Torvald's concern about Nora's decision*   Torvald is most concerned about what other people will say, especially about what they will say about him. Given his preoccupation with himself, his attitude toward Krogstad and his fear of anything that might involve a scandal, this attitude is consistent with his personality.

*13. *Nora's problem: personality or society's values*   Nora's problem is caused both by her and Torvald's personalities and by the values of the society in which they live. Their society supports dominating men, rather than liberated women, a fact that makes Nora the unusual partner in the marriage and gives Torvald little motivation to change his attitudes. On the other hand, in any society, a woman would have to be very insecure and needy to be happy with a husband who cares more about what other people think of him than he cares about his wife.

At the end of the play, Nora has exchanged one set of problems for another. She has cut herself off from the traditional support of a family, and she needs to find a job so that she can be financially independent. It might be possible, in time, for her to find both emotional and financial security.

*14. *Nora's greater responsibility: herself or her family?*   Opinions will vary. Nora must consider how much value she will be to her children if she is miserable living with Torvald, or if she continues to treat them like dolls, the way Torvald has been treating her. She could let Torvald make an effort to change, but the evidence in the play suggests that he is incapable of empathy and independent thinking.

15. *More important character*   Nora is more important in that she rebels against the values of the society. Torvald is very important in that he epitomizes what Ibsen is criticizing in contemporary life.

*16. *Themes*   (a) A marriage based on misperceptions and inequality is not a true marriage. (b) In Ibsen's view, a person's primary obligation is to himself or herself; everyone else comes second. (c) The most important goal for a person in life is to know himself or herself. (d) The development of one's personality and the fulfillment of one's goals are just as important for a woman as they are for a man.

ANALYZING LITERARY TECHNIQUE: POSSIBLE ANSWERS

*1. *Foreshadowing* a) (I) *Opening conflict* Torvald and Nora disagree about money. Torvald opposes extravagance; he is against anyone going into debt. Nora thinks that it is all right to borrow money and have debts. She views money as the best gift because she can decide how and when to use it. This becomes a major issue when it is revealed that Nora secretly borrowed money for the sake of Torvald's health and is secretly paying back the loan.

(b) (I) *Torvald's reaction to Krogstad's crime* Krogstad's crime is similar to Nora's, so it is reasonable to assume that Torvald will react to Nora as he did to Krogstad.

(c) (II) *Scene between Nora and Anna* Anna left her own child in order to earn a living caring for Nora (and eventually for Nora's children). Anna is pragmatic about the decision she made: "When I had the chance of such a good place? A poor girl who's been in trouble must take what comes." The scene hints that Nora may leave her own children, seeking a pragmatic solution to her own troubles.

(d) (II) *Krogstad's comment about having "heart"* Krogstad's statement prepares Nora and the audience for his willingess to take back his letter and for his returning Nora's IOU to her.

(e) (II) *Dr. Rank's comment about Torvald's "delicate nature"* Dr. Rank is politely expressing Torvald's selfishness. Torvald does indeed shrink from Dr. Rank's illness, considering it an intrusion on his happy life. The comment also foreshadows Torvald's shrinking from Nora's confession of forgery and debt.

2. *Irony* Following are some examples that students might choose to illustrate the effect of dramatic and verbal irony in this play.

(a) Dramatic irony *(I) Nora tells Torvald: "I shouldn't think of doing what you disapprove of."* Nora, who has been going against Torvald's wishes by eating sweets and spending too much money, is telling one more lie. Her words reflect her double life: one of lies to his face, and another of independent actions behind his back. The problem of the promissory note determines the course of her life. This problem, too, is based on her acting contrary to Torvald's values and deceiving him.

(II) Torvald says to Nora: "Between your father and me there is all the difference in the world. Your father was not altogether unimpeachable. I am; and I hope to remain so." Torvald knows that he himself has done nothing wrong, but he is unaware of Nora's forged note and its risk to his reputation.

(II) Torvald says to Nora: "Let what will happen—when the time comes, I shall have strength and courage enough. You shall see, my shoulders are broad enough to bear the whole burden." Torvald will have no strength and no courage in any crisis that causes him to fear for himself. Given his earlier statements, the audience suspects this. Nora learns it when he is too afraid of his reputation to support her against Krogstad.

(II) Nora tells Dr. Rank: "You know how deeply, how wonderfully Torvald loves me; he would not hesitate a moment to give his very life for my sake."   Nora does not see qualities in Torvald that Dr. Rank sees, namely his hate of ugly situations, his lack of courage, and his excessive concern for public opinion.

(III) After the dance, Torvald says to Mrs. Linden: "An exit should always be effective, Mrs. Linden; but I can't get Nora to see it."   Nora's properly dramatic exit comes at the end of the play. It never occurs to Torvald that Nora might act without his direction.

(III) Torvald says to Nora: "I often wish some danger might threaten you, that I might risk body and soul, and everything, everything, for your dear sake."   Torvald doesn't know that real danger is around the corner, and that it threatens him directly.

(III) After Krogstad has returned the IOU, Torvald says to Nora: "Here I can shelter you like a hunted dove, whom I have saved from the claws of the hawk."   Torvald does not realize that *he* is the "hawk." Nora is far from being safe; Torvald's abandonment of her when she needed him has destroyed their marriage.

(b) Verbal irony *(II) After Torvald sends Krogstad's dismissal letter and will not retrieve it, he says it is "Too late." Nora echoes the words: "Yes, too late."*   Torvald means only that it is too late to call the maid back; he is thinking only of his own affairs, of his dislike of Krogstad and his desire to assert his authority over Nora. Nora means that it is too late to save Torvald, the children, and herself.

(II) Speaking about the dance that she is supposed to perform, Nora says that she can't perform without rehearsing with Torvald. When he asks if she is nervous, she responds, "Yes, dreadfully!"   Torvald connects her anxiety with the coming performance, but Nora is anxious about Torvald's impending reading of Krogstad's letter.

(III) After he takes Nora away from the dance, Torvald says, "I was right after all not to let you stop longer." Nora responds, "Oh, everything you do is right."   Torvald believes that everything he does is correct, and he is delighted to hear Nora acknowledge it by her reply. However, Nora's reply contradicts her own feelings.

(III) After Torvald reads Krogstad's letter, he accuses Nora of rewarding Torvald's help to her father "like this." Nora echoes his words, "Yes—like this!"   Torvald accuses Nora of having no religion, no morals, and no sense of duty, whereas Nora realizes that these very values are what motivated her to borrow the money in the first place. Torvald's words condemn; Nora repeats them with pride. It is ironic that Torvald is incapable of acting on the values that he tells Nora he has, whereas Nora really possesses and acts on those values.

(III) When Nora returns from changing out of her dance costume into street clothes, Torvald remarks in surprise, "You have changed your dress." Nora responds, "Yes, Torvald; now I have changed my dress."   Torvald expects Nora to be dressed for bed. Nora's response refers to her psychological state as well as to her clothes. She has changed into someone else, someone who is prepared to take on the outside world.

3. *Function of minor characters*

   (a) Mrs. Linden   Mrs. Linden brings a role model of female independence into Nora's life. She supports herself and is relieved to be rid of a husband she did not

love. In some respects, Mrs. Linden is a foil for Nora: Mrs. Linden, being alone, wants someone to love and nurture, while Nora has a family but wants independence.

On a psychological level, Nora and Mrs. Linden also function as alter egos to each other. However, Mrs. Linden is more of a doppelgänger in her relationship to Nora. Mrs. Linden represents what Nora secretly would like to be, because Mrs. Linden is an autonomous woman who is free to take risks and assume the consequences, a condition that is made possible by her ability to support herself financially.

(b) Krogstad   Krogstad plays a pivotal role in the play, both in terms of plot and in terms of characterization. He is important to Nora as the person who knows of the loan and who can expose her; he also functions as a type of double for Nora, since her crime is the same as his. Krogstad is important to Torvald because he represents the type of individual over whom Torvald wants to assert his superiority; ironically, of course, Krogstad possesses information that gives him the upper hand over Torvald.

Krogstad and Mrs. Linden's story, in the subplot, acts as a type of commentary on the main plot. Krogstad and Mrs. Linden are able to forget old wounds and re-establish a bond, forming a partnership that will enable both of them to find greater emotional and financial security. The forgiveness and cooperation in Krogstad and Mrs. Linden's relationship throw into relief the problems in Nora and Torvald's marriage.

(c) Dr. Rank   Dr. Rank is in love with Nora; he has been her friend and advisor, giving her the emotional support she has lacked from Torvald. There is no evidence that Nora has returned his feelings, although she does seem to have suspected them. (Her comments to Mrs. Linden about an "admirer" are therefore ironic.)

Dr. Rank's function in the play is to make Nora aware of her true relationship with Torvald. There are three important scenes in which he heightens her awareness. (1) In Act I, Rank's view of Krogstad as a "moral wreck" increases Nora's worry about her secret deed and confirms her sense of isolation. (2) In Act II, the discussion of the law of retribution increases Nora's anxiety; her children will suffer for her deeds. (3) In Act III, Rank is a model for Nora to value each day of life, to make the most of it, and to face whatever comes with dignity. Rank's death and the resulting loss to the Helmer family anticipate the loss when Nora leaves.

WRITING ABOUT LITERATURE

1. *Expository theme on Nora's development*   Call students' attention to the suggestions in the textbook assignment. (See **U.P.** questions 1, 3–5, 9, 11, and 16 above.)
2. *Expository theme evaluating Torvald's response to Krogstad's letter*   Call students' attention to the directions and suggestions in the textbook assignment with regard to content. (See **U.P.** questions 2, 6, 9, 10, 12, and 13 above.)
3. *Expository theme contrasting Nora's and Torvald's idea of honor*   Call students' attention to the pre-writing suggestions. (See **U.P.** questions 4, 6, 10, 12, and 14, and **A.L.T.** questions 1 and 3 above.) **(PLJ)**

4. *Creative writing: a letter to Nora from a friend*   Call students' attention to the textbook assignment, which contains the four quotations that will form the basis of the letter that they are going to write. *(a)* "It's your [you and my father's] fault that my life has been wasted." *(b)* "I'm not fit to educate the children." *(c)* "I must stand quite alone to know myself and my surroundings; so I cannot stay with you." *(d)* "I no longer believe that before all I am a wife and mother; before all else I am a human being." **(PLJ)**

5. *Creative writing: a conversation between the nurse (Anna) and the maid (Ellen) about the effect of Nora's departure on Torvald*   Call students' attention to the suggested questions in the textbook assignment.

FURTHER READING

Ibsen, Henrik, *An Enemy of the People; The Wild Duck; Ghosts; Hedda Gabler; Peer Gynt.*

How Much Land Does a Man Need?

LEO TOLSTOY

INTRODUCING THE STORY

"How Much Land Does a Man Need?" is one of Tolstoy's most famous short stories. It is a traditional folktale that has been transformed into a parable that teaches that "greed is the root of evil." The plot concerns a peasant who can never resist the opportunity to acquire more good land. In the course of pursuing greater wealth, Pahóm forces his son to become a laborer, falsely accuses a neighbor of chopping down his trees, mistreats and alienates the local peasants with his selfishness, and leaves his wife behind to manage one estate while his greed compels him to acquire another. He behaves as the ultimate narcissist, in that he uses all other human beings to further his own ends and never considers their needs, desires, or feelings.

The tale is a superb example of Tolstoy's interest in human nature and his ability to characterize people. It examines how Pahóm behaves, the thoughts and feelings that motivate him to behave as he does, and the consequences that result from his actions. The plot is powerful for two reasons. First, the emotions that motivate Pahóm's materialism are common in varying degree to all human beings and, therefore, all readers can relate personally to the story. Second, in examining the morality of Pahóm's decisions and their effect on his personality and, indirectly, on his responsibilities to his family and his neighbors, Tolstoy leads his readers to evaluate the morality and the pragmatic wisdom of their own materialistic attitudes and behavior.

James Joyce regarded this tale as "the greatest story that the literature of the world knows." It is possible that what Joyce so admired in this tale was Tolstoy's superb fusion of content and style. The story addresses the universal and basic human question of what should be a person's goal in life, and it is told in the simple and direct style of a folktale. Every detail in the story contributes to the total design and the underlying moral content. The opening argument between the two sisters introduces the theme of the story and brings out the factors of temptation, anxiety, and loss that accompany gain (Pahóm's acquisition of land). Finally, the nature of Pahóm's sleepless night, his reaction to his prophetic dream, and every decision he makes in the course of his final quest foreshadow his fate. Tolstoy concludes with two crowning ironies: Pahóm has gained the land, but he has lost his life; and he actually needs no more land than the space his body occupies in death.

PLJ: What do you need in order to be happy? Is it better to be satisfied with what you have or to strive to improve it?

Literary Terms: allegory, characterization, foreshadowing, irony, parable, paradox, theme

COMPREHENSION QUESTIONS

1. (I) What does the city sister cite as advantages of city life? (good clothes, food, and entertainment)
2. (I) What does the country sister cite as advantages of country life? (freedom from anxiety, lack of temptations, ability to keep one's wealth)
3. (I) Who wants to get Pahóm into his power? (the Devil)
4. (II) What sacrifice does Pahóm make to buy land? (hires son out as laborer)
5. (III) What does Pahóm do to Simon? (falsely accuses him of chopping down his trees)
6. (IV) When Pahóm first moves beyond the Vólga, how does he get more land? (rents it)
7. (VI) When Pahóm goes to the land of the Bashkírs, how much land will he be able to acquire? (as much as he can walk around from sunrise to sunset of one day, for a payment of 1,000 rubles)
8. (VII) What dream does Pahóm have? (Devil is tempting him and laughs at his death)
9. (VIII) Why does his dream become reality? (can't pass up good land)
10. (IX) How does the tale end? (Pahóm buried in land just his size)

UNDERSTANDING THE STORY: POSSIBLE ANSWERS

1. *Rural setting and a peasant protagonist* Tolstoy believes that life on the land is more natural for humans, that it appeals to basic drives and needs in all people. A tale set in the country would therefore have applications for all readers.
2. *Peasant less greedy than tradesman? Why Devil knows how to treat Pahóm* Tolstoy proves that the peasant is at least as greedy as the tradesman. His point is that most human beings, regardless of their social status, spend their lives acquiring goods

rather than helping others and improving their minds. The Devil knows that given the opportunity, it is human nature to be greedy, and peasants are greedy for land.

3. *Why the Devil?*   The Devil was probably part of the original folktale and would make the tale more appealing to the intended audience, the peasants. The Devil's presence in the story underscores that Pahóm's choices are choices between good and evil. Thus, the Devil functions as an allegorical figure, an external symbol of an internal psychological factor.

4. *Effect of ownership of land on Pahóm's personality*   Pahóm changes in that he now cares more about his land than about any human being and, therefore, becomes inhumane. He forgets what it is like to be a landless peasant, and he attempts to keep other peasants off his land by having them fined. He also falsely accuses a neighbor of chopping down his trees and then falsely accuses the judges who acquit the neighbor of having been bribed.

*5. *Factors Pahóm wisely or foolishly ignores in his choices*   Pahóm ignores the needs and desires of his wife and children. He does not explore other ways of leading a rewarding life. He might have used some of his wealth to help others and to improve his community. He is foolish in that, even if he had not died, he would have ended up alone. Since he cared about no one, no one would have cared about him.

*6. *Title*   The title reveals the theme of the story: Should a person's goal in life be material or spiritual? How much land a person needs depends upon the individual's purpose in life; a rewarding life is not dependent on ownership of land. Thus, the title's meaning changes with the perspective.

7. *Why Bashkír chief laughs at the end*   The chief, having more land than he needs, does not value it the way Pahóm does. He cannot imagine a person being so foolish as to die from the attempt to acquire more and more land.

8. *Significance of Pahóm's dream: role of fate*   Pahóm's dream confirms his sole responsibility for his fate. He ignores his dream because his greed blinds him to the consequences of his behavior.

9. *Better to be satisfied or to improve*   Tolstoy would probably opt for moderation, acquiring enough for material comfort and well-being, but without sacrificing humane values and relationships.

ANALYZING LITERARY TECHNIQUE: POSSIBLE ANSWERS

1. *Function of argument between two sisters*   The argument involves the theme of the story, what a person's goal in life should be or what is necessary for a person to be happy, and foreshadows the plot. The points (temptation, anxiety, loss and gain) made by Pahóm's wife ironically prove to be more applicable to Pahóm (they cause his death) than to her brother-in-law.

2. *Characterization of Pahóm*   Tolstoy focuses on Pahóm's very human nature. Pahóm first feels joy and satisfaction as a landowner, but these feelings prove to be very transitory because he soon becomes accustomed to whatever he has. Owner-

ship makes Pahóm very protective of his possessions, and he becomes selfish, greedy, and cruel. Because Pahóm's feelings are common to some extent in all human beings, he seems real to Tolstoy's readers.

3. *Foreshadowing* Examples include: (1) Pahóm's sleepless night, which foreshadows his exhaustion; (2) Pahóm's dream, which foreshadows his death; (3) Pahóm's inability to reject good land, which foreshadows his overextending himself because of his greed; (4) Pahóm's removal of his shoes, which foreshadows his difficult walking; and (5) Pahóm's exhausted run at the end, which foreshadows the strain on his heart and his death.

4. *Irony* Examples of irony include: (1) the double meaning of the title; (2) the applicability of Pahóm's wife's arguments to Pahóm; (3) Pahóm's inability to appreciate what he has; and (4) Pahóm's change in personality as he acquires land. In this story, irony adds power, humor, and pathos.

*5. *Parable* A parable is a short story designed to teach moral value. Greed, one of the seven deadly sins, is the subject of the tale. The tale's lesson is that those who succumb to the temptation of greed cause their own moral and physical destruction. Pahóm's pride and greed keep him from learning from his experience. Realizing that he will die, Pahóm still is not willing to sacrifice his pride and 1,000 rubles in exchange for his life. The story moves the reader to examine his or her own life to be certain that he or she is not as foolish as Pahóm.

WRITING ABOUT LITERATURE

1. *Expository theme comparing Chekhov's and Tolstoy's points of view* Encourage independent points of view, and emphasize the importance of supporting details. (See **U.S.** question 6 and **A.L.T.** question 5 above.)

2. *Creative writing: A letter from Pahóm's wife to her sister* Encourage both positive and negative points of view. Remind students to attempt to characterize Pahóm's wife through her use of language. **(PLJ)**

FURTHER READING

Tolstoy, Leo, ''The Death of Ivan Ilych''; ''Master and Man''; *Anna Karenina.*

The Outlaws
SELMA LAGERLÖF

INTRODUCING THE STORY

''The Outlaws'' has great dramatic, intellectual, and artistic appeal. On the surface, it is a tale of adventure, with touches of a mystery story. As two outlaws hide together from the death penalty, the reader wonders if and how they will evade death.

Intellectually, the tale grabs the reader's mind with a tenacious grip. The reader ponders the nature of Tord, considers the motivation for his betrayal of Berg, and is fascinated by the deliberate ambiguity of the story's conclusion. Many aspects of the story are open to genuinely different interpretations, all of which have foundation in the text. The ambiguity is not only acceptable, it adds depth and richness to the tale.

Tord, son of a fisherman and a "witch," is an enigmatic character whose behavior will provoke interesting discussions. Living both in the world of reality and in that of imagination, Tord is periodically driven by irrational feelings that reflect his subconscious drives and motives. Possibly because his self-image is so low, he worships the murderer Berg, who despises him. Although Tord possesses information that would change Berg's opinion of him, he is in no hurry to reveal it. Tord's religious "conversion" raises many questions. He becomes obsessed with an image of God as an avenger of misdeeds, rather than with the more forgiving side of Christianity, represented by Christ, the Virgin Mary, and the saints who intercede on behalf of sinners. It is not clear if Tord's instinctive choice is a psychological reaction to the sacrifice his mother exacted of him. He may murder Berg because he has become a religious fanatic, or because he hopes to have a chance with Unn once Berg is dead, or because the murder of a criminal will enhance his self-esteem by bringing him pardon and social acceptance.

Early in the tale, Berg is depicted as a primeval superman, a glorious human being who is nature's crowning achievement. In fact, he is more animal than human as he eludes those who would capture him. Later in the story, he becomes Tord's religious teacher, imprudently substituting Christian morality and justice for Tord's pagan fatalism. Finally, having driven Tord mad with violent visions of Christian justice, Berg finds himself torn between his affection for Tord and his own instinct for self-preservation.

Tord and Berg inhabit a world in which women are perceived as dangerously non-human, wielding great power over men. Tord's mother is characterized by her son as a witch, someone who claims the bodies of drowned sailors. She sacrifices her son's life in order to preserve the life of her husband, and Tord accepts his role as scapegoat and fugitive. Unn, described as a kind of mermaid, lures males with her sex appeal and then destroys them. She encourages love, not marriage. Loved by her cousin Berg, she tells him that the white monk's nameless but accurate public insult to them both demands harsh justice. Since her father is not present, Berg "knows what he must do." Berg kills the monk, thereby becoming a fugitive. Once Tord sees Unn, she inhabits his dreams. To what extent she is a key motivating factor in Tord's murder of Berg is worth discussing.

Tord's world is one of terrifying visions that blur the distinction between illusion and reality. A secluded mountain pool is home to tree roots that resemble serpents or the "blackened skeletons of drowned giants." Drowned men speak to Tord and "threaten him with withered white hands." As Tord walks alone through the woods in a storm, he is chased by invisible hunters: a huge venomous snake, a monstrous starved wolf, eerie human voices, and finally "God, the great Avenger, the God of justice," and the white monk. The story is told with such artistic power that even in translation its scenes remain in the reader's imagination long after the tale has ended.

PLJ: To what extent do you think that human beings have the ability to control their own actions? To what extent do you think that human behavior is predetermined? What factors determine human behavior?

Literary Terms: contrast, flashback, folktale, foreshadowing, Gothic, irony, setting, symbol

COMPREHENSION QUESTIONS

1. What crime has Berg committed? (murdered a monk)
2. What crime has Tord committed? (none; took on himself his father's crime)
3. Why did Berg commit his crime? (The monk criticized his relationship with Unn; Unn threatened to leave him.)
4. How does Tord feel about Berg? (worships him; protects him)
5. How does Berg feel about Tord? (despises him because he thinks Tord is a thief)
6. How does Berg feel about Tord once he's learned the truth? (no longer despises him; thinks he's a fool for throwing his life away)
7. How does Tord feel about Unn? (has romantic dreams about her)
8. How does Tord feel about Berg's crime? (Berg honored Unn by killing the monk.)
9. What does Berg teach Tord? (about Christianity and justice)
10. What happens because of those lessons? (Tord kills Berg because Berg murdered the monk.)

UNDERSTANDING THE STORY: POSSIBLE ANSWERS

1. *Tord destined to betray Berg* It depends on the reader's attitude toward determinism and toward the role of personality in a person's destiny. Before Tord received Berg's sermon, Tord would have believed in fate.
2. *Importance of Tord's family background* Tord grew up isolated from the community, because his father was a thief and his mother was believed to be a witch. He chose to take the guilt of his father's crimes upon himself, for reasons that aren't precisely explained and which Berg does not understand. Tord may have: (1) feared his mother's powers as a witch; (2) acted out of loving obedience to his mother's wishes; or (3) acted out of a desire to protect his father. Thus, his loneliness and isolation may explain why he forms such an attachment to Berg and why he is eventually drawn to the possibility of a union with Unn.

   In psychological terms, Tord was betrayed when his mother asked him to sacrifice his own life in place of his father's for his parents' happiness. Thus, Tord has no self-esteem. He also may have a subconscious desire to punish one or both of his parents for not loving and valuing him. Thus, Tord identifies with God the Avenger and becomes the arm of divine justice in the world he inhabits. Given how his own mother treated him, Tord is not interested in Mary. He also rejects any identification with Christ even though Tord, like Christ, has sacrificed himself for the sins of another (his father).

In addition, Tord's poverty and his parents' occupations mean that he is of a lower social class than Berg. This class difference may further explain why Tord accepts Berg's treatment of him and serves him uncomplainingly.

*3. *Tord's relationships* In all of these relationships, Tord takes directions from someone whom he perceives to have greater power than himself. He obeys his mother's request to protect his father, he works for Berg as a type of servant, and he obeys what he believes is God's direction to avenge the murder. All of these suggest that Tord has doubts about his power to act on his own and to take responsibility for his own actions. Such doubts reflect a lack of self-esteem.

*4. *Berg's sermon* On the one hand, Berg despises Tord's heathenism, which has caused Tord to be amoral, irresponsible, and fatalistic. On the other hand, because Berg knows Tord did not commit any crime, it is possible that Berg's sermon is directed more to himself than to Tord.

5. *Why Tord betrays Berg*   (a) Tord's love of Unn is possibly very important. Tord desires her, and with Berg dead, he may think that he can win her. (b) Tord's desire for wealth and social acceptance are also possibly important. These were not important before he met Unn, but afterwards, he wonders if he would be able to win her and build a life with her if he had social standing. (c) Tord's desire for freedom is primarily important in terms of his winning Unn. (d) Tord's belief in religious principles is possibly most important. He believes that if he acts on religious principles—especially the principle of justice—then wealth, social acceptance, freedom, and possibly Unn all will follow. (e) Tord's particular personality is possibly as or more important than his religious beliefs. Tord's childhood experiences leave him so deficient in self-esteem and so accustomed to worshipping one who does not value him that, once Berg loves and trusts him, Tord may have a subconscious need to betray Berg in order to regain his contempt.

6. *Berg as villain or victim*   Berg is a villain in that he is a would-be adulterer, a murderer, and a snob (in his treatment of Tord). Some students may argue that he is also victimized by Tord, who turns Berg's teachings against him. However, there is a strong suggestion in the story that Berg teaches Tord in order to condemn himself.

7. *Berg regarding Tord's betrayal*   Berg's attitudes are not necessarily inconsistent. He initially considers Tord foolish because Berg would betray Tord if their situations were reversed. However, Berg's initial contempt for Tord comes from a position of security: Berg knows that Tord idolizes him and would not harm him. Later, Berg acts out of self-preservation, the most basic drive that he has (as evidenced by the opening of the story).

8. *Why Berg doesn't think Tord will kill him*   Tord worships Berg. Also, the white monk of Tord's vision bears an axe-blow, not a knife stab. Berg killed the monk with a knife.

9. *God of justice*   Tord's identification with a God of justice satisfies more than one of Tord's needs. (1) That anyone would intercede on behalf of a sinner is not confirmed in Tord's experience with his parents. Tord's mother does not nurture; she

demands his life. (2) The God of justice supplants Berg as the object of Tord's worship, just as Berg once replaced Tord's mother as the object of his worship. (3) Tord's identification with a God of justice also satisfies his subconscious need to avenge his parents' treatment of him. (4) Being on the side of the community and opposed to a murderer provides Tord with a source of self-esteem.

10. *Berg's sermon*   Tord has understood only one part of Berg's sermon, the part about God's justice. Just as important, however, are the ameliorating influences of Christ, the Virgin Mary, and the holy men and women (the saints), all of whom Tord ignores. Berg does not expect that his lesson will be only half understood, and he has no reason to believe that Tord will suddenly act upon religious principles, so he sees no threat to his own life.

   Before Berg's sermon, Tord is fatalistic about human behavior. He is accepting of others, rather than judgmental and punitive. He accepts Berg's murder of the monk as well as his own parents' treatment of him. After Berg's sermon, Tord has much to gain by killing Berg: freedom, social acceptance, wealth, and possibly love. Tord's identification with an avenging God also satisfies a subconscious need to avenge his parents' treatment of him.

11. *Tord's killing of Berg in self-defense: justification for the crime*   Opinions will vary. Technically, the circumstance of self-defense justifies Tord's action. However, the heathen Tord would have been more accepting and would not have provoked the change in his relationship with Berg. It is interesting to consider how the heathen Tord, given his needs, would have treated Berg, once Berg loved and trusted him.

12. *Why Tord praises God's greatness*   Tord believes he has acted as God's agent, avenging the unjust murder of the monk. In addition, because society considers his killing of Berg to be a good deed, Tord will be pardoned and rewarded. Self-defense has also removed the dishonor that would have accompanied a betrayal that did not incur personal risk. Tord has lost his best friend, but he has gained the world.

ANALYZING LITERARY TECHNIQUE: POSSIBLE ANSWERS

1. *Foreshadowing*   Examples of foreshadowing include: *(a)* Tord's early fear of the woods and night, which foreshadows the later storm scene; *(b)* Tord's visions of Berg's ancestors, which foreshadow Tord's later visions; *(c)* Berg's talk of motives for Tord's betrayal, which foreshadows Tord's later betrayal of Berg; and *(d)* Tord's vision of the monk with the axe wound in his forehead, which foreshadows Tord's similar killing of Berg.

2. *Symbolic use of light and dark*   *(a)* Light symbolizes the external world, rational forces, and what is good (day, sunshine, laughter, happiness, Unn, life); *(b)* Darkness symbolizes the internal world, reflecting the irrational, subconscious world of Tord's psyche and what is evil (night, the storm, fear, death, God's vengeance, and Hell). The contrast between light and dark dramatizes the conflict between good and evil.

3. *Irony*   Ironic aspects include the following: *(a)* Berg despises Tord for supposedly committing a crime, although Berg is a murderer and Tord is actually innocent; *(b)* Tord's approval of Berg's crime leads Berg to disapprove of Tord's attitude and to give him a lecture on Christianity; *(c)* Berg's teaching of Christian values to Tord leads Tord to betray Berg; *(d)* Berg's murder of the monk in order to keep Unn leads to Berg's state as an outcast without Unn; *(e)* When Berg expects Tord to betray him, Tord is loyal; when Berg expects Tord to be loyal, Tord betrays him; *(f)* Tord finds the vengeance in Christianity appealing, when that religion is noted for its love, compassion, and forgiveness; *(g)* Tord's new religion leads him to betray and kill his friend.

4. *Women's roles in story*   Women in this story are perceived as being dangerous, as violating the natural order of things, especially the natural order of society. Tord's mother seems to be responsible for isolating Tord's family from the rest of society, and it is because of her pleadings that he becomes an outlaw in place of his father. Unn is seen as responsible for the disruption of Berg's marriage and for the death of the monk; later, she seems to be responsible for Tord's betrayal of Berg, as Tord wishes to reestablish himself in society and thus win her affection.

   Students who are inclined to blame Tord's mother and Unn for the negative events in the plot should be reminded that the only way the reader comes to know these two women is through either Berg's or Tord's consciousnesses. The vision of the mermaid occurs just before Unn actually appears in the story; the men, not the narrator, connect the two.

5. *Gothic*   The Gothic elements in the story are the mysterious and supernatural elements, including the witch-mother, the frightening forest, and the bloody monk's ghost. The Gothic elements make the atmosphere of the story more charged and more memorable, and they tend to shift the reader's attention from the characters and their responsibility for their own actions.

WRITING ABOUT LITERATURE

1. *Expository theme examining justice*   Call students' attention to the directions with regard to content in the textbook assignment. Remind them to find support for their ideas in the story and to use direct quotations as well as explanations. (See **U.S.** questions 3, 4, and 8–10 above.) **(PLJ)**

2. *Creative writing: a continuation of "The Outlaws" after Berg's death*   Call students' attention to the questions suggested in the textbook assignment. Encourage them to write a story that is consistent with Tord's personality and character.

FURTHER READING

Lagerlöf, Selma, *Missing Links* (short stories); *The Wonderful Adventures of Nils; Gosta Berling's Saga; The Further Adventures of Nils.*

The Kiss

ANTON CHEKHOV

INTRODUCING THE STORY

"The Kiss" is particularly appealing to adolescents, given the socially insecure nature of the protagonist and his creation of a private fantasy world following a kiss that he receives in error. It shows how infatuation so enhances his self-image that his personality and outlook change. From a timid, modest, and undistinguished staff-captain, he becomes a person who is interested in the people around him. Even though reality pops the balloon of fantasy, Riabovich has recognized that ordinary men like himself have found women to love them, and, in time, another woman will make him forget his evil fate and his self-consciousness.

Written in 1886–87, "The Kiss" exhibits Chekhov's mature style as he explained it to his brother: "1. Absence of lengthy verbiage of political-social-economic nature; 2. Total objectivity; 3. Truthful descriptions of persons and objects; 4. Extreme brevity; 5. Audacity and originality: Flee the stereotype; 6. Compassion."

The story is typically Chekhovian in that it focuses on the feelings of an ordinary artillery officer. Chekhov contrasts Riabovich with his companion, the "setter" Lobytko, Riabovich being as socially awkward and uncomfortable as Lobytko is sophisticated and suave. Riabovich's fantasies evoke both humor and pity, making him a poignant character. Readers both laugh and sympathize with the poor staff-captain, who, in a final ironic twist, ignores the invitation he has so longed to receive. It is Chekhov's gift that his use of irony remains true to human nature and true to life experience, creating a story that appears to have natural power and effect.

Chekhov's ability to portray with gentle satire both the artificiality of the von Rabbek tea-time and the lack of communication among Riabovich, Lobytko, and Merzliakov is among his great artistic gifts. As any dramatist must, even in his short stories, Chekhov characterizes people by their words and actions, rather than by description.

The setting of the story reveals Chekhov's roots in Russian realism. Riabovich, the protagonist, is a Russian artillery officer and is therefore a common figure in contemporary Russian life. Chekhov emphasizes his thoughts and feelings and portrays his life as he would, in fact, live it, without adding an artificial plot, and without using an intrusive artistic style.

PLJ: Have you ever experienced a wonderful chance meeting? How did it affect your life? Did you have an opportunity to build on the experience? How did it end?

Literary Terms: characterization, dramatic irony, leitmotif, paradox, realism, satire, setting, tone

COMPREHENSION QUESTIONS

1. Why is Riabovich invited to General von Rabbek's for tea? (Local etiquette requires such hospitality.)
2. How does Riabovich feel while being entertained? (socially ill at ease and awkward)
3. What surprising event occurs? (Upon entering dark room, an unknown woman, expecting someone else, kisses him.)
4. How does Riabovich react to this event? (as if true love has entered his life)
5. How does Riabovich feel at the end? (angry at reality, resigned to his fate, unwilling to continue the fantasy)

UNDERSTANDING THE STORY: POSSIBLE ANSWERS

*1. *Riabovich affected by kiss*   Riabovich is ill at ease socially and has never had a romantic relationship, so he exaggerates this event beyond reality.

2. *Once kissed, what behavior at the tea reveals about Riabovich*   The Riabovich who thinks well of himself and is socially at ease is warm and friendly. His behavior toward Madame von Rabbek elicits a genuinely friendly response.

*3. *Effect of woman's reaction to kiss*   The woman's dismay and embarrassment contrast with Riabovich's reactions and cause his behavior to be both humorous and poignant.

*4. *Why Riabovich imagines woman's appearance*   The event would be diminished if the woman was no one in particular or one whom Riabovich did not find suitably attractive.

5. *Why Riabovich is sorry he told Merzliakov and Lobytko about kiss*   Merzliakov says the woman must have been a lunatic. Lobytko responds by telling about a similar personal experience that appears to be more interesting, making Riabovich's story nothing special by comparison.

*6. *Why Riabovich ignores second invitation to von Rabbeks'*   Its delay has made Riabovich confront reality, the certain disappointment in contrast with all of his fantasies. His despair and self-pity lead him to take perverse pleasure in showing Fate that he will not let himself be tempted to revive the past.

*7. *Effect of experience of kiss on Riabovich; role of illusion*   Students' opinions will vary. After the kiss, Riabovich seems to feel more at ease in social situations. He is probably better off having had the experience, even if it ended as it did, because in his fantasy world, he has begun to prepare himself to deal with future social relationships. Illusions are either helpful or harmful, depending on their nature. Believing in oneself can foster behavior that enhances that belief, and self-consciousness can do the opposite.

ANALYZING LITERARY TECHNIQUE: POSSIBLE ANSWERS

1. *Chekhov's primary focus and technique*   Chekhov focuses on how a single incident affects an individual physically, socially, and psychologically. The use of an omniscient narrator enables Chekhov to fully explore Riabovich's experiences and to reveal Riabovich's feelings to the reader.

2. *Leitmotif*   Chekhov turns several details into leitmotifs. Besides unifying the story, leitmotifs perform the following three functions: (1) They mark the passage of time: For example, the spring flowers set the scene for romance; their later absence reveals a different time and situation. (2) They function as a type of shorthand, with the parts symbolizing the whole: For example, Riabovich distinguishes the women at the von Rabbeks' by means of brief descriptive details. (3) They become a distinguishing characteristic of an individual. Chekhov characterizes Riabovich, Lobytko, and Merzliakov by particular attitudes and behavior. Riabovich is always involved in his fantasy life; Lobytko is always pursuing women (the setter); and Merzliakov is always reading his magazine.

*3. *Artillery brigade*   The army becomes an active, realistic setting in which the characters live before, during, and after Riabovich's fantasy life is operating. It adds dimension to Chekhov's portrayal of the characters as seen through Riabovich's eyes.

4. *Contrast: Riabovich and Lobytko*   Riabovich is as socially uncomfortable and awkward as Lobytko is sophisticated and suave. Lobytko's easy manner accentuates Riabovich's problem.

5. *Mispronunciation of name*   The servant's mispronunciation of von Rabbek's name is true to human nature: A person less involved with another is apt to pay less attention to that person's name and may remember what is only an approximation of the name. To the servant, General von Rabbek is simply one more general performing his social and civic duty; he is no more important than any of the other ex-army officers who perform the same function in their respective towns. To Riabovich, however, the identity of this particular general is of primary importance. The contrast between the two views emphasizes Riabovich's feelings at this time.

6. *Irony*   Chekhov's use of irony adds gentle humor and poignancy to the story. (1) It is ironic that a kiss, obviously given in error, has such a profound effect on Riabovich's life. He is euphoric about the woman who kissed him and depressed when he thinks that he will not receive a second invitation to the von Rabbek house. (2) It is ironic that Riabovich makes himself so angry at himself and at the von Rabbeks that, when it finally arrives, he ignores the invitation that he has so longed to receive.

   The central irony of the story, of course, is its lesson: that people may base their attitudes and behavior on how they *think* others view them, when, in reality, others view them quite differently—or do not think about them at all.

7. *Chekhov's use of satire*   The central target of satire in the story is the insincerity of most social interactions. The first (and probably the second) von Rabbek invitation

is not sincere; the time is obviously inconvenient, the social obligation obviously tedious. Mme. von Rabbek's smile disappears when she is out of sight; Gen. von Rabbek speaks with "affected joviality"; in conversation, the hosts pretend to be serious about topics they know little and care less about; and Riabovich is impressed with the von Rabbek family's ability to perform so well.

However, the satire is gentle rather than biting. Chekhov and the soldiers understand the difficulties under which the von Rabbek family is operating; under similar circumstances, they would feel the same way. Riabovich's exaggerated response to the mistaken kiss is also treated with gentle satire.

8. *Tone*   This story is typical of Chekhov in that it depicts a situation that is simultaneously both comic and poignant. Checkhov follows Riabovich from the time that he treats the fantasy as reality until he finally realizes the incident for what it actually was. In the process, Riabovich's emotions move from elation, to anticipation, to frustration and dismay, and finally to feelings of foolishness and anger that arise from insight. Both Riabovich's situation with regard to the young woman and his emotional reaction to the collapse of his fantasy are inevitable, given the circumstances of the kiss. The beauty of the story resides in Chekhov's sympathetic depiction of attitudes and emotions that are part of being human.

9. *Realism*   The following aspects of this story are characteristic of realism: *(a)* Chekhov focuses on the feelings of an ordinary person; *(b)* he describes people and objects as they appear to the eye and ear, without exaggeration or artificiality; *(c)* he presents the story objectively, without intruding; *(d)* he depicts a "slice of life" by focusing on only one experience in a person's life, beginning and ending with that incident.

WRITING ABOUT LITERATURE

1. *Expository theme on realism*   Students who read carefully probably will defend Chekhov's use of detail, recognizing that each piece of information helps to add to the setting and to increase the reader's sensitivity to Riabovich's loneliness and desire for connections. Students also should recognize the contrast between Chekhov's description of life as it is and Riabovich's fantasies. (See **U.S.** questions 1, 3, 4, 6, and 7, and **A.L.T.** questions 3 and 9 above.)

2. *Creative writing: incident from Riabovich's point of view.*   Students should try to write about the incident as if they were Riabovich. Students can write as if the experience were happening at that very moment, or they can treat the experience as a memory that Riabovich is recalling. **(PLJ)**

FURTHER READING

Chekov, Anton, "Misery"; "The Steppe"; "The Duel"; "A Woman's Kingdom"; "The Lottery Ticket"; "Vanka"; "The Peasants"; "Gooseberries"; "The Lady with the Dog"; "In the Ravine"; "The Betrothed"; "The Darling"; *The Three Sisters*; *The Cherry Orchard* (play).

The Other Wife

COLETTE

INTRODUCING THE STORY

In "The Other Wife," Colette explores the psychological effects of the presence of a first wife on her ex-husband and his new wife. Paradoxically, the first wife is simply a catalyst; the author does not name her, and the reader never knows whether she even notices Marc and Alice when they enter the hotel dining room. The sole concern of the story is the effect of her presence on the other two characters. Ironically, although the first wife is not even referred to by name, her presence turns out to have ominous implications for Marc and Alice's relatively new marriage.

From his first sight of his former wife, Marc is very uncomfortable and hopes that she will not see them. Because she was never satisfied with him, he feels with self-conscious certainty that he continues to be the object of a scorn that, now, also includes his new and somewhat plump wife.

Once Marc confesses that his first marriage failed because of his own inadequacy, Alice feels as if she possesses rejected, inferior merchandise. She begins to doubt her happiness, and her initial pity for the ex-wife gives way to envy of the woman's superior sophistication, taste, and judgment.

PLJ: Have you ever acquired something you wanted but later changed your mind about it? What caused your attitudes to change?

Literary Terms: characterization, contrast, foreshadowing, irony, paradox, theme

COMPREHENSION QUESTIONS

1. Why does Marc wish to sit where he does? (to avoid his first wife)
2. Why does Marc prefer his new wife? (She accepts him.)
3. Why did the first marriage end? (Marc could not make wife happy.)
4. How does Alice feel at first about Marc's other wife? (sorry for her)
5. How does Alice feel about Marc's other wife at the end? (inferior to her)

UNDERSTANDING THE STORY: POSSIBLE ANSWERS

*1. *Why Marc refuses to sit near first wife*   Marc feels self-conscious about being seen, revealing a low self-image. He is ashamed of himself and of Alice.

*2. *Why Alice laughs too loudly*   Alice hopes to convey how happily married they are, thus revealing that she is a better wife and making the first wife jealous.

*3. *Why Marc improves posture*   Marc wishes to make a good impression on his first wife. He wants to convey an attitude of self-assurance and convince her that he is thriving in his new marriage.

*4. *Marc's wisdom in telling Alice why marriage failed*   Marc reveals his low self-esteem by blaming the failure on his inadequacy. His idealization of his first wife makes Alice feel inferior and also causes her to view him as a cast-off rather than a catch. Marc's revelation does not appear to be in his own best interests. However, it is also important that Alice and Marc have never had this conversation before. It suggests that their marriage lacks a strong base of honesty and mutual trust.

5. *Themes*   More than one underlying idea is present in this story. Possible examples: (1) the neighbor's grass is always greener (better to be the first wife); (2) feelings of inferiority become self-fulfilling prophecies in that if one does not think well of oneself, no one else will either (Marc's self-disparagement leads Alice to disparage him also). Students should explain the way in which the story supports each idea they suggest.

ANALYZING LITERARY TECHNIQUE: POSSIBLE ANSWERS

*1. *Irony in Marc's statement about their satisfaction*   Marc's phrasing the statement as a question reveals his need to have Alice confirm their satisfaction. His need for Alice's confirmation reveals that it is a real question. Marc has just inadvertently told Alice that she has acquired a second-rate as well as a secondhand husband. Thus, Alice is no longer satisfied with Marc.

2. *Function of contrast*   Colette uses contrast to highlight her subject. The two wives are opposites: The first is sophisticated, demanding, and impressive; the second is warm, loving, and accepting. Each becomes more distinctive in contrast to the other. In addition, contrast accentuates the dramatic nature of Alice's change. Happy and satisfied at the beginning of the story, Alice is unhappy and dissatisfied at the end.

*3. *Point of view*   This story is told by a third-person omniscient narrator. The narrator is able to provide information that enhances the reader's understanding of the dialogue and what the true stakes are in the situation. Not only does the narrator comment on the characters' actions and motivations and behavior, but the narrator allows the reader to read Alice's thoughts at the end of the story.

4. *Paradox*   It is a paradox that people may base their attitudes and behavior on how they think others view them, when, in reality, others view them quite differently or may not think about them at all.

WRITING ABOUT LITERATURE

1. *Expository analysis of characterization*   Students should look closely at what the two main characters reveal about themselves and at what the narrator reveals about them. The characters' basic insecurity and attempts to disguise their insecurity fuel the growing distrust in their marriage. Students probably will predict that Alice and

Marc's marriage is in trouble, given Alice's thoughts at the end of the story. (See
U.S. questions 1–4, and **A.L.T.** questions 1 and 3 above.)

2. *Creative writing: Rewrite the story based on seeing Alice's ex-husband*   Students' revisions of Colette's story may end at approximately the same place, but with Marc's feeling doubts about Alice's value as a wife. Much of the new stories' conflict and resolution will depend on what reasons they give for the failure of Alice's first marriage. If the new stories are based as much as possible on Colette's characterizations of Marc and Alice, both characters should end up feeling self-doubts and mistrust of one another. **(PLJ)**

FURTHER READING

Colette, *The Collected Stories of Colette.*

At Sundown
RAINER MARIA RILKE

INTRODUCING THE POEM

In the lyric "At Sundown," Rilke explores a moment in time in which a mood in nature (twilight) evokes a similar mood (ambiguity) in the observer. Rilke re-creates the mood of twilight through his use of personification and contrast. By using personification, he transfers the sense of mystery found in a veiled woman to an experience in nature. By using contrast, he accentuates the feelings of isolation, uncertainty, and ambivalence in the observer.

The high point of the poem is Rilke's analysis of what it is to be human. Through the images of stone and star, he conveys the physical and spiritual duality that exists within each human being. People are physically limited by the fact that they are only flesh and blood, and yet they are free to lead a life of the mind that is limited only by the reach of their intelligence and imagination.

Rilke uses the technique of apostrophe to transfer the observer's experience to the reader. Readers may want to evaluate the effectiveness of the poet's use of "you" in the poem.

PLJ: What is your favorite time of day? When you are outside at this time, do you experience particular feelings or think about particular subjects? Give examples, if you can.

Literary Terms: apostrophe, contrast, lyric, metaphor, mood, personification, simile

COMPREHENSION QUESTIONS

1. Where is the observer when his experience occurs? (outside, looking at trees and houses)
2. What about this time of day inspires the observer's frame of mind? (its lack of clarity)

3. How does the experience make the observer feel? (isolated; frightened of the unknown; but also awed and inspired)
4. What two objects does the poet use to represent two different aspects of being human? What aspect does each represent? (stone: physical aspect; star: spiritual aspect)

UNDERSTANDING THE POEM: POSSIBLE ANSWERS

*1. *Evening*   The evening is compared to a woman who is changing from "raiments" (the colors of sunset) to "veils" (the shadows of leaves and tree branches against the twilight sky).

*2. *Speaker's sense of isolation*   The speaker feels estranged and isolated because nothing looks the same as it does in daylight, and yet all objects are still visible. The speaker also wonders where he belongs between heaven and earth.

*3. *Speaker's sense of division within himself*   The speaker feels as if he consists of two different aspects, one corporeal and the other spiritual. While he is physically earthbound, his mind or spirit is free to contemplate whatever his intelligence and imagination present.

ANALYZING LITERARY TECHNIQUE: POSSIBLE ANSWERS

1. *Apostrophe*   Rilke uses apostrophe to transfer the experience from the speaker's consciousness to that of the reader. Some students may find Rilke's use of "you" to be contrived or intrusive, resisting the speaker's attempt to project his own feelings on to the reader.

2. *Personification*   The personification underscores the theme of the poem. By imagining evening as a woman, the poet makes the evening human and therefore somehow comprehensible. At the same time, however, there is a feeling of mystery: The evening is a *veiled* woman.

*3. *Contrast*   Contrast heightens the speaker's feelings of isolation and uncertainty at this time of day.

*4. *Stone and star*   Stone and star convey the duality within each human being. Stone represents the body (physical matter), which is tied to earth. Star represents the mind (human intelligence and imagination), which can lead a life that is independent of the body.

*5. *Stage in life suggested by poem*   The time of life suggested by the poem is late middle age. This is most obvious in the twilight imagery, but it is also present in the third stanza of the poem, where the individual's life is described as "still ripening." This is an image of near-completeness. The poet's reflections on the meaning and direction of an individual's life seem appropriate for a mature adult who is wondering what the next stage of his or her life will bring.

WRITING ABOUT LITERATURE

1. *Expository essay on tone*   Students should be sure to examine carefully the various images in the poem: evening's changing raiments, veils in the trees, darkness like a silent house, star and stone. Also, encourage students to examine the relationship between what the poet says and what is actually happening in the physical world. More sophisticated students will also want to examine why the poem is addressed to an unknown "you." (See **U.P.** questions 1–3, and **A.L.T.** questions 3–5 above.)

2. *Creative writing: poem about time of day*   Call students' attention to the suggestions in the textbook assignment. Encourage them to use the poet's ideas as a springboard for their own. (**PLJ**)

FURTHER READING

Rilke, Rainer Maria, *Sonnets to Orpheus; Duino Elegies.*

A Country Doctor
FRANZ KAFKA

INTRODUCING THE STORY

On the surface, "A Country Doctor" is a nightmare in which a doctor finds that his life is beyond his control, that he is incompetent in terms of his profession and receives neither respect nor appreciation from those he would help, and finally, that he is subject to all the limitations of being human. Thus, the situation in which he finds himself is fraught with the Kafkaesque emotions of inadequacy, frustration, failure, anxiety, guilt, and despair. On a deeper level, the story is a "night journey" in which the dreamer gains important insight into what it means to be a human being and, consequently, insight into the nature of society and into his own place in the universe.

In the nightmare, the doctor, finding himself caught between his personal desires and his obligations to others, cannot resolve the conflict. He feels compelled to place the needs of a patient ahead of his own desire to remain at home in order to protect his household servant, Rose, from being sexually assaulted, and he never makes his peace with the fact that he has left her.

His torment is intensified by the fact that, having sacrificed his responsibility to himself and to those who are "his," the alarm is false, and, therefore, his sacrifice is ineffectual and unappreciated. His patient's illness first defies his best efforts to analyze it. It then turns out to be a wound that has existed from birth, and although it is incurable, it could be far worse than it is. Meanwhile, the patient himself has defied the doctor's best efforts, wishing to die when the doctor would cure him, and wishing to be cured as soon as the doctor realizes that the wound is incurable. In the end, he accepts the doctor's analysis; he is not seriously ill; the alarm was false.

On his way home, the doctor finds that his needless journey has sensitized him to the fragile nature of his own human condition. He is a naked (vulnerable) old man exposed to the hostile universe, both in terms of stormy winter weather and in terms of his profession. He feels betrayed by the inexorable nature of time and the fact that he cannot control important aspects of his life. Moreover, having taken this journey, he must accept the psychological results: He cannot forget the anxieties to which he has become vulnerable and the self-knowledge that he has acquired.

The nightmare is a ''night journey,'' not because it is literally a journey that takes place at night, but because of the nature of its symbolic content. In the words of Albert Guerard, it is ''an essentially solitary journey involving profound spiritual change in the voyager.'' The young patient's wound, ''all he brought into the world and his sole endowment,'' is the wound of being human. In recognizing the nature of his young patient's illness, the doctor becomes aware of the fact that all human beings (including himself) are imperfect, vulnerable, and fragile.

Moreover, a person's greatest expertise (the doctor's own knowledge and experience) provides no bulwark against the inevitable ravages of time and mortality (the doctor's feelings of being naked, exposed, and betrayed). Those who are aware of their wound (like the boy) are better off than those who are not (the boy's wound actually ''is not so bad''), for it is better to see life clearly than to live it blindly. It is better to lead a thoughtful and examined life, to know one's limitations, and to accept the nature of the human condition.

Finally, once an individual (the doctor) has taken the night journey (answered the false alarm on the night bell) and gained insight into the human condition, that person can never be the same again. It will never be possible to ignore reality, to deny human limitations, or to expect an infinitely better society. To know the human condition is to become humble and to accept anxiety and terror (''it cannot be made good, not ever'').

In analyzing this story as a dream, the theory that each character in a dream represents some aspect of the dreamer produces interesting results. The groom then symbolizes the eternally youthful, sexual, and aggressive side of the dreamer; Rose symbolizes the dreamer as the victim of forces beyond his control; the boy symbolizes the dreamer's incurably wounded ageless self; and the doctor symbolizes the adult form of the dreamer who is trying to cope with all of these aspects of himself.

''A Country Doctor'' can be considered symbolic of Kafka's personal life, in that he feels caught between his need for love and marriage and his self-imposed obligation as an artist to heal society through the creation of literature. On another level, the story can be considered an allegory of the human condition, where the doctor is Everyperson, doing his best to handle conflicting needs and demands under impossible circumstances.

Kafka achieves high drama through the contrast between his style and his content. His simple and direct sentences lead readers to expect a description of commonplace experiences. Instead, they reveal a profusion of fantastic images that are presented in a narrative perspective that locks the reader into the consciousness of the narrator. Using the associative pattern of thinking that is characteristic of psychological realism, Kafka makes the dreamer's nightmare become the reader's nightmare.

PLJ: Have you ever had a nightmare? What characteristics of a dream or a real experience cause you to label it a nightmare? What types of situations cause you to have nightmares?

Literary Terms: allegory, irony, narrative perspective, night journey, paradox, plot, psychological realism, setting, symbol, theme

COMPREHENSION QUESTIONS

1. Where does the doctor need to go? (into the country to treat a seriously ill patient)
2. What two things delay his immediate departure? (winter storm; no horse)
3. Whom is he worried about leaving, and what is their relationship? (Rose; household servant)
4. What two major problems confront the doctor upon seeing the patient? (diagnosis and treatment)
5. How does the doctor feel about himself in the situation that he encounters? (overwhelmed; overburdened; unappreciated; inadequate)

UNDERSTANDING THE STORY: POSSIBLE ANSWERS

1. *Doctor's challenges*   (1) Reaching the boy's home; (2) diagnosing the boy's illness; (3) curing the boy; (4) protecting Rose.
2. *Accompanying frustrations*   (a) Storm and no horse make travel impossible; (b) the boy at first appears to be healthy; (c) the boy's wound is incurable; (d) the doctor could not both protect Rose and attend to the boy; in choosing to help the boy, the doctor left Rose to the groom.
*3. *Why a nightmare*   (a) The doctor experiences a world that has no fixed reality, and a series of bizarre events occur (horses, groom, boy's wound); (b) the doctor has no control over his life. Everything that could go wrong actually occurs. He cannot cope successfully with the expectations placed upon him. The storm, the groom, and the nature of the boy's wound are all beyond his control.
*4. *Themes*   (a) Human beings are not in control of their lives. Circumstances beyond their control determine their behavior; (b) human beings are often torn between their responsibility to themselves and those they love and their responsibility to the society in which they live. Such conflicts have no happy resolution; (c) no matter how gifted they are, all human beings are subject to time and mortality.

ANALYZING LITERARY TECHNIQUE: POSSIBLE ANSWERS

*1. *Setting*   The abstract location in time and space conveys the world of the imagination or of a dream, a world that is not subject to rational laws, and therefore, a world in which anything can happen.

2. *Narrative perspective*   Kafka's choice of a first-person narrator with limited omni-science locks the reader into the doctor's nightmare exactly as the doctor experiences it. This technique guarantees an immediate and powerful experience for the reader.

3. *Allegory*   The story can be considered an allegory to the extent that the doctor is Everyperson, and his experiences symbolize the universal human condition. Other characters in the story also seem to represent specific aspects of an individual's life.

4. *Irony*   The choice of a doctor as the main character is an ironic twist that reveals one of Kafka's themes. The healer is unable to cure the wound; he who has sacrificed his personal life for his profession is not respected or valued for his profession.

5. *Style*   Kafka's simple clauses, concrete descriptions, and matter-of-fact presenta-tion of his subject matter contrast with the fantastic nature of the events that he is describing and heighten the drama of the plot.

   Kafka's technique of relating the entire story in one paragraph heightens the intensity of the drama by compressing the action. In fact, he relates parts of the story by stringing clauses together in order to avoid the pauses that would naturally occur between sentences. The story's style creates a nightmarish, surreal, stream-of-consciousness effect.

6. *Importance of plot or character*   Kafka's themes deal with human beings as they function in society. This is best revealed through action (plot) rather than through introspection (complex depiction of character). To the extent that the story is an allegory, each character symbolizes an idea, and these ideas are dramatically con-veyed through plot.

*7. *Night journey*   Rose's comment that "You never know what you are going to find in your own house" suggests that the doctor is about to begin a night journey. In this story, the doctor looks within himself and, through his experiences and feelings, acknowledges the true nature of the human condition: the ability within each human being to be both good and evil, knowledgeable and ignorant, responsible and irre-sponsible, powerful and weak; and the inability of any person to achieve perfection and defeat death. Having confronted the issues of human frailty, vulnerability, im-perfection, and mortality, and having acknowledged that such failings are an inte-gral part of life, he is no longer able to ignore them.

*8. *Psychological realism*   Psychological realism is accomplished by associative thinking. For the doctor, thoughts of the groom call forth thoughts of Rose, and the sight of the horses calls forth the desire to return home. The technique reinforces the nightmarish quality of the experience, in that one thought or event tumbles upon another in rapid succession, based on patterns of thought rather than on an orderly progression of events.

WRITING ABOUT LITERATURE

1. *Expository writing: An essay analyzing "A Country Doctor" as a nightmare*   Call students' attention to the directions in the textbook assignment regarding content (setting, characters, plot). Remind them of the importance of using direct quota-

tions to support their ideas. (See **U.S.** questions 2–4, and **A.L.T.** questions 1, 7, and 8 above.) **(PLJ)**

2. *Creative writing: A nightmare* Call students' attention to the suggestions in the textbook assignment. Remind them that dreamers do not always appear as themselves in their dreams. **(PLJ)**

FURTHER READING

Kafka, Franz, ''The Metamorphosis''; *The Trial;* ''In the Penal Colony''; *The Castle.*

The Wall

JEAN PAUL SARTRE

INTRODUCING THE STORY

''The Wall'' is an exciting adventure story with a surprise ending. It is also one of the classics of existentialism. It is the story of a man, Pablo Ibbieta, who is arrested and condemned to die by the Spanish Fascists (falangists) because he is active in the anarchist movement, a group that wished to liberate Spain from Franco and his government. Imprisoned with two other men, he must come to terms with his impending death. In time, he is offered his life in exchange for revealing the location of Ramon Gris, an important fellow anarchist and his friend. Pablo knows with certainty where Ramon is hiding but also knows that torture could pry the truth from him. Enjoying the prospect of their frustrating and fruitless search, he misleads the soldiers with a false location. Not long thereafter, he is amazed to learn that the soldiers have found and killed Ramon just where he told them to look, Ramon having left his hiding place without Pablo's knowledge.

In the ways they confront their deaths, Pablo, Tom, and Juan represent three facets of the human being. Both Tom and Juan are doubles of Pablo, representing emotional facets of him that he must bring under intellectual control as part of taking control of his life. Juan is Pablo's doppelgänger in that, like Juan, the purely emotional part of Pablo is also terrified of death; Pablo controls these emotions in himself by despising Juan in order to eradicate that aspect of himself. Pablo has a harder time coming to terms with Tom, for Tom functions as Pablo's alter ego as well as his doppelgänger. Both Pablo and Tom are political activists who live in the same environment and have experienced similar situations. Tom also asks the kinds of intellectual questions about life and death that Pablo would ask if he permitted himself to do so. However, such questions arouse emotional concerns, and Pablo criticizes Tom in order to distance himself from the concerns that the two of them share. Pablo consciously works to divorce his intellectual self from his emotional self, and that process involves forcing himself to give up all relationships with other human beings.

''The Wall'' is constructed on the basic existential paradox that while people act on the belief that they live in a comprehensible, predictable universe, the universe is in reality irrational and unpredictable. Pablo's manipulation of the soldiers with regard to Ramon's location and their finding Ramon there illustrates this paradox.

In addition, Pablo embodies many existential ideas and attitudes. Existentialists believe that human beings are "condemned to be free," in that the tragic human condition is the only absolute in a universe that contains neither God (according to the atheistic branch of existentialism) nor good nor evil nor hope. Rather than having been created for some divine purpose, human beings must create their own personal values, their own meaning, their own sense of purpose. They determine the course of their own lives. In an irrational world in which actions have unpredictable consequences, the process of striving is a valid end in itself, and active commitment throughout their entire lives will reward individuals with identity, integrity, and self-esteem. Although the human condition is tragic, freedom enables human beings to be dignified, courageous, noble, and even heroic.

PLJ: To what extent, if any, does the existence of death give meaning to life? How would you feel about yourself and about others if you learned that you would die tomorrow?

Literary Terms: alter ego, contrast, doppelgänger, existentialism, foil, irony, limited omniscience, narrative perspective, paradox, symbol, theme

COMPREHENSION QUESTIONS

1. As the story opens, what has happened to the narrator? (He has become a political prisoner.)
2. Why is Juan in the same situation? (His brother is an anarchist, although he is innocent.)
3. What does the Major announce? (death sentences for all three)
4. What is Pablo's goal in the story? (to accept death with dignity)
5. What bargain do the officers try to make with Pablo? (his life if he will turn in his friend, Ramon Gris)
6. How does Pablo react to this opportunity? (refuses to turn him in; fabricates story that Ramon is hiding in cemetery vault or gravediggers' shack)
7. What happens to Juan? (killed)
8. What happens to Pablo? (freed from death sentence and military court; matter sent to regular court)
9. What does Garcia reveal to Pablo? (Ramon found according to Pablo's story)
10. What is Pablo's response? (laughs at absurdity of life)

UNDERSTANDING THE STORY: POSSIBLE ANSWERS

*1. *Why Pablo criticizes comment about Saragossa*   Pablo doesn't want to envision his own death.
*2. *Pablo's dislike of pity*   Pity entails emotional involvement with other people. Feeling pity for someone else would lead Pablo to pity himself. In order for him to face death, Pablo thinks he must disconnect from life.

*3. *Pablo's being alone and hard*   Feeling alone and hard enables Pablo to prepare for his death by divesting himself of his emotions. If he can view his past life as having no meaning, it will be easier to face death with self-control and dignity.

*4. *Meaning of "I want to die decently"*   Dying "decently" means with self-control, without self-pity and with dignity. This is Pablo's self-assertion against fate: although he cannot choose when to die, he can choose how he will react to death.

*5. *Changes imminent death makes in Pablo's attitude toward life*   The only way that Pablo can face death is to forget the joyful and rewarding aspects of being alive. Pablo cuts himself off from all human relationships, including the woman he loves and the men who are sharing the death sentence with him. He refuses to permit himself to feel sympathy, pity, and love for others any longer.

*6. *Pablo's near approach to death*   By accepting his death as inevitable, Pablo gains control over his life, including both his emotions and his actions. Once he has no fear of death (the greatest of fears), he fears nothing else. He has power over his enemies because they no longer have power over him.

*7. *Pablo's refusal to turn in Ramon Gris*   In an irrational world, people's actions define the quality of their lives. Pablo achieves pride in himself through his behavior. He is proud not to succumb to the temptations set forth by his enemies, proud to retain his chosen principles in the face of death.

*8. *Themes*   The universe operates without any principle of reason governing it. Cause and effect are an irrational pairing. The only meaning in life is that which people create for themselves through their conduct.

ANALYZING LITERARY TECHNIQUE: POSSIBLE ANSWERS

1. *Function of Tom and Juan*   Both Tom and Juan serve as contrasting characters, or foils, for Pablo. Tom is Pablo's alter ego, in that both men are political activists in the same environment; they have had similar experiences; and they are both facing death. Tom is also Pablo's doppelgänger, in that Tom faces death more emotionally than Pablo, asking questions about the meaning of life and death that Pablo does not allow himself to consider. Pablo forces himself to be critical of Tom in order to distance himself from Tom's concerns because they are his own concerns as well.

   Juan's situation differs from that of Tom and Pablo and illustrates the theme in the story that life is irrational. Juan is not involved in politics and is innocent of the charges; it is his brother who is the politically active anarchist. Juan functions as Pablo's doppelgänger in that Juan responds with unrestrained emotion to his impending death. Pablo forces himself to disconnect completely from Juan in order to conquer his own terror and face death with dignity.

2. *Function of Pablo's humor*   Humor requires emotional distance. Pablo separates himself from his situation; he views the officers as insects. Pablo's final laughter is bitter. The universe is completely irrational, and it is foolish to have any illusions

about oneself and reality. Ramon Gris' fate destroys whatever of Pablo's illusions have not already been destroyed.

*3. *"The Wall" as symbol and title*   The wall symbolizes the barriers that separate the living from the dying. "The Wall" is an appropriate title in that Pablo constructs a barrier between his old emotional self and the intellectual self who is preparing to die. He also constructs a wall between himself and the prisoners who are confined with him. Similarly, each of the other two prisoners lives behind his own wall. Each of the three men faces his death alone, neither giving nor receiving support from the other two.

On a literal level, a wall (the hospital-prison) separates this group that is condemned to die from the world of the living, and those who are going to be shot are first placed against a wall.

4. *Why narrative perspective appropriate to theme*   A first-person narrator possesses limited knowledge. Thus, Pablo does not know why he has been arrested, what will happen next, or what his real future will be. His lack of knowledge permits him to speculate, and the difference between what he expects and what actually happens creates irony. Irony is at the heart of an irrational universe, where one cannot predict effects from causes.

*5. *Relationship between irony and theme*   The following ironies are important parts of the story: *(a)* Pablo escapes death because he unwittingly enables the army to find Ramon Gris; *(b)* Juan is killed even though he is innocent, while his brother, the anarchist, escapes capture; *(c)* Gris never expects to be captured in the cemetery because he never imagines that Pablo would fabricate such a tale. All three ironies support the theme that the universe is irrational and unpredictable.

WRITING ABOUT LITERATURE

1. *Expository theme analyzing Pablo's remarks in terms of existentialism*   Call students' attention to the quotation and overview of existentialism that are given in the textbook assignment. (You may wish to discuss existentialism more thoroughly with your students before giving them this assignment.) Remind them to combine direct quotations with their own analysis. Existentialist ideas present in the quotation include the following: *(1)* the idea of being alone, undergoing a lonely, individual struggle in solitude and isolation; *(2)*the idea of having no understanding because one lives in an incomprehensible, unpredictable universe; *(3)* the importance of asserting oneself and being true to oneself. (See **U.S.** questions 1–8, and **A.L.T.** questions 3 and 5 above.)

2. *Creative writing: Pablo's diary after his release*   Call student's attention to the quoted passage in the textbook. **(PLJ)**

FURTHER READING

Sartre, Jean Paul, *The Wall and Other Stories; The Flies* (drama).

The Guest

ALBERT CAMUS

INTRODUCING THE STORY

"The Guest" combines the appeal of an adventure story with that of a mystery story. The schoolmaster, Daru, is ordered to house a murderer overnight and then to take him to government officials in Tinguit. He despises the Arab for resorting to murder and for permitting himself to be caught, yet he considers his own role to be dishonorable and humiliating. Recognizing their common humanity, Daru treats the criminal like a guest and puzzles over how best to reconcile his respective responsibilities to the Arab, to France, and to himself. He decides to provide the Arab with the means and knowledge necessary either to escape or to deliver himself to the proper authorities. Seeing that the Arab is traveling toward Tinguit, the Arab's compatriots leave Daru a message that blames him for the Arab's fate and threatens him with retribution. Daru is now vulnerable and alone.

Daru is Camus's Everyman, in love with the beauty of the universe and the pleasure of simply being alive. He struggles to remain true to the moral principles by which he lives, respecting the needs of all people to determine the course of their own lives. However, the outside world will not let him remain neutral in an escalating political struggle. Human contact forces people to commit themselves, to take risks, and to fight for what they believe in. Daru views turning in the Arab as contrary to honor and therefore humiliating because the Arab's crime is neither a personal nor a political threat. Moreover, Daru does not want to be responsible for delivering the Arab to a possible death sentence, a punishment that Daru considers to be a crime against nature. In the end, Daru feels alone in a hostile world.

PLJ: What do you need in life in order to be happy? What aspects of your life do you value most? What principles guide your behavior? If you are asked to do something, what determines whether or not you do it?

Literary Terms: allegory, conflict, contrast, existentialism, irony, limited omniscience, narrative perspective, setting, symbol, theme

COMPREHENSION QUESTIONS

1. Where is Daru's school? (alone, high on mountain plateau in Algeria)
2. What is the political situation in Algeria? (French officials fear Arab uprising for independence)
3. What responsibility is Daru given? (turn Arab murderer in to police)
4. How does Daru feel about his responsibility? (doesn't want to do it)
5. What crime did the Arab commit? (killed his cousin)
6. How does Daru treat the Arab? (feeds and houses him as if he is a guest)

7. In the middle of the story, what does Daru hope the Arab will do? (escape)
8. How does Daru resolve his problem? (gives Arab choice of freedom)
9. What does the Arab do? (turns himself in to the authorities)
10. What happens to Daru? (threatened by Arab activists)

UNDERSTANDING THE STORY: POSSIBLE ANSWERS

1. *Relationship between where Daru lives and Daru's personality* Daru lives in an isolated area, where few people are involved in his life. Daru is independent and self-reliant, preferring isolation to the intrusion of society.

    Daru most values his independence and being true to his moral principles. His is a self-imposed exile because he does not like the usual human relationships, which he considers greedy, hateful, and bloody.

*2. *Principal conflict* The principal conflict, which is internal (it occurs in Daru's mind), is whether or not to turn the Arab over to the authorities. Daru resolves it by giving the Arab a choice. When the Arab chooses the authorities, the other Arabs blame Daru.

3. *Balducci and Daru* Balducci views Daru's independence and moral convictions as "cracked" because they are idealistic and impractical. However, Balducci likes Daru (he refers to him as "son"), so he simply does his job and lets Daru act on his own. The freedom of choice that Balducci allows Daru foreshadows the freedom Daru allows the Arab.

*4. *Why crime revolts Daru; why he treats Arab as guest* Daru hates murder as unnecessary and irrevocable. He also is angry that the Arab let himself get caught, causing Daru to be saddled with the responsibility of dealing with him.

    Daru treats the Arab as a guest because he believes all people are related through their common humanity. He also does not fear the Arab, since the man's crime was the result of a family squabble.

*5. *Why turning in Arab is dishonorable and humiliating* Daru views turning in the Arab as contrary to honor and humiliating because the Arab's crime is neither a personal nor a political threat. Also, the Arab's fate may be death, and Daru does not want to be responsible for a punishment he considers to be a crime against nature. Daru is caught with the paradox of detesting the Arab for his crime and being the cause of a similar crime if he turns the Arab in to the authorities.

*6. *Why Camus omits violence* Camus is interested in the plight of a human being who hates violence and who wishes to lead a moral life in a world filled with destructive actions. He concludes that one cannot lead a moral life and remain uncommitted and impartial. If one does not choose sides, society will make that choice.

*7. *Tragic end: why "had loved" instead of "loved" landscape.* (a) Daru is a tragic figure in that by trying to stay uninvolved and impartial, he acts in a way that gives the Arab the freedom to imperil Daru.

(b) The landscape symbolizes Daru's independence; now he will be forced to be on the French side, and for his own safety, he may have to move into town. His place in the universe is no longer what it was, an island separated from society by his attitudes and his location. A darker reading is that Daru will be killed to avenge the Arab's death.

8. *Title*   Opinions will vary, depending on whether the Arab or Daru is viewed as more important. Both ''The Guest'' and ''The Host'' emphasize the human connection and the responsibility of one human being for the life of another.

ANALYZING LITERARY TECHNIQUE: POSSIBLE ANSWERS

1. *Function of Balducci*   Balducci is a foil for Daru. Balducci performs a task he does not like because it is his job. He, too, is careful not to hurt the Arab. The freedom of choice that Balducci gives Daru foreshadows Daru's offer to the Arab.

2. *Suspense and fear*   Camus's use of details creates suspense and fear: Daru's handling of Balducci's gun; the Arab's night venture; Daru's hearing furtive steps around the schoolhouse at night and slight sounds behind him the next day.

*3. *Relationship between political setting and plot*   Balducci's talk of an imminent Arab uprising and police mobilization makes the Arab's crime and his village's agitation over his whereabouts sources of fear and uncertainty. Balducci does not think that the Arab is politically involved, but he can't be certain. In addition, the political situation forces Daru to choose between his identification with French culture and his love of the Algerian land and people.

4. *Function of Camus's narrative perspective.*   Camus uses third-person limited omniscience, with the center of consciousness located in Daru's mind. As a result, the reader knows only what Daru thinks, sees, and hears. This creates suspense and immediacy.

5. *Irony*   *(a)* The French treat the Arab like a criminal when he is no apparent threat to the French colonists. *(b)* Daru thinks that his neutrality makes his position safe. *(c)* Despite Daru's rejection of the responsibility that Balducci places on him, the Arab's compatriots blame Daru for the Arab's decision. *(d)* Daru detests the Arab because of the Arab's crime, yet if the authorities kill the Arab, Daru will have inadvertently played a role in the Arab's death.

6. *Allegory*   *(a)* Daru's physical environment symbolizes Camus's universe in that it is clean and beautiful, even in its austerity. The universe is not concerned with the cycle of human existence; one human being is as good as another as one replaces the other.

(b) Daru symbolizes the human condition. He is Camus's Everyman, in love with the beauty of the universe and the pleasure of simply being alive. Human contact forces people to commit themselves, to be involved, to take risks, and to fight for what they believe in. In the end, each one is alone to lead one's life as one sees best, in an uncaring universe where one must persevere even if one is misunderstood.

WRITING ABOUT LITERATURE

1. *Expository theme on "No man is an island . . ."* Call students' attention to the quotation and the suggestions in the textbook assignment. (See **U.S.** questions 2, 4, and 6 above.)

2. *Expository theme on Daru's choice* Call students' attention to the directions in the textbook assignment. (See **U.S.** questions 2, 4–6, and 7, and **A.L.T.** question 3 above.)

3. *Creative writing: "The Guest" from the Arab's point of view* Call students' attention to the questions suggested in the textbook assignment. Students should consider what code of behavior guides the Arab's actions. Students should note that the Arab's cousin was a thief who ran away, and therefore the Arab killed him. The Arab does not run from the consequences of his actions; alternatively, the Arab may fear the nomads more than he fears the French. **(PLJ)**

FURTHER READING

Camus, Albert, *Exile and the Kingdom* (short stories); *The Stranger; The Plague.*

Africa

Song for the Dead
DAHOMEY (TRADITIONAL)

INTRODUCING THE POEM

The "Song for the Dead" is a song about the value of life. In the words of the Daho-mean, "Dance all the colors of Life"—for once people have died, they can no longer enjoy life's pleasures. While the Dahomeans dance for the dead, they also dance for themselves. Recognizing that all people share an inevitable mortality, they find it impor-tant to enjoy their own lives.

The style of the Dahomean song is dynamic, expressing an important message clearly, succinctly, and with great vitality. Repetition is the key to its effect, and the closing meta-phor ("all the colors of Life") is a beautiful expression of the human life-experience.

PLJ: To what extent do you consider your life to be a gift? If each day you stopped to realize that this day will never return, what effect would it have on your daily life?

Literary Terms: metaphor, repetition, theme

COMPREHENSION QUESTIONS

1. What does the song say about death? (Enjoyment dies with one's death.)
2. What does the song say about wives? (Passion dies with one's death.)
3. What does the song say about food and drink? (Pleasure dies with one's death.)
4. What pleasure do pipes bring? (quiet)
5. What does the song advise the living to do for the dead? (enjoy life for them)

UNDERSTANDING THE POEM: POSSIBLE ANSWERS

1. *Why dance for the dead*   The dead can no longer enjoy life, so the Dahomeans enjoy it for them. Whether, in fact, the dead gain vicarious enjoyment from the joys of the living is a matter of personal belief. However, in either case, the living are more appreciative of the fact that they are alive and able to enjoy these experiences.
2. *Attitude toward life*   The theme of the poem is: Enjoy each day of life to the fullest, for no enjoyment exists after death.

ANALYZING LITERARY TECHNIQUE: POSSIBLE ANSWERS

1. *Appropriateness of "all the colors of Life"*   The metaphor is simple enough to be appreciated by young and old, uneducated and educated. It reveals the people's ap-

preciation of the natural world. The range of colors in nature is wondrous, varied, and changeable. Life, too, is wondrous, varied, and changeable.

2. *Effect of repetition*   Repetition of "I say to you say" gives the poem the vitality of rhythm. Repetition of the internal structure of each stanza and of the phrase "Goes with you" emphasizes the theme of the song.

*3. *Arrangement of stanzas*   Like a well-organized essay, the first stanza introduces the thesis or thematic idea: "There is no enjoying beyond Death." The next four stanzas supply supporting, specific examples that relate to the thematic statement. The last stanza concludes the song with practical advice as to how to cope with the fact of the thematic statement.

WRITING ABOUT LITERATURE

1. *Expository analysis of the poem's organization*   Direct students' attention to the suggested comparison in the textbook assignment. (See **A.L.T.** question 3 above.)
2. *Creative writing: An essay or poem expressing a philosophy of life*   A philosophy may express any belief that can direct one's choices in life. Students should be encouraged to choose their supporting details thoughtfully, and to consider what images best express the philosophy of their choice. **(PLJ)**

FURTHER READING

Courlander, Harold, *A Treasury of African Folklore.*
Herskovits, Frances and Melville, *Dahomean Narrative.*

Mista Courifer

ADELAIDE CASELY-HAYFORD

INTRODUCING THE STORY

In "Mista Courifer," Casely-Hayford dramatizes the generation gap as it occurs in an African family. The story is appealing and powerful because of the universality of its themes and the author's ability to depict with compassion the humor and irony that are inherent in the situation.

Mista Courifer, an undertaker and preacher, considers certain English customs to be symbolic of the civilized, modern, and successful Sierra Leonean and, thus, has spent his adult life emulating English ways. He has adopted the English view of native dress and native homes, so that, instead of having pride in his native customs, he is ashamed of them. He and his family live in the European-style house that he built for them, and he dresses in the attire of an English undertaker. Mista Courifer is proud that he has chosen what he considers to be the best of both worlds, an English veneer for public success, and the authoritarian manner that is traditional with the Sierra Leonean male for personal comfort at home. Mista Courifer's son Tomas is his pride and joy. Tomas wears imported English clothes to his government job. Under his tutelage, Mista Courifer expects Tomas to rise to the top of the bureaucracy and become "somebody."

Suddenly Tomas rebels. He announces that he prefers to combine the native African and English ways to suit his own values and tastes, which are the reverse of his father's. He and his well-educated bride will live in a mud hut, dress in native attire, and have an English-style family life. Mista Courifer becomes frustrated and furious at the change in his son's image. Tomas remains loving but intransigent.

When Tomas and Accastasua appear in church in native costume, Mista Courifer is so shocked and ashamed that he no longer has the desire and confidence to be a preacher. A defeated man, he takes refuge in his undertaking business, which deals with the dead rather than the living.

PLJ: How are your parents' goals for you different from your own? If you intend to pursue your own goals, how will you deal with your parents? How do you expect them to react to you?

Literary Terms: characterization, irony, symbol, theme, tone

COMPREHENSION QUESTIONS

1. What is Mista Courifer's favorite occupation? (preacher)
2. What is characteristic of Mista Courifer's way of life? (emulates European housing and clothing)
3. What is Mista Courifer's goal in life? (to be proud of his Europeanized son Tomas)
4. What does Tomas do to his father? (disappoints him by returning to native clothing and a mud hut)
5. How does Mista Courifer react? (furious and too ashamed to continue preaching)

UNDERSTANDING THE STORY: POSSIBLE ANSWERS

1. *Why Mista Courifer values certain English styles*   Mista Courifer chooses values that will achieve the most for his personal well-being. Since the English rule Sierra Leone, the most successful Sierra Leoneans are those who value English ways enough to emulate them. Since Sierra Leonean tradition elevates the father in the home, Mista Courifer perpetuates those aspects of that tradition in his own home. He expects Tomas to share his values, and he grooms him to be even more successful in the community.

2. *Why Tomas reverses Mista Courifer's values*   Tomas comes into his own when his initiative improves his job situation. He then begins to function as an adult rather than as a grown child. He decides against wearing the clothes he has always hated, and he plans to have the type of marriage that suits his personal needs and values.

3. *Mista Courifer as father*   Mista Courifer has been a good father in that he has loved Tomas and has done his best to train his son to succeed in the community. Tomas acquires self-esteem from his own ability to handle his career responsibilities and from Mista Courifer's great pride in him.

4. *Compare/contrast Tomas and Mista Courifer*   Both Tomas and Mista Courifer are loving people who have personal convictions and act in accordance with them. Both believe in combining English and Sierra Leonean ways according to personal taste. They are different in that Tomas looks forward to independence—independence both from his father and from colonial rule.

5. *Why Tomas changes his mind about his job*   Tomas expects that his boss, Mr. Buckmaster, values him so little that he will dismiss him on the basis of his recent attitudes and behavior. Tomas is amazed to hear how Mr. Buckmaster has valued him, which causes him to become ashamed of the quality of his recent work, which, in turn, causes Mr. Buckmaster to be genuinely concerned about Tomas. Mr. Buckmaster's attitude causes Tomas to explain his problems, thereby earning both self-respect and increased respect from Mr. Buckmaster. Tomas is now free to keep his job, since his wishes have been granted.

6. *Why Mista Courifer gives up preaching*   Tomas's new behavior contradicts Mista Courifer's values, and he feels that this devalues his position as a leader of the congregation. He finds it hypocritical to preach one way of living while his son chooses a different way for himself. Mista Courifer views native dress and native homes as the English do. Instead of having pride in his national customs, he is ashamed of them.

7. *Author's attitude toward Mista Courifer*   The author views Mista Courifer sympathetically and with humor. It is clear from her description of his European house and clothing that she finds his English affectations inappropriate, unpatriotic, and silly.

8. *Author's attitude toward Tomas*   The author's favorite characters are like Tomas, authentic and sensible. They take the best of both cultures, but the best is determined by what enables them to be proud of who they are. Tomas will keep his job with the government, which he performs well. He will return to mud huts, which are more comfortable and airier in Sierra Leone's climate, and he will wear traditional clothing. These decisions reflect pride in his culture. However, he also will choose the English style of family life, because he believes it is better for the entire family.

9. *Title*   The choice of title makes one character more important than the other, and the tale begins and ends with Mista Courifer. It is he who lacks pride in the traditions of his culture, finds self-esteem in trying to be English, and is devastated by his son's adoption of certain traditional ways.

10. *Themes*   (a) Grown children must function as adults and make their own decisions. (b) Each person is entitled to his or her own values and style. (c) Parents cannot expect their children to be carbon copies of themselves. (d) Parents do not have to accept the values and style of their children. (e) For those who must try to balance two diverse cultures, some place more emphasis on assimilation and others place more emphasis on cultural heritage.

ANALYZING LITERARY TECHNIQUE: POSSIBLE ANSWERS

1. *Connection between Mista Courifer's sermons and his life*   Mista Courifer is outraged by his son's advocacy of all that he has worked so hard to discard. Thus, he responds to Tomas's return to national tradition as Jonah and Noah responded to their sinful environment: He takes refuge inside his workshop as Jonah and Noah retreated into the whale and the ark.

2. *Relationship between author's attitudes and tone of story*   Although the author clearly disagrees with Mista Courifer's values, she understands the political causes of those values. Thus, she criticizes him gently, with sympathy and humor. Her sympathy and humor create the tone of the story.

3. *Function of Keren-happuch*   Keren-happuch is treated with sympathy and is a source of irony and humor because of the way that her attitudes and values contrast with those of Tomas. She values Tomas's English clothes because her father doesn't give any such clothes to her.

*4. *Two examples of humor and their contribution*   (a) Mista Courifer: contrast between quiet husband and coffin-maker and wondrous religious leader (singing, praying, sermonizing). (b) Mista Courifer: obstinately wishing to appear English despite the obvious disadvantages and impossibility of achieving the goal. (c) Keren and Tomas: visual humor in their attendance at church wearing English clothes. (d) Mista Courifer's visit with Mr. Buckmaster: Tomas's testimonial. (e) Contrast between Mista Courifer's suggestion and Tomas's choice of vacation pursuits.

   Casely-Hayford's use of humor enables her to treat serious issues—the clash of generations, racial differences, colonialism—in such a way that people can laugh at them and thus come to a better understanding of the problems and solutions involved.

*5. *Irony*   Examples of irony include the following: (a) Mista Courifer's desperate effort to appear English; (b) Tomas's return to traditional home and dress; and (c) Mr. Buckmaster's testimonial. All contribute humor to the story.

WRITING ABOUT LITERATURE

1. *Expository theme analyzing irony*   Call students' attention to the directions in the textbook assignment with regard to content and organization. (See **A.L.T.** questions 4 and 5 above.)

2. *Creative writing: Letter about life in the Courifer family after Tomas's marriage*   Call students' attention to the questions suggested in the textbook assignment. **(PLJ)**

FURTHER READING

(Works by other prominent Ghanaian writers)
Armah, Ayi Kwei, *The Beautiful Ones Are Not Yet Born* (novel).

Awoonor, Kofi, *Ride Me, Memory* (poems); *This Earth, My Brother* (novel).
Kayper-Mensah, Albert, *The Drummer in Our Time* (poems).

A Drink in the Passage
ALAN PATON

INTRODUCING THE STORY

"A Drink in the Passage" conveys a sense of the tragic barrier that exists between whites and blacks in the Republic of South Africa. For many years, that nation has had the policy, known as apartheid, of social segregation and economic and political discrimination against blacks and other non-European groups. Edward Simelane, an educated black man and winner of a national sculpture contest, meets Jannie van Rensburg, a white man, when they are both admiring the prize-winning sculpture. van Rensburg desperately wishes to "talk out (his) heart to" the sculptor of the work and, even though he is ignorant of Simelane's identity, he invites him back to his apartment for a drink. Although Simelane accepts, the encounter fails.

Although van Rensburg wishes to bridge the racial barrier, his manner of walking and his way of serving the drinks reveal an underlying discomfort. His well-meaning family does its best to converse with Simelane, but it is obviously difficult, since Simelane is a stranger and the black experience is foreign to them.

Although Simelane recognizes and appreciates van Rensburg's courage and good intentions, he makes little effort to respond to him. Being in a white area close to curfew and breaking the liquor laws, Simelane is very anxious to return home before the police discover him. A political activist might love the opportunity van Rensburg presents; Simelane has no interest in it.

Later, Simelane feels guilty for his treatment of van Rensburg and asks Paton to write this story, hoping that others will understand the feelings of both parties. When he asks Paton whether it is too late for the two races to relate to each other, the author, caught between hope and despair, does not respond.

The power of the story lies in the similarity of people who are separated only—but completely—by a racial barrier. Paton, with his gift for depicting attitudes and feelings, conveys the humanity of all involved and reveals the racial barrier to be a wall that the best intentioned people can breach only with great effort.

PLJ: Have you ever attempted to become acquainted with a stranger? How did you go about it? How successful were you? What circumstances would increase the success of such a venture?

Literary Terms: climax, exposition, foreshadowing, irony, metaphor, narrative perspective, symbol, theme

COMPREHENSION QUESTIONS

1. What caused the nationwide sensation at the Golden Jubilee? (black man won sculpture competition, competing against whites)
2. How had this occurred? (committee forgot "for whites only")
3. Why didn't Simelane attend the ceremony? (said he wasn't feeling up to it; his attendance would have provoked a racial demonstration, and he is not politically oriented)
4. What does Simelane observe in the bookshop window? (exhibition of his prize-winning sculpture)
5. Whom does he meet there? (white man who loves his sculpture)
6. Why do they drink in the passage? (given segregation, van Rensburg not comfortable inviting Simelane inside)
7. How does van Rensburg's family feel about the stranger? (want to be friendly, but don't quite know how)
8. How does Simelane respond to van Rensburg and his family? (without interest)
9. What does Simelane ask Paton to do at the end? (write this story)

UNDERSTANDING THE STORY: POSSIBLE ANSWERS

*1. *Sculpture's appeal to van Rensburg*   The mother-child relationship is a universal bond, one that is shared by all people on earth. Simelane's rendition of the loving relationship reveals the common bond of humanity that should exist between whites and blacks instead of apartheid, and it is this that appeals to van Rensburg. van Rensburg feels that "God must be in the man who made it" because he thinks that Simelane has perpetuated God's values in his own work.

2. *Sculpture competition and Simelane's visit to van Rensburg re: structure of society*   Both reveal a society in which blacks and other non-Europeans are segregated from whites under apartheid. Note: error in contest rules; curfew; rules about blacks walking with whites and using the same entrances to buildings; rules about blacks in a white neighborhood and in buildings inhabited by whites; and rules about blacks and liquor.

3. *Simelane not a demonstrator*   Simelane has no interest in personally trying to improve the political, economic, and social condition of his people. If he were interested in civil rights, he would have claimed his prize in person in order to further the status of himself and his people. He also might have been more interested in communicating with van Rensburg because he might have had ideas about ways in which van Rensburg could organize whites to help the black cause. As it is, he fears trouble with the police more than he wishes to respond to the gestures of friendship.

4. *Why Simelane doesn't reveal his name*   Simelane does not reveal his name because: *(a)* he is self-conscious about being the sculptor of the winning entry; *(b)* years of segregation have trained him to keep a social distance from whites, and he has no genuine interest in communicating with van Rensburg. Once Simelane has lied, he cannot reveal the truth.

5. *Why van Rensburg's background is important*   van Rensburg's background reveals the ways in which Simelane's background is superior to his own. It also reveals areas of common interest. Had both men been of the same race, they might have become friends. This commonality points up the significance and injustice of the racial barrier.

6. *Why van Rensburg invites Simelane to drink in the passage*   Either van Rensburg or his family (or both) is not completely comfortable with Simelane. Years of segregation have trained them to keep a social distance from blacks. Ironically, this causes van Rensburg to be more comfortable standing where they can be discovered than drinking in the apartment.

7. *Simelane thanks woman at van Rensburg's*   How Simelane thanks the woman reflects his social relationship to her. *Dankie, my nooi* and *Dankie, missus* are unacceptable because they assume that the woman is socially superior to Simelane, and he doesn't wish to act as if he is a servant. Simelane fears that *mevrou* may anger the woman with its implication of social equality, but, given the choice, he decides to err on the side of appearing to be disrespectful and presumptuous. The woman is comfortable with his choice.

8. *Why country breaks van Rensburg's heart*   van Rensburg wants to be sure Simelane understands that he thinks apartheid is shameful and that he is opposed to it.

9. *How van Rensburg feels at end*   van Rensburg feels frustrated, sad, and possibly angry that genuine, mutually motivated communication did not and could not occur between him and Simelane. His best efforts could not breach the racial wall.

10. *Why Simelane's wife weeps*   Simelane's wife weeps for her husband, for van Rensburg, and for the institution of apartheid that has created an insurmountable wall between two men of good will.

11. *Why Simelane asks Paton to write story*   Simelane asks Paton to write the story because he wants to make amends for refusing to reciprocate van Rensburg's efforts to relate to him. The story he tells Paton reflects both his awareness and appreciation of van Rensburg's attitude and efforts, and his own terrible fear of being caught by the police for breaking the rules of the white establishment. Paton's story may explain the feelings of the educated black toward the enlightened white, so that these whites won't be unrealistically optimistic about resolving the racial problem easily or soon.

ANALYZING LITERARY TECHNIQUE: POSSIBLE ANSWERS

1. *Function of story within framework*   At the beginning, the framework (conversation between Simelane and Paton) serves as exposition, providing background information about the contest and the reactions to it, thus supplying the setting of the story. At the end, the framework supplies a commentary for the story and gives it a broader meaning. It adds an optimistic note in that it reveals Simelane's conversation with another white man—in this case an educated and enlightened author—in a meaningful way. It also enables Paton to give his opinion on the subject of race relations.

2. *Foreshadowing* The background information about the sculpture contest foreshadows the setting in which van Rensburg's attempt at friendship with Simelane occurs and anticipates their difficult relationship. The fact that Simelane has no active interest in working for civil rights foreshadows that he would not be motivated to risk trouble with the police in order to respond to van Rensburg's gestures of friendship.

*3. *Relationship of climax and theme*   (a) The climax occurs when Simelane and van Rensburg part without being able to relate in a meaningful way.

    (b) The fact that the high point of the story is the lack of communication between two men of similar interests but different races—one making a concerted effort to be kind and friendly, and the other terrified of being caught by the police for breaking the rules of the white establishment—reveals the formidable nature of the wall between them that is the theme of the story.

*4. *"Black man conquers white world"*   This is an appropriate caption in that Simelane won the national sculpture contest in competition with the best of the white sculptors. It is ironic in that, generally speaking, the white world of the Republic of South Africa continues to ignore the rights of black people and to subject them to denigrating rules. Specifically, it is Simelane's fear of breaking those rules and his lack of interest in those whom the rules benefit that prevent him from taking the time to get to know van Rensburg.

5. *Liquor as symbol* Liquor is a social symbol in that it represents the spirit of friendly good fellowship. As a symbol of this spirit, van Rensburg invites Simelane to join him at his apartment for a drink. It is ironic, and significant of the relationship between the races, that van Rensburg serves Simelane the drink in the passage rather than inside the apartment.

    Liquor is also an economic and political symbol of black inferiority. Blacks cannot afford expensive liquor and do not have it available to them. Also, laws limit their drinking to specific times and places so as to discourage the threat arising from group dynamics.

6. *van Rensburg's use of "mate"*   van Rensburg's use of "mate" symbolizes the potential for friendship between him and Simelane, based on a shared appreciation of Simelane's sculpture.

    However, "mate" takes on ironic overtones as the emotional distance between the two men becomes evident. Even though he is remarkably open to friendship with a black man, van Rensburg is not comfortable walking next to Simelane and is not comfortable serving him his drink inside the apartment. Simelane is appreciative of van Rensburg's efforts but is more concerned about leaving the city before the curfew than about responding to a white man's overtures of friendship.

*7. *Metaphor* Examples of metaphor include: (a) "touch"; (b) sight: "blind" and "years in the dark"; and (c) movement: "run a race in iron shoes." These metaphors describe the chasm between whites and blacks, who cannot relate to each other because they are strangers. Years of government regulations and acceptance of the established order, combined with lack of knowledge and personal contact, have created a situation that will be difficult to change.

WRITING ABOUT LITERATURE

1. *Expository theme on function of sculpture*   Students' essays should include a discussion of the common experiences shared by whites and blacks. You might encourage students to consider whether a real mother and child (rather than a sculpted mother and child) might have evoked the same kind of response from van Rensburg. (See **U.S.** question 1, and **A.L.T.** questions 4 and 7 above.)
2. *Creative writing: van Rensburg "talks out his heart" to Simelane*   Call students' attention to the suggestions in the textbook assignment. They might lead to a discussion of the common humanity between the two peoples and emotions of sorrow and anger. **(PLJ)**

FURTHER READING

Paton, Alan, *Tales From a Troubled Land; Cry, the Beloved Country.*

Prayer to Masks
LÉOPOLD SÉDAR SENGHOR

INTRODUCING THE POEM

Senghor wrote "Prayer to Masks" after World War II, when, for many, the world seemed dead and without hope. He believed that even though European colonialism had exploited Africa, the future of both continents was still interconnected. The poem is a call to Africans to have pride in their heritage and to recognize that they have a unique contribution to make in the world. In this post–World War II period, Europe and Africa must discard the rubble of the past and build a new and better world. The poem states that the world will be better if it contains the joy of life, the optimism, and the vitality that only the Africans can teach the people of other cultures.

Senghor includes principles of the Négritude literary movement in this poem. He personifies Africa as a pitiful princess, but a princess nonetheless. To pity her is not to devalue her. By using the masks that represent ancestor veneration and worship, Senghor acknowledges and commends the role of tradition in African culture. Through simile and metaphor, he reveals Africa's connection to Europe and Africa's unique role in the future of the world. Senghor uses irony and paradox for dramatic effect and repetition for dramatic energy.

PLJ: Much of the strength and vitality of the United States comes from the fact that the country brings together people from many backgrounds and cultures. What has your family heritage contributed to the United States?

Literary Terms: figurative language, irony, metaphor, Négritude, paradox, personification, repetition, simile, theme

COMPREHENSION QUESTIONS

1. What do the masks represent to the speaker? (his ancestors)
2. How does the speaker describe Africa? (a pitiful princess)
3. How does the speaker describe Africa's relationship to Europe? (joined at the navel)
4. What does the speaker want the African people to do? (take part in the rebirth of the world)
5. Name two contributions that the speaker sees Africans giving to the world. (joy; memory of life and hope; the vitality of rhythm)

UNDERSTANDING THE POEM: POSSIBLE ANSWERS

1. *Why speaker calls on masks*   The speaker asks the cooperation of his ancestors, whom the masks represent, in the great tasks he finds necessary for Africans in the creation of a new and better world.
2. *Traditional relationship between the living and the dead*   Spirits of the dead remain a part of the lives of the living. They are worshiped, and in ceremonies, masked figures speak for them.
*3. *Implication of "Who give away their lives like the poor their last clothes" (line 14)*   The speaker implies that the Africans could not afford to sacrifice their lives for their European colonizers and that they should not have been so generous as to fight in a war that had no impact on their own lives.
*4. *Themes*   *(a)* Africans have a necessary and unique contribution to make in the creation of a more harmonious world. *(b)* While modern Africa may be pitiful compared to its past, the continent still possesses dignity, self-respect, strength, joy of life, and creativity.

ANALYZING LITERARY TECHNIQUE: POSSIBLE ANSWERS

1. *"Masks of unmasked faces" (line 8)*   The ancestor masks represented the essential qualities of the personality and values of the ancestor, rather than his or her physical appearance, physical condition, or age.
*2. *Personification of Africa*   Like a princess, Africa has stature and value, even when she is living through unfortunate circumstances.
3. *Africa and Europe "joined at the navel" (line 12)*   As European colonies, the African countries were linked economically and politically to Europe. The image is ambivalent, though: Is Europe (the economically and politically stronger culture) or Africa (the older culture) the "mother" implied by the umbilical-cord image?
*4. *Yeast and white flour (line 16)*   "Yeast" refers to the Africans, and "white flour" refers to the Europeans and the people of other primarily "white" continents. The resulting "bread" would be a reformed social order in which the Africans contributed their unique talents to the cultures of the white continents.

The key components in the "yeast" that enable "white flour" to become "bread" are the African abilities to enjoy life, to be optimistic (hope), and to have creative energy (rhythm).

*5. *"Men of coffee cotton oil" (line 20)*   Europeans do not view the Africans as human beings, but rather as the producers of valuable commodities. Thus, Africans are important only to the extent that they satisfy the Europeans' needs.

6. *Repetition*   Repetition infuses the poem with rhythm and, therefore, dramatic energy. Repetition of "masks" reinforces the speaker's imperative command for the masks' attention. Repetition of "who would" and "They call us" builds to the climax at the end of the poem.

7. *Irony*   It is ironic that Africa is undervalued, when Africans contributed equal fighting skills alongside the Europeans. In the view of the speaker, it is also ironic that those who are treated like slaves hold in their hands the keys to the future well-being of the world.

*8. *Paradox*   It is paradoxical that Africa, although pitiful, is a princess (worthy of respect and admiration). It is paradoxical that Africans, who are ordered about like slaves, have the ability to contribute qualities to the world that will make it a better place to live. It is paradoxical that Africans are called "men of death," when they are really people of life, who are able to communicate their joy of living, their vitality, and their creativity to the rest of the world.

WRITING ABOUT LITERATURE

1. *Expository analysis of Senghor's techniques that instill pride*   Call students' attention to the directions in the textbook assignment. (For a discussion of figurative language and paradox, see **U.P.** questions 3 and 4, and **A.L.T.** questions 2, 4, 5, and 8 above.)

2. *Creative writing: A poem expressing pride in one's cultural heritage*   Call students' attention to the suggestions in the textbook assignment. **(PLJ)**

FURTHER READING

Senghor, Léopold Sédar, *Selected Poems; Prose and Poetry.*

Dry Your Tears, Africa!

Bernard Dadié

INTRODUCING THE POEM

"Dry Your Tears, Africa!" can be interpreted as a return from a journey that is either real or symbolic. The speaker may speak for all Africans who are returning home from war on the European continent. Given the poem's publication in the 1950s, Dadié's phrases "storm and squalls of fruitless journeys" and "the springs of ill fortune and of glory" may refer to the participation of African troops in World War II, including the prejudice and discrimination that they experienced as they fought on the French side. Their experience later caused an argument within the Négritude movement as to whether World War II had been a just cause for African participation.

On a symbolic level, Africa's returning children may refer to the many Africans whom the French assimilated by educating them in French African schools, where they were taught French language, culture, and values. As a result, many became more French than African. Some of these Africans received their university education in Paris and continued to live there. It was the goal of the Négritude movement to bring these Africans back into African culture by showing them the unique and appealing aspects of their own traditions and values that would make them proud to be African.

Dadié's poem reflects the values of the Négritude movement in its personification of Africa as the loving mother and those who have left as her children. His emphasis on Africa's natural beauty and the love of Africans for their native land are common themes in Négritude poetry. His use of repetition emphasizes the idea of the returning Africans and the beauty of their native land.

PLJ: Under what circumstances would you ever want to leave your native country? Where would you choose to go? Do you think that you would want to remain there or return to your homeland? If you returned, what do you think you would find most appealing about your homeland?

Literary Terms: contrast, figurative language, metaphor, Négritude, personification, repetition, theme

COMPREHENSION QUESTIONS

1. Why has Africa been crying? (Africa's children have left.)
2. Why should Africa stop crying? (children are returning)
3. What did the Africans find on their journeys? (ill fortune and glory; storms and squalls)
4. What do Africans admire about Africa? (its natural beauty)
5. What do Africans bring back to Africa? (playthings, love, dreams, and hopes)

UNDERSTANDING THE POEM: POSSIBLE ANSWERS

*1. *Africans better off if they had never left Africa?* "The neighbor's grass is always greener." The returning Africans may well be more satisfied having returned from foreign cultures than they would have been if they had never experienced them. Learning who they were not was probably an important factor in learning who they were.

2. *"Playthings"* The returning Africans probably bring home technological inventions that were not currently available in their native land, such as typewriters and electrical appliances. Dadié calls these "playthings" because they bring pleasure and ease but are not necessary for a happy and fulfilling life.

ANALYZING LITERARY TECHNIQUE: POSSIBLE ANSWERS

1. *Water imagery*   (a) *squalls* (lines 3, 10): storms at sea, indicating a difficult, uncomfortable series of experiences; *(b) crest of the wave* (line 4): Africans have traveled far from Africa, over the sea to a different continent; *(c) drunk/From all the springs of ill fortune/and of glory* (lines 12–15): sources of fresh water that quench one's thirst, the Africans have experimented and experienced a new life; *(d) the charm of your waters* (line 19): part of the natural beauty of Africa that brings the Africans back, with pride, to their native land.

*2. *Personification*   Dadié depicts Africa as a loving mother who weeps over the loss of her children to other lands and to European culture. The speaker is one of the returning Africans who now appreciates Africa's unique qualities. Like the other previously assimilated Africans, he is choosing to forego his adopted culture and return lovingly to Mother Africa with his dreams and hopes. Personification humanizes abstract concepts, making it easy for readers to understand and identify with them.

3. *Contrast*   Dadié contrasts foreign with native, new with traditional, disappointment with hope, and the past with the future. Africans who were educated to value European culture and who traveled to France to live and to fight in World War II are returning to Africa disillusioned with foreign culture and interested in renewing their ties to their own native heritage. They now look to their homeland to fulfill their hopes and dreams.

4. *Repetition and theme*   "Dry Your Tears, Africa!" expresses Dadié's theme in the poem. The peoples of Africa have not deserted their native land and their native heritage for other lands and cultures. Having experimented with European culture, they joyfully return home, appreciative of Africa's beauty and excited about their future there. Repetition of the title thus reinforces the theme. By repeating the words that introduce each item on the list of Africa's attributes, Dadié emphasizes each separate aspect of Africa's beauty.

WRITING ABOUT LITERATURE

1. *Expository theme analyzing nature of the journey*   Remind students to use direct quotations from the poem to support their argument that the journey is literal or symbolic. (See **U.P.** question 1 above.)

2. *Creative writing: Poem or description of thoughts about being away from home*   Remind students of the questions suggested in the textbook assignment. Encourage them to use striking images and details to make their writing more vivid. **(PLJ)**

FURTHER READING

Dadié, Bernard, *Climbié* (autobiographical novel).

A Sunrise on the Veld
DORIS LESSING

INTRODUCING THE STORY

"A Sunrise on the Veld" is a powerful rite-of-passage story, a journey of initiation consummately related by an author who is both a master storyteller and a master stylist. The adolescent protagonist leaves home at dawn on a hunting expedition, feeling exuberantly omnipotent. His euphoria is shattered when he discovers an injured buck in the process of being eaten to the bone by hordes of voracious ants. The sight functions as a Joycean epiphany. Suddenly, the boy realizes that death is an inherent part of life and that, like the fate of the buck, the circumstances of his own mortality are beyond his ability to predict or control. He remembers the times when he has injured a wild animal and left it to its fate in order to be home in time for breakfast, and he suddenly feels the guilt of acting selfishly and irresponsibly. He knows that this incident with its accompanying insights has irrevocably changed the course of his life, and he plans to take the time to ponder its significance. However, he crosses the threshold into adulthood reluctantly, nostalgic for his lost innocence and not quite ready for the pain, loss, and guilt that are part of the adult world.

The extraordinary power of the story emanates from two major themes involving the nature of the universe and the relationship of human beings to that universe. The issues of control over one's life and the extent to which one's fate is unpredictable and inescapable are serious subjects for every human being. Lessing's third-person limited omniscient narrative perspective dramatizes the contrast between the boy's feelings of control and power in a benign universe before seeing the dying buck and, afterwards, his feelings of fatalism in a cruel and uncaring universe.

The second powerful theme involves a different, but equally important, conception of the universe and the relationship of human beings to it. In Lessing's hands, nature becomes a living entity that is the essence of the universe. Both animals and humans are part of that totality, neither more nor less. Once nature is understood in this way, the responsibility of human beings to the plant and animal kingdoms becomes clear. The boy's feelings and perceptions are described in figurative and sensory language that enables the reader to experience the environment as directly as if he or she were actually accompanying the boy on his journey. Thus, in this respect also, a crucial issue in the story becomes important to the reader.

PLJ: It is said that it is not what happens to you but what you make of it that counts. Look back over your life and find the point at which you left childhood behind. What happened? To what extent, if any, was the change caused by a specific incident or by a series of events? What effect did the experience have on you? What did you learn from it?

Literary Terms: connotative language, contrast, epiphany, figurative language, irony, limited omniscience, narrative perspective, realism, setting, symbol, theme

COMPREHENSION QUESTIONS

1. Why does the boy awaken so early? (to go hunting)
2. What is his attitude toward his life? (feels he is omnipotent)
3. What sight shocks him? (a buck being devoured by ants)
4. What does the sight mean to him? (life involves the unexpected and death)
5. What does he want to think about? (his responsibility to other living things and his own fate)

UNDERSTANDING THE STORY: POSSIBLE ANSWERS

1. *Importance of the boy's age*   The boy is at a transitional age from child to adult, making his reaction to the dying buck appropriate. If he were younger, he would not have made the connection between the buck's fate and his own life; if he were older, he already would have lost his innocence.
2. *Importance of the boy's being alone*   If the boy had not been alone, his reaction probably would have been affected by his companions' responses. His friends might have made light of it in order to protect themselves from any psychological discomfort in the presence of their peers. His father's reaction would have depended on his own particular background of experiences, and that reaction might have distracted the boy from any introspection.
3. *Quotation concerning the boy's past and future*   The boy's past is his childhood—all that he has been until this moment in time. His future is the person he becomes once he has experienced the death of the buck. This story is about a rite of passage or initiation into adulthood, during which the boy becomes mature enough to acknowledge and understand the complexities of life.
4. *Buck as "a figure from a dream"*   On the surface, the buck is a dreamlike figure in that it is so distorted that it has passed beyond recognition and imagination. On a deeper level, the buck, like dreams, is the symbol of an aspect of reality—in this instance, of the dark aspects of the life experience (illness, death, and the boy's lack of control over the environment and his own fate).
5. *Quotation about refusing to accept the responsibility*   The boy is reluctant to understand the buck as a symbol of an important aspect of his own life. He does not want to admit the darker aspects of life into his own life. He does not want his understanding of this experience to change his life, and he knows that it must affect his attitudes, not only toward himself and his place in the universe, but, more specifically, toward his hunting animals, which is a recreational activity that he loves.
*6. *Will boy think about buck tomorrow?*   Student responses will vary. If the boy is introspective, he will consciously continue to think about the buck. If he is not com-

fortable with the thoughts that follow from this experience, he will become busy enough to avoid thinking about it consciously, but he may dream about it.

7. *Themes* *(a)* All living things die, and no living thing can avoid its fate. *(b)* One cannot remain an innocent child forever; sooner or later, a life experience that introduces one to the dark side of life becomes a rite of passage into adulthood. *(c)* Life contains both beauty and cruelty, both creation and death.

ANALYZING LITERARY TECHNIQUE: POSSIBLE ANSWERS

1. *Contrast* Lessing contrasts the boy's thoughts and feelings about himself and the universe before and after he sees the death of the injured buck. The difference in his thoughts and feelings reflects his emotional growth and confirms the experience as a rite of passage or initiation into adulthood.

2. *Nature* Nature functions as another living part of the universe: plants, fowl, animals, and the boy are all alive and joyful with life. With the death of the buck, the boy realizes that the ants, too, are part of nature and part of life, and that, in nature, one living thing lives off another. Thus, nature is both cruel and joyful. He himself, being part of nature like the buck, will experience the cruelty as well as the joy.

3. *Epiphany* The epiphany is the death of the injured buck, which reveals the nature of life to the boy. For the first time, he contemplates death as a personal reality, the inescapable fate of every living thing.

4. *Symbolism of buck* The buck symbolizes the boy and every living thing. Making the buck symbolic of the boy's life increases the importance and power of the experience, both for the boy and for the reader, for whom the buck is also a symbol. The symbolic aspect of the story gives it a universal significance.

5. *Narrative perspective* Third-person limited omniscience permits the author to reveal: *(1)* the boy's thoughts and feelings as he takes his journey and watches the death of the buck; *(2)* descriptions of nature and the death process, using sensory and figurative language that would not be a natural part of the boy's thoughts and feelings. A first-person narrator would have thought the same thoughts and felt the same emotions, but would have expressed them more directly. For the reader, the experience would be more intense but less philosophical and less pictorial.

*6. *Connotative and figurative language and nature* Lessing views nature as a living thing of which humans, animals, birds, insects, and plants are all an integral part. The living aspects of nature capture her interest. Her figurative and sensory language gives the reader a visual and aural picture of the African veld that is like watching a motion picture or a videotape. Examples: *(a)* ''Alert as an animal he crept . . .''; *(b)* ''Now he felt the chilled dust . . .''; *(c)* ''the bush stood trembling . . .''; *(d)* ''The grass stood . . . and the trees were showering . . .''; *(e)* ''The first bird woke . . . the bush woke into song . . .''; *(f)* ''the patches of rawness were disappearing . . .''; *(g)* ''nothing but one bird singing . . .''; and *(h)* ''big black ugly insects . . . standing and gazing . . . with small glittering eyes.''

7. *Paradox*   The story contains the following paradoxes: Life is both beautiful and cruel, and it contains both creation and death. These paradoxes are themes of the story, and they are what the boy learns in his rite of passage.

WRITING ABOUT LITERATURE

1. *Expository theme analyzing Lessing's treatment of nature through connotative and figurative language.*   Call students' attention to the questions suggested in the textbook assignment. (See **A.L.T.** question 6 above.)
2. *Creative writing: Boy's thoughts about death of buck.*   Call students' attention to the questions suggested in the textbook assignment. **(PLJ)**

FURTHER READING

Lessing, Doris, *African Stories.*

Good Climate, Friendly Inhabitants
NADINE GORDIMER

INTRODUCING THE STORY

"Good Climate, Friendly Inhabitants" is the deftly told story of an aging white book-keeper, who is afraid of dying a lonely death. The story derives its power from this woman's relationship with two men. Out of the depths of her loneliness and against her better judgment, she finds herself attracted to a good-looking, ne'er-do-well white male, young enough to be her son, who conveniently lives off her as long as he can. Meanwhile, she confides in Jack, a black man who has worked with her at the garage for years. Jack is a good friend to her: listening, advising, caring, and protecting. However, tragically, she cannot breach the color barrier to value and take comfort in his friendship.

Gordimer tells the story from the woman's point of view, seeing and evaluating the two males and the woman herself through the woman's eyes. The technique of first-person limited narration adds irony, mystery, and the question of reliability to the story, for the woman often presents herself and others as she subconsciously chooses to see them.

PLJ: A common saying about people is, We never see ourselves as we are; in order to know ourselves, we need to see ourselves as others see us. Do you know any people who believe certain things about themselves that are inconsistent with the way that others view them? If so, think of such a person, and give examples both of what this person thinks and what others think about him or her. Explain why you think this person has distorted views of himself or herself.

Literary Terms: characterization, climax, interior monologue, irony, limited omniscience, narrative perspective, setting, theme, tone

COMPREHENSION QUESTIONS

1. Who is this story about? (unmarried woman who works in office of an automobile service station)
2. How does she view herself? (unusually well-preserved for her age)
3. With what two groups of people does she work? (blacks at the gas pumps; white mechanics)
4. How does she feel about them? (nothing in common with either group)
5. What two men take a prominent role in the story? (Jack, a black, and the Rhodesian, a white)
6. How does the woman react to these two men? (confides in Jack, but doesn't consider him a friend because he is black; is both attracted to and repelled by the Rhodesian.)
7. What happens at the end of the story? (Jack gets rid of the Rhodesian for the narrator.)

UNDERSTANDING THE STORY: POSSIBLE ANSWERS

*1. *Narrator's appearance*   The narrator is 49 trying to look 25. Her hair has had too much of bleach and permanents, and her face shows her age. However, she prides herself on her figure, and she wears uniforms made for girls, not women. Thus, she fools herself, rather than anyone else.
*2. *Narrator's friends*   When the narrator boasts of friends among garage customers and those who pass with their dogs, she is revealing her loneliness. Actually, she has only one friend, with whom she goes to the movies on Fridays. She has Sunday lunch whenever she chooses with an old couple who feel sorry for her. It is ironic that she cannot value Jack, whom she should consider a good friend, because of his race.
*3. *Narrator's relationship with her daughter*   The narrator's relationship with her daughter increases her social isolation. She disapproved of her daughter's marriage, implies that she disapproves of her grandchildren, and has seen the family only once in what could certainly be ten years.
*4. *Narrator's attitude and behavior toward blacks, including Jack*   The narrator views blacks as children, and she calls them "boys" no matter what their ages. When she wants to assert her superiority, she sends them on personal errands. As much as she longs for a friend, she could never consider relating to a black in that way. She complains that she works in absolute social isolation, and when Jack befriends her, she cannot recognize his friendship.

*5. *Rhodesian's character*   Possible adjectives that describe the Rhodesian include: self-serving, selfish, and manipulative. For example, he lies in order to get housing, money, and sexual favors. His numerous lies include: *(a)* a need to change his money; *(b)* that his watch is gold; *(c)* that he needs a hotel room; *(d)* that he has driven down from Rhodesia; *(e)* that he is 37; *(f)* that his raw-looking scars are from old wounds; and *(g)* that his car was being repaired or sold.

*6. *Narrator's relationship with Rhodesian*   The narrator is drawn to the Rhodesian's physical appearance because he is young, blond, suntanned, and clean-cut. His appeals for her financial aid encourage her to reach out to him. Given her loneliness, she needs whatever relationship he offers her, and she does her best to interpret his behavior as that of a person who is having a run of bad luck.

The narrator comes to fear the Rhodesian because he is totally unscrupulous. She believes he may steal from her or even kill her. She is equally afraid of her own inability to resist her attraction to him, her loneliness having made her needy and vulnerable.

*7. *Safety in confiding about Rhodesian*   Confiding in someone would enable narrator's body to be found soon if she were murdered. The person might also help her get rid of the Rhodesian. Her need to confide is a symbol of the extent of her fear of him.

*8. *Why Jack gets rid of the Rhodesian*   Jack feels free to get rid of the Rhodesian after the narrator gives him her address so that he can check on her well-being should she not come to work. Her request makes Jack aware of her fear of the Rhodesian.

*9. *Importance of "know thyself"*   The narrator states, "To myself I admit everything," but she cannot face the reason for her attraction to the Rhodesian and her willingness to let him take advantage of her. If she could have acknowledged her great loneliness and her fear of dying alone, she could have made a concerted effort to make genuine friends. She also would have been able to recognize the Rhodesian for the type of person he was and could have resisted his efforts to take advantage of her. If she could have acknowledged and revised her attitude toward blacks, she would have been able to recognize, accept, and appreciate Jack as her friend.

ANALYZING LITERARY TECHNIQUE: POSSIBLE ANSWERS

1. *Relationship of setting to character and plot*   The narrator would not be so lonely and might accept Jack's friendship if it were not for the restrictions of apartheid.

*2. *Function of Jack*   With an unreliable, first-person narrator, a character like Jack is necessary in order to tell the reader how to evaluate the narrator's responses. Jack is an objective witness.

3. *Why the narrator and the Rhodesian have no names*   With a first-person narration, either the narrator would have to reveal her own name or someone else would have to call her by her name. Jack cannot call her by her name because his lower social status prohibits it. (Jack calls her "missus" occasionally, but usually nothing.) The

Rhodesian has no interest in the narrator's name. He never reveals his name, and the term "the Rhodesian" associates him with the spurious circumstances of his arrival.

4. *Tone*   The tone is disturbing, projecting a sense of sadness both in the narrator's lack of control over her life and in her inability to value Jack's heart beneath his blackness. The first-person narration, with its distorted view of self and others, makes the narrator's fragility and vulnerability apparent to the reader.

*5. *Climax*   The climax, or moment of highest emotional intensity, may be different for different students. For some, it will be the moment when Jack tells the narrator, "He was here," because the narrator is terrified of the Rhodesian's presence in her life. For others, it will be the moment when Jack tells her, "I told him you're gone . . .," because Jack proves that he is the narrator's true friend even though he is black. For still others, it will be the narrator's last words about having no one to speak to and living in a town filled with "people you can't trust," because she disregards Jack's concern for her and his actions on her behalf and cannot view him as her friend.

*6. *Relationship between last sentence and title*   The relationship is ironic in that it reflects the difference between reality and the narrator's interpretation of it. The narrator reveals herself to be a pitiful woman, whose situation is made more difficult and more poignant by the society in which she lives. If it were not for the attitude toward blacks fostered by her country's apartheid policies, she would be able to accept Jack as her friend. However, because Jack is a member of the race she fears, the narrator is unable to recognize him as a valued person in her life, and, ironically, she mistakenly concludes that "this whole town is full of people you can't trust." It is also ironic that, in reality, the narrator contributes to her own loneliness by choosing to isolate herself from Jack and the other blacks who work in the garage. Finally, it is ironic that the narrator's attitudes and behavior towards blacks actually cause her to be an "unfriendly inhabitant."

*7. *Narrative perspective*   Gordimer creates immediacy and power by letting the reader enter the narrator's mind and view the world as the narrator sees it, with her prejudices and her vulnerability. The narrator's spoken and unspoken thoughts ironically conflict with the reality of the outer world as revealed by Jack's and the Rhodesian's words and deeds. Specific examples include: *(a)* Narrator's and Rhodesian's contrasting attitudes toward her age; *(b)* Narrator's comments about friends in contrast with her relationship with Jack; *(c)* Narrator's view of the Rhodesian in contrast with his treatment of her.

WRITING ABOUT LITERATURE

1. *Expository analysis of function of narrative perspective*   Call students' attention to the directions in the textbook assignment. (See **U.S.** questions 1–4, 6, 7, and 9, and **A.L.T.** questions 5–7 above.)

2. *Expository character sketch of Rhodesian*   Call students' attention to the directions in the textbook assignment, and remind them of the importance of using direct quotations. (See **U.S.** questions 5–8, and **A.L.T.** question 2 above.)
3. *Creative writing: Retell story from different point of view*   Call students' attention to the choice of topic and to the ideas suggested in the textbook assignment. **(PLJ)**

FURTHER READING

Gordimer, Nadine, *Selected Stories.*

Africa
DAVID DIOP

INTRODUCING THE POEM

The poet speaks lovingly of Africa through a progression of ideas. First, he refers to the proud old tribal cultures that are the subject of legend and song. Next, he describes the humiliating condition, like slavery, of Africans in the French colonies. Then, he announces the rebirth of a strong land that is becoming free of faded white colonialism. Finally, he correctly predicts the difficulties of freedom.

Diop's use of personification humanizes Africa, enabling the reader to feel the strength, beauty, painful mistreatment, and revitalization that are all part of the African experience. Mother Africa's correction of the speaker's point of view introduces a powerful irony: Africa is not weak but strong; she is not conquered but rises renewed; she is not enslaved but free. In addition to the picturesque language that personification enables him to apply to enslaved Africa, Diop uses the striking metaphor of Africa as a young tree that is emerging in strength from a field of pale, white flowers (French colonialism).

PLJ: Think about your parents, your grandparents, and your great-grandparents. What have these relatives experienced in their lives? How do their experiences affect your life, in terms of your thinking or your behavior?

Literary Terms: irony, metaphor, Négritude, paradox, personification, theme

COMPREHENSION QUESTIONS

1. How does Diop describe the ancestral warriors? (proud)
2. How does Diop describe Africa's black blood? (beautiful)
3. How does Diop describe the condition of Africa's children? (enslaved)
4. How does Africa describe herself? (a young, strong tree)
5. How does Africa describe the taste of liberty? (bitter)

UNDERSTANDING THE POEM: POSSIBLE ANSWERS

*1. *Speaker's connection to African heritage*   The black blood connects him to his African ancestors, who were subject to the rule of France and thus slaves.

*2. *Implication of "Saying yes to the whip"*   Agreeing to be whipped implies that Africa is willing to be colonized (subjugated by European countries), willing to devote its economy to the benefit of foreigners, willing to permit foreign countries to wield political power over African communities, and willing to accept the socially inferior status that such colonization creates.

3. *Why Africa calls speaker "impetuous"*   The speaker's passion leads him to focus on the negative aspects of African experience without seeing the positive aspects of the present. Currently, a rebirth of African dignity, renewed pride in African culture, and interest in political independence lead Africans to feel pride rather than pity for Mother Africa.

4. *Why liberty tastes "bitter"*   Achieving liberty involves casting off what is known, established, and predictable for what is unknown, risky, and unpredictable. The process can involve wars in which people are injured and killed. The transition period involves loss of political and economic security. Sometimes, the new government is as bad as the prior government.

*5. *Theme*   Africa should not be viewed as a victim but as a survivor, emerging from its colonial phase with renewed vigor and strength.

ANALYZING LITERARY TECHNIQUE: POSSIBLE ANSWERS

1. *Personification*   Personifying Africa as a mother endows Africa with all that "mother" symbolizes: love, tenderness, nurture, concern for the African's well-being. It also endows Africans with the feelings of children for their mother: love, tenderness, desire to please, pride, and loyalty.

*2. *Irony*   The irony in "Africa" is related to the idea of reversal and paradox. The speaker is wrong to view Africa as having been destroyed by colonialism. Africa is strong enough to have survived the ordeal and to have emerged with renewed youth and strength, now devoted to the cause of political independence (liberty).

3. *Metaphor*   (a) Blood irrigates fields and is the substance of sweat: Both images tie the workers to their work, work that is both life-enhancing (irrigation) and life-depleting (sweat from slavery).

   (b) Africa as a young, strong tree: a dynamic image of continuing new growth and development.

*4. *Contrast*   (a) Then and now: African ancestors were proud warriors; African soldiers fighting for France in WW II are colonists and, being black, are treated like a subspecies of human being.

   (b) Appearance and reality: Africa no longer acquiesces to its colonial status; patiently and obstinately it is pursuing the path toward political independence.

(c) Black and white: Black (Africa) is beautiful, youthful, and strong; white (European countries) is not beautiful, but "faded" (*faded* implying a loss of vitality).

*5. *Significance of color*   (a) Black is beautiful: color of the speaker's skin; color of African blood; (b) white is not beautiful, being pale and faded: flowers symbolize European colonial powers in Africa, such as France; (c) red is painful: red scars from the wound of whiplashes.

WRITING ABOUT LITERATURE

1. *Expository writing: Use of contrast*   Remind students to use direct quotations to support their ideas. (See **U.P.** question 5, and **A.L.T.** questions 2, 4, and 5 above.)

2. *Creative writing: Poem exploring own cultural roots*   Remind your students that they may invent a cultural heritage for this assignment. **(PLJ)**

FURTHER READING

Diop, David, *Hammer Blows and Other Writings.*

Marriage Is a Private Affair
CHINUA ACHEBE

INTRODUCING THE STORY

"Marriage Is a Private Affair" explores a common theme of African literature: the effect of tradition on contemporary behavior. It is the poignant story of the pain involved when children mature and make decisions that their parents do not approve. Although Achebe sets his story in Nigeria, the conflicting values of the older and the younger generation in a family, and the pain engendered by this conflict, are present in all families when the younger generation adopts new ways.

Okeke has reared his son Nnaemeka within the Ibo tribe and thus with tribal values that are appropriate to that community. However, once Nnaemeka moves to the city (Lagos), he adopts modern attitudes and behavior, including the freedom to choose his own mate. When Nnaemeka tells his father about his decision to marry Nene, a woman from a different Nigerian tribe, Okeke believes that such a marriage will be a disaster. Nnaemeka's choice is, in fact, a good one, and his marriage prospers. Eight years pass, in which Okeke cannot reconcile himself to Nnaemeka's marriage. Finally, Nene's letter, imploring Okeke to let his two grandsons meet him, breaks through the wall of emotional resistance behind which Okeke has barricaded himself. Okeke belatedly realizes how foolish he has been to let his commitment to the traditions of his tribe deprive him of a loving family, and he hopes that he does not die before the family can recover the joys that it has lost.

The key to the story's tone is the attitude of the three characters toward each other. Both Nnaemeka and Nene realize that Okeke is a good man whose Ibo culture does not permit him to accept their marriage, and Okeke remains true to the only principles that he feels can sustain him. Meanwhile, Nnaemeka and Nene continue to treat Okeke with respect and to support each other's attempts to improve their relationship with him.

PLJ: How would you feel if your older brother or sister, who was also your very close friend, married a person of a different race or religion? Would your parents be likely to object to such a marriage? Under these circumstances, what do you think the young couple should do?

Literary Terms: characterization, conflict, contrast, foreshadowing, irony, realism, setting, theme, tone

COMPREHENSION QUESTIONS

1. What does Nnaemeka need to tell his father? (engaged to Nene)
2. What plans does Okeke have for Nnaemeka? (an arranged marriage)
3. How does Okeke react to Nnaemeka's news? (will have nothing to do with Nnaemeka and Nene)
4. How long does this period last? (eight years)
5. How does the story end? (Okeke relents when his grandsons want to meet him.)

UNDERSTANDING THE STORY: POSSIBLE ANSWERS

*1. *Why Okeke objects to Nnaemeka's marriage*   (a) Ibo custom dictates that parents arrange the child's marriage. (b) Nene is from a different tribe; marriages work best when partners share common bonds; different tribe means different religion and cultural heritage. (c) Nnaemeka's independent behavior reveals that he no longer values the traditions of his tribe and the values of his family; thus, Okeke feels that he has failed in his rearing of Nnaemeka.

*2. *Nnaemeka's blame for relationship with Okeke*   Nnaemeka is to blame in that he knows what the effect of his decision will be. His choice is to please himself or to please Okeke; no compromise is possible. Thus, Nnaemeka must please himself and try to help Okeke adjust to the values that accompany city life.

3. *What Nnaemeka's attitude toward Okeke reveals about Nnaemeka*   Nnaemeka loves, respects, and understands Okeke. He believes that Okeke has the ability to be flexible, and that, in time, he will support his son's marriage.

*4. *What Okeke's reaction to native doctor reveals about him*   Okeke holds some independent views. He does not share the superstitions of his neighbors and does not trust native doctors. This fact supports Nnaemeka's evaluation of Okeke and reveals Okeke's potential to free himself of destructive traditional tribal constraints.

5. *Okeke's reaction to Nene's letter*   He is pleased that his grandsons wish to know him. He is pleased that Nene has responded to his hostility with kindness and understanding. He finally realizes that his attitude has cut him off from love and family life.

*6. *Attitude implied in title*   The title conveys Achebe's attitude that young people are living in a new age and must be free to make their own decisions. Good parents should feel confident in their child's ability to choose wisely.

7. *Effect of last sentence on impact of story*   The last sentence puts the attitudes and events in perspective. Humans die; life is short; death is often unexpected. Thus, time and life are priceless. Love and life experiences lost through estrangement are not recovered. People should look beyond present irritations to the future and preserve a flexible attitude. Okeke's realization of his mortality enhances his value of life. He realizes the tragic loss of eight years, and his response makes him a more sympathetic character.

8. *Themes*   Themes include: *(a)* new ways are not necessarily worse than old ways; *(b)* family relationships are more important than some traditional values; *(c)* live each day as if it were your last.

ANALYZING LITERARY TECHNIQUE: POSSIBLE ANSWERS

*1. *Contrast*   Contrasts include: *(a)* town vs. tribe; *(b)* age vs. youth; and *(c)* tradition vs. innovation.

2. *Foreshadowing*   Nnaemeka's reaction to writing Okeke about his marriage foreshadows its effect on Okeke and prepares the reader for the action that follows.

3. *Tone*   The tone is poignant. It is achieved through the universal nature of the conflict, the inevitable pain and compromise that are necessary, and the fact that all three major characters are basically good human beings.

4. *Character determines fate vs. Fate determines character*   Students' answers will vary. "Fate determines character" whenever external events impinge on people's lives and force them to react. "Character determines fate" in that one's response to any given situation is determined by one's particular personality structure.

   Okeke's situation is an example of the relationship between the two views. When Nnaemeka's marriage conflicts with Okeke's tribal values, Okeke's response will determine his fate. He can be true to his value system or be flexible and adapt that value system to new circumstances. At first, he is inflexible and reacts with hostility, creating a chasm. Later, he relents, bridging or closing the chasm.

5. *Irony*   It is ironic that Okeke can be flexible about native doctors and inflexible about relating to Nnaemeka and Nene, when both are important to Nnaemeka's well-being. It is also ironic that the tribal values, which were intended to be supportive, can become destructive.

WRITING ABOUT LITERATURE

1. *Expository theme analyzing how contrast enhances theme*   Call students' attention to the directions in the textbook assignment with regard to content and organization. (See **U.S.** questions 1, 2, 4, and 6, and **A.L.T.** question 1 above.)

2. *Creative writing: Letter from Okeke to Nene after the visit*   Call students' attention to the questions suggested in the textbook assignment. **(PLJ)**

FURTHER READING

Achebe, Chinua, *Things Fall Apart; Arrow of God; Girls at War and Other Stories.*

The Rain Came

GRACE A. OGOT

INTRODUCING THE STORY

Ogot weaves many strands of meaning into "The Rain Came." Some give it romantic appeal, while others give it intellectual power. The story's romantic appeal is based on its satisfying conclusion, where love conquers adversity. Stories of beautiful maidens in distress, like Oganda, who are rescued by handsome and courageous young men, like Osinda, are the subject of many folktales and myths. Because it ends with a feeling (although not an actuality) of "happily ever after," the story satisfies the human need for love, security, and justice.

The story gains intellectual appeal from its examination of the role of tradition in society. "The Rain Came" contains elements of a fertility myth, where the sacrifice of a valued and beautiful young virgin is necessary in order to bring rain for the growth of crops. Ogot dramatizes the intense emotion with which individuals respond to the traditional demands of their society under circumstances where "love it or leave it" are the only options. Labong'o experiences heartrending conflict between his responsibility to his people and his responsibility to his family, but, as chief, he does not have the freedom to choose. Oganda experiences anguish and terror at being the sacrificial victim; she would prefer a normal life to eternal fame, but, as princess, she does not have the freedom to choose. Meanwhile, the villagers celebrate because, with the exception of Osinda, they have everything to gain and nothing personal to lose from the sacrifice of Oganda. Fortunately for Oganda, Osinda has both the motivation and the freedom to choose the course of his life. Valuing Oganda more than family, friends, and the safety of conformity, he leaves the village and rescues the woman he loves.

The fact that it rains despite Oganda's rescue means different things to different people. The villagers presumably are unaware of Oganda's fate and remain committed to their traditions. Oganda and Osinda learn that they have achieved personal happiness and freedom without cause for guilt since "the Almighty" does not punish their community for their rebellion.

The conflict between people's responsibility to their society and their personal desires and the conflict between tradition and innovation have universal application. People in every society are called upon to sacrifice their personal desires for the needs of their community, particularly in time of war. Moreover, as young people become young adults, they often find that new circumstances cause them to question traditional patterns of behavior.

PLJ: If the well-being of you and your family were threatened, would your first responsibility be to yourself or to your family? Why? If the well-being of a country is threatened (for example, by war), how should citizens balance their responsibility to their own families with their responsibility to their country?

Literary Terms: characterization, climax, folktale, foreshadowing, irony, myth, narrative perspective, omniscient narrator, short story

COMPREHENSION QUESTIONS

1. What does Labong'o learn from the medicine man? (must sacrifice his daughter so that rain will fall)
2. How does he react? (sad but complies)
3. Why do the villagers react as they do? (survival of their village is more important to them than Oganda's life)
4. Why do the villagers sing of Oganda's good luck? (Oganda's name will be remembered.)
5. What happens to Oganda? (rescued by Osinda)

UNDERSTANDING THE STORY: POSSIBLE ANSWERS

1. *Why Nditi dreamed Oganda must be sacrificed*   Nditi's dream is not fortuitous. The chief's only daughter is the most impressive sacrifice. She is most appealing to the lake monster and most acceptable to the villagers. Only the chief or one of his wives would be contenders for this honor, and they were unacceptable for many reasons: Fertility sacrifices required young, healthy specimens; the political safety of the village depended on the chief; and, if they were young enough, the chief's wives could bear other children.
2. *Villagers' attitude toward human sacrifice*   The villagers accept the necessity of human sacrifice without question because they believe that such sacrifice will motivate the forces of nature to sustain them. Only Oganda, her parents, and Osinda are grieved. The other villagers are relieved that they are not to be sacrificed.
3. *Labong'o's choice*   Labong'o has no choice with regard to Oganda's sacrifice. As the chief of his people, he must place the well-being of the community before that of his family and himself. If he were to take his family and leave the community, he would have to find a community that would accept them, and he would have to be able to accept himself. He might find such a community in a city; finding self-respect would be much more difficult.

4. *Oganda's choice*   Without Osinda's support, Oganda has no viable choice with regard to her sacrifice. If she were to run away, she would sacrifice every source of emotional support. She would be alone in the world, presumably with no neighboring community that would befriend her.

5. *Special protective coats*   Osinda's special coats will camouflage Oganda and himself so that the ancestors will not easily discover them as they walk through the forest.

6. *Significance of rain's arrival*   To many readers, the fact that it rains despite Oganda's rescue reveals the futility of the practice of human sacrifice. Others may believe that "the Almighty" rewarded Oganda's willingness to sacrifice herself for the good of her village.

7. *Osinda: hero or villain?*   Ogot presents Osinda as the hero who rescues Oganda. Certainly, Oganda views him as a hero. Even if it did not rain, Labong'o's love for Oganda would probably also lead him to view Osinda as a hero. Labong'o would probably admire Osinda's courage and be thankful that his daughter would be able to have a full life. Most of the villagers, however, despite the rain, would probably view Osinda as a type of traitor. People who conform to the demands of society often resent those who do not. From the point of view of the conformists, Osinda's actions would threaten the solidarity of the community and the certainty that adherence to tradition contributes to daily life. Many villagers would fear that Osinda's behavior would motivate others to place their own needs before the needs of their community, to the detriment of the village.

8. *Oganda's heroism*   Oganda is heroic in that she places the welfare of her community before her own personal welfare and, with dignity, accepts the burden that they place upon her. Even beyond public view, she courageously travels through the sacred land and faces her destiny with fortitude.

9. *Villagers' view of Oganda's escape*   The conformists in the village would probably regard Oganda as they would regard Osinda, as a type of traitor. She, too, would be viewed as a bad influence in the community, a threat to its solidarity, and therefore to its future welfare.

10. *Role of tradition*   This story commends both those who, like Oganda, are willing to make personal sacrifices for the good of their community and those who, like Osinda, have the courage to break with tradition in order to achieve personal happiness.

ANALYZING LITERARY TECHNIQUE: POSSIBLE ANSWERS

1. *Chief's characterization*   The chief's sorrow over the fate of his daughter and his role in her death make him a very human figure. His situation reveals how difficult it can be for people to reconcile their personal feelings with their responsibility to their community. As the chief of the tribe, he has no choice but to sacrifice the welfare of his family for the welfare of his village.

2. *Significance of title*   The title points to the climax of the story—the rain's occurring in spite of Oganda's escape—thereby directing the reader's attention to the events leading up to the rain, the irony involved, and the inhumanity of human sacrifice.

3. *Irony*   The last line gives the story its power. When it rains even though Oganda has escaped, the event suggests that Oganda's sacrifice was not necessary. It is ironic that the villagers' ignorance of Oganda's escape prevents them from questioning the necessity of human sacrifice, so that they probably will perpetuate this religious tradition. Until Oganda's escape, the story reads like a myth that explains the relationship between the world of mortals and the world of the divine. Her escape changes the genre and function of the story.

4. *Narrative perspective*   The third-person omniscient narrative perspective, traditionally used with a tale, permits the narrator to know everything about every character and to reveal just as much as is necessary to create the desired effect. Its use permits Osinda's rescue of Oganda to be a surprise.

5. *Figurative language*   Figurative language should be consistent with the time and location of the story in which it occurs. The simile "like a mouse cornered by a hungry cat" is appropriate since it reflects animals the people may know in their village life. The images of Oganda and her parents' being "like three cooking-stones, sharing their burdens" and, without Oganda, her parents' being "two useless stones which would not hold a cooking-pot" are superb because the cooking stones are clearly an integral part of village life.

WRITING ABOUT LITERATURE

1. *Expository theme on myth and short story*   Call students' attention to the directions in the textbook assignment. Remind them to use direct quotations to support their ideas.

2. *Creative writing: Continuation of the story*   Call students' attention to the end of the story and to the directions and the questions suggested in the textbook assignment. Point out that Osinda's rescue of Oganda does not automatically ensure that the couple will live "happily ever after." Encourage students to make their own stories consistent with Ogot's characterizations and setting. **(PLJ)**

FURTHER READING

Ogot, Grace, *Land without Thunder; The Promised Land.*

The Trials of Brother Jero
WOLE SOYINKA

INTRODUCING THE PLAY

The Trials of Brother Jero displays Soyinka's versatility as a writer, for he writes comic satire as well as he writes serious drama and poetry. In this farce, Soyinka exposes human weaknesses as every character tries to cope with ordinary problems of living. Brother Jero is a self-proclaimed charlatan, a prophet who cares more about himself than he cares about anyone else. He takes advantage of people, but he causes no serious harm. He proudly exhibits his behavior, enjoying the ingenuity with which he uses his understanding of human needs and wishes to manipulate and deceive others.

The play is both visually and verbally funny. In the comic heart of the play, Soyinka achieves humor through the dramatic technique of unrevealed identities and the growing threat of their discovery. Dramatic and verbal ironies abound in relation to the plot. In addition, the repetitious conversational style of the major characters adds an important comic effect. Surrounding the central action of the play, numerous scenes are comic gems. Among them are those in which: Brother Jero escapes through a window, works hard not to lust after women, changes his name, and makes a follower of a member of parliament; Amope ceaselessly badgers Chume; Chume is successful as a preacher; and a drummer is chased by a woman who is being chased by Brother Jero.

PLJ: What is the difference between human frailties that are serious and those that are humorous? Among your relatives and friends, which traits do you find amusing? Which traits anger you? Which traits of yours do others find amusing? Which traits of yours disturb others?

Literary Terms: allusion, characterization, comedy, discovery, farce, irony, plot, repetition, reversal, satire, tone

COMPREHENSION QUESTIONS

1. What does Amope want from Brother Jero? (money Jero owes her for robe he purchased)
2. What self-sacrifice does Brother Jero demand of himself? (to ignore temptation of women)
3. What sacrifice does Brother Jero demand of Chume? (to refrain from beating his wife)
4. What leads Brother Jero to permit Chume to treat Amope as he wishes? (Jero discovers that Chume's wife is Amope, to whom Jero owes money.)
5. What leads Chume to become estranged from Brother Jero? (Chume discovers that Jero is a hypocrite and liar, and that he wants Chume to beat Amope because of Jero's relationship with her.)

UNDERSTANDING THE PLAY: POSSIBLE ANSWERS

1. *Jero's character*   Jero is psychologically astute, very clever, and very entertaining. However, since he is a charlatan, he is not admirable. He is self-serving and manipulative, taking advantage of the human weaknesses in others. The best one can say about his behavior is that he does not seriously harm anyone.

2. *Chume's character*   Chume's good will and honesty are very appealing. However, his gullibility is not admirable. He sees people as either good or evil. Thus, he either blindly follows Jero or he believes him to be more evil than he actually is.

3. *Amope's character*   Amope is an unpleasant human being because she apparently nags everyone. Although her behavior is counterproductive, Amope is perceptive in that she sees the true nature of both Chume and Jero. She is also an energetic business woman.

*4. *Realistic characterizations*   Jero, Amope, and Chume are all portrayed as psychologically complex individuals, which makes them very realistic. Their failings are exaggerated in order to make them humorous, but the fact that each possesses a combination of psychological strengths and weaknesses enables readers and audiences to relate to them and sympathize with them.

   People exist in our society who manipulate others as Jero does. Among them are certain television evangelists, advertisers, salespeople, and politicians.

5. *Source of humor in unrevealed identities of Jero and Amope*   The humor is based on the fact that people's actions are based on certain assumptions. If the assumptions change, their attitudes and behavior change. Thus, Jero's attitude toward Chume's wife changes once he knows that she is Amope, and Chume's attitude toward Jero changes once Chume knows about Jero's debt to Amope and how Jero lives.

6. *Chume committed to asylum*   It is not likely that Chume will be put into an asylum. *(a)* The authorities will realize that Jero was at fault; *(b)* once Chume realizes that Jero is not romantically involved with Amope, he will no longer try to kill Jero; *(c)* committing Chume is too serious for the light-hearted humor of this play.

*7. *Jero's trials*   The nature of Jero's trials (lust, creditors, a threatening disciple) makes them very humorous. His trials are ironic in that he brings them all upon himself—he is not like the prophets in the Bible who were tested by God.

*8. *Serious subjects of this comedy*   *(a)* The serious responsibility that religious leaders owe members of their congregation and others with whom they deal; *(b)* the need for mutual respect between marriage partners; and *(c)* the need for politicians to be responsible to their constituents.

*9. *Soyinka's goal*   Soyinka is attempting to exert moral leadership. His farce is like a sugar-coated pill. Beneath his highly entertaining comedy are oblique but serious criticisms of certain types of interpersonal relationships. In the ideal world, politicians and religious leaders are ethical people who are responsible to their constituents and congregations. Similarly, husbands and wives respect and help one another. Every human being acknowledges the dignity of every other human being and treats others with respect.

ANALYZING LITERARY TECHNIQUE: POSSIBLE ANSWERS

*1. *Language as characterization*   Speech patterns and vocabulary reflect social class, sophistication, and sincerity: *(a)* Jero's refined speech is foreign and is cultivated with the intent to deceive; *(b)* Chume's unrefined speech is natural, heartfelt, and sincere.

*2. *Dramatic irony*   One important example of dramatic irony is when Brother Jero realizes at the end of Scene III that Amope is Chume's wife. Chume thinks that he is being granted permission to beat his wife because it is spiritually necessary; the audience knows that Jero wants to revenge himself on Amope.

Another good example of dramatic irony comes toward the end of the play, when Jero is chased offstage by Chume while the Member of Parliament is praying, so that the Member thinks Jero has been transmuted.

In both examples, the dramatic irony drives the plot of the play and contributes to the humor of the play.

*3. *Discovery*   (a) Jero's saying "So that is your wife" unifies plot by connecting Amope, Chume, and Jero. The humorous surprise of irony leads to humorous reversal.

(b) Chume says, "Did I hear you say Prophet Jeroboam?" The humorous surprise of irony leads to humorous reversal.

*4. *Plot vs. characterization*   Plot is more important in this play because it is the vehicle for the humor. However, Soyinka's complex characterization enhances the quality of the play, making it both more humorous and more serious.

*5. *Satire*   This play is a satire in that it ridicules the vices and foolishness of the characters within it. Soyinka is criticizing certain types of human behavior: hypocrisy, selfishness, dishonesty, disrespect.

*6. *Farce*   This play is a farce in that it is very comic with satiric overtones. It also has an improbable, contrived plot and contains elements of slapstick humor (for example, Jero's sneaking out the window and the chase scene).

However, a farce usually has a happy ending. This play ends before the comic misunderstandings are resolved, possibly suggesting that Soyinka intends the play's satiric elements—his criticism of society—to stand out more vividly than the play's purely comedic elements.

WRITING ABOUT LITERATURE

1. *Expository theme analyzing how Soyinka criticizes forms of behavior*   Students probably will find this a challenging assignment. The goal is for students to write a persuasive essay based on a close analysis of one aspect of this play. Encourage students to focus closely on just one thematic strand, rather than trying to combine two or more elements of the play. Depending on the aspect of behavior that students choose to focus on, they may or may not find that Soyinka suggests a solution or reformation of the behavior. Encourage students to analyze whether this strengthens or detracts from Soyinka's critique of society. Some students may want to research further the goals of satire. (See **U.P.** questions 4, 7, 8, and 9, and **A.L.T.** questions 5 and 6 above.)

2. *Expository theme analyzing how Soyinka creates humor*   Remind students to choose two or three of the five techniques. (See **A.L.T.** questions 1–4 above.)

3. *Creative writing: Dialogue resolving conflicts among Brother Jero, Amope, and Chume* Call students' attention to the questions suggested in the textbook assignment. **(PLJ)**

FURTHER READING

Soyinka, Wole, *Jero's Metamorphosis; Opera Wonyosi; A Shuttle in the Crypt; The Devil and the King's Horseman; Aké: The Years of Childhood; Ìsarà.*

The Lovers
BESSIE HEAD

INTRODUCING THE STORY

"The Lovers" is a brilliantly conceived and executed story that is deeply satisfying on many levels. On the surface, it is the tale of Keaja and Tselane, a romantic love story that is reminiscent of the tale of Romeo and Juliet but without the lovers' tragic deaths.

On a deeper level, "The Lovers" is the tragic story of a tribal society that is emotionally crippled by its uncritical devotion to traditions that, in the narrator's words, attempt to control "human helplessness in the face of overwhelming odds." Originally based on male jealousy and fear of the power of female sexuality in an agrarian culture, tribal rules rigidly control relations between the sexes, expecting individuals to direct their feelings into the socially acceptable, communal aspects of tribal life. The narrator states:

> A delicate balance had to be preserved between a woman's reproductive cycle and the safety of the community; at almost every stage in her life a woman was a potential source of danger to the community. . . . Failure to observe the taboos could bring harm to animal life, crops, and the community.

Thus, males and females lead separate lives except for arranged marriages in which procreation is the only common interest and shared goal. Sexual taboos include communal abstinence from sexual relations from the time immediately prior to the harvest until the thanksgiving ritual. Fear of bringing disaster into the community subjugates the will of the individual to the dictates of the tribe, and all nonconformists are punished with ostracism, banishment, or death.

The power of "The Lovers" emanates from the heroism of three characters who have the courage to defy the dictates of their social, political, and religious environment. Current events and history offer ample testimony to the fact that such human beings exist outside fiction. Some members of every society observe the quality of life around them and question its inevitability. Among these, some have the courage to take the risks involved in a public stand, and others are too fearful to do so. Keaja and Tselane, motivated both by their convictions and their passions, are willing to risk death in order to lead a more meaningful life.

Mma-Monosi is the most interesting character in that her nature, attitudes, and behavior reflect the profound psychological effect of an earlier, terrifying personal experience. She once watched in horrified silence as the tribe killed a young man who would not agree to marry the girl his parents had chosen for him. (It is possible that Mma-Monosi herself loved the young man, although this is not explicit in the text.) As a result of this experience, Mma-Monosi has become a type of divided personality: She is powerful and independent yet simultaneously so concerned about public approval that she cannot tolerate any form of criticism. Her bitter lesson has taught her that safety lies in blindly accepting the established order.

Tselane's predicament forces Mma-Monosi to relive her own horrible experience, and she welcomes the opportunity to save her beloved step-daughter from a similar experience. Not only does Mma-Monosi "supervise the last details of the departure," but she is the only person who watches the couple as they leave the village. Thus, Mma-Monosi is in a position to convince the tribe of the truth of a hallucination that she creates in order to save the lovers' lives. She is the most heroic of the three characters in that, should her ruse be discovered, she is risking her life by remaining in the village. In the end, she owes her life to a powerful ally, a superstition—a perennially active and enduring force in her tribe.

At the end of "The Lovers," Head explains how Tselane and Keaja's story has become a legend. Her direct narrative style is characteristic of legends, focusing on plot rather than on character. Her subtle psychological characterization of Mma-Monosi gives an unusual dimension to the tale by adding mystery and suspense.

PLJ: Have you or anyone you know ever been forced to choose between rules and values that your family has established and those that you feel are personally more appropriate? How did you or the other person handle this conflict?

Literary Terms: antagonist, characterization, climax, conflict, folktale, foreshadowing, irony, legend, narrative perspective, protagonist, romance, setting, short story, theme

COMPREHENSION QUESTIONS

1. How does the love affair begin? (couple finds refuge from rain in same cave)
2. What has fostered Keaja's attitudes toward marriage? (his father's unhappy marriage to his mother)
3. Why does Tselane take his views seriously? (her similar personal experience; her attitude toward the other young men)
4. In what way is Tselane closer to Mma-Monosi than to Mma-Tselane? (Mma-Monosi is a close friend; Mma-Tselane is a loving but stern parent.)
5. What is Mma-Monosi's attitude toward marriage? (accepts tradition)
6. What causes Keaja to propose to Tselane? (prospect of his own arranged marriage)
7. Why does Tselane become ill? (conflict between love for Keaja and tribal tradition)
8. What causes Tselane and Keaja to reveal their engagement? (Tselane's pregnancy)

9. How is the issue resolved? (Keaja and Tselane leave tribe for a new life)
10. What permits the story to have a happy ending? (Mma-Monosi creates a story of Keaja and Tselane's death that frightens the tribe into moving away.)

UNDERSTANDING THE STORY: POSSIBLE ANSWERS

1. *Why villagers accept tribal regulations and taboos* Superstition about environmental retaliation (drought, disease, and death), fear of loss of social status, and fear of tribal punishment combine to motivate the villagers to conform to tradition. Men and women adapt to the regulations by finding status and friendship among members of their own sex.

2. *Why tribe ignores possibility of human initiative* This controlled life is a type of sacrifice to the gods to ensure prosperity and safety. Also, tribal elders have a vested interest in preserving things as they are. Tribal rules and taboos support their position. Human initiative would create changes that would threaten the authority and power of the elders. However, by ignoring the possibility of imaginative actions, the tribal elders have no way to deal with them whenever they occur.

3. *What Rra-Tselane's reply to Rra-Keaja's proposal reveals about Rra-Tselane* Rra-Tselane is more interested in maintaining his position in the tribe than in preserving Tselane's life, but then he doesn't care enough about Tselane to spend any time with her. Rra-Keaja loves his son above all else.

4. *Mma-Tselane takes action on behalf of Tselane* Mma-Tselane realizes unless she makes a concerted effort, Tselane will die. She knows that she risks losing social status and the related self-esteem, but she loves and values her daughter enough to assume the risks. She gains a different type of self-esteem from knowing that she has done her best for her daughter.

*5. *Connection between Mma-Monosi and story* The horrible story about the young man who is killed may be her own. The evidence for this interpretation includes: the weak side of her powerful and independent personality; her initial refusal to tell the story; her enthusiasm for Tselane's love; and her declaration of her willingness to die on Tselane's behalf.

6. *Why Keaja and Tselane don't return* Keaja and Tselane choose to risk life in a different tribe. Not only do they wish to marry whom they choose, they wish to live a different kind of married life and to rear their children free of their tribe's social regulations and taboos.

7. *Factors in tribe affecting legend* The villagers accept Mma-Monosi's report because they believe that sinister forces always lie in wait, ready to destroy life, and that those who question life upset the natural order and invite these forces to bring death and disaster into the village. These factors cause the villagers to respond with a negative interpretation to the report. Another, more optimistic worldview would have had the lovers' love rewarded by the gods, who would have taken their spirits up to the heavens, where they would live in eternal bliss.

8. *Themes* Love is stronger than tradition. Necessity is the mother of invention. Superstition blinds the mind.

ANALYZING LITERARY TECHNIQUE: POSSIBLE ANSWERS

1. *Relationship between setting and plot*   The setting, which is the tribe with its values, is also the antagonist, thereby creating a strong connection with the plot. The unity of setting and plot creates a tightly knit structure for the story.

2. *Antagonist*   Society is the antagonist, creating the conflict with the lovers (the protagonists). Society, having overwhelming power of authority, is a formidable adversary.

*3. *Mma-Monosi's characterization*   Mma-Monosi's characterization adds mystery and suspense without detracting from the narrative emphasis of the tale. Her story about the young man who is killed by the tribe provides a counterpoint for Tselane and Keaja's unfolding story.

4. *Climax*   The climax is Mma-Monosi's report of the lovers' end. It gives an added dimension to the story, causing the reader to question the validity of the report and to analyze Mma-Monosi's character.

5. *Foreshadowing*   Tselane's willingness to face trouble and death foreshadows the risks she and Keaja take at the end. Mma-Monosi's story, her initial refusal to reveal it, the two sides of her personality, and her declaration that she will die if necessary in order to keep Tselane safe and sound, all foreshadow her decision to support Tselane in her similar situation.

*6. *Narrative perspective*   The third-person-omniscient narrator, the storyteller, is traditional in folktales and legends. This approach permits the reader to learn background material and the thoughts and actions of anyone the author chooses. What is lost is immediacy—the reader's emotional involvement with the plot as it affects the emotions of a particular character. Student opinion will vary as to which is preferable.

7. *Folktale; legend; romance*   A legend is a folktale based on an accepted historical occurrence. Thus, depending on the attitude toward this tale, it is either a folktale or a legend. "The Lovers" is a romance in that it is an adventure story with an internal mystery and a miraculous ending that is inconsistent with the laws of nature.

WRITING ABOUT LITERATURE

1. *Expository theme analyzing narrative perspective*   Call students' attention to the directions in the textbook assignment with regard to content and organization. (See **A.L.T.** question 6 above.)

2. *Creative writing: "The Lovers" from Mma-Monosi's point of view*   Call students' attention to the directions and suggested questions in the textbook assignment. **(PLJ)**

FURTHER READING

Head, Bessie, *The Collector of Treasures and Other Botswana Village Tales.*

The Far East

Fighting South of the Ramparts

LI PO

INTRODUCING THE POEM

''Fighting South of the Ramparts'' cautions against war by emphasizing the carnage that affects both the aggressor and the defender, and both the officer and the common soldier. Li Po based his poem on an old Han dynasty folk song (first century A.D.) that, in theme, honors the soldiers who die serving their prince. Li Po changed the point of view from that of the prince to that of the soldier, creating an attitude of protest in place of the folk song's attitude of adulation. Thus, he subtly criticizes the expansionist policies of the T'ang dynasty (627–650) by his treatment of the comparable situation under the Han.

The poem reflects Li Po's interest in Taoist philosophy, particularly Chapter 31, ''Quelling War,'' of the *Tao te Ching*. The poem concludes with a paraphrase of the Taoist principle that nations should wage war only under duress. Only a few years later, Li Po saw China's border armies rebel and civil war destroy the China that he had known. Both events were tangible proof of the Taoist principle that rulers who cause the slaughter of their subjects will encourage revolution.

Li Po's use of detail vividly conveys war's carnage. He contrasts the aggressive Han dynasty with the preceding, more defensively oriented Ch'in dynasty, and the bloodthirsty Huns and Tartars with the more civilized Chinese. He depicts the ravages of war in searing connotative language.

PLJ: To what extent do you think that soldiers should be responsible for their own behavior in battle? To what extent do you think that soldiers should obey orders regardless of the nature of those orders?

Literary Terms: connotative language, contrast, figurative language, first-person narrator, irony, narrative perspective, theme

COMPREHENSION QUESTIONS

1. How long have the emperor's armies been fighting? (long enough to have grown old and gray)
2. What is the nature of the enemy troops? (barbaric; war is their only occupation)
3. What attitude toward war was held by the House of Ch'in (defensive; built Great Wall)
4. What attitude toward war is held by the House of Han? (expansionist policies encourage war)
5. What has happened to Han armies? (death and devastation to soldiers and captains alike)

UNDERSTANDING THE POEM:
POSSIBLE ANSWERS

1. *Purpose of specific battle locations*   These locations, familiar to Li Po's audience, testify to the great range and number of frontiers on which border wars were being fought. This knowledge, in turn, supports Li Po's antiwar attitude.
2. *Importance of the Huns*   Li Po contrasts the barbaric, warlike Huns with the civilized, usually peaceful Chinese. The Chinese prefer farming to fighting, whereas war is the way of life for the Huns.
3. *House of Ch'in vs. House of Han*   In contrast to the aggressive and territorially acquisitive House of Han (206 B.C.–A.D. 220), the leaders of the House of Ch'in (third century B.C.) were interested in preserving peace in China. Therefore, they built the Great Wall to keep out potential invaders. The two dynasties represent opposite political philosophies. Li Po implies that the Ch'in dynasty was a better period for China. Meanwhile, he is living in the T'ang dynasty, at a time when T'ang leaders have been operating with the same political attitudes and actions as the House of Han.
4. *Meaning of "The general schemed in vain"*   This line puts the blame on the leader in command and shows the futility of his plans: His own men were destroyed in the battles. The line also supports Li Po's Taoist theme, which he states in the last two lines.
5. *Risks in speaker's point of view*   The speaker's point of view is that of a common soldier who views the border wars as disastrous for all of China. If enough of the other soldiers shared his view, they might desert or revolt. If military leaders shared his view, they might lead their troops against the government in power.

ANALYZING LITERARY TECHNIQUE:
POSSIBLE ANSWERS

*1. *Why speaker's point of view?*   Li Po chooses the perspective of a common soldier because it is the soldiers who provide the power behind the emperor's policies of territorial expansion. They are the most likely to be hostile to the border wars because they have the least to gain and the most to lose from them. As peasants, they are treated like objects by their social superiors. Under imperial orders, they are required to leave their families forever, to spend their lives living on one border or another, farming and defending the land against barbarian tribes. Whether they win or lose a particular battle, they have sacrificed their lives and their families to their emperor's lust for power.
*2. *Function of contrast*   Li Po uses contrast to reveal better alternatives to the Han (and T'ang) imperial policy of territorial expansion. Examples include:

(a) The contrast between the Huns and the Chinese reveals differences in lifestyle and values. The Huns lack the civilized values and interests of the Chinese. They have little in the way of learning and possessions, and they value nothing but accomplishments in war. They are nomadic desert tribes, not farmers.

(b) The contrast between the House of Han and the House of Ch'in reveals differences in political values. The Ch'in dynasty was oriented toward peace and built a huge and extensive defensive wall to protect their country against their aggressive neighbors. In contrast, the Han dynasty is ambitious and aggressive, accepting constant war as the price for acquiring more land.

*3. *Use of irony*   Li Po stresses the ironic fact that war can be equally devastating to the aggressor and the defender, to the winner and the loser, and to the officer and the common soldier. No one "wins" a war.

*4. *Relation of connotative language to theme*   Li Po's connotative language vividly conveys the devastation that occurs as a consequence of war. Examples: (*a*) the Huns live on desert lands where "white bones lie among yellow sands"; (*b*) "the horses of the conquered neigh piteously to Heaven"; (*c*) birds "peck for human guts, carry them in their beaks and hang them on the branches of withered trees"; (*d*) "Captains and soldiers are smeared on the bushes and grass." War in this poem is not glorious; instead, it is a cursed event to be waged only when a nation finds itself faced with dire necessity.

*5. *Function of last two lines*   The last two lines, paraphrased from the *Tao te Ching*, express the theme of the poem. Structurally, they form the culmination of Li Po's examples of war's disasters. The poem moves from the range and duration of the border wars, to the responsibility of the Han dynasty for the wars, to the devastation caused by war, and, finally, to the conclusion that war should be an option only when no peaceful alternative exists.

WRITING ABOUT LITERATURE

1. *Expository analysis of treatment of theme*   See **A.L.T.** questions 1–5 above. From questions 1, 2, 3, and 4, students should choose to analyze any two or three techniques. The theme is referred to in question 5. Call students' attention to directions in the textbook assignment with regard to examples, direct quotations, and analysis.

2. *Expository analysis of Taoism in poem*   The theme of the poem, that war is disastrous to everyone in the warring nations, leads to the implication that any leader who enjoys conquest will cause the death of so many that those in the country who dissent from his or her policy will unite and render that leader powerless.

   Students who wish to learn more about Taoism may be directed to various references, including most encyclopedias; Time-Life's *Ancient China; A Treasury of Asian Literature*, edited by John D. Yohassan (New American Library); and *Sources of Chinese Tradition*, volume 1, by De Bary, Wing-Tsit Chan, and Watson (Columbia University Press). (See **A.L.T.** question 5 above.)

3. *Creative writing: A war poem*   Call students' attention to suggestions in the textbook assignment with regard to content, use of language, and possible procedure. Remind them that they can adopt any narrative persona. Points of view may be for or against war. **(PLJ)**

FURTHER READING

Birch, Cyril, ed., *Anthology of Chinese Literature, Vol. 1.*

Prince Huo's Daughter

JIANG FANG

INTRODUCING THE STORY

Because it is a well-told story of a love gone awry, "Prince Huo's Daughter" has a timeless appeal. Jade, a beautiful young woman from a lower social caste, becomes fatally heartsick when Li Yi, the famous poet, breaks his marriage vows to her in order to marry his mother's socially desirable choice for him. Before Jade dies, she tells Li that her spirit will haunt those he loves in the future, and her curse becomes a reality.

The story is appealing on three levels. First, it is a love story that reads with the simplicity and familiarity of a folktale. Second, it is a morally satisfying tale of good and evil in which goodness ultimately triumphs and evil is punished. Finally, buried in this old tale is a modern psychological study of the effect of cruel behavior on the mind of the perpetrator. Jade's curse becomes a self-fulfilling prophecy for Li. It is the external manifestation of Li's guilt. Because of his unfaithfulness to Jade, Li imagines that each of his successive loves is unfaithful to him. His doubts (in psychological terms, projection and paranoia) destroy his relationships and his happiness, creating an appropriate, lifelong self-punishment for his heartless treatment of Jade.

PLJ: Have you ever broken a promise? What caused you to do so? How did you feel? What did you do about it?

Literary Terms: catharsis, characterization, climax, folktale, foreshadowing, irony, melodrama, narrative perspective, plot, resolution, setting, theme, tragedy

COMPREHENSION QUESTIONS

1. What is Li's reputation? (great scholar and poet)
2. How does Li meet Jade? (through a matchmaker)
3. Why does Li leave Jade? (wins official post through examination)
4. What promise does Jade ask of Li? (love her for eight years before he reaches age of marriage)
5. What conflict occurs? (Li's mother chooses a wife for him.)
6. What happens to Jade when Li does not return? (becomes very ill)
7. Why doesn't Li attempt to see Jade? (ashamed of his broken promise)
8. Who brings Li to Jade? (a young nobleman in a yellow shirt)
9. How does Jade react to Li's visit? (curses him for his mistreatment of her, through the women he will love)
10. What happens in the end? (The curse works—Li becomes a suspicious and jealous husband and lover.)

UNDERSTANDING THE STORY: POSSIBLE ANSWERS

1. *Why "Prince Huo's Daughter" instead of "Li Yi"* The story focuses on Jade's effect on the life of Li, an appropriately narrow focus for a short story.

*2. *Li* Li is self-centered, with social and economic ambitions. He could have avoided the arranged marriage by not raising the money. However, Li is also a sensitive artist, and his guilt destroys him.

*3. *Why Li doesn't tell Jade the truth* Li appears to be unable to handle confrontations. He does not argue with his mother, and he does not discuss his situation with Jade. He solves the problems in his life with as little conflict and effort as possible.

*4. *Jade's illness* Students may disagree about this. Although the author and Li's contemporaries blame Li, some students may argue that Jade is equally to blame for her illness. Realizing the difference between her social position and Li's, Jade acknowledges that Li will eventually marry someone else. Her desire to have Li for eight more years is insufficient reason for her to make herself ill trying to keep him.

*5. *Does Li's shame excuse his callous behavior?* No. In fact, his behavior creates greater shame, as his actions continue to be callous. Li's shame is a rationalization for his unwillingness to confront Jade with the truth. Li was simply living his life in the way he wished to live it.

*6. *Significance of dream and curse* As in folktales and myths, Jade's dream prophesies the future. Jade interprets her dream as a prophecy of reunion and separation, and the dream comes to pass. Jiang Fang's relating of the dream *after* the events it seems to prophesy undercuts some of its supernatural power for the reader.

   To a modern reader, Jade's curse is the external form of Li's subconscious, which punishes him for his mistreatment of Jade. It is important to remember, however, that it is Jade's act of cursing Li that suggests this form of self-punishment to Li.

*7. *Li's attitude toward women after Jade's death* The ostensible cause of Li's attitude is Jade's curse. For a modern reader, the real cause is Li's sense of guilt. Subconsciously, he knows how cruel he was to Jade, and he cannot forgive himself. Thus, he punishes himself by depriving himself of any marital happiness. The method he uses involves believing that the women are treating him the way that he treated Jade. In psychological terms, he projects his own attitudes and behavior onto them and suffers from paranoia.

8. *What story reveals about life in China during T'ang dynasty* (*a*) Parents were authoritarian figures who arranged marriages for their children; (*b*) women did not have the social mobility and freedom of men; (*c*) education was highly prized and very competitive; (*d*) social status was very important and was enhanced by wealth, education, and fame.

9. *Importance of intelligence and moral character* In the story, moral character is more important than intelligence, although it would be best to have both. That is why even those who admire Li's accomplishments sympathize with Jade, and also why Li cannot forgive himself for his treatment of Jade.

10. *Themes* (*a*) People reap as they sow, in that cruel behavior destroys the perpetrator as well as the object of that behavior. (*b*) Love is often destroyed by ambition. (*c*) It is better to love wisely than too well.

ANALYZING LITERARY TECHNIQUE: POSSIBLE ANSWERS

1. *Tragedy* The story is tragic in that Li's behavior helps cause Jade's death. The reader pities Jade but not Li. Unlike the great tragic heroes, Li does not outwardly acknowledge his immoral behavior, and he gains no insight into his own personality. He punishes himself without understanding that he is doing so.

   The plot is melodramatic in that it deals with strong passions: "true love," deceit, a death-curse, and an avenging spirit. Like characters in a melodrama, Li and Jade are not psychologically complex. Li does not appear to be torn between his love or responsibility to Jade and his commitment to someone else; Jade is loyal beyond all expectations. Also, Li and Jade suffer melodramatic (dire) fates. Li destroys his marriages by tormenting his wives, and Jade dies.

   On the other hand, most melodramas have happy endings, whereas this story does not. Although Jade is able to exact retribution for Li's unconscionable behavior, Jade is dead and Li is miserable.

2. *Narrative perspective* The traditional third-person-omniscient narrative style is appropriate to this short story because the story is a type of folktale. Folktales are part of the oral tradition of a culture. Oral tales keep listeners' attention by being simple in structure, characterization, detail, and language, and by adhering to familiar and predictable plot patterns.

3. *How setting affects plot* The setting affects the plot in that both Li's and Jade's social fates are determined by the social customs of their society. Thus, Li's mother arranges a marriage for him that is the proper one, and Jade cannot compete because of her low social position.

4. *Function of Li's contemporaries* Li's contemporaries function as a type of Greek chorus, in that their attitudes reveal how the reader should view Li's behavior.

5. *Foreshadowing* Both Jade's repeated concern about losing Li's love and Li's related protestations of his own fidelity foreshadow Li's infidelity.

6. *Catharsis* The climax of this story is Jade's confrontation with Li, in which she complains about his treatment of her, explains its effect on her life, and announces her curse. Until this point, both Jade and the reader have had to accept whatever Li has chosen to do. Such a situation creates tension that needs to be resolved. Finally, Jade is able to do what she can to force Li to face up to his disgraceful behavior. As a result, both she and the reader are relieved—catharsis is achieved.

7. *Resolution* Li's subsequent, unsuccessful relationships with other women, whether attributed to Jade's curse or to Li's psyche, comprise the plot's resolution. Because Li deserves punishment for his treatment of Jade, the resolution gives the story a sense of completeness and the reader a sense of satisfaction.

WRITING ABOUT LITERATURE

1. *Expository writing: Analysis of characterization*   Li's values offend his friends and the reader. Li deserves to be punished, and his punishment is appropriate for his misbehavior. Jade wins the affection of all through her loyal devotion to Li. Readers identify with Jade. They hope that Li will be punished, and they are satisfied by Li's fate and Jade's role in it. (See **U.S.** questions 2–7 above.)

2. *Creative writing: Story from Li's point of view*   The challenge is to find justifiable reasons for Li's behavior. Li might state that Jade knew from the beginning that their relationship was temporary. Li might also point out that it was his duty to accept the marriage that his mother had arranged for him. Li probably would blame his wives for his suspicions and jealousy. (**PLJ**)

FURTHER READING

Yang Xianyi and Gladys Yang, trans., *T'ang Dynasty Stories.*

The Damask Drum
MOTOKIYO ZEAMI

INTRODUCING THE PLAY

The Damask Drum is a poetic play about a man who dares to love a woman far above his social position. The Gardener's infatuation with the Princess is inappropriate both because of their different social positions and because of their disparate ages. The Princess, with excessive pride, encourages the Gardener by promising him a view of her if he can accomplish an impossible task. When the Gardener cannot make a damask (satin cloth) drum sound so that she can hear it, he commits suicide. The Princess's guilt, in the form of the Gardener's Ghost, condemns her to go mad and endlessly beat the drum. Thus, the Gardener's passion and the Princess's rashly proud response cause their tragedy.

PLJ: How would you feel if a person in whom you had no interest revealed a crush on you? How would you treat that person?

Literary Terms: allusion, figurative language, metaphor, simile, symbol, theme

COMPREHENSION QUESTIONS

1. Who falls in love? (The Gardener falls in love with the Princess.)
2. How does the person who is loved respond? (The Princess will reveal her face when she hears the drum.)

3. What does the lover do in order to get attention? (The Gardener beats on a damask drum.)
4. What happens to the lover? (He commits suicide when the Princess does not respond.)
5. What happens to the loved one? (She is guilt-ridden; the Gardener's Ghost causes her to go mad and beat the drum continuously.)

UNDERSTANDING THE PLAY:
POSSIBLE ANSWERS

*1. *"Love's equal realm knows no divisions" (lines 7–8)*   The Princess is being facetious. Love *does* know divisions for the Gardener, who cannot bridge the Princess's high social rank and youth. Love also respects divisions in real life, where nationality, religion, race, social status, and age may be important factors.

*2. *Princess's pity for Gardener*   The Courtier is being ironic. The Princess feels no real pity, only excessive pride that such a man loves so great a person as herself. She knows that the Gardener will fail the task she has set, since the drum is incapable of making a loud sound.

*3. *Gardener's attempt to beat drum*   He should not have permitted himself to be controlled by his passions ("the whirlpool of desire" [line 180]; "the anger of lust denied" [line 125]). He should have acknowledged that certain social barriers existed between the Princess and himself.

*4. *Princess as victim*   Students who read carefully will realize that the Princess is not a victim: She is as much to blame as the Gardener for the tragedy. She rashly encourages his passion and thus contributes to her own fate. ("When I bad him beat what could not ring,/ Then tottered first my wits" [line 113]).

*5. *Why Princess goes mad*   Ostensibly, the Gardener's Ghost haunts the Princess. To modern readers, it is the Princess's guilt about the Gardener's suicide—projected as the Ghost—that causes her madness.

6. *Themes*   (a) Do not try to be someone other than who you are. (b) People suffer from their treatment of others. (c) Cruel words and deeds cause guilt in the person who uses them.

ANALYZING LITERARY TECHNIQUE:
POSSIBLE ANSWERS

*1. *Courtier and Chorus*   The Courtier provides the exposition (setting, relationships between characters, and background) for the play. The Chorus both echoes and reinforces the Gardener's feelings and tells the audience how to interpret the play's action. For example, the Chorus tells a legend confirming the inappropriateness of the Gardener's love and explains how the Princess's behavior created the angry Ghost.

*2. *Symbol of Gardener's Ghost*   The Gardener's Ghost symbolizes the Princess's guilt about her treatment of the Gardener. The Ghost is an external form (projection) of her self-punishment.

3. *Metaphor expressing theme*   The metaphor in the Princess's question, "By what dire seed this harvest sown?" (line 157), is appropriate in that the play is, to a certain degree, about the relationship between cause and effect. The Princess and the Gardener both suffer from their treatment of each other.

4. *"Fabric of pride" (line 78)*   Damask is a fabric of pride in that it is a heavy, richly patterned silk used in the clothing of wealthy people (in comparison, note the Chorus's "coarse-woven dress" [line 47]). Also, the Princess's pride leads her to encourage the Gardener to hope that she will respond to his beating on the silent drum.

*5. *Metaphors or similes conveying Gardener's age*   Zeami uses striking metaphors to depict the Gardener. Some examples include: *a*) "the evening bell . . . tolls in / A heavy tale of day linked on to day" (lines 24–26); (*b*) "I was gaunt as an aged crane" (line 31); (*c*) "The days had left their marks . . . like waves that beat on a sandy shore" (lines 36–37); (*d*) "This autumn of love that closes / In sadness the sequence of my years" (lines 42–43); (*e*) "Glimpse of a moon that slipped / Through the boughs of an autumn tree" (lines 138–39). Both singly and with the increased intensity created by Zeami's repetition of the idea of the Gardener's age, these figures of speech dramatically convey his old, weathered, sad self.

WRITING ABOUT LITERATURE

1. *Expository essay analyzing Gardener's and Princess's behavior*   Call students' attention to suggestions in the textbook assignment regarding the importance of social status and one's obligations to another. Remind them to combine direct quotations with their own ideas. (See **U.P.** questions 1–5, and **A.L.T.** questions 1, 2, and 5 above.)

2. *Creative writing: A dialogue between the Princess and the Gardener after death*   Call students' attention to suggestions in the textbook assignment. (**PLJ**)

FURTHER READING

Mishima, Yukio, *The Damask Drum.*
Zeami, Motokiyo, *Kantan; Sotoba Komachi.*

The man had no useful work

RABINDRANATH TAGORE

INTRODUCING THE POEM

"The man had no useful work" is a philosophical narrative poem about what constitutes the ideal life. Tagore's protagonist uses his time in Paradise as he used it on earth, to bring artistic vision and beauty into the world. However, he is the wrong man in the wrong place in this Paradise, where only functional tasks are valued. Before he is told to leave, he has convinced one girl that beauty should be an important part of life. In the closing paradox, the girl chooses to leave Paradise and return to earth with the man, because for her, as for him, Paradise is no paradise without the presence of beauty.

Tagore constructs the poem as a type of allegory. The man and the girl represent everyman and everywoman, and Paradise represents the ideal world that people work to create for themselves. Tagore is alluding to the fact that modern technology may bring more jobs, more wealth, and more material goods, but it may also remove the leisure that is necessary to create things of beauty and to enjoy them. He also expresses this idea in the passage from his essay "Modern Poetry" that is quoted in the textbook introduction.

PLJ: What is your vision of Paradise? How would your life there differ from your current life? To what extent can you create a paradise on earth for yourself?

Literary Terms: allegory, irony, paradox, satire, setting, theme, tone

COMPREHENSION QUESTIONS

1. Where has the guide taken the man? (to the wrong Paradise)
2. What is important in the place where he now lives? (functionally useful work)
3. What does the man first do for the girl? (decorates her water pitcher)
4. How does the girl feel about it? (fascinated)
5. What does the man next do for the girl? (makes her a hair ribbon)
6. How does the girl react to his second deed? (cares about her hair)
7. What does the chief of the elders tell the man? (must return to earth)
8. How does the man feel about the elders' decision? (overjoyed)
9. What does the girl decide? (to accompany the man)
10. How does the chief of the elders react to her decision? (cannot comprehend it)

UNDERSTANDING THE POEM: POSSIBLE ANSWERS

*1. *Wrong man in wrong place*   The man is surprised that, given his "life spent in perfecting trifles," he deserves to be in Paradise. The fact that he is in the "wrong Paradise" implies that he deserves to be in the "right Paradise."

The man is in the wrong place in that his values and artistic gifts are not valued in this Paradise; he is the wrong man in that he does not fit in with the life-style and priorities in this Paradise and threatens the established conventions of the community.

*2. *Girl's attitude toward man's art*   The girl cannot imagine the existence of anything that lacks meaning. She does not accept the man's answer, so she examines the pitcher every which way in order to discover the meaning of his designs.

*3. *Why girl permits man to make her a ribbon*   In the process of examining the pitcher, the girl has gained an appreciation of its beauty. Therefore, she is curious about what type of ribbon he will make for her. Beauty now intrigues her.

The girl's original treatment of her hair implies lack of any interest in her personal appearance and no concept of beauty. Having a beautiful hair ribbon makes her conscious both of her appearance and of beauty. A beautiful ribbon on unkempt hair will call attention to the mess, and she now wants to look attractive.

*4. *"Irregular rents"*   The girl is obviously taking time out from her tasks to improve her appearance. As the man creates more objects of beauty, the girl and others will take even more time away from their tasks.

*5. *Man's turban*   The man's turban marks him as the wrong man in the wrong place. Color adds a beautiful dimension to a functional piece of clothing. It makes the turban attractive and distinctive, nonutilitarian qualities that have no place in this Paradise.

*6. *Why man and girl prefer earth to Paradise*   (a) The man prefers to live where his leisurely pursuits are accepted and valued, and he wants to be free to pursue them. Such an environment is also more beautiful, and the man clearly values beauty. (b) The girl chooses to accompany the man, even though it means leaving Paradise, because she has discovered the importance of beauty in life.

*7. *Why chief doesn't understand the girl*   The chief of the elders is committed to function and rationality as the prime values. Not only does he lack any appreciation for beauty, but he sees it only as something that contradicts the principal values of the community. Given these values, he cannot understand anyone who does not share them. Moreover, the fact that the girl no longer appreciates the environment that the elders perpetuate in Paradise threatens the premise that Paradise is perfect.

*8. *Themes*   (a) Beauty on earth is worth more than Paradise without it. (b) Without the leisure to create and enjoy beauty, life lacks a crucial dimension.

ANALYZING LITERARY TECHNIQUE: POSSIBLE ANSWERS

*1. *Why poem set in Paradise*   Paradise symbolizes the attainment of everything that would make one happy. Tagore views people in the modern age as busily leading materialistic lives that will enable them to have the wealth to purchase more goods on the theory that, once they have acquired whatever they want, they will be happy (i.e., they will have created "Paradise" on earth.)

*2. *Why the man and the girl have generic names*   The man and the girl symbolize men and women in general. They are not supposed to be limited to particular people.

*3. *Allegory*   In the poem, the man and the girl represent everyman and everywoman, who are living in the ideal world (Paradise) that real people on earth are busily working to create for themselves. The underlying moral is that Paradise is no paradise without the presence and value of beauty, as manifested in all of the arts.

 4. *Satire*   Satire, lightly or seriously, ridicules human follies and vices. Tagore's poem is gently satiric of those who enslave themselves to frenetic, functional lives in the misguided belief that such lives are the ultimate experience.

 5. *Irony*   The chief irony is that "the man had no useful work," as if the creation of beauty in any form is not useful. The poem deals with what beauty can add to life, showing that it creates a dimension beyond the prosaic that not only is valuable in

and of itself, but that can lead to beauty beyond itself (the girl's ribbon leads to her more attractive general appearance).

*6. *Paradox*   It is paradoxical that this Paradise is not *the* Paradise. Those who live in the Paradise meant for "good, busy souls" may think it the best of all possible worlds, but ignorance is bliss. Those who know what it is to live with beauty prefer life on earth with beauty to a Paradise without it.

WRITING ABOUT LITERATURE

1. *Expository writing: An analysis of the relation of the poem to quotation in textbook Introduction*   The textbook quotation describes Paradise in the poem as life on earth in the modern age. Here, earning a living is more important than the leisure to enjoy the arts, and people have "no will power to bypass unadorned ugliness." (See **U.P.** questons 1–8, and **A.L.T.** question 6 above.)
2. *Expository writing: An analysis of this poem as allegory*   Call students' attention to the textbook assignment. Remind them to use direct quotations to support their ideas. (See **A.L.T.** questions 1–3 above.)
3. *Creative writing: A sequel*   Setting: after the man and the girl have left Paradise. Call students' attention to the suggested questions in the textbook assignment. **(PLJ)**

One Soldier
KATAI TAYAMA

INTRODUCING THE STORY

"One Soldier" is the powerful story of the thoughts and actions of a mortally ill soldier during the last hours of his life. The protagonist is Japanese, but he is the universal soldier. Katai relates the story from the point of view of the soldier, and his use of psychological realism creates a literary gem.

The soldier's walk in search of his regiment is a journey across "the lonesome valley" toward death. Thoughts of the pleasant but distant past become juxtaposed with the painful present. The horrors of war accompany him: a friend's untimely death; oozing blood; rapacious flies; callous superiors; and eternally crackling rifle fire. Warm thoughts of home and nature's beauty intermittently distract him, and two strangers' kindness relieves the horror of loneliness. But these sources of relief cannot restore his health. Finally, the soldier surrenders his ties to life and war, gratefully exchanging his pain for the peace of death.

Katai's style, even in translation, is as powerful as his plot. Details create a vivid picture of the dying soldier and his fragmented world. Simple key phrases, repeated throughout the story for emphasis, add unity and power. The psychological realism of free association unifies contrasting sections. Repeated contrasts between the remembered world at peace and the actual world of war highlight the serenity of peace and the horrors of war.

Katai's style is reminiscent of the writing of the American writer Stephen Crane (1871–1900), who was also a naturalist writer and a war correspondent.

PLJ: When doing an unpleasant task, do you ever break the tedium with daydreams? How do these thoughts relate to your actual life?

Literary Terms: contrast, foreshadowing, irony, limited omniscience, narrative perspective, naturalism, realism, repetition, symbolism

COMPREHENSION QUESTIONS

1. Why is the soldier making this journey? (can't stand conditions in hospital; wants to rejoin army unit)
2. What difficulty does the soldier encounter along the way? (In spite of his illness, no one will give him a ride.)
3. What important problem is the soldier trying to confront? (his imminent death)
4. What happens to the soldier in the end? (dies painful death)
5. What happens in the soldier's world in the end? (war continues without him)

UNDERSTANDING THE STORY: POSSIBLE ANSWERS

1. *Soldier's journey and nature of war* The soldier journeys from illness to death, from denial of the possibility of death to the acceptance of that possibility, and from panic over the reality to self-control in dealing with it. The journey reveals the difference between philosophy, which is abstract, and reality, which is concrete. It is easier to be willing to give one's life for one's country than to come face to face with one's own death.
2. *Why soldier dies of beriberi rather than from a wound* The soldier's illness is an irony that helps to strip away the romance of war. Illness makes it harder to think of death as glorious and heroic.
*3. *Given choice, would soldier have remained in army or returned home?* Answers will vary. Considerations include to what extent the soldier will be able to live with the decision he makes, and to what extent society's opinion is an important factor. If society frowns upon disillusioned soldiers and views war as a form of patriotism, the soldier might feel forced to reenter the war whether or not he wished to do so.
4. *Passages offensive to military personnel* (a) Poor medical care and unsanitary conditions in the army hospital; (b) laughing corporal: "This train's not for soldiers. I don't known any regulation which says the infantry should ride on trains"; (c) ". . . nothing more cruel than the narrow discipline of army life"; (d) "We have to be ready to die and put a good face on it"; (e) "Still a private, eh? Time you got yourself some stripes!" (f) scene of the soldier's painful death.

5. *Any soldier in any war*   It is important that the subject of this story could be any soldier in any war because it makes the story universal in its applicability and its appeal. Nothing about the soldier or his situation is particularly Japanese.

ANALYZING LITERARY TECHNIQUE: POSSIBLE ANSWERS

*1. *Contrast*   (1) The ideal vision of war vs. the reality of war emphasizes the war's reality and strengthens Katai's antiwar theme. (2) The loneliness of the soldier's journey vs. his happy family life back home emphasizes the emotional price of being a soldier. (3) The soldier's willingness to die for his country when death is an abstract concept vs. his unwillingness to die when death is a reality emphasizes how important life is to each individual.

*2. *Narrative perspective*   Katai tells the story primarily from the soldier's point of view. While Katai alternates between a first-person narrator and a third-person narrator, the center of consciousness is always that of the soldier, whose perspective is limited. This technique creates a close bond between the reader and the soldier and therefore gives the story immediacy and power.

3. *Psychological realism*   The soldier's thoughts and feelings, arranged in the order in which each occurs to him in the process of associative thinking, make his experience very real for the reader. By closely imitating the way that the human mind works, Katai makes the soldier appear to be a real person, one with whom the reader can easily sympathize. Examples: (*a*) the soldier's developing attitude toward death, from his patriotic attitude, through his terror of death and sadness at the loss of his life, to his final desire to escape his pain; (*b*) the soldier's thoughts of the past, of home and early attitudes toward war, intermixed with his present journey.

4. *Realism*   Katai's detailed views of nature and of the continuing war make war and its toll on all of nature, including human beings, more real.

*5. *Repetition*   (1) "Heavy": emphasizes the heaviness of the soldier's rifle, pack, and legs, which, in turn, emphasizes the difficult nature of his journey and his overwhelming fatigue. (2) Difficult breathing: emphasizes the soldier's illness, which foreshadows his death. (3) The insects: emphasize the continuity of life in spite of the soldier's death. (4) Loading ammunition on the train: emphasizes the passage of time in the external world while the soldier is making his journey. Without this objective reality, the reader could lose track of time because so much of the story takes place within the soldier's mind.

WRITING ABOUT LITERATURE

1. *Expository writing: Analysis of literary technique*   Call students' attention to the assignment in the textbook. Remind them to choose three examples, to explain the function of each, and to use direct quotations to support their ideas. (See **A.L.T.** questions 1, 2, and 5 above.)

2. *Creative writing: New ending for story*   Call students' attention to the assignment in the textbook. It may help students to look closely at passages in the original story, to see how Katai combines details about the soldier's life and surroundings with descriptions of the soldier's emotions and feelings.

If students choose the letter-writing option, encourage them to include concrete details. (See **U.S.** question 3 above.)

FURTHER READING

Tayama, Katai, *A Country Schoolmaster.*

The New Year's Sacrifice
Lu Hsün

INTRODUCING THE STORY

"The New Year's Sacrifice" is a poignant and powerful story of hypocrisy that reaches from the old China into cultures of all times and places. The story revolves around the celebration of the Chinese New Year, a time when families participate in an elaborate religious ceremony, called "the sacrifice," to welcome the God of Fortune and to appeal for a blessed life during the coming year.

Against this setting, the narrator relates the sad tale of a family servant, Hsiang Lin's Wife, who works for Fourth Uncle and Fourth Aunt at two different times. Fourth Uncle's and Fourth Aunt's character flaws, apparent during Hsiang Lin's Wife's first employment, intensify during her second sojourn in their house. Fearing that their servant's catastrophic life experiences will contaminate their own well-being, Fourth Uncle and Fourth Aunt refuse to let Hsiang Lin's Wife participate in any of the many rituals that are connected with the New Year's festival. Their refusal to accept her worthiness, even after she has used her year's wages to purchase a threshold in the Tutelary God's (guardian god of the village) temple, destroys her spirit and eventually destroys her life. She commits suicide in spite of her fears for the afterlife.

Thus Lu Hsün leaves the reader with a sense of the hypocrisy that is pervasive in the society that he is satirizing and that is always potential in human nature. The attitudes and behavior of Fourth Uncle and Fourth Aunt are typical of their community, where people feel certain of securing divine blessings as long as they pay scrupulous attention to the old customs. Attuned only to their own lives, they remain insensitive to the needs of others. However, the power of the story resides in its universal human truths. People are hypocrites whenever they espouse liberal and righteous principles and then act in a way that negates those principles.

The life of Hsiang Lin's Wife is presented as a collection of personal disasters because, for Lu Hsün, social commentary was as important as literary artistry. In order to depict the deplorable social attitudes and behavior that were common in the rural China of his day, he had to include the various situations that produced these effects. The short-story genre, with its brevity and its unity of focus, made it necessary for him to create one character who would become the victim of all of these catastrophes, and "Hsiang Lin's Wife" is the result.

PLJ: What principles of behavior govern your own life? To what extent do you find it difficult to remain true to principles that are important to you? What factors create difficulties? Do you know any well-meaning people who act in ways that contradict the principles that they believe govern their lives?

Literary Terms: characterization, flashback, irony, paradox, satire, setting, symbol, theme

COMPREHENSION QUESTIONS

1. What is the purpose of the New Year's sacrifice? (ceremony to invite a year of good fortune)
2. What social position do Fourth Uncle and his family have in Luchen? (highly educated; upper middle class)
3. What is the relationship between Hsiang Lin's Wife and Fourth Uncle's family? (their servant)
4. Name two catastrophes that occurred in Hsiang Lin's Wife's life. ((*a*) First husband died; (*b*) second husband died; (*c*) wolf carried off and ate her son.)
5. In the end, how is Hsiang Lin's Wife treated by Fourth Uncle and Fourth Aunt? (treated as if contaminated because of catastrophes in her family)
6. What type of life is Hsiang Lin's Wife living when the narrator meets her? (a beggar)
7. What does Hsiang Lin's Wife do that bothers the narrator? (asks him three difficult questions about death that he tries to answer)
8. What finally happens to Hsiang Lin's Wife? (commits suicide)
9. What is Lu Hsün's attitude toward Fourth Uncle and Fourth Aunt? (religious people who are callous and cruel to Hsiang Lin's Wife without cause)

UNDERSTANDING THE STORY: POSSIBLE ANSWERS

*1. *Lu Hsün's definition of a good person*   A good person's attitudes and actions would be sensitive to the needs and feelings of others, regardless of their social or economic status. People's secular lives and religious lives should be mutually consistent in that they should live their daily lives according to their religious principles.
 2. *Hsiang Lin's Wife's three questions*   Hsiang Lin's Wife wants to know if she's going to be punished in the lower world by being cut in two and divided between her two husbands, as Liu Ma believes.

Being a modern intellectual, the narrator feels estranged from the values of the old China, yet he feels helpless in terms of changing the society to which they all belong. Consequently, he does not feel comfortable about relating to Hsiang Lin's Wife, and he does not pursue the situation that exists behind the questions that she asks him. Their meeting continues to bother him. Later, he fears that his responses confirmed her fears about the lower world and her fate after death, and that, somehow, his words led to her suicide.

*3. *Why Fourth Uncle thinks Hsiang Lin's Wife is a "bad character"* Hsiang Lin's Wife decides to commit suicide at a time when everyone prays for blessings in the coming year. Her death interferes with Fourth Uncle's concentration on convincing the gods that he deserves to be blessed. In addition, Fourth Uncle may subconsciously realize his responsibility for Hsiang Lin's Wife's death and, therefore, her action threatens the blessing that he desires. He distances himself from the darker aspects of his own character by blaming her.

*4. *Why Hsiang Lin's Wife dies at this time* Hsiang Lin's Wife feels sinful, worthless, and ostracized by society. Even her contribution to the temple did not change anyone's response to her, and she expects that the attitude of the gods will be even more censuring than the attitude of the townspeople. She may have chosen to sacrifice herself to the gods during the New Year's festival in order to obtain their blessings in her afterlife in the lower world. Sacrificing oneself is more meaningful than sacrificing animals, and Hsiang Lin's Wife has tried everything else in her power to atone for the sins that the townspeople and her employers have made her feel that she has committed in her life. Hsiang Lin's Wife may also have committed suicide because she felt particularly depressed at a time of year when everyone else was celebrating good fortune.

*5. *Why Fourth Uncle won't let Hsiang Lin's Wife participate in New Year's rites* The catastrophes that have occurred in Hsiang Lin's Wife's life lead Fourth Uncle to think that the gods are punishing her for improper behavior. Therefore, when he is trying his best to behave in a way that will cause the gods to bless him and his family, he fears that Hsiang Lin's Wife's participation in those preparations will pollute his efforts and bring the gods' anger, rather than their blessing.

*6. *Why people in Luchen view Hsiang Lin's Wife with contempt* At first, Hsiang Lin's Wife's catastrophes remind the people of Luchen of their own good fortune, so they enjoy her complaints. Later, her problems make them feel guilty about their own good lives and the fact that they are making no effort to help her. Her problems also remind the people of Luchen that good fortune leaves unpredictably. Therefore, they fear and despise Hsiang Lin's Wife because her presence reminds them of a fact that they would like to forget. In their minds, if her behavior caused her problems, they will avoid such problems by controlling their own behavior.

*7. *Lu Hsün critical of Fourth Uncle and household* Lu Hsün is critical of all hypocrites. He expects people to treat one another with respect, kindness, and generosity. Fourth Uncle and Fourth Aunt think only of themselves. Lu Hsün is also critical of a religion that encourages people to please the gods and earn their blessings by making animal sacrifices instead of requiring moral behavior in human relationships.

8. *Social attitudes in rural China*   Hsiang Lin's Wife's life experiences reveal that (*a*) men have a privileged place in society and in religious practices (Fourth Uncle and the New Year's sacrifice); (*b*) parents dominate their grown children and their children-in-law. A woman may be sold in marriage to a young boy so that her labor may be exploited by her husband's family (as in Hsiang Lin's Wife's first marriage). She also may be treated like a slave (as in Hsiang Lin's Wife's second marriage).

*9. *Title and theme*   (*a*) Both "The New Year's Sacrifice" and "Benediction" reflect the irony that the people of Luchen expect to be blessed on the basis of the quality of their performance of religious rites rather than on the quality of their treatment of other human beings. "The New Year's Sacrifice" has an additional meaning in that it can also refer to Hsiang Lin's Wife's sacrifice of her own life.

(*b*) Both titles relate to the theme that sacrifice and benediction should focus on the moral actions of human beings and their treatment of one another with respect, kindness, and generosity.

ANALYZING LITERARY TECHNIQUE: POSSIBLE ANSWERS

1. *Why Lu Hsün begins and ends with the current New Year's holiday*   The current holiday establishes the religious framework within which Hsiang Lin's Wife's story occurs, as well as emphasizes the townspeople's hypocrisy—the gap between their beliefs and actions. The story within the story (Hsiang Lin's Wife's story) emphasizes the inhumanity of these people. The contrast between their religious sentiment and their treatment of Hsiang Lin's Wife gives the story its great power.

2. *Flashback*   The structure of a flashback permits Lu Hsün to select the memories that the narrator recalls. Thus, his thoughts are all focused on the part of Hsiang Lin's Wife's life that relates to her mistreatment by her family, her employers, and fate. Extraneous detail, although interesting, would weaken the power of the story by diluting it.

*3. *Depiction of Fourth Uncle and Fourth Aunt*   Both Fourth Uncle and Fourth Aunt think only of their own welfare. Both are insensitive to the needs of Hsiang Lin's Wife. Their callous behavior, which destroys Hsiang Lin's Wife's life, illuminates the hypocrisy of their religious practices. The attitudes and behavior of the aunt and uncle are the major sources of irony and satire, and thus they give the story its power.

*4. *Elements of satire*   The story is a bitter satire in that it ridicules vices that cause human tragedy (rather than follies, which provoke humorous, gentle criticism). The story reveals the hypocrisy of these people, who value correct rituals more than moral behavior. Lu Hsün finds the idea of pleasing divinities with animal sacrifices instead of treating people humanely to be morally unacceptable.

In addition to the actions of Hsiang Lin's Wife's mother-in-law and brother-in-law, the arrogant attitudes and cruel behavior of Fourth Uncle, Fourth Aunt, and Liu Ma ruin her life. During Hsiang Lin's Wife's first employment, Fourth Uncle and Fourth Aunt underpay her and treat her like a slave. They hand her and her wages over to her mother-in-law upon demand, pitying only themselves. During Hsiang Lin's Wife's second employment, Fourth Uncle views her misfortunes as a sign of divine displeasure, and he and his wife treat her as a pariah. They cause her spirit to break, making her useless as a servant, and then fire her, leaving her to become a beggar.

*5. *Irony*   Irony is the source of the satire and power of the story. Liu Ma, "a devout woman . . . who abstained from meat and did not kill living things," terrifies Hsiang Lin's Wife with her convictions about Hsiang Lin's Wife's sinful life and about her consequent treatment in the lower world. When she tells Hsiang Lin's Wife that she should have killed herself, she is being as harmful and unjust as everyone else. She appears to be more worried about the lives of domestic animals than about human life.

The final paragraph reveals that the people of Luchen consider themselves to be good people whose prayers and offerings will reward them with the favor and blessings of the "saints of heaven and earth." They do not consider their treatment of Hsiang Lin's Wife and others to be relevant to the gods' treatment of them. The most disturbing irony in this story is that bad things do happen to good people and that good things do happen to bad people. The people of Luchen may continue to be "blessed," in that they will not be punished for their callous and cruel behavior.

*6. *Paradox*   It is paradoxical that basically good people, through ignorance of their prejudices, can be cruel to others.

WRITING ABOUT LITERATURE

1. *Expository essay analyzing use of satire*   Call students' attention to the directions in the textbook assignment with regard to content and organization. (See **U.S.** questions 1, 3–7, and 9, and **A.L.T.** questions 3, 4, 5, and 6.

2. *Creative writing: A contemporary version of Lu Hsün's story*   Direct students to suggestions in the textbook assignment. Actions involving hypocrisy and injustice can result from issues based on religion, economics, politics, social status, or gender. **(PLJ)**

FURTHER READING

Lu Hsün, *Selected Stories of Lu Hsün.*

In a Grove

RYŪNOSUKE AKUTAGAWA

INTRODUCING THE STORY

"In a Grove" is a first-class mystery story, a "whodunit" without an obvious solution. A robber confronts a married couple and rapes the wife. Then the husband is murdered. Each of the principal characters, to enhance his or her self-esteem and public image, confesses to the crime, creating in the process an elaborate rationalization of behavior and leaving the reader with a fascinating intellectual puzzle.

Akutagawa tells the story from six different points of view. His portraits of the three principal characters reveal the psychological complexity of human nature and the bias that is inherent in any individual's point of view. Each has important personal and public reasons for claiming to have done the stabbing. The thief takes pride in his self-image and in his reputation. Once he is caught, he justifies his actions by declaring affection for the wife and by his depiction of her and her husband. The wife, shamed by the rape's effect on her own self-image and reputation and resentful of her husband's attitude toward her, may confess in order to relieve her sense of shame and guilt by being punished for the crime. The husband may claim to have committed suicide in order to relieve his private and public shame about his wife's rape and to die the honorable death of a warrior.

Through the use of a multiple narrative perspective, Akutagawa reveals that the human mind is complex, objective truth is elusive, and ambiguity is an inherent part of life. In the culture he is depicting, one's public image determines one's self-esteem. People act and depict their actions in whatever way will lead others to accept and admire them. However, in any culture, the egotism that is an inherent part of human nature makes it difficult to learn the objective truth about an event, even from participants and witnesses. When events involve the elemental human passions of love, hate, and jealousy, the human psyche blurs the line between reality and illusion, often making it impossible to distinguish objective truth from subjective fiction.

PLJ: Which is more important to you: how you feel about yourself, or how others feel about you? To what extent is your self-esteem determined by how others evaluate your behavior?

Literary Terms: characterization, first-person limited omniscience, irony, narrative perspective, plot, setting, theme, unreliable narrator

COMPREHENSION QUESTIONS

1. Why is the police commissioner questioning people? (man murdered)
2. What position does the robber Tajomaru take? (confesses to murder)
3. What position does the wife take? (confesses to husband's murder)

4. What position does the husband take? (confesses suicide)
5. How does the reader learn the husband's views? (through a medium)

UNDERSTANDING THE STORY: POSSIBLE ANSWERS

*1. *Why husband, wife, and thief all confess*   With this action, each gains self-esteem and public approval.

*2. *Characters' testimony*   (a) *The thief*. The thief's declaration of affection for the wife makes his motive for rape more acceptable. His statement that everyone else is greedy makes his motives and behavior similar to others'. His statement that the wife made him kill the husband and that he made it a fair fight exonerates him.

The thief has little to lose by confessing. Circumstantial evidence (husband's property in thief's possession) and the thief's reputation will convict him anyway. His goal is to die with honor.

One would expect the thief to deny responsibility for the crime in hope of saving his own life, even though it is most likely that he killed the husband to prevent the husband's revenge for the rape.

(b) *The wife*. The wife hopes that her confession of murder will result in punishment, thus relieving her sense of shame and her guilt about having been raped and having run away.

The wife risks imprisonment or loss of life, but she does not consider a life filled with shame and guilt to be worth living.

One would expect the wife to be the innocent, ravaged victim. Only self-serving males (both the thief and her husband) would insinuate that she would have found the thief sexually attractive or otherwise appealing. Under the circumstances, it is much more likely that she would have killed herself instead of her husband.

(c) *The husband*. The husband confesses because it is more honorable to commit suicide than to be killed in a fair fight or to be murdered by his wife or by the thief (most likely reality). Even if it were true, the husband would not believe his wife's view that his facial expressions revealed that her rape disgusted him and that he despised her for it. He gains self-esteem and honor at the expense of his wife's reputation, but he cares more about himself than about his wife. His attitude toward her testimony lends credence to his wife's view of his attitude toward her after the rape. His testimony reveals him to be cruel and despicable.

Being already dead, the husband has nothing to lose except a relationship with his wife after her death.

One would expect the husband to act like the victim of a vicious crime. His likely responses would have been to accuse the thief of the murder and to be very sympathetic and loving about his wife.

3. *Themes*   (a) Objective truth is elusive; (b) ambiguity is an inherent part of life; (c) the human psyche interprets experience in whatever way is compatible with its need for self-esteem and public approval.

ANALYZING LITERARY TECHNIQUE: POSSIBLE ANSWERS

1. *Choice of narrative perspective*   Telling one story from different points of view reveals how the individual psyche interprets experience to its own advantage. The human mind is complex, objective truth is elusive, and ambiguity is an inherent part of life.
2. *Why mystery unsolved?*   Dramatically, the technique creates suspense and involves readers in the story, challenging their intelligence. Psychologically, the technique reveals a truth about life: that objective truth is elusive and ambiguity is inherent in human experience.
3. *Irony*   It is ironic that three characters confess to the stabbing, when two of the three risk their lives by doing so. This irony creates the dramatic surprise, and it reveals the complexity of the human psyche.
*4. *Testimony of minor characters*   The testimonies of these characters are at best only partly reliable. They lead the reader to assume that, in contrast, the testimonies of the participants will be accurate, when, ironically, no one's testimony is reliable.

   (*a*) The woodcutter reveals basic facts and conjectures about a battle.

   (*b*) The priest adds facts and conjectures that the couple he saw were husband and wife.

   (*c*) The policeman reveals facts about the thief when he describes the arrest, and his prejudice about the thief, given the thief's reputation.

   (*d*) The old woman's testimony reveals her view of the personalities of her daughter and son-in-law. Although she claims to recognize her son-in-law, he does not have the same name as the corpse, and he and her daughter were walking in a different direction toward a different town.

WRITING ABOUT LITERATURE

1. *Expository writing: Analysis of reliability of confession of the thief, the wife, or the husband*   (See **U.S.** questions 1 and 2 above.) **(PLJ)**
2. *Creative writing: an objective version of the story*   Use of a hidden observer is possible; however, students should be aware of his or her bias. (Even Kurosawa's woodcutter is unreliable.) The objective version should be consistent with all indisputable facts. (See **A.L.T.** question 4 above.)

FURTHER READING

Akutagawa, Ryūnosuke, *Rashomon and Other Stories*; "The Nose"; "The Spider's Thread"; *Kappa*; "The Hell Screen."

The Grasshopper and the Bell Cricket

Yasunari Kawabata

INTRODUCING THE STORY

"The Grasshopper and the Bell Cricket" captures a special moment in time. In the process of hunting for insects, a boy (Fujio) offers a particular girl (Kiyoko) the insect that he has caught and wants her to have, and Kiyoko accepts it. She discovers that it is not a common grasshopper, but a rare bell cricket. In the process, only the narrator notices that the light from Kiyoko's lantern casts the reflection of her name on Fujio's waist and that the light from Fujio's lantern casts his name on Kiyoko's breast, suggesting a relationship of which the children themselves are unaware.

The narrator uses the grasshopper and the bell cricket on two levels, the real and the symbolic. They symbolize what is ordinary and common on the one hand, and what is rare and valued on the other. For him, the exchange of reflected names symbolizes all that is mysterious in life, the extra dimension of human experience that is often unrecognized and that is beyond comprehension. Being male, Kawabata identifies with Fujio, and divides females into "grasshoppers" and "bell crickets." He pities Fujio for being unaware of the larger, mysterious reality of this moment because if Fujio could react more completely to the experience, this ability would sustain him through times of skepticism and loss of faith, times when he might so doubt the existence of what is rare and beautiful that he would be incapable of recognizing its presence in his life.

Kawabata has written a type of haiku poem in prose, one in which he preserves a significant moment in time that functions on two levels. On the surface, it is a moment that is pictorially beautiful and emotionally satisfying. On the symbolic level, it is an epiphany, a moment of sudden revelation in which the deeper meaning in this ordinary event flashes into the narrator's mind.

The symbolic meaning of the moment not only enriches the narrator's life, but it has universal significance. Moments of pure beauty are rare and fleeting, but, like the bell cricket, they can be found and captured in a world that is filled with ordinary grasshoppers. It is important for each person to remain open to the discovery of these moments in order to recognize what is rare and beautiful when it is present. Kawabata ironically mentions that a person is as likely to consider what is ordinary to be rare as to consider what is rare to be ordinary. However, he is rightfully more concerned with a person's inability to recognize beauty than to mistake it.

PLJ: Have you ever witnessed a very special and private moment, one in which you were, in effect, an invisible outsider who was looking into someone else's world? For example, have you ever come upon animals in their natural setting or observed a child alone at play? If so, did you stop and observe, or did you continue on your way? To what extent, if any, did it affect your life?

Literary Terms: apostrophe, connotative language, irony, narrative perspective, repetition, setting, symbol, Symbolist, theme, tone

COMPREHENSION QUESTIONS

1. Where does the narrator observe this story? (at the base of a slope near a school playground)
2. What is happening? (Children are hunting insects.)
3. What are the children using to help them? (handmade paper lanterns)
4. What does Fujio give Kiyoko? (bell cricket he thinks is a grasshopper)
5. What does the narrator see that most impresses him? (Kiyoko's name reflected on Fujio's waist, and Fujio's name reflected on Kiyoko's breast)

UNDERSTANDING THE STORY: POSSIBLE ANSWERS

1. *Role of surprise*   The two surprises (the bobbing lanterns and the reflection of the names) act as flags to direct the reader's attention to the special significance of what the narrator is about to describe. Their presence creates climaxes out of these important scenes. They enhance the story by adding vitality, but the scenes would be just as effective in themselves without the markers.
2. *Children*   The story is about being able to appreciate wonder and beauty in life. Children are usually more sensitive to the wonder of small things. The world is still new to them, and their joys of discovery are frequent. In contrast, adults often think that they have discovered it all, and no longer look at the world outside themselves. Thus, most adults would not choose to go on an insect hunt, and they would not choose to take the time to put their hearts and minds into the creation of beautiful lanterns when they could purchase them.
3. *Children's attitude toward lanterns*   Their attitude reveals their desire to have something that is beautiful and their joy in being creative. Kawabata prizes all of these qualities.
4. *Significance of Fujio's repeated question*   Fujio's repeated offer, despite numerous acceptances, reveals his desire to give his insect to Kiyoko. This adds the first personal touch to the story, in that it now concerns particular children rather than an overview of a group.
5. *Fujio's feelings about bell cricket*   Fujio is probably embarrassed that he kept calling attention to an insect by the wrong name. However, he was less interested in the insect than in using it as an opportunity to be important to Kiyoko. Therefore, Fujio is probably interested in what it is only to the extent that Kiyoko is more or less pleased by it.
*6. *Uses of light*   (a) Bobbing: The colorful moving lanterns create atmosphere, a beautiful visual picture.

(*b*) Illuminating: When Fujio uses his lantern to illuminate Kiyoko's face, he reveals his purpose in rejecting so many offers for the grasshopper. This adds particularity in the form of character interest.

(*c*) Reflecting: The reflection of the names of Fujio and Kiyoko on each other's bodies gives the event the narrator is observing a mysterious and symbolic dimension that emanates from but is beyond the event itself.

7. *Contribution of narrator's point of view*   The narrator's ideas add the philosophical content of the story. It is he who gives the story a symbolic dimension. For him, it is important that each person recognize the beauty in life, no matter what its surface appearance might be.

ANALYZING LITERARY TECHNIQUE: POSSIBLE ANSWERS

*1. *Relationship of setting and tone*   The colorful bobbing lanterns create a visual picture of a special, idyllic moment in time.

*2. *Relationship of narrative perspective and tone*   The narrative perspective of a third-person omniscient author permits the narrator to philosophize about the story's symbolic significance. An omniscient narrator knows more than his characters and can think about them in terms of his own special knowledge. This adds a serious quality to the idyllic tone.

*3. *Relationship of apostrophe and tone*   When the narrator speaks directly to Fujio, he is creating a personal connection between Fujio and himself. This technique adds a personal and more important aspect to the tone of the story.

*4. *Irony*   It is ironic that the children, like most people, are unaware of all of the beauty and wonder that fill their lives. This loss adds sad and wistful aspects to the tone of the story.

5. *Relationship of symbols and theme*   The grasshopper symbolizes what is ordinary and common in life; in contrast, the bell cricket symbolizes what is rare and special. Kawabata's principal themes are: (1) It is important for each person to be aware of the bell crickets in life, even when they look like grasshoppers; otherwise, one misses much of what is rare and beautiful. (2) People's attitudes make their experiences common or beautiful; they can turn grasshoppers into bell crickets or bell crickets into grasshoppers.

Advertently or inadvertently, Kawabata has achieved the major goal of the Symbolists with this story. By recapturing and reproducing the experience that originally inspired particular thoughts and emotions in himself, Kawabata succeeds in re-creating these feelings in the reader. Thus, the story becomes the symbol of the reactions that it inspires.

6. *Function of repetition*   (1) Growing numbers of children: The cumulative process emphasizes growth. (2) Fujio's repeated question reveals his interest, expressed indirectly, in Kiyoko. (3) The children's repeated comment, ''It's a bell cricket!'' emphasizes the value of that insect. (4) Reflected names emphasize the epiphany, the symbolic significance of the event.

WRITING ABOUT LITERATURE

1. *Expository writing: An essay analyzing Kawabata's use of light*   Call students' attention to the types of light suggested in the textbook assignment. Remind them of the importance of direct quotations. (See **U.S.** question 6 above.)

2. *Expository writing: An essay analyzing how Kawabata achieves tone*   Call students' attention to the techniques suggested in the textbook assignment. Remind them that direct quotations must support their ideas. (See **A.L.T.** questions 1, 2, 3, and 4 above.)

3. *Creative writing: A real or imagined special moment in time*   Call students' attention to suggestions in the textbook assignment. Remind them to aim for detail that will create a sense of immediacy for their readers. **(PLJ)**

FURTHER READING

Kawabata, Yasunari, *Palm-of-the-Hand Stories*; "Of Birds and Beasts"; *The Sound of the Mountain*; "One Arm."

Downtown

FUMIKO HAYASHI

INTRODUCING THE STORY

Set in Tokyo shortly after the end of World War II, "Downtown" is a story about the will to survive. It shows that human relationships can make life worth living even amid destruction and poverty.

Having received no word about her soldier-husband for six years, Ryo takes her young son to Tokyo to start a new life. From the country and female, she is unaccustomed to independence and to being solely responsible for herself and her son. Her friendship with Tsuruishi enables her to come to terms with the past and to move ahead with her new life.

The story is a poignant tale of the cost of war to the wives who remained behind. Tsuruishi's wife loses faith in his return and takes up with another man. His sister supports herself and her two children by making clothes. Ryo survives by peddling tea door to door.

The role of luck in life, both good and bad, permeates the story. Life or death, kind or callous treatment, success or failure in selling tea are all a matter of serendipity. Yet, in spite of the trials and losses that are part of living, the good people whom Ryo meets, those who are kind, sympathetic, and caring, bolster her with the courage to continue and the comfort that she is not alone in her plight.

PLJ: Imagine what your life would be like if you survived a war or a natural disaster in which you and your family were directly affected. What problems would you anticipate? How would you attempt to cope with these problems? What aspects of life would sustain and comfort you?

Literary Terms: characterization, irony, setting, theme, tone

COMPREHENSION QUESTIONS

1. Why has Ryo come to Tokyo? (to earn a living for herself and her son)
2. How does Ryo earn a living? (sells tea from door to door)
3. Where is Ryo's husband? (prisoner of war or dead)
4. Who is Tsuruishi? (man who becomes Ryo's friend)
5. How do other women like Ryo earn a living? (by sewing)

UNDERSTANDING THE STORY: POSSIBLE ANSWERS

*1. *Ryo's world*   Ryo's postwar world is one in which survival is primary. Order and predictability no longer exist. Ryo's husband may or may not return; Ryo may or may not be successful selling tea.

"Downtown" is universal in its application. Catastrophes force those who are victims to be flexible and adapt to new circumstances. War always causes death and destruction, leaving widows and fatherless children.

*2. *Remaining values*   The humane values continue to exist in this postwar world: love, friendship, and empathy.

*3. *Why Ryo's husband an embarrassment*   The imprisonment of Ryo's husband reminds people of the unpleasant fact that Japan lost "the war" (World War II).

*4. *Why Ryo remains after Tsuruishi dies*   Ryo has learned that she can survive in Tokyo. She will be able to earn a living, and she will be able to meet good people who will become her friends.

*5. *Tsuruishi: better or worse for Ryo*   Student opinion will differ. Some will agree that " 'Tis better to have loved and lost than never to have loved at all.'' Ryo's feelings for Tsuruishi make her realize that it will be possible for her to love someone other than her husband should he not return. Also, since Tsuruishi has recently returned, it is possible that her own husband will still return. Others will think that, under these circumstances, 'tis better not to have loved, since loving creates a greater sense of loss and also a great sense of guilt should Ryo's husband return.

*6. *Ryo a sympathetic character*   Hayashi presents Ryo very sympathetically. She is a wife in limbo, without a husband for six years, and her husband may or may not be alive. She attempts to earn a living, in a decent manner, that will enable both her and her young son to survive. Ryo is a good human being: generous and caring, but also very lonely.

7. *Role of luck or fate*   Luck or fate reflects the unpredictability of life and an absurd universe. Ryo may or may not be successful selling tea each day. Tsuruishi dies while on a journey that was unnecessary. Ryo's husband may or may not be alive to return home.

8. *Attitude toward war*   War brings loneliness, pain, poverty, and death into the lives of innocent people. Hayashi deals with war by examining its effect on individuals who are also representative of larger groups. Hayashi's characters do not preoccupy themselves with the philosophical, political, religious, and economic causes of war.

9. *Themes*   Themes include: (*a*) Live each day to the fullest, for tomorrow is a mystery; (*b*) War destroys both the lives of those who fight and the lives of those who remain behind; (*c*) It is possible to remain kind and loving in spite of great adversity.

ANALYZING LITERARY TECHNIQUE: POSSIBLE ANSWERS

*1. *Relation of setting to plot*   The story is set in postwar Japan and concerns Ryo's survival without her husband. He has not returned because he is a prisoner of war who may or may not have died by the time the story begins. Therefore, Ryo is compelled to find a way to earn enough money to support her young son and herself. All of the other characters in the story are also suffering from the effects of war on their lives.

2. *Tsuruishi's function*   Tsuruishi's life teaches Ryo that her husband may return; that she can live and find love even if he does not return; that life continues; and that good people continue to exist. Tsuruishi's death teaches Ryo that nothing is predictable in life; one can only do one's best to make the most of each day.

3. *Irony*   It is ironic that Tsuruishi survives the war and imprisonment only to be killed in a freak accident in the course of an unnecessary journey. It is also ironic that Tsuruishi encourages Ryo to become involved with him after his own wife became involved with another man. Irony reinforces a major theme of the story, that life is unpredictable and that people need to create their own meaning in an absurd universe.

4. *Tone*   The tone is compassionate and poignant. It is created by the facts of Ryo's life and by the way that Ryo reacts to adversity. Ryo never loses her determination and ability to work hard and to care about others.

5. *Title*   "Downtown" is general, whereas "Ryo" is specific and individual. Hayashi views Ryo, not as an individual in a vacuum, but as an individual who is symbolic of thousands of poor widows who must struggle to survive in postwar Japan.

WRITING ABOUT LITERATURE

1. *Expository theme: Sympathetic character sketch of Ryo*   Ryo is determined, courageous, friendly, kind, and optimistic. Remind students to use direct quotations to describe their choice of supporting incidents. Students should relate Ryo's character to conditions in postwar Tokyo, considering the plight of single women in Japanese urban society. (See **U.S.** questions 1–6, and **A.L.T.** question 1)

2. *Creative writing: A sequel to this story*　Remind students that suggested questions in the textbook assignment may be helpful. (**PLJ**)

FURTHER READING

Hayashi, Fumiko, "Late Chrysanthemum"; *Drifting Clouds*.

A Certain Night
TING LING

INTRODUCING THE STORY

"A Certain Night" conveys the atmosphere in which a group of Chinese Communists are executed by their political enemies, the Nationalists. Hatred for their oppressors gives way to hope for their cause as their final thoughts move away from themselves and toward the ideals for which they are sacrificing their lives. Ting Ling concludes with snow falling on dark corpses and the question, "When will it be light?" "Light" implies more than the dawn of the next day. It refers to the dawn of a new political day, one in which the Chinese people work together to create a better environment for the common people, the peasants and the workers. For the men in the story, political slogans dispel the darkness and give meaning to their deaths. For them and for Ting Ling, the new Communist state is a brilliant source of light.

Ting Ling effectively creates the mood of the situation by her repeated attention to the weather. She has created a physical environment that reflects the atmosphere of the political execution, as if nature abhors the actions of the Nationalists. The execution occurs on a black night and is carried out by people who operate in secret. A ferocious wind lashes faces as rifle butts smash chests and gunshots lacerate bodies. Her use of color and sound create lasting images in the mind of the reader.

Note: Anglo-Saxon obscenities suggested in the translation have been omitted without damage to the meaning of the story.

PLJ: If someone dear to you died, how would you honor that person's memory?

Literary Terms: connotative language, figurative language, metaphor, realism, repetition, setting, symbol, theme, tone

COMPREHENSION QUESTIONS

1. What feet are tramping? (Nationalist soldiers who will shoot Communist activists)
2. Who is the main character? (young poet condemned to death for his Communist activities)
3. Describe the weather. (stormy winter night)

4. What do the prisoners do just before the end? (shout Communist slogans and sing a socialist song)
5. What happens to the prisoners in the end? (executed by Nationalist soldiers)

UNDERSTANDING THE STORY: POSSIBLE ANSWERS

*1. *Author's attitude toward prisoners*   It is clear from the way the author describes the two political groups that she sympathizes with the prisoners. Her closing question about light refers to the new Communist age in China. Her description of the poet as loyal and hardworking depicts him as an innocent victim of Nationalist oppressors.

*2. *Nationalists vs. Communists*   Ting Ling describes a Nationalist soldier as having a "cunning face, malicious and smug . . . with a revolting moustache of the sort imperialists wear"; later she writes that the face "seemed to symbolize the cruelty of all the rulers to the oppressed." She refers to Communists as "dispelling the darkness" and welcomes the "brilliance of a new state being founded."

*3. *Nationalist attitude toward condemned prisoners*   Nationalists consider the prisoners to be criminals, traitors to their country, and deserving of death. From their point of view, the Nationalists are correct, for the goal of communism is to take over the government of China.

*4. *Change in poet's attitude toward death*   At first the poet is angry at being deprived of a trial and being sentenced to death. However, being with his comrades comforts him, and in the end he dies happily for his cause, which he believes is greater and more important than any individual.

5. *Purpose of the story*   The story both honors Ting Ling's husband as a political martyr and honors communism for saving China from imperialist domination.

6. *Themes*   (*a*) Power tends to corrupt, and absolute power corrupts absolutely; (*b*) One may find death easier to bear when one devotes one's life to a great cause; (*c*) For some people, it is worth sacrificing their lives for a cause.

ANALYZING LITERARY TECHNIQUE: POSSIBLE ANSWERS

1. *Tone*   The tone is depressing, but with a vision of hope. Despite the depressing subject of a political execution, in which those killed have the author's sympathy, the story leaves the reader with the real possibility of a better future. The prisoners believe that they are sacrificing their lives for a just cause that is about to become a reality through the efforts of courageous people like themselves. The men and women consider themselves martyrs rather than victims, and they take comfort in their shared values and goals and in their accomplishments. Ting Ling describes both the cruelty of their imprisonment and murder, which is dark in tone, and their optimism, evident in one comrade's ability to inspire courage and another's reminder to celebrate the founding of a brilliant new state, which is hopeful in tone.

2. *Relationship between setting and tone*   The stormy setting complements the dark tone of the current political situation. A black, stormy night forms the backdrop for the horror of a politically motivated execution.
3. *Symbolism*   The primary symbols in the story are light and the storm. Ting Ling uses light to symbolize communism. Communist slogans dispel the darkness and reveal the brilliance of the new Communist state that is being founded. Ting Ling's closing question about the light means "When will China become Communist?"

    In addition, by reflecting in the natural world the turbulence in the political world, the storm symbolizes nature's abhorrence of the foul, secret deeds of the Nationalists. It also symbolizes the dark of the tunnel that one must traverse before reaching the light at the end.
4. *Connotation of trampling feet*   Trampling feet connote the force, intent, power, and feeling of victory of the huge escort of Nationalist soldiers. The image is repeated to emphasize their presence and their contribution to the dark tone of this part of the story.

WRITING ABOUT LITERATURE

1. *Expository analysis of the propagandistic elements in this story*   Call students' attention to the textbook assignment, reminding them to include an evaluative conclusion and to support their ideas with direct quotations. (See **U.S.** questions 1–4 above.)
2. *Creative writing: This story from a Nationalist soldier's viewpoint*   Remind students that Nationalists have their own political and social bias, and that they will justify their own attitudes and behavior.

FURTHER READING

Ting Ling, *"Miss Sophie's Diary" and Other Stories; I Myself Am a Woman: Selected Writings of Ding Ling*.

Forty-Five a Month
R. K. NARAYAN

INTRODUCING THE STORY

"Forty-Five a Month" is the story of Venkat Rao, who works under a workaholic boss. Venkat Rao devotes long hours to tedious tasks for which he receives low pay. He has so little time to spend with his family that he feels guilty and promises to take his daughter Shanta to the movies. When he realizes that he is going to have to break his promise, he writes a letter of resignation, but he retracts it when he is offered a small raise in salary.

In the end, he is caught in a life of quiet desperation, for he will still earn too little to provide the life he wishes for his family, and yet he lacks the courage to quit his job and take a chance on the future.

The story has universal appeal in that many people around the world work at jobs they do not like and that keep them from their families. Venkat Rao's attitudes and behavior lead readers to examine their own lives in order to decide the relative importance of career enjoyment, financial success, and family responsibilities and pleasures.

Narayan uses an interesting narrative technique to convey Venkat Rao's personality. First, an omniscient narrator introduces the reader to Shanta. Then, the narrator tells the story from Venkat Rao's point of view, revealing his world to the reader as he reacts to events. The double point of view gives the reader a partial reality check on Venkat Rao's attitudes and reveals him to be his own worst enemy. Lacking the courage of his convictions, he is a sorrier figure than his wife and daughter because, in behavior, he is a willing pawn in his manager's game.

PLJ: Do you value yourself more highly, the same, or less highly than others value you? How does your value of yourself affect your life? To what extent do you aim higher or lower because of how you view yourself? How do you view those people whose opinion of your merits differs from your own?

Literary Terms: characterization, conflict, foreshadowing, irony, narrative perspective, omniscience, paradox, theme, third-person limited omniscience, unreliable narrator.

COMPREHENSION QUESTIONS

1. Why is Shanta anxious to leave school? (movie date with father)
2. How does Venkat Rao view Shanta? (neglected, ignored, deprived)
3. What does Venkat Rao plan to do about his job? (resign)
4. Why doesn't Venkat Rao carry out his plan? (offered small raise)
5. How does Venkat Rao feel in the end? (torn between job and family)

UNDERSTANDING THE STORY: POSSIBLE ANSWERS

*1. *Why Venkat Rao makes date with Shanta*   Venkat Rao makes the date in order to feel in control of his life. He is asserting his independence from his job.
*2. *Accuracy of Venkat Rao's view of Shanta*   Venkat Rao's view appears to be inaccurate. The omniscient author presents Shanta as happy at school, with friends and an understanding teacher. At home, her mother also is understanding. Shanta is adequately cared for, as is clear from the fact that she has a choice of clothes to wear, including warm ones.
*3. *Why Venkat Rao neither quits nor demands more money*   Venkat Rao accepts the terms of his employment because he lacks the courage to risk what he has in order to improve his circumstances.

*4. *How Venkat Rao's personality contributes to his problems*   Venkat Rao is his own worst enemy. He is dissatisfied with many aspects of his job and with his contribution to family life, yet his attitude at the office is so meek and accepting that his boss is able to work him beyond reason. Venkat Rao lives with constant inner conflict that he is unable to resolve.

*5. (*a*) *Should Venkat Rao take a job with more leisure but lower pay?* (*b*) *Role of family in his decision*   Discussion will reveal students' values, and students may disagree.

6. *Themes*   Themes include: (*a*) In order to be happy, people must have the courage of their convictions; (*b*) If people do not value themselves, others will not value them.

ANALYZING LITERARY TECHNIQUE: POSSIBLE ANSWERS

*1. *Organization*   By beginning with the omniscient narrator, the author gives the reader an objective reality against which to compare Venkat Rao's distorted point of view.

*2. *Narrative perspective*   First, the omniscient narrator reveals Shanta to be a happy, contented child. Then, the narrator tells the story from Venket Rao's point of view, revealing his inner conflicts and torments, and his inability to take control of his life. Venkat Rao feels sorry for his family and himself; he complains about many aspects of his job; and he does nothing to improve life for anyone except his boss.

3. *Foreshadowing*   (1) Venkat Rao's description of his work habits indicates that he will have to break his promise. (2) When Venkat Rao's wife admonishes him about making false promises, the reader expects that his promise is indeed false. Both incidents prepare the reader for what follows, and they make the plot internally consistent.

*4. *Irony*   It is ironic that Venkat Rao complains so much about his job, and then, when he is given the opportunity to do something about it, he declines. If Venkat Rao were as unhappy about his job and his time with his family as he professes to be, the reader would expect him to have the courage to take a necessary risk in order to improve his life.

5. *Tone*   The tone is mildly ironic and sweetly sad. Narayan achieves the balance by presenting the mother and child as being basically satisfied with their lives. At least, they do not take advantage of the opportunity to complain. This makes it less important whether Venkat Rao keeps his job or resigns and tries to find another one. He is the most unhappy member of his family, and he is a principal cause of his own unhappiness.

WRITING ABOUT LITERATURE

1. *Expository writing: "Pattern of existence" vs. moment in time*   Students probably will argue that Narayan portrays Venkat Rao's character in such a way that the reader sees a pattern of existence rather than a moment in time. Venkat Rao lets a significant moment pass him by when he breaks his promise to Shanta. He does not resolve his crisis; he simply perpetuates it. (See **U.S.** questions 1–5, and **A.L.T.** questions 1, 2, and 4.) **(PLJ)**

2. *Creative writing: Retelling story from point of view of Shanta's mother*   Students may choose different points of view:

   (*a*) Venkat Rao's wife appears to be satisfied with her life, which is filled with her friends and her daughter.

   (*b*) Venkat Rao's wife is dissatisfied with her life. She resents the demands of Venkat Rao's job. She wishes that Venkat Rao were more assertive, and she would like him to be more involved with his family.

FURTHER READING

Narayan, R. K., *Under the Banyan Tree* (short stories); *The Ramayana* (epic); *The Guide* (novel); *Malgudi Days* (short stories); *Gods, Demons, and Others* (legends).

The Soldier

KRISHAN CHANDAR

INTRODUCING THE STORY

"The Soldier" is the story of the return home of a maimed soldier, Zaman, and his psychological development during a period of twelve hours. One by one he loses the three sources of his emotional strength and sense of self-worth, and then, by surprise, he is given the emotional tools he needs to start to build a new life.

Zaman returns home filled with hatred and anger at his fate. In a war in which many friends have died and his best friend (Shahbaz) has survived unscathed, he has lost a leg. With it, he also has lost his pride in his physical ability. He returns to his village alone and is surprised to find that life has continued in peace and happiness without him, as if the war had not occurred. Donning a mask of joviality and psychological strength, he plays the part of the local hero, despite his mother's concerns about his lost leg and his devastating discovery that, in his absence, his betrothed, Zena, has married another man.

It is Zena's continued love for Zaman, her confession of her sin in breaking their troth, and her willingness to die for her crime that suddenly releases Zaman from the clutches of hostility. He will not forget; he may not forgive; but he can now accept. In the night that follows his first momentous day, Zaman feels neither despair nor hope. His tears express his sorrow for his fate, but he has the courage, strength, and goodwill to try to create a new life. Thus, the story ends on a note of optimism, with the resiliency of the human spirit.

PLJ: How do you think you would react to tragedy in your life (for example, the divorce of your parents, the death of a loved one, a debilitating disease, or any other major change in your life)? To what extent, if any, would you feel great anger and hatred? What sources of strength would help you to accept what cannot be changed in your life?

Literary Terms: characterization, irony, paradox, plot, setting, theme, tragedy

COMPREHENSION QUESTIONS

1. Where is the soldier going? (home after the war)
2. How long has he been in the army? (six years)
3. What has happened to him? (one leg shot off)
4. What disappointment greets him at his destination? (girl to whom he was engaged has married another)
5. What surprise occurs at the end? (girl admits love and sin; Zaman forgives her)

UNDERSTANDING THE STORY: POSSIBLE ANSWERS

1. *Why both Zaman's friendship with Shahbaz and love affair with Zena* The contrast set up in the opening paragraph reveals the strength of the male relationship in contrast with the weakness of the romantic relationship. A second and related contrast is that between relationships in war and in peace. The male relationship is forged under fire, when risk of death is a daily reality. The qualities needed for life during peace are different from those needed for life during war. Peace requires a different kind of courage and strength; it also requires understanding, compassion, and flexibility. Zaman is in transition between war and peace, and he will need to shift emotional gears.
2. *Why Zaman responds passively to Shahbaz's questions* Zaman is angry about the loss of his leg. Fate being as unkind and incomprehensible as it is, he has no interest in trying to fathom the rationale behind the operations of the universe. He knows that his injury is unjustified and irrational, and he resents that Shahbaz, fighting at his side, incurred no such injury.
3. *Chandar's purpose* Chandar chooses a few crucial hours in the homecoming of a maimed soldier to depict the soldier's psychological transition from wartime to peacetime, from heroic past to uncertain future, from anger to acceptance.
4. *Themes* Themes include: (*a*) Human beings have little control over their fate; (*b*) Life is filled with surprises: Some are pleasant, and others cause suffering; (*c*) Human beings have within themselves the power to weather adversity.

ANALYZING LITERARY TECHNIQUE: POSSIBLE ANSWERS

1. *Relationship between setting and plot* The setting juxtaposes the battlefield with the home. Zaman returns from war with medals designed to compensate for the loss of his leg. He returns with Shahbaz, a true friend in war and one who is loyal, trusting, and self-sacrificing. Zaman returns to a world in which family and friends are more interested in his injury than in his heroism and are unprepared for war's devastation. His betrothed, Zena, proves to be the opposite of Shahbaz. By marrying another, she has been disloyal, skeptical of Zaman's return and his love for her, and self-centered.

*2. *How minor characters contribute to Zaman's character development*   (*a*) Shahbaz's presence makes it possible to introduce Zaman as a war hero and companion in arms. (*b*) Zaman's mother brings out his psychological strength in terms of his lost leg because it is necessary for him to comfort her. In the process, he is also coming to terms with the same emotions within himself, and he is comforting himself as well as her. (*c*) Zena's love and confession of sin permit Zaman to let go of his hatred and anger and accept his fate. By acknowledging the validity of Zaman's feelings, Zena diffuses them by sharing them. (*d*) The first girl reminds Zaman of his and Zena's pledge of love; the second girl reminds Zaman that other human beings also have troubles.

3. *Paradox*   It is paradoxical that wars are soon forgotten by civilians whose lives are unaffected by combat, injury, and loss of life.

4. *Tragedy*   To return from war maimed, physically or psychologically, is tragic. In order for a person to be a tragic hero, the tragic situation must elevate his or her human nature: Insight must occur. When Zaman becomes able to accept the loss of a limb and of his betrothed without anger and hatred, his acceptance of human frailty and the imperfect nature of the human condition makes him a tragic hero. Had he been unable to make the leap from his specific losses to the broader understanding of himself as part of the stream of life, he would have still been a tragic figure, but he would not have been heroic.

WRITING ABOUT LITERATURE

1. *Expository analysis of minor characters' contributions to Zaman's characterization*   Remind students to relate their ideas to the direct quotations that support them. (See **A.L.T.** question 2 above.)

2. *Creative writing: A sequel about Zaman*   Call students' attention to the directions and questions suggested in the textbook assignment. (**PLJ**)

FURTHER READING

Natwar-Singh, K., ed., *Tales From Modern India.*

Latin America

Serene Words

GABRIELA MISTRAL

INTRODUCING THE POEM

The appeal of "Serene Words" is its comforting tone, its emphasis on the beauty of the natural world, and Mistral's use of language. The beauty of nature reminds Mistral that life, despite its problems, is a good experience. Nature, like her mother and God, is a source of joy and comfort for her in the face of pain, sorrow, and death.

The source of "Serene Words," the collection *Desolation* (1922, with significant revisions in the 1923 and 1926 editions), includes some of Mistral's finest early work. Three of the book's four sections draw a picture of life as a lonely, sorrowful experience, a picture that has much in common with existentialism. However, Mistral's existentialism is softened both by feeling (especially feelings of love and desire) and by her strong belief in Christianity. The final section of *Desolation* is filled with striking images of cold and deserted landscapes. The images also often identify the landscape or world with women. Most of the poems in the collection follow a similar structure, in which a series of items are compared in each stanza, with the final stanza's unifying all of the images. Mistral's poetic language is intentionally simple and close to the spoken word.

PLJ: What do you value most in life? Why? What decisions have your values affected? Who or what gives you comfort when you need it, for example, a particular person, music, reading, exercise, or a pet?

Literary Terms: connotative language, contrast, figurative language, lyric

COMPREHENSION QUESTIONS

1. How old is the speaker in this poem? (middle-aged)
2. To what does the speaker compare life? (nature)
3. What is the speaker's attitude toward life? (positive: beauty and love compensate for pain and death)

UNDERSTANDING THE POEM: POSSIBLE ANSWERS

1. *Attitude toward good and evil*   The speaker sets life's advantages and disadvantages side by side and decides that the beauty of nature and love can make one forget fatigue, sadness, pain, and death. The power of love and nature's great beauty make life good. Faith and love protect people against the harmful aspects of life and even temper death's sting.
2. *(a) Experiences; (b) sources of emotional support*   *(a)* The poem suggests that

many experiences, especially of natural events, shape people's ideas and values. Some possibilities include: a field of wheat (line 3), blooming violets (lines 7–8), a lily (line 12), a brook (line 14), a skylark's song (lines 15–16).

(b) Some sources of support include: love (lines 4, 18), a mother's care (line 19), and God (line 20).

3. *Connection between age and attitudes*   A child or a senior citizen might be more likely to emphasize either the positive or the negative in life. The child lives in the present and has limited experience. The senior citizen, who may be in declining health, has a lifetime of memories.

ANALYZING LITERARY TECHNIQUE: POSSIBLE ANSWERS

*1. *Function of contrast*   Mistral juxtaposes words that are connected with life (nature, farming) with those that are connected with death (war, sadness). Her choice of language changes what could be a complex philosophical discussion into an experience that all people can understand. The juxtaposition of opposites enhances the examples of love and nature as powerful, positive experiences. Responses will vary as to which contrasts are most effective, such as thirst and the hillside vs. the lily (lines 11–12), or the skylark's song vs. death (lines 15–16). In the last stanza, lack of contrast creates a purely positive mood. Love brings peace, and death is but a form of sleep.

*2. *Connotative language*   Mistral's word choices convey the joy of life. Examples include: "a flower's freshness" (line 2), "a smiling verse" (line 5), "heavenly violets" (line 7), "the man who breaks into song" (line 10), "a skylark's bursting heavenward" (line 15), and "God is putting me to sleep" (line 20).

*3. *Figurative language.*   Mistral's use of metaphor and personification conveys the beauty of life through the beauty of nature. Examples include: "I glean/this truth . . . life is the gold and sweetness of wheat" (lines 1–3), "the wind blows a hon-eyed breath" (line 8), and "a lily can ensnare our gaze" (line 12).

4. *Lyric poem*   "Serene Words" is a lyric poem in that it expresses the personal mood of the speaker, who, in this case, is Mistral. It also emphasizes pictorial detail rather than a story.

WRITING ABOUT LITERATURE

1. *Expository analysis of contrast*   Call students' attention to the directions and suggestions in the textbook assignment with regard to content and organization. Remind them of the importance of using direct quotations. (See **A.L.T.** questions 1–3 above.)

2. *Creative writing: A poem about comfort*   Call students' attention to the directions in the textbook assignment. Remind them of the importance of detail. **(PLJ)**

FURTHER READING

Mistral, Gabriela, *Selected Poems of Gabriela Mistral.*

Rosendo's Tale
JORGE LUIS BORGES

INTRODUCING THE STORY

On the surface, "Rosendo's Tale" is an action-packed story about the life of a tough in the old days in Argentina. Below that surface, it is the thought-provoking story of the narrator's psychological development from a youth who lets himself be manipulated by others into proving his courage and skill into an adult who is self-confident and independent enough not to let anyone manipulate him, no matter what the cost to his reputation. In the process, Rosendo has learned about life's fragility and its value, and, in the end, he discards his old life in favor of one over which he has greater control.

Written late in Borges's life, "Rosendo's Tale" was created to be the companion piece to "Streetcorner Man," one of his earliest short stories. "Streetcorner Man" tells the same story, but it is told by a narrator who views Rosendo as a coward. In a commentary about "Rosendo's Tale," Borges says that the later version depicts a "character who sees through the romantic nonsense and childish vanity of dueling, and finally attains manhood and sanity."

In "Rosendo's Tale," the antagonist, the Butcher, functions as Rosendo's double: early in the text in the sense of his being Rosendo's mirror image, and later in the sense of his representing Rosendo's darker side or doppelgänger. Early in the story, the Butcher is almost identical to Rosendo in appearance, backgound, skill, attitude, and behavior. However, his relationship to Rosendo changes once Rosendo becomes more inner-directed and no longer caters to the opinions of others. Then, the Butcher represents Rosendo's insecure and aggressive side, an aspect of the double known as the doppelgänger.

Paradoxically, the character in this story who appears to be the coward is actually the one who is brave, since Rosendo has the courage to think for himself and to act with independence and judgment. Everyone present is amazed when he ignores the Butcher's challenge to his reputation. However, they are unaware that the behavior and death of Luis Irala, Rosendo's valued friend and alter ego, has laid the foundation for Rosendo's decision in this similar situation. Borges, in his comments on "Rosendo's Tale," considers Rosendo's decision to be the mark of maturity and sanity.

PLJ: To what extent, if any, do you let the opinions of others influence your attitudes and behavior? What factors determine whom you choose to follow and whom you choose to ignore?

Literary Terms: allusion, alter ego, characterization, doppelgänger, exposition, flashback, foreshadowing, irony, limited omniscience, narrative perspective, paradox, symbol, theme

COMPREHENSION QUESTIONS

1. Why does Rosendo talk with the author? (to give him the correct version of a particular incident)
2. How did Rosendo learn to handle a knive? (as a child, used charred sticks as knives in play-duels)
3. How did Rosendo happen to kill Garmendia? (Garmendia challenged Rosendo to a knife duel and lost.)
4. What advantage exists for Rosendo in signing a confession? (Rosendo freed in a few days)
5. What is Rosendo's next job? (party tough guy who gets out the vote)
6. Why does Irala fight? (doesn't want to be called a coward)
7. What advice does Rosendo give Irala? (ignore other people's views and unloving women)
8. What happens to Irala? (gets killed in knife duel)
9. What does Rosendo notice about the Butcher? (Butcher looks and acts like Rosendo)
10. What decision does Rosendo make at the end of the story? (refuses to fight the Butcher and leaves to begin a new life)

UNDERSTANDING THE STORY:
POSSIBLE ANSWERS

1. *Effect of passage of time on understanding the past*   With the passage of time, a person can become less emotionally involved and more able to analyze the event in question. Experience can also be a great teacher. Seeing oneself in the behavior of others can provide insight, and later experiences may create a pattern that also leads to insight.

*2. *Effect of Rosendo's experience with Garmendia on Rosendo*   Rosendo's experience with Garmendia teaches Rosendo how easy it is to kill or to be killed, even for no worthwhile reason.

3. *Rosendo's attitudes toward providence and toward Garmendia's death*   Rosendo's attitude toward Garmendia's death reveals the unpredictable nature of a duel: "almost without thinking"; "a minute when anything might have happened." In contrast, Rosendo's remark about providence implies the existence of a divine plan underlying human behavior. In this instance both the serendipitous outcome of the duel and its providential effect on Rosendo's future have worked in Rosendo's favor.

*4. *Effect of Luis Irala's death on Rosendo's attitudes and behavior*   Irala's death reinforces what Rosendo learned from killing Garmendia: how easy it is to kill or to get killed, and for no worthwhile reason.

*5. *Why Butcher makes Rosendo feel ashamed*   The Butcher's behavior is adolescent and foolish, motivated only by the Butcher's need to prove his skill with a knife and his superiority to Rosendo. Seeing that attitude in the Butcher makes Rosendo ashamed of the fact that he has felt and acted the same as the Butcher.

*6. *Why Rosendo decides to lead a new life*   Rosendo has become old enough to value being alive. Gratuitous violence no longer excites him. He has learned from his own and Luis Irala's experiences that it is all too easy to die for unimportant reasons. He also knows his own courage and skill. Since he has no need to prove anything to anyone, these insights about life and death motivate him to create a new life for himself.

*7. *Rosendo's psychological development*   (a) As a youth, Rosendo went along with the games of his peers, including pretend knife fights. He exhibited no independent thinking. His goal was to acquire skill among his peers.

(b) As an adolescent, Rosendo chose gaucho outlaws as his role models. This involved accepting any and all challenges, risking his life, and proving his skill. Again, he exhibited no independent thinking. His goal was to win the respect and admiration of others through his courage and skill in knife duels.

(c) As an adult, Rosendo exhibits independent thinking. He decides that he values life too much to risk death needlessly, and he has the self-esteem to disregard what others will think of his behavior.

*8. *Themes*   (a) People who have the courage to live according to their own, independent convictions live more satisfying lives. (b) People who let the opinions of others determine their behavior can never be at peace. (c) Experience teaches valuable lessons to those who are observant and willing to reevaluate their attitudes.

*9. *Appeal of knife-fighters*   Knife-fighters appeal to Borges because they have to make decisions that involve life and death. Therefore, they live at the crux of life. How they choose to act reveals their values. In the end, Rosendo's behavior affirms the value of life.

ANALYZING LITERARY TECHNIQUE: POSSIBLE ANSWERS

1. *Exposition*   The exposition relates this story to an earlier version. It explains the new point of view and indicates that the story will be an argument against the earlier and different point of view.

2. *Flashback*   The flashback permits Rosendo to present his story selectively, with attention only to the details he now finds important. It also permits him to interpret his earlier behavior in light of hindsight.

3. *Foreshadowing*   Both Rosendo's attitude toward the cockfight and his advice to Luis Irala predict how he is likely to react to the Butcher's challenge. Foreshadowing makes Rosendo's behavior in the end consistent, plausible, and courageous.

4. *Irony*   (a) It is ironic that Rosendo gives Luis Irala advice that he himself did not follow in his own life, even though Irala has greater reason to fight than Rosendo did. The advice reveals Rosendo's new emotional maturity.

(b) It is ironic that Rosendo doesn't understand the behavior of the cocks when he lives among people who behave in the same mindless way and, in the past, he has behaved that way himself. This also reveals Rosendo's new emotional maturity.

*5. *Butcher as Rosendo's double, or doppelgänger*   The concepts of the double and the doppelgänger refer to the Butcher's relationship to Rosendo, since the Butcher functions first as a mirror image of Rosendo's public self (one aspect of the double) and later as the worst side of Rosendo (the aspect of the double that is known as the doppelgänger). Although Rosendo and the Butcher share a similar appearance and reputation, Rosendo becomes able to see the Butcher as his old, other-directed and needlessly aggressive adolescent self, and he feels ashamed.

*6. *Symbolism of cockfight*   The cockfight symbolizes the senseless, merciless dueling of the gaucho outlaws and the other toughs in that society. Subconsciously, it becomes connected in Rosendo's mind with the challenges one knife-fighter hurls at another in order to prove his courage and skill.

 7. *Narrative perspective*   In this instance, the first person narrator is reliable (in contrast with the view of another narrator in the earlier version of the story). The author, who introduces the tale, lets Rosendo tell his own story, and the lessons that he learns from his experiences attest to the reliability of his explanation.

*8. *Paradox*   It is paradoxical that a courageous person can appear to be a coward in the eyes of the group by choosing independent behavior in preference to the actions that the group advocates.

WRITING ABOUT LITERATURE

 1. *Expository essay applying quotations from Borges's "Streetcorner Man" to "Rosendo's Tale"*   Call students' attention to the quotations and directions in the textbook assignment. Pertinent quotations from "Rosendo's Tale" include: *(a)* "I got the jump on him almost without thinking"; *(b)* "There was a minute when anything might have happened and . . . it was all over"; *(c)* "That night I saw how easy it was to kill a man or to get killed"; *(d)* "If you kill him, you get put away; if he kills you, you go six feet under"; *(e)* "So you're going to risk your peace and quiet. . . ."; *(f)* "He was out to kill and he got killed." (See **U.S.** question 8 above.)

 2. *Expository character sketch of Rosendo's emotional development*   Call students' attention to the suggestions in the textbook assignment. Rosendo changes from being dependent on the opinions of others (he is capable of being manipulated into acting against his own self-interest) to being self-confident (advice to Luis Irala) to, finally, being self-directed and self-sufficient (able to ignore the Butcher's challenge and begin a new life). (See **U.S.** questions 2 and 4–9, and **A.L.T.** questions 5–6 and 8 above.)

 3. *Creative writing: A dialogue about whether Rosendo is a coward*   (See **U.S.** questions 2 and 4–9, and **A.L.T.** questions 5–6 and 8 above.) **(PLJ)**

FURTHER READING

Borges, Jorge Luis, *The Aleph and Other Stories; Ficciones; Labyrinths; Dreamtigers; A Personal Anthology; Borges: A Reader.*

The Word

PABLO NERUDA

INTRODUCING THE POEM

Neruda's "The Word" is a tribute to language. From the opening image of "born in the blood," Neruda values language as an inherent and integral part of life itself. He moves from a poetic description of its birth (stanza 1), to its ancient history and development (stanza 2), to its value as connection and communication with peoples past, present, and future (stanza 3). He then returns to the first word (stanza 4) with the powerful chain reaction that its sound set in motion. He moves beyond nouns to verbs because verbs "blend existence with essence" (stanza 5). Neruda considers communication to be the essence of life and its absence to cause the death of the human spirit: "not to speak is to die" (stanza 6). In fact, he believes that language defines a human being and proves a person's existence: "I utter and I am" (stanza 7). He concludes with a toast to language, for it gives "life to life itself" (stanza 8).

"The Word" is also a tribute to metaphor, for Neruda conveys the nature and power of language through his striking use of figurative language. Images tumble forth like jewels from a treasure chest: for example, "lands that had returned to stone"; "pain took to the roads"; "dressed up in terror and sighing"; "electricity of its beauty"; and "hereditary goblet." Even in translation, the poem's beauty and power impress themselves on the mind of the reader.

PLJ: How important is language to you? If you could speak, but could not read and write, what of value to you would be lost? What if your community also lacked any written language?

Literary Terms: allusion, figurative language, irony, metaphor

COMPREHENSION QUESTIONS

1. According to the poem, what is the function of words? (to communicate)
2. According to the poem, what is the value of words? (communication in present; connection with past and future)
3. According to the poem, what part of speech is most important? (verb)
4. What word associated with birth and life opens and closes the poem? (blood)
5. At the end of the poem, what great ability do words have? (give life to life)

UNDERSTANDING THE POEM: POSSIBLE ANSWERS

1. *What motivated first word*   (1) terror: fear of danger and death, need to protect self and others; (2) sighing: desire to express love, wishes, and concerns.

2. *"Inheritance" of words (stanza 3)*   Words connect readers with the thoughts, feelings, and experiences of others across time and through space. Words give pleasure and instruction, and literature enriches the experience of living. In addition, prior knowledge is often the building material of new knowledge.

3. *Verbs*   Some verbs are intransitive, expressing being and existence. Other verbs are transitive, expressing action. The combination of the two types includes all aspects of living, including both what is temporary and what is permanent.

4. *"Not to speak is to die" (line 45)*   Neruda's hyperbole emphasizes the importance of written and oral language to human beings. He is exaggerating in order to make a point.

5. *Themes*   (a) Language is critical to human life: "not to speak is to die" (line 45); (b) Language defines what it is to be human: "I utter and I am" (line 53); (c) Language gives form to life experiences: "words give . . . life to life itself" (lines 67–68).

ANALYZING LITERARY TECHNIQUE: POSSIBLE ANSWERS

*1. *Metaphor in Stanza 1*   Flight and the beating of wings suggest a bird, which is appropriate, given that its travels are described at the beginning of Stanza 2.

*2. *Metaphors in Stanza 2*   (a) "lands that had returned to stone" (line 8): refers to the changes in weather that caused severe drought, turned arable land into deserts, and forced people to leave their homelands in search of a more hospitable and nurturing environment; (b) "when pain took to the roads" (line 10): refers to the mental and physical condition of those who were forced to relocate, and implies food shortages, inadequate clothing, difficult travel conditions, and danger from animals and hostile peoples; (c) "new lands and water reunited/to sow their word anew" (lines 12–13): refers to the place of relocation, which had water in the form of lakes or rivers and rainfall so that the environment could provide food for populations of animals and human beings.

Just as people planted farmland for physical sustenance, they planted their language for both physical and intellectual sustenance, in that they used the language they had brought with them and added words to it based on their new experiences and their contact with new peoples. Lead students to see that metaphor functions as a type of shorthand or shortcut by suggesting great detail through the use of a few highly suggestive words; appeals to the senses and the imagination; and enriches what is abstract by approaching it through what is concrete.

3. *Stanza 7: Allusion to Descartes*   The statement "I think; therefore I am" affirms that humans' ability to think proves that they exist. Neruda alludes to this statement with the paraphrase "I utter and I am," the connotation being that speech is what distinguishes human beings from all other forms of life and from all objects. Neruda elevates human speech to the position of the prime human quality. Since language is the verbal and written expression of thought, a natural connection exists between Descartes' statement and Neruda's statement.

*4. *Metaphor of the cup*   Words contain meaning as cups contain liquid, so words are cups of meaning. The hereditary goblet refers to language that is inherited from one's parents and one's total culture.

*5. *Metaphor of blood*   According to the poem, words possess the life-force of blood. When Neruda says that words are "born in the blood" (lines 1–2), the poet is connecting words with human beings. Words are an inherent part of being human; they are latent in infants when they are born, and they develop along with the human being. At the end of the poem, the verb is "blood" because it is both the source and vitality of life (lines 63–68).

*6. *Metaphor of water*   Water possesses the qualities of movement, flexibility, fluidity, continuity, and variations in mass. Thus, water is a good metaphor for language, which also develops, changes, and increases across time and space. In stanza 4, the "first word" was only a drop or a ripple that became a great cataract (lines 26–30).

WRITING ABOUT LITERATURE

1. *Expository theme analyzing Neruda's use of metaphor*   Call student's attention to the directions in the textbook assignment with regard to content and organization. Possible metaphors include: water, blood, cup, and wine. (See questions **A.L.T.** 1–2 and 4–6 above.)

2. *Creative writing: a poem involving history and synonyms of a verb*   Call students' attention to the directions in the textbook assignment with regard to procedure, content, and style. Possible verbs include: *walk, talk, eat, work,* and *play.* **(PLJ).**

FURTHER READING

Neruda, Pablo, *Twenty Love Poems and a Song of Despair,* "The Heights of Machu Picchu," in *Selected Poems;* "The Word," in *Memoirs.*

The Inextinguishable Race

SILVINA OCAMPO

INTRODUCING THE STORY

"The Inextinguishishable Race" is a satire on modern society reminiscent of *Gulliver's Travels.* In Ocampo's tale, children rule the city in which they and their parents live. In a striking reversal of roles and values, the children perform all of society's tasks while their parents stay home and relax with hobbies. The smaller one's size, the better. All aspects of living are child-sized, and the children refuse to consider the needs of anyone larger than they are. They view adults who complain about "inconveniences" as greedy, and they are wary of any adult small enough to masquerade as a child. Although these children are growing progressively smaller, and therefore are finding it increasingly difficult to perform the tasks on which the welfare of their society depends, they will destroy their society rather than share their power. They do not see anything myopic in this attitude, being convinced that unless they rule as dictators, their race will die. Thus, Ocampo is depicting a world in which the principal values are topsy-turvy: what the children value as good is evil; what they view as salvation will bring annihilation; and what they consider to be human is inhumane.

In his closing remarks, the young narrator bridges the gap between his society and the real, modern world by assuming that the increasing myopia of his group reflects an increasingly human world view. Ocampo implies that the "humanity" of adults in modern societies is just as self-centered, myopic, inhumane, and paranoid as the humanity of these children. Like the children in Ocampo's story, adults in the real world strongly resist relinquishing their power, at home or at work, nationally or internationally. Like the children in the story, many adults are prejudiced against anyone who is different, with gender, race, religion, and nationality being divisive issues in modern societies. Finally, like the children in the story, many adults in the real world focus only on the quality of their own lives. They do not care that others live under inferior and unsatisfactory conditions, and they see no connection between how they treat others and their own future.

PLJ: To what extent do you try to see the society in which you live as others view it? What are the advantages of trying to be objective about oneself and one's society? What are the disadvantages?

Literary Terms: characterization, foreshadowing, irony, narrative perspective, satire, symbol, theme, unreliable narrator

COMPREHENSION QUESTIONS

1. What two aspects of the city does the narrator first notice? (perfect; small)
2. Who runs the city? (the children)
3. How are the parents viewed? (selfish; passionate)
4. What is good about being a parent? (all play; no work)
5. What is bad about being a parent? (food portions, clothing, and furniture too small)
6. Who are the enemies of the ruling class? (small adults who pretend to be children)
7. What worries the children? (Their size is decreasing.)
8. What is the children's primary concern? (Their race will be overthrown or will die out.)

UNDERSTANDING THE STORY: POSSIBLE ANSWERS

1. *Conditions within city*   The city appears perfect, in that their society benefits the ruling class, the children. Everything is scaled to their needs, and they are in control of their own lives.

However, the city is imperfect, in that the children feel overworked. Because they are shrinking in size, they feel forced to use equipment that is too large and too heavy for them. They refuse to give adults any responsibilities because they view them as potential enemies.

2. *Parents as passionate*   The narrator views passion as a factor that distinguishes parents from children. However, the children are passionate (even apparently violent) in their hatred of those whom they view as a threat to their power. Although they are in control of their community, they still indulge in childish temper tantrums.

*3. *Characterization of children*   The children are inhumane, dictatorial, and self-deluding. They view adults as "creatures" who are selfish, greedy, and unscrupulous. They refuse to scale any aspect of their society to adult needs. They refuse to admit adults into any area of power: They would destroy their society (and themselves) rather than relinquish any part of their power.

4. *Themes*   In the words of Lord Acton (1834–1902), "Power tends to corrupt and absolute power corrupts absolutely."

ANALYZING LITERARY TECHNIQUE: POSSIBLE ANSWERS

1. *Foreshadowing of the reality beneath appearance*   The fact that the child-narrator is "bleary-eyed" and accuses the parents of "selfishness" foreshadows that all is not as it appears.

*2. *Use of irony*   (*a*) "A child's world," the symbol of innocence, purity, and goodness, is transformed here into sophisticated evil:

(*b*) Becoming "more and more human," the symbol of progress, wisdom, and increasing humanity, is transformed here into what is regressive and destructive of both others and self.

(*c*) Other ironies include the fact that children, not adults, rule the society; the city appears to be perfect, but life is difficult for both adults and children; and the children view adults as selfish, greedy, and unscrupulous, when they themselves behave like the adults they are criticizing.

*3. *Choice of title*   Ocampo probably chose this title because it is consistent with the ironic nature of the story. The children think that their attitudes and actions will preserve their race, whereas their selfishness, paranoia, and myopia actually will be self-defeating. In addition, the title emphasizes the story's satiric aspects. The story reminds the reader that similar behavior in other societies has not yet been rooted out, and that certain negative aspects of human nature may be inextinguishable.

4. *Narrative perspective*   The third-person narrator is unreliable. She begins by connecting "small" and "perfect," and follows with a "highly progressive race of pygmies." Because she is correct that everything is small, the reader expects that everything is also perfect and progressive, which is untrue.

The child-narrator is also unreliable. He praises his society, but his point of view is that of a member of the ruling class. By using a first-person child-narrator,

Ocampo is able to show the reader how the narrator views himself, his group, his parents, and his society. No other consciousness intrudes to give objectivity or a conflicting point of view. The child-narrator makes no ethical judgments, and he cannot face the question of whether the children are growing weaker. Any adult in that society would have a different perspective, one that reflects the adults' problems and involves criticism of the ruling class.

5. *Symbolism of children*   In this story, the children symbolize adults in modern societies. In a role reversal, the children live in their world the way Ocampo believes that adults live in theirs, with selfishness, myopia, and paranoia. Both groups think only of satisfying their own needs and view everyone else as a threat to their future well-being.

   The children in this story, while symbolic of adults, actually think and behave like young children. Young children are naturally selfish and incapable of foresight. They cannot see the consequences of their attitudes and behavior. For example, if two children have a tug-of-war over a mutually desired toy and the toy breaks in the process of being pulled, each child will be delighted that the other did not get it, rather than sorry that the toy broke. In the story, the child-narrator displays the same type of selfish and myopic thinking when he says that they never will allow anyone else to have an important role in their society, and that, if this is the choice, they will preserve the future of their race by destroying their machines, electrical plants, and fresh water reserves.

6. *Satire*   The story is a satire in that it ridicules the values and myopia of the ruling classes in modern society. Just as the reader is aghast at the attitudes and behavior of the children in this fictional society, so the author is aghast at the identical attitudes and behavior of adults who thrive in modern societies.

WRITING ABOUT LITERATURE

1. *Expository writing: character sketch of the child-narrator and his group*   Call students' attention to the directions in the textbook assignment. Remind them to use direct quotations to support their ideas. (See **U.S.** question 3 above.)

2. *Expository essay: Ocampo's use of irony*   Call students' attention to the directions in the textbook assignment. Irony is the major source of the story's power. Remind students about the importance of using direct quotations to support their ideas. (See **A.L.T.** questions 2 and 3 above.)

3. *Creative writing: parental revolt*   Call student's attention to the directions in the textbook assignment regarding content. Emphasize the goal of presenting a convincing argument. Arguments in favor of revolt would include what adults would have to gain if they were to win: (*a*) food, clothing, and furniture of the proper size; (*b*) personal freedom; (*c*) a better run society, with more goods more easily produced for more people. Arguments in favor of peace would include what adults have to lose by revolting: (*a*) loss of leisure; (*b*) imprisonment or death; (*c*) greater physical discomfort and deprivation; (*d*) the collapse of society. **(PLJ)**

FURTHER READING

Ocampo, Silvina, *Leopoldina's Dream.*

The Third Bank of the River

JOÃO GUIMARÃES ROSA

INTRODUCING THE STORY

"The Third Bank of the River" is the poignant story of a son (the narrator) whose dutiful and orderly father leaves his wife and young children without explanation in order to live the remainder of his life floating in a boat in the middle of the nearby river. The son respects and admires his father. The greater part of a lifetime passes while the father in his boat and the son on the shore continue to renounce the joys of other human relationships.

The son lives only for his father, who remains silent. Although he describes his father's actions, neither the narrator nor the reader ever knows the father's thoughts or emotions. It is possible that the father devotes his life to asserting, by his actions, the lack of any meaning in the universe, and that he lives for the day when his son will take his place and continue his philosophical statement. However, other reasons may govern his actions, including his psychological need to exist as an independent person and his feeling that he must separate himself from his family in order to achieve this autonomy. It is consistent with Rosa's philosophy of life to interpret the father's behavior either as having no explanation at all, or as having a multitude of explanations, any one of which may or may not be correct. Rosa's decision to have the father remain mute and to tell the story from the point of view of the son, whose knowledge is limited, reflects this view of life.

To Rosa, life is an enigma. It is a natural phenomenon that, like the river, is constantly moving and changing. Part of life is rational; part is irrational. Reality has different faces that may be completely visible, partly visible, or invisible. The "third bank of the river" symbolizes the irrational dimension of reality, and the narrator speaks for the author when he states: "Nobody is crazy. Or maybe everybody."

Although the son thinks they are alike, both father and son learn that they are not identical. The son offers to take his father's place, but when his father accepts that offer, the son is unable to continue his father's silent protest against a world devoid of meaning, and he lacks his father's courage to divorce himself irrevocably from life. His father can survive (and possibly can only survive) in an emotional desert, absorbed by and locked into his own autonomous solitude, but the son cannot. Although he has already sacrificed most of his life for his father, his failure to relinquish the rest of it destroys him.

The reader who accepts the son's remarks about his family and himself as those of a reliable narrator can find a psychological basis both for his father's and his own behavior. The story includes the following details: (*1*) The mother appears to rule the submissive father and the children; (2) The father deserts his family but remains within their sight; (3) The son states that he feels anxious, bad, and guilty, and he juxtaposes these feelings with thoughts of his father's desertion; (4) The son is the only family member who chooses not to marry and remains home alone so that he can devote his life to his father, even though he views his father as an "impediment"; (5) In the end, when he cannot adopt his father's way of life, the son feels that he is not a man but "what never should have been."

These details suggest that the father has no viable masculine identity as long as he is a passive male in a home dominated by his wife. He asserts himself by leaving home. He remains within sight so that his family will see that he continues to exist. With these actions, he suddenly achieves both independence and importance. It is important to realize that the behavior of both the father and the narrator can symbolize the relationships of real people. Real individuals may find family life intolerable for a variety of reasons, including the possibility that they may never have resolved their own questions of identity and autonomy as they grew up, and, therefore, they retreat from any emotional investment that they fear will stir up their own old issues. If these parents remain with their families, they remove themselves emotionally from them. They may become "workaholics," because their work serves a double purpose. It provides personal satisfaction and success and also a socially acceptable excuse for their lack of emotional involvement with their families. They may also retreat in front of television screens and behind housework.

The narrator's self-knowledge is limited to recognizing his feelings without understanding anything about them. Those who wish to analyze his psyche can examine the possible effects of his parents on his life as a little boy. They can consider his conscious and subconscious feelings about his mother, his father, and his developing male identity. They can consider his need for a male role model and the role that his father's behavior, both off and on the river, plays in his life. Finally, they can evaluate the closing paragraph, in which the narrator questions his masculinity because he cannot choose to live his father's kind of life.

The narrator and his father appear to have an instinctive mutual understanding. Until the climax, when the narrator breaks his promise, he views his father as his alter ego, or second self. Afterward, the narrator's reaction to his own behavior suggests the concept of the Shadow, or dual personality, in which the subconscious, fundamental self is quite different from the conscious, social self.

All young children make particular choices in order to acquire and keep the love and approval of their parents. Like the narrator, children who must cope with particular psychological idiosyncrasies in their parents may have to choose between identifying with their parents and being independent. Their need to remain connected with a parent may force them to sacrifice an independent life; however, independence may cause them to lose their necessary connection with their parent. Inevitably, such a choice is sad and unsatisfactory.

PLJ: How do you react to people whose behavior you do not understand? To what extent are you comfortable being different from members of your family? How do you react when they make you feel as if you are disappointing them by not conforming to their expectations?

Literary Terms: alter ego, characterization, climax, limited omniscience, narrative perspective, point of view, realism, setting, Shadow, symbolism, theme

COMPREHENSION QUESTIONS

1. What action does the narrator's father take? (leaves family and lives on river nearby)
2. How does the narrator's family react? (marry and move away as if father were dead)
3. How does the narrator react? (remains nearby to care for father)
4. What offer does the narrator make? (to take father's place)
5. What finally happens? (The father accepts the offer, but the son lacks the courage to make a commitment.)

UNDERSTANDING THE STORY: POSSIBLE ANSWERS

1. *Description of father*   The contrast between the father's earlier behavior and his desertion of his family reflects Rosa's premise that human behavior can be irrational.
2. *Why father abandons family*   There are several plausible explanations. (*a*) The father cannot handle the responsibility of a wife and children.

   (*b*) The father hates his wife because he lets her control his life. He belatedly compensates for his passivity in his marriage and acts upon his emotional need to assert his masculine identity and autonomy as a separate person. He feels that he can only do this by leaving home and remaining visible in order to prove that he is the master of his own life and that his family cannot make him meet its needs.

   (*c*) The father believes that life (the universe and human behavior) is absurd. He has the courage to live according to his convictions, and his living in the boat is his public statement (in the form of a silent protest) that all of life is pretense and illusion.

   (*d*) The father has become insane, and his actions are mad.

   (*e*) The father's physical separation symbolizes the emotional separation that fathers and mothers may feel forced to make in real life when circumstances in their adult lives remind them of their own old, unresolved issues of identity and independence.
3. *Why father remains visible to family*   Some possible responses include: (*a*) The father wants to retain some connection with his family, tenuous as it is. (*b*) The father acts as he does in order to feel as if he is a separate and important person. Having someone in his family sympathize with him and be attentive to his physical needs reinforces the success of his desertion. (*c*) Although he feels compelled to choose a strange act, the father wants to provide a good masculine model for the narrator by proving that he is an autonomous, independent male. (*d*) The father's public statement of his autonomy has meaning only for people who know him.

Strangers would simply think that he is insane. (*e*) The father's actions reflect his insanity.

4. *How father could return home*   The father could return home only if he felt that his autonomy would be assured. If he were not able to acknowledge his feelings, to himself or to his family, it would be difficult to discuss the issues involved. If his presence was important to the family, the family would have to respect his needs, and the power structure within the family would have to change.

5. *Father's right*   Opinions will vary as to whether the father's primary responsibility is to himself or to his family. Many people solve their need for autonomy by remaining at home but keeping a psychological distance from their families.

6. *Narrator's affection and respect for father*   (*a*) The narrator admires his father for having the courage to leave his domineering wife and to assert his masculinity and independence. (*b*) He admires his father for having the courage to act upon his convictions, even though the idea that life lacks any meaning is frightening. (*c*) The narrator's fears about his father mask fears about himself; the narrator's affection and respect for his father mask negative feelings about his father that the narrator cannot accept.

7. *Why narrator attributes his own behavior to father*   All children need to have wonderful parents. Those who don't have them may fabricate them. The narrator creates the father he wishes he had. That father is psychologically true in that the narrator believes, with part of his mind, that the ideal father exists. However, part of the narrator recognizes reality and the lie.

8. *Why narrator never marries and remains near father*   (*a*) The narrator feels responsible for his father because he loves and respects him. If the narrator were to leave, his father would not be able to survive in the life he has chosen.

   (*b*) The fact that the narrator never marries reflects the psychological damage his father has caused by being such a passive husband and father, and which he has exacerbated by abandoning his family.

   (*c*) That the father needs the narrator is part rationalization. Presumably, the father would have accepted help from another family member. However, the narrator needs a father-figure with whom to identify psychologically as a male and so remains home near his father.

9. *Significance of "Nobody is crazy. Or maybe everybody."*   The narrator's statement reflects Rosa's view that human behavior can be irrational as well as rational, and that any behavior can have many different interpretations.

*10. *Why the narrator volunteers to exchange places*   The narrator may love and admire his father and wish to ease his old age by substituting for him, as a child takes over his or her parents' business. Alternatively, the narrator may feel responsible for his father's welfare because he needs to be like his father in order to confirm his own masculinity.

   The father accepts because the narrator's offer implies that he accepts his father's right to be autonomous. If so, then the father no longer needs to assert himself. However, the narrator is terrified by the exchange. He cannot face the personal consequences of acting on his words. The narrator may not have the same need as his father to assert his autonomy regardless of what that entails. He may lack the courage or the madness to live in his father's world, or his sharing of his father's philosophy of life may have been an illusion. He finds that he cannot actively adopt what may be his father's view, that life is devoid of meaning. He also finds he cannot permanently cut himself off from society.

11. *Meaning of narrator's concluding remarks* By the end of the story, the narrator is quite psychologically disturbed. He views his actions as a catastrophic failure. Not only has he disappointed his father and thus severed his one remaining relationship, but his failure to be like his role model has made him lose whatever shaky confidence he had.

12. *Responsibility for narrator's life* The narrator, his father, and his mother are all responsible for the narrator's life. As a child, his reactions were determined by the interrelationship of many factors: his own psychological and chemical framework; the nature of his parents; and their relationship to each other, to his siblings, and to him. It may have been better for the narrator if his father had been more assertive at home. However, the adult narrator is responsible for his own life. If he feels psychologically damaged, he can make an effort to repair the damage.

ANALYZING LITERARY TECHNIQUE: POSSIBLE ANSWERS

1. *Relationship between setting and plot* Rosa set the story by a river because of the symbolic connection he makes between a river and human life. Both are natural phenomena that change as they continuously move from their origin to their end.

   Many in the field of psychology consider water to symbolize the human unconscious. The narrator fears the loss of his masculinity when he cannot act like his father. At the end, he incoherently loses himself in the waters of the river, as the symbol of his father (''between the long shores'') and as the source of the comfort and sustenance of the mother's womb (''inside the river'').

2. *Narrative perspective* By using a first-person narrator, with his limited omniscience and unreliability, Rosa forces the reader to experience everything through the narrator's perceptions. The father's motivations, thoughts, and feelings remain open to individual interpretation, since Rosa makes him silent. An omniscient author or an informed third-person narrator would be able to understand the motivations, thoughts, feelings, and behavior of every character. Rosa's choice of narrator is consistent with his (Rosa's) view that no one can really know and understand someone else (or even, ultimately, oneself).

3. *Realism* The content of Rosa's bizarre story contrasts with the traditional realist style in which he tells it. Such a style accepts the extraordinary as ordinary.

*4. *Climax* The climax occurs when the narrator cannot keep his word and take his father's place. It is critical to both the philosophical and psychological aspects of the story. The narrator cannot actively adopt his father's view that life is devoid of meaning and permanently cut himself off from society. The narrators' reaction to his failure provides a major clue to the structure of his psyche, which then explains all of his actions and emotions as he has described them. His concern about his masculinity reveals him to be functioning psychologically like a little boy, who can identify himself as a male only by being just like his father. Concern about his masculinity also ties in with the narrator's self-imposed obligation to his father throughout his life, his rejection of the idea of marriage, his description of his mother's role in the home of his childhood, and his feelings of anxiety, guilt, and pain.

5. *River as symbol*   Since a river has only two banks, the "third bank" symbolizes the irrational and mysterious aspect of life. The river itself symbolizes human life. Both are fluid, flexible, and constantly changing.

WRITING ABOUT LITERATURE

1. *Expository writing justifying or criticizing the narrator's change of mind*   Call students' attention to the directions, the questions, and the suggestions in the textbook assignment with regard to content. The narrator can be condemned or justified, depending on what a person believes he owes the father, what he owes himself, and which obligation is the more important of the two. (See **U.S.** question 10, and **A.L.T.** question 4 above.) **(PLJ)**
2. *Creative writing: Story from the father's point of view*   Call students' attention to the questions suggested in the textbook assignment.

FURTHER READING

Rosa, João Guimarães, *"The Third Bank of the River" and Other Stories.*

The Tree
MARÍA LUISA BOMBAL

INTRODUCING THE STORY

"The Tree" is a story of life without love. It describes a young woman's thoughts about her younger self and her past marriage as she listens to a piano recital. Brígida's fantasy life responds to the various musical passages and culminates, with the end of the concert, in greater self-knowledge. Bombal uses a combination of psychological and poetic devices to create this complex portrait of a young adult whose experience with criticism as a child has devastated her youth and adolescence and led her into a disastrous marriage.

Bombal tells Brígida's story by using a third-person narrator who enters Brígida's mind for most of the story. However, Bombal's choice of narrative perspective permits her to combine her interest in psychological realism with visually and symbolically textured settings.

First, the characteristics of each piece of music suggest the direction of Brígida's thoughts: Mozart's capricious spirit suggests thoughts of her own youth; Beethoven's rhythms evoke the development of frustration and disappointment in her marriage; and Chopin's sadness provokes her to dwell on her melancholy acceptance of her sterile married life.

Accompanying each musical selection is an appropriate symbol of water. Mozart's youthful vitality suggests the happy and youthful image of singing water in tall fountains. Beethoven's rhythms suggest the ebb and flow of the sea, which envelops Brígida and controls her as her marriage does. Finally, Chopin's melancholy strains evoke the sadness and agitation of rain and symbolize Brígida's futile efforts to adjust to her marriage.

Once Brígida is involved with thoughts of her marriage, the tree outside her dressing-room window becomes the rich symbol of her fantasy life, which makes it possible for her to survive the sterility of her marriage. When the tree is suddenly removed, nothing can shield Brígida from the reality of her life. Paradoxically, all her physical comforts do not bring happiness. She courageously confronts her emotional starvation and divorces Luis.

Bombal is considered a surrealist writer because of her interest in the human psyche, her use of unusual symbolism, and her striking use of language. One of Bombal's most striking images is Luis's description of Brígida as "a necklace of birds," which is doubly symbolic in that the birds reflect Brígida's personality and the necklace reflects her relationship to Luis.

PLJ: What is your attitude toward failure? Do you prefer to aim high and risk not achieving your goals, or do you prefer to aim only for what you are certain that you can accomplish? What do you gain by the attempt? What do you lose by the failure? Which is better?

Literary Terms: characterization, connotative language, figurative language, irony, metaphor, narrative perspective, paradox, psychological realism, setting, surrealism, symbol

COMPREHENSION QUESTIONS

1. Where does this story take place? (at a piano concert)
2. What is the first part of the story about? (Brígida's youth)
3. Describe Brígida's husband. (father's friend; workaholic businessperson)
4. Describe Brígida's marriage. (sterile; unloving)
5. What happens to Brígida's great source of comfort? (The tree is cut down.)

UNDERSTANDING THE STORY:
POSSIBLE ANSWERS

1. *Effect of father's view of Brígida*   Brígida's father gave her the impression that she was incapable of doing what everyone else could do and that he expected nothing in the way of accomplishment from her. His view became a self-fulfilling prophecy. Brígida was happy not to worry about failing to meet another person's demands, even if that meant being considered stupid. At eighteen she is happy to be "a necklace of birds": silly, playful, and lazy.

Brígida operates on the mistaken belief that if she doesn't try, she won't fail. (It is mistaken because her lack of effort guarantees her failure.) She accepts the fact that others think that she is stupid with ambivalence, believing that they therefore will not expect anything from her and will not be disappointed in her. This compensation comes at great personal cost: Brígida leads a boring life, no one admires her, and she has no friends.

2. *"To be intelligent you should begin from childhood"*   Brígida is correct to the extent that it is easier to begin when one is young, but motivation and effort can accomplish miracles. Also, since her insights into herself and Luis reveal that she actually is quite intelligent rather than retarded, the comment reflects Brígida's low self-esteem.

3. *Why Brígida conceals anger from Luis*   Brígida fears confrontation because she risks criticism and losing Luis's acceptance of her. Therefore, she responds like a child by taking refuge in the safety of sleep and silence. In this way, Brígida inadvertently leads Luis to think that she no longer loves him and prepares for the dissolution of their marriage.

4. *Brígida's problem with Luis*   Brígida's problem is that Luis treats her like a child or an object, rather than like an adult. She wants to feel that he loves her and that her love is important to him. His question implies that he needs her love; however, his immediate acceptance of a loveless marriage destroys that possibility.

5. *Always and Never*   (a) *Always:* Life will always be irremediably mediocre. Luis will always ignore her needs and escape from them.

   (b) *Never:* Life will never contain love, excitement, and joy. Luis will never love her.

6. *Brígida's philosophy about happiness*   Brígida adopts this philosophy as a way of trying to accept the sterility of her marriage. However, when the tree is destroyed, Brígida confronts the quality of her life and rejects this philosophical rationalization. She divorces Luis and tries to create a more satisfying life for herself.

ANALYZING LITERARY TECHNIQUE: POSSIBLE ANSWERS

1. *Connection between setting and technique of psychological realism*   The setting is the concert hall, and the nature of each musical selection determines the path of Brígida's thoughts. Bombal weaves the two together so closely that a stream of consciousness, or a complex type of associative thinking, results. Not only does one thought lead to another, but the musical background also influence's Brígida's thought patterns.

2. *Narrative perspective*   The third-person narrator spends most of her time in Brígida's mind, giving the reader an intimate insight into her personality. However, because the narrator is separate from Brígida, the narrator is also able to provide striking descriptive passages that give the story added depth and texture.

3. *Irony*   It is ironic that Brígida is far more intelligent than she thinks she is. Her insights into people's lives, the condition of happiness, and, in the end, her own

needs are very sophisticated. Additionally, she is very sensitive and creative, as is clear by her imaginative responses to the music and to the tree.

*4. *Music as symbol* (*a*) Mozart's felicitous and capricious music evokes Brígida's memories of her youth and adolescence, in which she also was felicitous and capricious, lacking responsibility and devoting her energy to silly playfulness.

(*b*) Beethoven's undulating rhythms evoke Brígida's thoughts of her early marriage to Luis, in which she searched for a love that Luis was incapable of giving her.

(*c*) Chopin's melancholy tonalities evoke Brígida's thoughts about the final period of her marriage, in which she tried to resign herself to the sterility of her life and was driven to escape into the world of fantasy.

*5. *Water as a symbol* (*a*) During the concert, different associations are made with the three composers: *Mozart*—singing water in tall fountains symbolizes the tone of Mozart's music and the prevailing tone of Brígida's youth; *Beethoven*—the currents of the sea symbolize the rhythms of Beethoven's music and the ebb and flow of married life that encompasses Brígida's search for love and emotional satisfaction. In addition, the rhythms may have sexual connotations; *Chopin*—the melancholy agitation of the rain and the hidden waterfall symbolize the tone of Chopin's *Études* and Brígida's melancholy and agitated search for a way to accept the sterility of her married life.

(*b*) Brígida compares her dressing room to "a world submerged in an aquarium." In this image of water, the dressing room is both a magical retreat or escape and a place of artificiality and imprisonment. Brígida has found an escape from her father's house and a retreat from her unsatisfactory marriage, but she is still within Luis's house. Her lack of control is made apparent when the tree, which provides this green retreat, is cut down.

(*c*) Water as rain is also symbolic. The storm comes after Luis has violently left the house. The storm both reflects the mood of the marriage and prevents Brígida from taking action—she chooses not to leave Luis because she wants to listen to the rain in the tree.

*6. *Tree as symbol* (*a*) The tree symbolizes Brígida's emotional life; it is as fertile as Brígida's day-to-day life is sterile. It provides her with a refuge against reality and offers her a fantasy world in which she finds emotional solace. With the tree's removal, she finds herself forced to face reality, and she divorces Luis.

(*b*) "The Tree" as the story's title emphasizes the tree's role as the symbol of Brígida's emotional life.

*7. *"Necklace of birds"* (*a*) Birds symbolize Brígida in that both they and she "chirp" happily and flit from one pursuit to another.

(*b*) A necklace symbolizes Brígida in that, as a child, she liked to hug Luis by putting her arms around his neck; as Luis's wife, she is a decorative object that he wears or puts aside as he wishes.

*8. *Mirrors and windows* The mirrors in Brígida's dressing-room function as intensifiers, magnifying whatever they reflect: the earlier, magical world of green forests, mist, and firefly-like lamps, and the later, harsh reality of apartment windows and automobiles.

The windows serve as a way for Brígida to let light and life into her sterile world. It is important that Brígida is not seen looking into the mirrors (being self-reflective or self-centered), but is rather seen looking out the window (being directed towards connection with other living things).

WRITING ABOUT LITERATURE

1. *Expository writing: An analysis of Bombal's use of symbolism*   Call students' attention to the directions in the textbook assignment with regard to content and organization. Remind them of the importance of using direct quotations to support their ideas. (See **A.L.T.** questions 4–8 above.)
2. *Creative writing: Sequel describing Brígida's life after divorce*   Call students attention to the suggestions in the textbook assignment. **(PLJ)**
3. *Creative writing: This story from Luis's point of view*   Call students' attention to the questions suggested in the textbook assignment.

FURTHER READING

Bombal, María Luisa, *"New Islands" and Other Stories.*

Two Bodies
OCTAVIO PAZ

INTRODUCING THE POEM

In "Two Bodies," Paz describes the relationship between two people, probably lovers, and their relationship to the world in which they live. Using metaphor as a form of shorthand, the poet describes four different aspects of their relationship, each accompanied by a different relationship to the universe. The poem moves from the couple's being synchronized with each other and in harmony with the universe in which they exist (stanza 1); to their being static (together, but each preoccupied with self) in a universe that ignores them (stanza 2); to their being intertwined with one another in a universe where they must nourish and sustain each other (stanza 3); to their being confrontational or hostile in a universe that provokes friction between them (stanza 4); to their being mortal in a universe that is devoid of any intrinsic meaning (stanza 5).

The last stanza functions as the climax of the poem, in that it provides the pessimistic backdrop against which human relationships achieve significance. Given the inevitable mortality of human beings and, in Paz's view, the lack of any inherent meaning in the universe, human relationships are vitally important. Despite the limitations of any intimate relationship, love and friendship enrich lives that are fragile and brief, and they provide the only meaning and soul-satisfying values that are possible in the universe.

PLJ: Think about the people whom you know. To what extent, if any, do your relation-ships with different people differ? List the kinds of relationships that you have. Do you know anyone with whom your relationship varies from time to time? If so, list the varia-tions.

Literary Terms: existentialism, figurative language, metaphor, surrealism, symbol

COMPREHENSION QUESTIONS

1. How does the poet describe the position of the two bodies? (face to face)
2. What objects are the bodies compared to by the poet? (waves [line 2], stones [line 5], roots [line 8], knives [line 11], stars [line 14])
3. How does the poet describe the sky at the end of the poem? (empty)

UNDERSTANDING THE POEM: POSSIBLE ANSWERS

1. *Why face to face*   Face to face implies the possibility of relationship and communi-cation, speaking and loving.
2. *Why at night*   Night is the time of the greatest intimacy between lovers and a time when distractions of the day have ceased and people are more aware of the emo-tional realities of their lives. Thoughts and feelings that have been pushed aside during the day reappear at night.
3. *Significance of "at times"*   "At times" signifies change, and Paz describes four different aspects of a human relationship. He omits the phrase from the last stanza in order to emphasize the inevitable mortality of human life.
4. *Human beings and the universe*   Human relationships are imperfect, subject to change, and finite. Moreover, they exist in a universe that is devoid of any meaning other than that which people bring to it. Given both the nature of human life and the nature of the universe, relationships are to be valued in spite of their many limita-tions. At their best, they provide meaning and value where, otherwise, none exists. At their worst, they are still better than nothing.

ANALYZING LITERARY TECHNIQUE: POSSIBLE ANSWERS

*1. *Night as symbol*   Night is the time when it is difficult to be distracted from the basic realities of life, which may appear in symbolic form in dreams and which include the mortal nature of human existence and the place of human beings in a meaning-less universe. Paz gives the poem a universal dimension by relating night to water (stanza 1), earth (stanzas 2 and 3), fire (stanza 4), and air (stanza 5), the four ele-ments once thought to comprise the physical world.

*2. *Metaphors and human relationships*   *(a)* The metaphor of waves in an ocean (stanza 1) suggests that the pair of human beings moves together in synchronization and in harmony with the universe, propelled by the pair's life forces and by their activities in their environment.

(b) The metaphor of two stones in the desert (stanza 2) suggests that the two human beings are separate, each withdrawn into his and her own self, although they are physically together, and that they exist in a universe that ignores them.

(c) The metaphor of two roots (stanza 3) suggests a close relationship that is rooted in an unsupportive and uncaring universe. Under these circumstances, the only emotional support possible is that which one human being gives to another.

(d) The metaphor of two knives in a night that "strikes sparks" suggests that the couple's relationship is at times confrontational and hostile because events and emotions in the normal course of living incite them to quarrel.

*3. *"Two stars" and "empty sky"*   (a) The metaphor of two stars suggests that the couple possesses beauty, brilliance, and vitality, all of which are aspects of human potential. However, falling stars are burning out and symbolize the couple's inevitable mortality.

(b) The metaphor of the empty sky suggests that the universe is devoid of meaning.

4. *Order of stanzas*   The location of the last stanza, which is the climax, must be fixed. The arrangement of the other four stanzas depends on personal taste, although there is a pairing of opposites between stanzas 1 and 2 (water and earth) and 3 and 4 ("roots/laced" and knives, suggesting connection and separation). In addition, some readers may think there is a logical progression from night striking sparks (stanza 4) to the "two stars falling" (stanza 5).

5. *Function of repetition*   Repetition unifies the poem. The five repetitions of "Two bodies face to face" emphasizes that the poem is describing five aspects of a relationship. The four repetitions of "at times" conveys the variable aspect of any human relationship. The omission of "at times" in the last stanza emphasizes humans' inevitable mortality in a meaningless universe.

6. *Existentialist aspects*   Against the poem's background of human mortality and an intrinsically meaningless universe, Paz implies that human relationships, with all their limitations, are the only source of soul-satisfying values in the universe. This attitude reflects the following characteristics of existentialism: *(a)* human beings must choose the values by which they will live, for the only certainties in life are suffering and death; *(b)* however, in the absence of absolute values, human beings have the awesome freedom and responsibility to create their own individuality through their choices and their actions.

WRITING ABOUT LITERATURE

1. *Expository theme examining Paz's use of metaphor*   (See **A.L.T.** questions 1–3 above.)

2. *Creative writing: a poem about relationship*   Call students' attention to the suggestions and directions in the textbook assignment. **(PLJ)**

FURTHER READING

Paz, Octavio, *Early Poems; Blanco.*

Crossroads
CARLOS SOLÓRZANO

INTRODUCING THE PLAY

In *Crossroads* (also known as *Crossing*), Solórzano depicts life in the twentieth century as a time when human beings are isolated and emotionally starved in an impersonal and absurd world. In *Crossroads,* impossibility is possible, and surprise is an inherent part of life. Appearance is both real and illusory, in that those who are old in appearance are young in mind and heart.

The character named the Man misses a most special moment in his life because he cannot recognize, accept, and value that moment when it occurs. He is so committed to his preconceptions of what reality should be that he is unable to relinquish his illusions. He leaves in desperation, blaming the Flagman for his situation.

The intensity of his anger and desperation reflect his subconscious recognition of certain unpalatable truths. Life is often unpredictable, and reality shatters illusions. True communication is often impossible because egotism constructs unbreachable walls. Factors such as age, sex, race, religion, and nationality create social barriers that even well-meaning people cannot overcome. Consequently, people find themselves caught in webs, both those of their own spinning and those created by the values of their society.

With the Man, Solórzano paints a portrait of a self-deluding soul who would be a poignant figure if he were not completely self-centered. In contrast to the Man, the Woman engages the sympathy of the reader and the audience. She leaves filled with the sorrow and anguish of rejection but, having realized that possibility from the beginning, she is prepared to continue to live through her dreams and other correspondences.

Solórzano creates effective drama with three characters who converse in sparse dialogue on a bare stage. The Man's inability to recognize the Woman when he sees her produces many dramatic and verbal ironies. The themes of the play are dynamic. Life contains more than people expect, and they must be open to broader ways of thinking. Otherwise, like the Man, they can miss an important experience. Solórzano's choice of names for his characters, his setting, and his staging create a generic situation that becomes symbolic of life in the modern age.

PLJ: Have you ever missed something of value because the experience that you had was so different from what you had expected that you were unable to appreciate it?

Literary Terms: characterization, foreshadowing, irony, paradox, setting, symbol, theme

COMPREHENSION QUESTIONS

1. Who is the Man? (pen pal of the Woman)
2. Whom does the Man wish would help him? (the Flagman)
3. How does the Man expect to recognize the person for whom he's waiting? (wearing white flower on dress)
4. Is the Man successful in his quest? Why or why not? (fails because he refuses to see beyond the Woman's age)
5. How does the Man feel at the end of the play? Why? (desperate: in need of a loving relationship and longing to find woman he expected to meet)

UNDERSTANDING THE PLAY: POSSIBLE ANSWERS

1. *Why Man and Woman do not have particular names*   The Man and the Woman represent men and women in general, rather than particular individuals. Their plight is symbolic of the plight of all human beings. This treatment gives the play a broader focus and a more important message.
*2. *"They call me by many names"*   Like the Man and the Woman, the Flagman does not represent a particular person, or even a person in a particular role in life. The Flagman is the detached bystander, one who is not interested in anyone else. He does not listen, he is not involved, and he does not care. He symbolizes the impersonal element in the universe.
3. *"The impossible is always true"*   Most students will probably agree with the Flagman's statement. One cannot predict many eventualities, such as illness, death, and the ramifications of economic and political events. Many factors interrelate in a multitude of ways, creating unforeseen results.
*4. *Why the Woman is afraid of finding one whom she seeks*   The Woman is afraid that reality will disappoint her. She has good reason to be pessimistic because she has been tempting young men with an old, doctored photograph of herself. Thus a great discrepancy exists between her actual appearance and what she has led the young men to expect. By ignoring the Man's presence, the Woman can keep alive her dream of a relationship between them.
5. *Why the Woman doesn't reveal identity to the Man*   The Woman wants to protect herself from being rejected for being old and unattractive. She would rather that the Man think that he'd never met the person whom he expects.
  The Woman offers the Man the flower to see if he will make the connection between it and her and will give her a chance to be what he wants her to be.
*6. *Why the Man feels the woman he awaits must come*   The Man is in such desperate need of a romantic relationship that his heart is fixed on the meeting and its being able to satisfy his needs.
7. *What the Woman's story reveals*   The Woman's story reveals her loneliness and her desperate need to be accepted and loved. The Man's reaction reveals his preoccupation with himself, which is so extreme that he does not even realize that the

Woman is talking about herself and that she is, in fact, the woman he is so anxious to meet.

8. *Why the Man is angry at the end*   The Flagman states the reality of the situation; beneath his anger, the Man realizes that the Flagman is correct. The Woman really is the woman for whom the Man was searching. On the surface, the Man's anger is focused on the Flagman's double-talk. Beneath the surface, the Man is angry at the facts of his life, angry at the Flagman for stating them, and angry at himself for pinning his hopes on an illusion.

*9. *The Man's final line*   The Man's final line reveals the agony that results from his discovery. He cannot accept the reality of the Flagman's comments about the Woman's identity. He desperately wants his dreams to come true. He repeats "What the devil are you good for!" because he cannot face that what the Flagman *is* good for is stating the nature of reality.

10. *"One moment to recognize one another"*   The Woman is referring to herself and the Man and their particular situation: For them, "now or never" probably reflects reality. In her view, if the Man really understood his need for companionship, he would have valued a relationship with her.

   Most students probably will agree that for a relationship to begin to develop between any two people, both must be ready at the same time and must be in contact. However, they may disagree about whether such an opportunity may occur more than once.

11. *What the Man and Woman learn from their "crossroads experience"*   The Man reluctantly learns that appearance all too often belies reality, and that reality destroys illusions. His desperation and anger at the end of the play reveal the shattering effect that this discovery has upon his psyche.

   The Woman's experience confirms her suspicions that reality destroys illusions. These suspicions have led her to hide at home behind old, doctored photographs and communication through letters.

12. *Themes*   Theme include: (*a*) The best-laid plans go awry; (*b*) One's expectations are often disappointed; (*c*) True communication between human beings is often impossible; (*d*) People find themselves caught in webs, both those of their own making and those created by the values of their society; (*e*) Barriers exist in our society and in the world that even well-meaning people find it difficult to overcome; (*f*) By being too certain about what one wants, one can be blind to other interesting, but different, opportunities.

ANALYZING LITERARY TECHNIQUE: POSSIBLE ANSWERS

1. *Setting*   The lack of a specific location is consistent with viewing the characters and action as symbolic. It adds to the timeless quality of the characters and the plot. Having fewer people around causes less intrusion and distraction and creates greater focus.

*2. *Role of the Flagman*   The Flagman symbolizes the impersonal modern world. Many of his lines reveal this impersonality: "They all look alike"; "I can't know if someone I don't know has been around"; "That's not my job"; "It's not important."

The Flagman also acts as a foil for the Man, who responds, in frustration, by amplifying the Flagman's comments. The Man responds to the lines "They all look alike" and "What other one?" with a description of the expected woman.

In addition, the Flagman's philosophical remarks provoke analysis of the nature of society. Some examples include: "Everyone sells something" (cynical attitude toward others; everyone motivated by self-interest); "I saw the one that you aren't looking for, and the one you're looking for I didn't see" (ironic aspect of life); "They all look alike" (focus on appearance and generalizing about reality); "That's very common. The contrary's also common" (knowing without seeing; seeing but not knowing); "He's (or she's) never coming" (inevitably disappointed expectations); "The impossible is always true" (unpredictable nature of experience).

3. *Why the Woman is old*   The Woman's age is used to underscore the Man's confusion about appearance and reality. Because the Man values appearances and illusions, he cannot see beyond the Woman's physical attributes to recognize her essential character. He literally does not see the person with whom he has been corresponding and with whom he believes he is in love, even when she is standing right before him.

While relationships between older men and younger women are fairly common and therefore generally accepted in Western societies, relationships between older women and younger men are less common. Therefore, the Woman's age provides another barrier for the Man, by asking him to accept the unexpected. The Woman attempts to breach the barrier of her age in a number of ways, by providing him with the doctored photograph, by veiling herself, and by making him close his eyes, but she is unsuccessful.

4. *Foreshadowing*   The Flagman's comment, "One can't know by just seeing a person whether it was the one who placed an ad in the newspaper," foreshadows the discrepancy between the Man's expectations and the reality of the Woman. Foreshadowing prepares for the surprise of dramatic irony.

*5. *Dramatic and verbal irony*   (a) Examples of dramatic irony include: the Man's meeting with the Woman "seems impossible" and actually becomes impossible, given the Man's expectations and his nature and the Woman's actual appearance; the Man tells the Flagman, "Perhaps she has passed by and you didn't see her," when the Man has seen the Woman without recognizing her; the Flagman tells the Man, "One can't know by just seeing a person whether it was the one who placed an ad in the newspaper"; and the Man cannot face the possibility that the Woman is the person whose photograph and letters he has received.

(b) Examples of verbal irony include: The Man states, "She's the woman that I've been waiting for for many years," whereas, given her age and appearance, she is actually not the woman he is waiting for at all; The woman tells the Man, "Now I believe that she won't come," which is correct because the real Woman has come, and the woman whom the Man is expecting does not exist.

*6. *Symbolism*   Examples of symbolism include: The Man and Woman, with their generic names, symbolize the sexes; The Flagman symbolizes the impersonal modern world; The broken clock symbolizes timelessness; the dark stage symbolizes the characters' inability to see life-experience clearly, to recognize and to understand it; Light, which symbolizes knowledge, blinds the Man—he is unable to tolerate too much knowledge, such as the Woman's true identity as his pen pal.

7. *Paradox*   Paradoxes include: (*a*) The impossible is possible; (*b*) Life is at once rational and irrational; (*c*) A person can be both young and old; (*d*) Two people can converse with each other without communicating; (*e*) People can be blind to opportunities and situations that are part of their lives.

8. *"Sad Vaudeville"*   Vaudeville is a form of stage entertainment where, usually in a number of acts, performers sing, dance, tell jokes, and enact skits. This play is a vaudeville in that it is a stage entertainment. It is sad in that communication, which is of prime importance to the Man and the Woman, cannot occur because they are unable to remove barriers that both they and society have constructed.

WRITING ABOUT LITERATURE

1. *Expository theme analyzing the Flagman's role*   Call student's attention to the directions in the textbook assignment with regard to content and organization. (See **U.P.** questions 2 and 9, and **A.L.T.** questions 2 and 6 above.)

2. *Expository theme analyzing dramatic and verbal irony*   Call students' attention to the directions in the textbook assignment with regard to content and organization. (See **U.P.** questions 2, 4, and 6, and **A.L.T.** question 5 above.)

3. *Creative writing: How this experience affects the Man's life*   Call students' attention to the questions suggested in the textbook assignment. **(PLJ)**

FURTHER READING

Solórzano, Carlos, *Three Acts* (includes *The Puppets*).

Paseo

JOSÉ DONOSO

INTRODUCING THE STORY

"Paseo" is the story of gain and loss in a family that is unable to express emotion. A spinster aunt, accompanied by two of her brothers, comes to live with her newly widowed third brother and his young son. Aunt Mathilda caters to her brothers and manages the household to their satisfaction. However, her nephew, the narrator, is starved for love. Despite the fact that his mother is dead, Mathilda does not give the boy any special attention, and none of the adults is emotionally responsive to him. They do not intend to be callous or cruel; they simply do not reach out to one another in an emotional way.

Mathilda finds herself unable to reject her adoption by a decrepit and injured white dog. In the process of caring for it, she comes to respond to it with a long-buried fun-loving and affectionate part of her personality, and she adopts it as her companion and friend. By the time a month has passed, Mathilda has begun to prefer the dog's company to that of her family. A walk at night to meet the dog's needs leads to increasingly longer nightly walks that meet her own. She returns later and later, looking both increasingly unkempt and physically attractive, until the time comes when she does not return at all.

The story is told from the point of view of Mathilda's nephew, who, as an adult, relates this part of his childhood. Therefore, the reader knows no more than the narrator does. Donoso's choice of narrator reinforces his focus on the lack of communication among the members of this family and their lack of intimate knowledge about each other. The adult nephew is different enough from his father and uncles to be critical of their extreme need for emotional self-control, their inability to express love, and their rejection of so many of the opportunities that life offers. However, he is far from an impartial observer.

In the course of the story, Mathilda becomes completely different in appearance, personality, and behavior. The nature of her change and the manner in which it occurs suggest the concepts of a dual personality and the "night journey." Carl Jung speaks of "the dark night of the soul," and the existence of the Shadow that is an inherent part of each person's personality. According to Jung, the Shadow "personifies everything that the subject refuses to acknowledge about himself and yet is always thrusting itself upon him directly or indirectly." Some people refer to this passionate subconscious self as the doppelgänger. The process that Jung describes, by which a person recognizes his or her other self in dreams, anthropologists and literary critics have labeled the "night journey."

In myths and literature, the "night journey" is often a real journey. Albert Guerard describes it as being "an essentially solitary journey involving profound spiritual change in the voyager." It is no accident that Mathilda takes her walks at night, the customary time for sleep and dreams. Moreover, in the story, night is regarded by her nephew as mysterious and magical and by her brothers as dangerous. Both elements are an integral part of psychological self-discovery.

The particular experience and the nature of the psychological change vary with each individual. Mathilda's interactions with the dog in the process of caring for it are instrumental in her psychological development. In the course of nursing the dog back to health, Mathilda talks to it and treats it like a human companion. She suddenly realizes that, paradoxically, she is both well-off and deprived. Although her life is financially secure, she is emotionally impoverished. Once Mathilda has permitted her personality to develop fully, she leaves home with her dog because she is no longer satisfied to remain in an emotionally stifling environment.

In addition to night, other symbolic motifs reappear throughout the story in the form of the house as a book, the usually predictable billiards games, and the magical sounds of the seagoing vessels. The boy feels the magic in the distant, unknown, and unpredictable world that his aunt discovers; however, his comfort in the predictable, protective, and secure environment of his home overshadows his longing for the opposite. His father and uncles remain too frightened of losing control either to find intimacy in human relationships or to incorporate new experiences into their lives. Although alive, they are emotionally dead. As he matures, the nephew may not become more courageous, even though he criticizes the behavior of the men in his family. When he prefers to think that they and his aunt are all dead, he reveals his continuing psychological discomfort with issues that have never been resolved.

PLJ: In your opinion, what qualities must a good friend possess? What do you value most in your closest relationships? How do you want your favorite relatives and friends to respond to you?

Literary Terms: alter ego, characterization, doppelgänger, figurative language, flashback, foreshadowing, irony, limited omniscience, motif, narrative perspective, "night journey," paradox, simile, symbolism, theme

COMPREHENSION QUESTIONS

1. How do the members of this family relate to one another? (with respect, but with no warmth)
2. What event causes a great change in the family situation? (Aunt Mathilda rescues a dog.)
3. What causes Aunt Mathilda's behavior to change? (dog's affection and personality enrich her life)
4. How does Aunt Mathilda's behavior change? (She is no longer interested in billiards, she no longer turns down brothers' beds, and she takes increasingly longer walks with dog at night.)
5. How does Mathilda's nephew react to her new behavior? (jealous that she loves dog more than himself)
6. What final action does Aunt Mathilda take? (never returns from last walk)
7. How does Aunt Mathilda's final action affect the family? (No one discusses it with the boy; the uncles try to ignore it, but it upsets their orderly lives.)
8. How might Aunt Mathilda's departure have been prevented? (communication and outward affection)

UNDERSTANDING THE STORY: POSSIBLE ANSWERS

1. *Why narrator prefers to think that family is dead*   Possibilities: (*a*) The narrator thinks that people should express emotion and lead freer lives. He views his father and uncles as having led pathetic lives, devoid of love and joy, and feels that death would end their misery. This choice does not account (as it should) for the narrator's inclusion of his aunt in his statement.

    (*b*) Depending on how he has chosen to lead his own adult life, the narrator may wish to forget this period in his youth. If he has not been happy, Mathilda's choice and the possibility of her greater happiness may be very disturbing. His inclusion of Mathilda in his statement implies that he never satisfactorily resolved the issues of attitude and behavior that Mathilda's disappearance brought to the surface so long ago.

2. *World of narrator's family*   The real world is chaotic, but the family's world is safe, predictable, protective, orderly, dignified, and comfortable. The family creates an environment that makes it feel secure. The family values intelligence, wealth, and reputation rather than those aspects of life that involve taking risks. The men view emotional involvement and an adventurous spirit as dangerous because both threaten predictability.

   Mathilda's disappearance proves that life is unpredictable, and that it is impossible to protect oneself against every possibility. The narrator's family has emotionally secluded itself in order to feel secure and safe. Ironically, tragedy strikes because of these attitudes and behavior as well as in spite of them.

   Finally, Mathilda's disappearance alarms her brothers because it causes them to realize that their own emotional inadequacies have provoked Mathilda's behavior. Initially, they tried to cope with her changed personality and behavior by ignoring them, but they cannot really ignore her departure and the rejection that it signifies. They haunt the windows of the house, their "faces aged with grief."

3. *Why Mathilda prefers dog to nephew*   Mathilda may prefer the dog to her nephew for several reasons: (*a*) The dog was all hers; her nephew was her brother's; (*b*) animals give unqualified love; the boy may have been reserved in his treatment of Mathilda; (*c*) the dog obviously needed Mathilda; she may have been unaware of the fact that her nephew also needed her.

4. *Why narrator states dislike of dogs*   The narrator's statement explains his attitude toward Mathilda's rescue of the dog, her relationship with it, and his own lack of involvement and criticism of the experience. Particularly after the dog was clean, and given its friendly nature, the boy's attitude is unusual in a child. His dislike may be a rationalization for his feeling of jealousy that Mathilda preferred a homeless mongrel to himself and gave the dog the love and attention that the narrator himself wanted and needed from her.

5. *Why brothers accept dog despite their feeling about it*   For the brothers, the world remains safe and comfortable as long as it remains as it is. Anything that might cause change is feared, for change involves risk. Confrontation provokes change, in that it provokes people to reveal and learn more about each other's attitudes and feelings. Consequently, the safest way to proceed is to deny that the nature of the household has changed.

6. *Mathilda's walks*   (*a*) Mathilda exults in being free to experience life on her own terms, without being held to account and judged for her choices, attitudes, and behavior. No one understands her relationship with the dog, and it appears that no one values a lovely night.

   (*b*) Mathilda has good reason to expect that her brothers would have been very critical of her attitudes, feelings, and behavior because her new outlook is taking her away from them. In addition, such a change implies that there is more than one way to lead a life and that other ways may be better than the ways her brothers have chosen. Fearing to live any other way than their own, the brothers would never consider other possibilities to be as good or better than those they have chosen.

*7. *What narrator's tale reveals about him as boy*   The boy senses the magic in the universe without having the courage to investigate it. He wishes that the adults in his home would incorporate the qualities that he finds missing there into their lives, so that he, too, could reap the pleasures of the warmth of love, exciting new experiences, and shared thoughts and feelings. This is reflected in his wish for less structure in the billiards game, which symbolizes the nature of his home environment.

At the same time, the boy treasures the qualities of safety and protection that being at home gives him, and he is unable to open himself to the qualities that he wants. Part of him fears what is new and beyond his control. Thus, he dislikes and is jealous of Mathilda's dog and is unable to participate in a new experience that would be loving, exciting, and fun. He might even have won some of Mathilda's attention by playing with the dog.

Finally, the boy is first disturbed and then terrified by the changes that he sees in Mathilda. He recognizes that the dog is making her happier than anyone in her family is able to do, and that she has come to care more for the dog than she does for them. The boy also recognizes in Mathilda the ability, which he wishes he had, to feel free to investigate and experience the magical aspects of the night: the risky, uncertain, unpredictable, undignified, disorderly, and uncomfortable. The boy's terror reflects how he would feel if he were she, his knowledge of his own inadequacy, and his fear for his own loss when she leaves.

8. *Themes*   (a) Life without risk is not living; (b) One can't judge a book by the cover, in that people are different from what they appear to be; (c) It is impossible to protect oneself from change.

ANALYZING LITERARY TECHNIQUE: POSSIBLE ANSWERS

1. *Foreshadowing*   Telling the story as a flashback contributes an ominous feeling to it, for knowledge of the strange and frightening ending pervades the telling.

2. *Choice of adult nephew as narrator*   The adult nephew as the narrator permits the most objective telling of the story from within the story. He has gained some emotional distance from his relatives, and now he understands that they were emotional cripples. However, the narrator's version is not intended to be the objective rendition that an omniscient narrator might present. In his youth, the narrator was obviously deeply affected by these events, and, as an adult, he may be limited in his ability to relate them to others. Note that he begins with his preference for his family to be dead, a comment that reflects his current discomfort in dealing with these memories and the issues that they stir up.

The narrator as a young boy would be too emotionally involved in his own needs and the threat of Mathilda's behavior to his own well-being. He would lack the experience and sophistication to do more than sense alternative possibilities of living.

3. *Title*   "Paseo" emphasizes Mathilda's walks with the dog. Since these represent the development and exhibition of her true personality, and this development is the focus of the story, the title is appropriate.

4. *Characterization of Mathilda*   Mathilda's delight when she unexpectedly loses a billiards game reveals her potential for preferring a life that is less orderly and predictable, and more loving and exciting. The change in Mathilda as she cares for the dog makes her gradual development realistic.

*5. *Night as symbol*   Night is the time of sleep and dreams, shadows and mystery. Mathilda walks while people normally sleep, returning when they begin to awaken. Her walks are a "night journey" in that they are solitary (she won't even discuss them) and involve a profound spiritual change in her personality.

*6. *Other symbolic motifs*   Other symbolic motifs include: (*a*) The billiards game, with its order of participation and winning: The change in Mathilda's attitude and interest reflects the change in her personality.

(*b*) The magic of the dark city and the ships in the harbor; which is sensed as appealing by the boy, entered by Mathilda as the expression of her newly discovered self, and considered dangerous and off limits by the uncles.

(*c*) The family home as a book, suggesting that one cannot judge a book by the cover (people are not what they seem). The motif also suggests an open book (easily read and understood; in the process of unfolding) and a closed book (closed up; hidden; withdrawn; unavailable; uninvolving; undeveloping). The members of the family are more than what each appears to be, but no one gets to see beneath the surface of anyone else. The house and the people in it are "closed books" in that they are not open to communication and to new experiences. When Mathilda changes, she does not communicate about the changes within her: She simply lives by herself among the members of her family until she suddenly leaves them.

(*d*) The massive library door functions as a tangible way of sealing off emotions; the door is a physical representation of the brothers' ability to conceal their personal feelings.

7. *Irony*   It is powerfully ironic that disaster (Mathilda's desertion) comes to a family that has done its best to shut itself off from any new experiences and that it is just this attitude that fosters the development of the disaster.

8. *Paradox*   Paradoxes include: (*a*) A person can be both well-off and deprived, in that he or she can be well-off financially and deprived emotionally; (*b*) Physical comforts do not bring happiness; (*c*) People can converse with each other without communicating; (*d*) People can be blind to situations that are part of their lives; (*e*) Life is both rational and irrational.

WRITING ABOUT LITERATURE

1. *Expository essay exploring symbolism in "Paseo"*   Call students' attention to the directions in the textbook assignment with regard to content and organization. Remind them of the importance of using direct quotations to support their ideas. (See **A.L.T.** questions 5 and 6 above.)

2. *Expository writing: Character sketch of the narrator as boy*   Call students' atten-
   tionto the directions in the textbook assignment with regard to content. Remind
   them to use direct quotations from the story to support the points in their analysis.
   (See **U.S.** question 7 above.)
3. *Creative writing: A letter from Mathilda to her family*   Call students' attention to
   the directions in the textbook assignment with regard to content. **(PLJ)**

FURTHER READING

Donoso, Jośe, *The Blond Man.*

Chess
ROSARIO CASTELLANOS

INTRODUCING THE POEM

"Chess" is a poem about the fragility of human relationships. Two lovers assume that
their relationship is strong enough to withstand a competitive game. However, in the
process of playing it, their relationship changes from friendship to one in which each
tries to win the game at the expense of the other. The reader is left to wonder whether, by
the time they finish the game, their friendship also will be finished.

The objective of the game of chess is to use superior intelligence to defeat one's
opponent. However, the game actually symbolizes any competitive situation that makes
adversaries of friends and thus threatens their relationship.

PLJ: Have you ever played a competitive game with a good friend? Would you run for a
competitive office against a good friend? Why or why not? To what extent, if any, would
a "winner" and a "loser" in your relationship threaten your good feelings toward each
other?

Literary Terms: irony, symbol, theme

COMPREHENSION QUESTIONS

1. What is the relationship between the two people? (friends; sometimes lovers)
2. Why do they decide to play chess? (for fun; to share another experience)
3. What is the goal of the game? (to destroy the opponent)
4. What closing words reveal the game's power? ("annihilate the other one forever")

UNDERSTANDING THE POEM:
POSSIBLE ANSWERS

1. *The game: anticipation and reality*   What the speaker anticipates as good-hearted fun becomes cut-throat competition. The game becomes personal and serious rather than playful and enjoyable.

*2. *Competition as a risk to friendship*   The last line, "annihilate the other one forever" (line 13), implies that the outcome of the game will transfer into actual life. By spending so much time in an adversarial relationship, the two people will destroy their friendship.

*3. *Sex of players*   Current research supports the view that preserving relationships is, in general, more important to women and that winning a competition is, in general, more important to men. This would mean that a chess game or other competition might be more threatening to two men or to a man in a male-female relationship than to two women.

*4. *Themes*   Themes include: (*a*) Friendship and love are fragile and need support in order to thrive; (*b*) Competitive people need to anticipate the effect of their success on important relationships.

ANALYZING LITERARY TECHNIQUE:
POSSIBLE ANSWERS

*1. *Chess as symbol*   The chess game symbolizes any serious competition between two people in which each spends an unusual amount of time or has a great emotional investment in trying to surpass the other. A chessboard is a traditional symbol for a battlefield. The game is an excellent choice for intellectual competition because of the strategies needed to win and the long periods of time spent planning them.

*2. *Structure of poem*   The three stanzas relate to one another as a progression in which the friendship disintegrates. The first stanza sets forth the friendship and the expectation of enhancing it. The second describes the process, which will be the chess game. The third reveals the competitive level, the time devoted to the pursuit of winning, and the antagonism between the competitors. The final line creates a bridge between the world of the game and the lives of the competitors after the game has concluded. It implies that the competition will leave lasting scars on the competitors' friendship.

*3. *Irony*   It is ironic that the friends play an intellectual game in the expectation that it will foster their friendship when, in fact, the game threatens their friendship.

WRITING ABOUT LITERATURE

1. *Expository writing: An essay analyzing structure*   Remind students of directions in the textbook assignment (inclusion of symbolism and irony). Also remind them of the importance of direct quotations. (See **U.P.** question 4, and **A.L.T.** questions 1–3 above.)

2. *Creative writing: Conversation between chess players*   Students may want to create two different versions, one in which the man is the winner, and one in which the woman is the winner. (See **U.P.** questions 2–3 above.) **(PLJ)**

FURTHER READING

Castellanos, Rosario, *A Rosario Castellanos Reader.*

A Very Old Man With Enormous Wings

GABRIEL GARCÍA MÁRQUEZ

INTRODUCING THE STORY

In "A Very Old Man With Enormous Wings," García Márquez tells the charming story of a decrepit angel who suddenly falls into the yard of an ordinary Colombian villager and his wife. The angel is exploited as a curiosity and is mistreated by everyone in the community because he does not look or act as they think an angel should. The author imaginatively uses irony as a source of humor, including in the tale a priest who cannot accept an angel that does not pass his tests, an unusual group of miracles, and a competing freak adapted from the Greek myth of Arachne.

Whether the very old man is an angel or whether he is an unusual and unfortunate human being, the story's power emanates from García Márquez attitude toward the indifference, intolerance, and inhumanity of ordinary people. All of the villagers are sadly deficient in their ability both to appreciate the greatest wonders in life and to treat the unfortunate with sympathy, kindness, and respect. The story has a powerful satiric bite in that it makes a serious and critical statement about human values and prejudices.

Yet, what would be a tragedy in the hands of Fyodor Dostoyevski has a silver lining in the hands of García Márquez. Through his comic vision the Colombian author achieves a precarious balance in his fiction: the depiction of a world without illusion, without nobility, and without hope of perfection, juxtaposed with the optimistic belief in the human ability to survive despite an endless succession of what should be overwhelming obstacles. Thus, the satiric elements are gentle and lighthearted rather than sharp and bitter, and, at the end, the winged creature grows new feathers and flies away. The reader is left with paradoxes: The impossible is possible; predictable situations are filled with surprises; people all too often are blind to the significance of experiences that are part of their lives.

As is typical in García Márquez' fiction, his style is inseparable from his subject. The casual and simple style of the folktale is the perfect vehicle for his use of magic realism, wherein the fantastic is treated in the same manner as the ordinary, and both are inseparably combined into the fabric of the whole. This "tale for children" reflects García Márquez' oral legacy from his grandmother.

Magic realism also provides an imaginative and sophisticated way to achieve free expression in countries that are ruled by dictators. Often, the wild humor of the magical aspects of these otherwise realistic stories satirizes an underlying serious political problem, criticizing the society in a way that is so oblique as to be acceptable in a repressive environment.

PLJ: A well-known saying states that "you can't judge a book by its cover." To what extent, if any, have you found this saying to be correct when applied to human beings? Do you make any effort to get to know people who appear to be quite different from yourself? Why or why not?

Literary Terms: allusion, comedy, folktale, humor, irony, magic realism, myth, paradox, satire, theme, tragedy

COMPREHENSION QUESTIONS

1. What did Pelayo find in the rear of his courtyard? (angel; old man with wings)
2. Where did he put what he found? (into chicken coop)
3. What first made the priest question the nature of Pelayo's guest? (didn't understand Latin, "God's language")
4. How did Pelayo and his wife profit from their guest? (charged admission of five cents each and built mansion)
5. What diverted the audience from Pelayo's show? (arrival of woman who had been changed into a spider)
6. What was appealing about the new show in town? (cheaper; her fate taught people a lesson)
7. What miracles did the angel perform? (blind man grew three new teeth; leper's sores sprouted flowers; paralyzed man almost won lottery)
8. What did the doctor's examination reveal? (It seemed impossible that angel had survived chicken pox; also, wings appeared natural.)
9. Why did Pelayo and his wife fear their guest's death? (didn't know what to do with a dead angel)
10. What happened to Pelayo's guest at the end of the story? (grew new feathers and flew away)

UNDERSTANDING THE STORY: POSSIBLE ANSWERS

1. *Why the angel appears as an old man* In the guise of an old man, the angel is treated by everyone as a decrepit old man would be treated, revealing the dark side of human nature.
2. *Why the angel speaks like a Norwegian sailor* The angel speaks a language that is not related to Spanish, and the villagers do not understand a word of it. They assume it's the language of a remote country like Norway. He also has come from the sea, and the Norwegians are famous sailors.
3. *How Pelayo and Elisenda feel about guest* Pelayo and Elisenda do not like him because of his disgusting smell and his disreputable appearance. He also does not fit their preconceived ideas about angels.

4. *Importance of whether Pelayo's guest is an angel*   If an angel were to test the true nature of human beings, it would be to its advantage to appear as a decrepit, disgusting-looking human-type creature. People would then react honestly. If it were to arrive in the form that people imagine angels to have, people would be on their best behavior in order to impress the angel.

5. *Villagers' treatment of angel*   Their treatment reveals them to be selfish, callous, cruel, and intolerant of anything strangely different. Their inability to appreciate the angel's unique qualities reveals their inability to appreciate the wondrous aspects of life.

6. *Angel's abilities and inabilities*   The angel's abilities and inabilities are what distinguish him from what the villagers expect an angel to be like. He neither looks nor acts in a way that is considered typical of angels, and they cannot accept an angel who does not conform to their preconceptions.

7. *Person who comes closest to identifying angel*   The doctor, observing the angel scientifically, determines that it cannot be human because of its wings and because of certain physical signs that, in a human, would indicate death. Ironically, the doctor appears in a better light than the priest, in that he is impartial and is not ruled by preconceived ideas.

*8. *Significance of villagers' fascination with spider-maiden*   It is ironic that, even though the villagers are religious, they are more interested in the angel as a freak than as an angel. They prefer the spider-maiden because it is cheaper to visit her, and they can understand her and therefore relate to her. Their attitude reveals lack of imagination, lack of wonder, and lack of understanding of anything abstract.

9. *Why angel lives so long with Pelayo's family*   Five to six years is long enough for the family to become accustomed to the angel and to make some effort to relate to him. However, they do not. The angel accepts the family's behavior, in that he does not strike out at them. His departure is as natural and unpredictable as his arrival (apparently dependent on the condition of his wings).

10. *Narrator's attitude*   The narrator treats the tale matter-of-factly, suggesting that the events are no more amazing than any other life events.

11. *Theme*   Themes include: (*a*) You cannot judge a book by its cover; (*b*) People are inclined to ignore or mistreat strangers, the poor, and people who are different from themselves; (*c*) People often do not see beyond their preconceived ideas (prejudices) when evaluating others.

ANALYZING LITERARY TECHNIQUE: POSSIBLE ANSWERS

*1. *Comedy vs tragedy*   (*a*) Sources of humor will include: (*1*) the arrival of such a creature; (*2*) the various attitudes about his identity, including the reasons for the priest's doubts; (*3*) the illnesses of those who come to be cured and the nature of the miracles that the angel performs; and (*4*) the spider-maiden's arrival and her tale of woe.

   (*b*) Sources of sadness will include the angel's treatment by all the villagers.

(c) It appears that comedy prevails, in that, with few exceptions, the angel accepts his situation and, in the end, when his wings have recovered, he sets off for a better life. García Márquez may intend to reveal the patience and fortitude of the downtrodden.

2. *Satire*   Satire ridicules people and institutions and makes them laughable, usually to promote reform. It is clear that García Márquez uses this device. The tunnel vision of the priest and the shallow values of the villagers are the prime targets. No one makes any effort to deal with the creature as he is, and he suffers because he does not conform to preconceived ideas about what he should be like. It is obviously better to be tolerant and imaginative rather than parochial, and better to be kind and considerate rather than callous and cruel.

3. *Folktale*   Both the style and the content of García Márquez' story are reminiscent of the folktale. The style is simple, as if it were being told aloud, which is appropriate for stories originating in an oral tradition. The people are common folk who must cope with an unusual and magical event, and they react with an appropriate lack of sophistication.

4. *Irony*   Irony is related to the thematic content and the humor of the story. For example, it is ironic that an angel who fell to earth would be unrecognized, unappreciated, and treated like a freak. His decrepit appearance, the assumptions made about him, the priest's reasons for being unable to accept him, the villagers' preference for a different freak, and Elisenda's finding it hell (verbal irony) to have an angel living with them are all ironic sources of humor.

*5. *Why "A Tale for Children"*   The story would be appealing to children because it is written in the style of a folktale and because of the myth of the spider-maiden within it. They would enjoy the magical idea of a decrepit angel's falling to earth and not being recognized, and also the humor of the people who come to be cured and the bizarre miracles that the angel performs.

Depending on their age and experience, children might not appreciate the humor of the religious allusions, and they might not understand that the behavior of the villagers symbolizes the inhumanity of human beings toward those among them who are strange or different.

6. *Magic realism*   This story is a good example of magic realism in that it blends the magical (an angel suddenly appearing in a small village, a young woman turned into a spider) with the real (the descriptions of the village and villagers, the parish priest's concerns, details such as the state of the chicken coop). The combination of the magic and the real is delightfully provocative.

7. *Paradox*   Paradoxes include: (a) The impossible is possible in life; (b) Life is both rational and irrational; (c) People can be blind to the significance of situations that are part of their lives.

WRITING ABOUT LITERATURE

1. *Expository essay analyzing this story as "a tale for children"*   Call students' attention to the directions in the textbook assignment. Remind them to use direct quotations to support their ideas and to explain the appeal of each of the three elements that they identify. (See **A.L.T.** question 5 above.)

2. *Expository essay analyzing Arachne allusion and role of spider-maiden*   Students may wish to consult a book of mythology or a reference book to learn more about the Arachne myth. The spider-maiden serves to focus the villagers' treatment of the angel as a type of circus freak. (See **U.S.** question 8 above.)

3. *Creative writing: The experience from the point of view of the angel in the form of a report to his superiors*   Call students' attention to the questions suggested in the textbook assignment. **(PLJ)**

FURTHER READING

García Márquez, Gabriel, *One Hundred Years of Solitude; Leaf Storm and Other Stories; Collected Stories; Innocent Erendira and Other Stories; No One Writes to the Colonel and Other Stories.*

North America

Special Request for the Children of Mother Corn

ZUÑI (TRADITIONAL)

INTRODUCING THE POEM

"Special Request for the Children of Mother Corn" is a poem from a Zuñi midwinter ritual in which a religious leader prays for the blessing of a life-sustaining corn crop. The poem reveals the Zuñi people's connections to the earth as the great mother of all that grows, the sun as the nurturing father, and the cobs of seed corn as the children of the Corn Maidens, the Zuñi's spiritual, life-sustaining mothers. Many aspects of the natural world are conceived in human terms: the trees, whose arms break beneath the snow (lines 6–8); the earth mother, whose flesh cracks with cold (lines 11–12); the young corn, whose hands stretch out in a plea for rain (lines 22–23). Underlying the Zuñi prayer is the concept that the corn possesses a living spirit that is aware of the Zuñi's thoughts and that will grow in appreciation. However, for the winter snow that will enable the corn to grow in the spring, the Zuñi recognize that they will need luck as well as prayer.

PLJ: Whenever you need something that money cannot buy, such as love or good health, what do you do to try to make it a reality?

Literary Terms: figurative language, metaphor, personification

COMPREHENSION QUESTIONS

1. Why will the Zuñi be lucky if the winter brings snow? (The spring snow-melt will provide necessary moisture for a new corn crop.)
2. Why do the Zuñi call the different types of corn "our mothers"? (Corn sustains them as a mother sustains her children.)
3. What do the Zuñi call the sun? (father)
4. Who creates the rain? ("rain makers," or rain clouds)
5. How do the Zuñi intend to live? (with thoughts of appreciation for the corn)

UNDERSTANDING THE POEM: POSSIBLE ANSWERS

1. *Function of poem* The Zuñi hope to please the Corn Maidens and receive a fine yield of corn.
2. *Significance of Zuñi relationship to corn* The relationship that the Zuñi feel to corn reveals its importance in their lives, namely as a nurturing mother. The Zuñi consider themselves intimately related to the natural world.
*3. *Meaning of lines 15–17* The corn kernels (seeds) are being planted in the earth.
4. *Significance of final lines* The corn myth outlined in the Introduction reveals that

when the Zuñi did not show their respect and appreciation for the Corn Maidens, they disappeared and left the people without sustenance. The Zuñi do not intend to make this mistake again.

ANALYZING LITERARY TECHNIQUE: POSSIBLE ANSWERS

*1. *Personification*   Personification conveys the feeling that all of life is related. The conception of aspects of nature as mother and father emphasizes their nurturing aspect and reflects the dependence of the Zuñi on the world of nature. Note the following specific examples: the earth as the great mother of all that grows, whose flesh cracks with cold (lines 11–12); the sun as a nurturing father (line 20); the cobs of seed corn as the children of the Corn Maidens (lines 26–27); the trees, whose arms break beneath the snow (lines 7–9); the young corn, whose hands stretch out in a plea for rain (line 23).

2. *Metaphor*   Opinions will vary. Possibilities include frost flowers; fourfold robe of white meal; and floor of ice.

WRITING ABOUT LITERATURE

1. *Expository writing: An essay analyzing the role of personification*   Call students' attention to the directions in the textbook assignment with regard to content and structure. (See **U.P.** question 3, and **A.L.T.** question 1.)
2. *Creative writing: A special request for something of value*   Call students' attention to the directions in the textbook assignment with regard to content and form. **(PLJ)**

FURTHER READING

Astrov, Margot, ed., *The Winged Serpent*.
Bierhorst, John, ed., *The Sacred Path*.
Highwater, Jamake, ed., *Words in the Blood*.
Turner III, Frederick W., ed., *The Portable North American Indian Reader*.
Witt, Shirley H. and Steiner, Stan, eds., *The Way*.

The Black Cat
EDGAR ALLAN POE

INTRODUCING THE STORY

Poe defines a short story as follows:

> A skillful literary artist has constructed a tale. If wise, he has not fashioned his thoughts to accommodate his incidents; but having conceived, with deliberate care, a certain unique or

single effect to be wrought out, he then invents such incidents—he then combines such events as may best aid him in establishing this preconceived effect. . . . In the whole composition there should be no word written, of which the tendency, direct or indirect, is not to the one preestablished design.

Poe was an avid reader who kept a record of ideas that appealed to him. He used these notes to inspire his own creative thought and to supply random details for his stories. For example, a pamphlet by Daniel Webster, *Argument on the Trial of John Francis Knapp* (1830), describes a murderer as being a calm, ordinary-appearing but demonic character, who, having carefully and successfully committed his crime, finds himself compelled, of his own volition, to confess his guilt. This combination of ideas supplied Poe with the outline for "The Tell-Tale Heart" and "The Black Cat."

Poe's achievement in "The Black Cat" is to turn a Gothic tale of horror into a story told by a madman. "The Black Cat" is a dramatic monologue in which the narrator inadvertently reveals his character as he tells his tale. The narrator's thought processes as he plans, executes, and exults over his grotesque deeds become the story's dramatic effects.

Poe's narrator in "The Black Cat" is a melodramatic example of a person who cannot acknowledge and accept, and who therefore cannot control, the dark side of his human nature (his doppelgänger or Shadow). He operates, as an adult, with the psychological limitations of a child. Very young children have not yet developed the mental ability to understand moderation and extenuating circumstances, and they therefore repress many aggressive feelings and impulses in order to be "good" enough to receive the love and care that they need from parents. The narrator views himself through the eyes of his child-self. To him, a person is either good or evil. Since he is compelled to view himself as good, he must deny all unacceptable thoughts and impulses and bury them deep within his subconscious, where they bubble like a subterranean volcano and finally explode in uncontrollable behavior.

Exhibiting this divided personality, the man who professes to love his pets and his wife abuses them. Then, he tearfully and with remorse kills his cat. He is now filled with contempt for the part of himself who committed the crime, so he hates his second cat for loving him when he is so loathsome. Finally, his self-hatred becomes so overwhelming that his "moodiness . . . increased to hatred of all things and of all mankind." He impulsively murders his loving wife when she tries to prevent him from killing the second cat. In an ironic twist, when the narrator's rational self thinks that he has committed the perfect crime, his Shadow compels him to dare fate by knocking on the burial wall. His second cat, which he inadvertently buried along with his wife, howls from behind the wall, demanding the punishment that the narrator's Shadow knows that he deserves. However, the story ends as it begins, with the narrator's being unable to acknowledge his Shadow-self.

PLJ: Do you believe whatever you hear or read? How do you know if you are hearing or reading an accurate presentation? To what extent, if any, do you evaluate the content of what you hear or read? To what extent, if any, do you evaluate the credibility of the speaker or writer?

Literary Terms: characterization, doppelgänger, Gothic, irony, narrative perspective, psychological realism, Shadow, unreliable narrator

COMPREHENSION QUESTIONS

1. What opening statement does the narrator make about himself? (He is sane.)
2. What does he blame for his new attitude toward his pets? (alcoholism)
3. What does he do to Pluto? Why? (He removes the cat's eye and then kills the cat because it fears and avoids him.)
4. What is the difference between Pluto and the second cat? (the second cat's white patch)
5. How does the narrator feel about the second cat? Why? (He hates it and wants to kill it because it loves him.)
6. What does the narrator do to his wife? (kills her)
7. How does the narrator really feel about his wife? (does not love her; feels no remorse at her death)
8. What happens to the second cat? (accidently buried alive in wall with corpse of wife)
9. What happens at the end? (The narrator taps on the wall, causing cat to reveal itself and wife's corpse.)
10. What does the narrator think leads him to bring about his own end? (pride in his ability to hide the murder)

UNDERSTANDING THE STORY:
POSSIBLE ANSWERS

*1. *What motivates the narrator?*   Self-justification motivates the narrator to relate his tale. He is writing on the eve of his execution for his wife's murder. The narrator wants to believe that he is not responsible for his behavior: He hopes someone "more calm, more logical, and far less excitable" will be able to explain what happened.

*2. *Narrator's treatment of Pluto*   The narrator's treatment of Pluto foreshadows his behavior toward the second cat and toward his wife. The narrator may feel that the cat sees into his inner self, the Shadow-self that he tries to hide from himself and the world, and that is why he cuts out the cat's eye and later kills it.

*3. *Narrator's treatment of second cat*   The narrator is initially attracted to the second cat because it reminds him of Pluto. However, by reminding him of the earlier cat's affection, the second cat also reminds the narrator of the first cat's death. Gradually, the cat's missing eye and white spot (which appears to the narrator to be shaped like a gallows) drive the narrator to dread and mistreat the second cat, too.

*4. *What leads the narrator toward self-destruction?*   The narrator's alcoholism, pride, and subconscious guilt and need for punishment combine to lead him toward self-destruction. The narrator blames all of this on the "spirit of PERVERSENESS." He cannot accept evil as part of his own nature. Because he cannot acknowledge his evil impulses, he cannot control them, and having acted upon them, he cannot assume responsibility for his actions.

*5. *What reader learns about the narrator*   The reader comes to recognize that the narrator is insane, despite his protestations to the contrary. He inadvertently reveals how the "spirit of PERVERSENESS" (his doppelgänger or his Shadow) takes control of his life and destroys all who love him. Finally, it destroys him as well. The narrator's blame of the cat for his crimes reveals his desperate need to think well of himself and to ignore the darker side of his nature.

ANALYZING LITERARY TECHNIQUE: POSSIBLE ANSWERS

1. *Narrative perspective*   Poe's choice of narrative perspective, the first-person limited omniscient narrator, fuses the plot with the character. The plot becomes the narrator's perceptions of the events. To the extent that he is an unreliable narrator, readers are left on their own to determine the nature of objective reality. Being intimate with the center of consciousness creates a sense of immediacy and suspense for readers. They know only what the narrator knows and make their discoveries along with him.

2. *Psychological realism*   The technique of telling a story through the thoughts, feelings, and perceptions of one of the characters is a form of psychological realism in that the story is then set in the mind of a character instead of in external reality.

3. *Dramatic irony*   Dramatic irony is present in the narrator's proclamation of his sanity while he tells a tale that reveals his insanity. The narrator's claims of gentleness and love for his wife and other creatures is also ironic. Dramatic irony also provides a surprise ending that is a satisfying retribution for the narrator's crime.

4. *Allusion to Pluto*   Pluto is another name for Hades, the Greek god of the Underworld. Poe was probably using it because of its connotation of the Underworld, suggesting that the cat was some kind of spirit or portent of death. Despite the narrator's early claims of affection for Pluto, the cat's name would set off warning bells for the reader—a form of foreshadowing.

5. *Gothic horror tale*   Gothic elements include: (*a*) the mysterious fire; (*b*) the event of Pluto's shadow's being etched on a wall in the ruins of the burned house; (*c*) the grotesque element of the decayed and gory corpse of the narrator's wife; (*d*) the noise of the buried cat's howling; (*e*) the supernatural terrors of the second cat's white spot. Also related to the Gothic tradition are the narrator's attempts to explain the bizarre events, as much as possible, by scientific or natural means.

6. *Poe's effects and technique*   Poe creates terror and horror, first, through the psychological realism of his narrative technique, which makes the reader a part of the deranged narrator's thoughts and actions and, second, through his use of Gothic details. The emphasis in the story is on perversity and on uncontrollable, violent behavior.

WRITING ABOUT LITERATURE

1. *Expository theme presenting a psychological analysis of the narrator*   Call students' attention to the directions in the textbook assignment with regard to content. (See **U.S.** questions 1–5 above.)

2. *Creative writing: point of view of cat or the police*   Call students' attention to the directions in the textbook assignment. **(PLJ)**

FURTHER READING

Poe, Edgar Allan, "The Tell-Tale Heart"; "The Masque of the Red Death"; "The Cask of Amontillado"; "Ligeia"; "The Fall of the House of Usher"; "The Pit and the Pendulum."

Give Me the Splendid Silent Sun
WALT WHITMAN

INTRODUCING THE POEM

In "Give Me the Splendid Silent Sun," Whitman rhapsodizes about life, particularly the irony of his wish for the beauty, peace, and solitude of life in the country when he loves being part of Manhattan, the ultimate urban environment.

The power of the poem comes from both its content and its style. Whitman presents a striking contrast between what he thinks he wants in life and what he finds that he really wants. The content of the poem is romantic in its idealization of both the natural world and the urban world. Among the wealth of supporting details, which reflect a sympathy for realism, he selects only those that support his view of the universe as a joyful set of choices. Nature is charming, and the city is exciting.

With a poet's ear for sound, Whitman chooses words and phrases that also reflect the contrast between the natural world and the urban world. He describes the natural environment in long, flowing lines and more ornate speech, changing to short, disconnected clauses and simple speech once he rejects the pastoral scene for the city scene.

Whitman's repetitive sentence structure, in the form of detailed lists of appealing qualities, creates a visual picture of both rural beauty and metropolitan variety and complexity. The sheer mass of pictorial images gives the poem a cumulative descriptive power. Meanwhile, Whitman's repeated use of "Give me . . ." and "Keep your . . ." emphasizes the importance of his need and the irony that is implicit in his change of mind.

PLJ: Which do you think that you would prefer, living in the country or living in the city? What are the advantages of each location?

Literary Terms: apostrophe, connotative language, contrast, free verse, irony, paradox, realism, repetition, romanticism, tone

COMPREHENSION QUESTIONS

1. Where does Whitman first think that he wants to live? (in the country)
2. What aspects of rural life does he find most appealing? (solitude and beauty of nature)
3. Where does Whitman realize that he really wants to live? (in the city)

4. What aspects of this environment does he find most appealing? (variety and complexity of life on the streets)

UNDERSTANDING THE POEM: POSSIBLE ANSWERS

1. *Whitman's view of nature*   While Whitman's presentation of nature is realistic, with many concrete details, his overall view of nature is idealized and romantic. He omits all aspects of nature that are unattractive, unreliable, or harmful. He also omits the human labor necessary to sustain life in the country.
2. *Whitman's view of urban life*   Whitman's presentation of urban life is also realistic, with concrete details such as the old and worn returning soldiers' noticing nothing as they march. However, here his view is even more idealized and romantic in that he has included unattractive and painful aspects of reality without being bothered by them. He devotes enough space to descriptions of marching men, both going to war and returning (often dazed and wounded), that it is surprising that these sights do not diminish his pleasure of the city.
3. *Whitman's views*   Opinions will vary: Some students will prefer the pastoral environment; others will, like Whitman, prefer the city with all its problems.
4. *Relation between 1865 and content*   Manhattan's Broadway hosts parades of soldiers going off to fight in the Civil War and returning from the battlefield. Whitman records the trumpets and drums, the appearance of the brigades, the military wagons loaded with war gear, and the clanking muskets of the marching men. The tone of these passages reflects the closing stages of the war. The speaker is enjoying the sights and sounds.

ANALYZING LITERARY TECHNIQUE: POSSIBLE ANSWERS

1. *Advantages of free verse*   By using free verse, Whitman is able to focus on his subject rather than on trying to fit it into a particular form. Writing in a prose style permits longer sentences, greater variety of content within each line, and less predictability. Whitman is free to create whatever devices he wishes in order to create unity and achieve emphasis.
2. *Contrast*   Whitman's use of contrasting details and a contrasting choice of words and phrasing highlights the difference between the noisy urban environment and the tranquil natural environment.
3. *Apostrophe*   Whitman uses apostrophe to address both the city (line 15) and Nature (line 21). In both examples, Whitman treats nonhuman entities as if they are listening to him. It makes them appear to be vital forces that are actively interacting with him.
4. *Irony and first line*   It is ironic that Whitman chooses a tumultuous environment over one that is filled with peace and beauty. He even chooses the city despite its many reminders of the human price of war. The first line symbolizes Whitman's

view of nature and has an ironic function in that he uses the line twice, first to wish for the joys of nature and then to repudiate them.

5. *Paradox* It is paradoxical that in Whitman's view, nature is both beautiful and boring, so that he repudiates an environment that appears to be perfect. Similarly, the city is raucous, turbulent, and even disquieting, and yet, for all its unpleasantness, in Whitman's view, it is enriching and even enchanting.

*6. *Repetition* (*a*) Repeated sentence structure: Detailed lists of appealing qualities create visual pictures of rural beauty and urban variety that have cumulative power.

(*b*) Repeated phrases: "Give me . . ." emphasizes Whitman's need; "Keep your . . ." emphasizes his rejection of the country and the irony of his change of mind.

7. *Tone* Whitman's tone is ebullient and joyous. He is enthusiastic about both nature and the city, but he prefers the city. He conveys his enthusiasm through the use of the phrase, "Give me . . ." followed by lists of delightful sights. He conveys through his use of detail the variation and complexity that he so enjoys.

WRITING ABOUT LITERATURE

1. *Expository analysis of the use of repetition in the poem* Call students' attention to the directions in the textbook assignment. Remind them of the importance of using direct quotations to support their ideas. (See **A.L.T.** question 6 above.)

2. *Creative writing: a poem about the best place to live* Remind students to work from a list of reasons that support their choice and to use repetition for emphasis and effect. **(PLJ)**

FURTHER READING

Whitman, Walt, *Leaves of Grass.*

My Life Closed Twice

EMILY DICKINSON

INTRODUCING THE POEM

"My Life Closed Twice" is a philosophical lyric. With eloquence and power, it expresses the devastating impact on Dickinson's life of the loss of two people she loved, an impact that is intensified by her skepticism about the possibility of reunion after death. In a series of paradoxes, Dickinson equates the impact on her life of the loss of two loved ones with the devastating condition of a living death. So great were these losses that her "life closed twice before its close," and "parting" is all she needs of hell. A more conventional religious view would lead one to hope for reunion in heaven after death. However, Dickinson expresses only uncertainty about one's fate after death. She states that parting, which occurs in this life, "is all we know of heaven." Thus, her ability to express heartfelt emotions in a lyric poem enables Dickinson to confront her traumatic life experiences and to accept her reactions to them.

PLJ: Imagine that a person very dear to you has permanently left your life. What type of impact would that loss have on your life?

Literary Terms: climax, connotative language, lyric, paradox, tone

COMPREHENSION QUESTIONS

1. In general, why did the speaker's life close twice? (two devastating events occurred)
2. What might immortality reveal to the speaker? (a third devastating event)
3. What do we know of heaven, according to the poem? (nothing except that it involves parting in this life)
4. What does the poem suggest we know of hell? (The pain of parting is hellish.)
5. What attitude does this poem express? (skepticism about reunion in heaven)

UNDERSTANDING THE POEM:
POSSIBLE ANSWERS

*1. *"My life closed twice"*   The speaker has "died" emotionally twice before her physical death.
*2. *Immortality*   The speaker is uncertain about the nature of immortality. It is possible that loved ones are not reunited after death, and she fears a third cataclysmic separation.
*3. *"Parting is all we know of heaven"* (line 7)   Many people believe that they will be reunited in heaven after death. The speaker does not know if this is true. She is certain only of what she experiences in this life, which is that parting from loved ones is devastating.
*4. *"Parting is . . . all we need of hell"* (lines 7–8)   The speaker means that, for her, hell also may or may not exist after death, but that it most certainly exists in life. In her experience, parting from loved ones has been so devastating that it is a type of hell on earth.

ANALYZING LITERARY TECHNIQUE:
POSSIBLE ANSWERS

*1. *Connotative language*   Dickinson uses connotative language to convey the devastating effect of the two events to which she alludes. Examples: "So huge, so hopeless to conceive" (line 5), "Parting . . . heaven . . . hell" (lines 7–8).
*2. *Paradox*   (a) "My life closed twice" (line 1): The speaker has died twice emotionally while physically continuing to live, thus experiencing a living death.

(b) "Parting . . . heaven" (line 7): Heaven is generally considered a reward. The speaker states that all she knows for certain about heaven is that it requires separation from those who are living, thus suggesting heaven is a punishment for those left behind.

(c) "And all we need of hell" (line 8): People believe hell is an experience that is a punishment after death. Dickinson is saying that parting from a loved one is so torturous that it creates a hell on earth.

3. *Last line as climax*   The last line dramatically conveys the extent of the devastation caused by the two events in the speaker's life. It intensifies the emotion behind all of the other statements.

4. *Tone*   The tone is one of despair and devastation. Two cataclysmic events have occurred in the speaker's life, and conventional religion offers little comfort for her. She is afraid of another devastating separation.

WRITING ABOUT LITERATURE

1. *Expository writing: an essay analyzing Dickinson's use of paradox*   Call students' attention to the suggestions in the textbook assignment. Remind students to use direct quotations to support their ideas. (See **U.P.** questions 1–4, and **A.L.T.** question 2 above.)

2. *Expository writing: an essay analyzing Dickinson's techniques of compression*   Call students' attention to the suggestions in the textbook assignment. (See **U.P.** questions 1, 3, and 4, and **A.L.T.** questions 1 and 2.)

3. *Creative writing: significance of loss of presence of a loved one.*   Remind students that they can choose between writing a poem or writing prose.

FURTHER READING

Dickinson, Emily, "There's a Certain Slant of Light"; "Because I Could Not Stop for Death"; "The Soul Selects Her Own Society"; "I Heard a Fly Buzz—When I Died"; "The Brain—Is Wider Than the Sky."

Ile

EUGENE O'NEILL

INTRODUCING THE PLAY

Ile is the story of a man who must choose between his wife's well-being and his own self-respect. As the captain of a whaling ship, Captain Keeney's self-esteem depends on his continuing ability to be successful at his profession, which is acquiring whale oil (ile). He already possesses wealth and an established reputation. When the play opens, he has been two years at sea, and his hunt for whales has been unsuccessful. Supplies are dwindling, the men are mutinous, and his wife Annie is on the verge of a mental breakdown. Captain Keeney must decide whether to return home or to continue the frustrating search. Shortly after he has subdued his men and reluctantly agreed to his wife's heartfelt pleas to return home, the sea-ice opens, revealing the elusive whales. He reverses his decision and orders his men to prepare for the kill. Mrs. Keeney responds by losing her mind.

Thus, a well-intentioned man becomes a pawn of fate through a common failing in human nature, an excess of pride. Captain Keeney loves and attempts to care for his wife, but his personal investment in his career is more compelling. When pushed, he can put his wife's needs ahead of his continued search for an elusive prey. However, with the prey within his grasp, he becomes deaf to his wife's pleas. Courage, determination, and perseverance are heroic in moderation, but tragic in excess. Captain Keeney's obsessive drive to acquire oil regardless of the attitudes of his crew and his wife make him a tragic figure.

Mrs. Keeney is a tragic figure in that she lacks the psychological strength to create meaning in her own life when the outer worlds of marriage, town life, and the natural universe do not support her needs. She is also tragic in a universal, symbolic sense because life-experience often fails to respond to the basic needs and drives of human beings, the world being indifferent at best and often hostile.

In addition to creating two tragic characters, O'Neill places them in a situation that has no satisfactory solution. Captain Keeney's values being what they are, either decision inevitably will bring disaster into both his and Annie's lives. His decision to stay causes her insanity and robs him of his wife. However, he would have been miserable if he had chosen to sacrifice the oil in order to take Annie home. He could not live without self-esteem, and he would have hated his wife for being the cause of his private shame.

The character of Captain Keeney reveals O'Neill's love of Greek tragedy with its interplay between the human personality and fate. Like many a hero in Greek mythology, Captain Keeney's greatest strength becomes his greatest weakness, and he is compelled to act in such a way that he brings disaster into his life. As the captain of the whaling ship, Captain Keeney is a man of high social stature in the eyes of his crew. The source of his excellence (the Greek concept of *aretē*) is his expertise as a captain; he always returns from his whaling voyages with a full load of oil. His pride in his success and his related fear for his reputation are both excessive (the Greek concept of *hubris*), and they lead him to take action that is blindly reckless or rash (the Greek concept of *atē*); in that he continues to pursue whales despite the crew's attitude and his wife's emotional needs. Retribution (the Greek concept of *nemesis*) inevitably follows in the form of his wife's insanity.

Ile differs from the classical Greek tragedy in that Captain Keeney knows what form the retribution will take before he makes the critical decision, and having precipitated his wife's insanity, he reacts with denial rather than with remorse. O'Neill thus reveals the destructive power of psychological necessity to be awesome, creating isolation from loved ones through imprudent and callous behavior. The question of whether one's responsibility to oneself is more important than one's responsibility to one's family is as old as Greek myths and as modern as the vital contemporary conflict between the demands of one's career and the needs of one's family.

PLJ: In what ways, if any, are your own needs and desires more important to you than those of other members of your family? In what ways, if any, are your family's needs and desires more important to you than your own? Has a conflict ever occurred where a family member had to make a choice between what was best for that person and what was best for others in the family?

Literary Terms: climax, conflict, crisis, exposition, foreshadowing, irony, melodrama, paradox, repetition, setting, symbolism, theme, tone, tragedy

COMPREHENSION QUESTIONS

1. What is important about the day on which the action occurs? (sailors' two-year commitment is over)
2. What is Captain Keeney's goal? (get whale oil)
3. What has the problem been with the voyage? (no whales, so no oil)
4. What does Mrs. Keeney want her husband to do? (return home)
5. How does Mrs. Keeney feel about the voyage? (hates it)
6. What effort has the captain made to please his wife? (brought an organ onboard the ship for her)
7. What is the attitude of the seamen? (They threaten mutiny if the captain doesn't turn back.)
8. What reversal occurs? (Captain agrees to turn back, then sees whales and stays to hunt them.)
9. What happens in the end to the captain? (goes whale hunting)
10. What happens in the end to Mrs. Keeney? (goes insane)

UNDERSTANDING THE PLAY: POSSIBLE ANSWERS

*1. *Three major conflicts* The major conflicts include: (*a*) the conflict between Captain Keeney and Annie; (*b*) the conflict between the Captain and himself (inner conflict between wish to please himself and wish to please Annie); (*c*) the conflict between the Captain and external forces (fate or nature). The conflict between Captain Keeney and his crew is minor.

*2. *Why conflicts so powerful* The power of the three conflicts arises from their interdependence. All involve the issue of acquiring oil and the priority of Captain Keeney's responsibility.

*3. *Blame for Mrs. Keeney's condition* The blame for Mrs. Keeney's condition is shared between her and the Captain. She was not happy home alone so she chose life at sea. The Captain places his obligation to himself and his goals over his love for Mrs. Keeney and her needs.

*4. *Sympathetic character*   One strength of *Ile* lies in the balance O'Neill achieves between the two major characters. Both are admirable people. Mrs. Keeney's point of view is understandable before the whales are discovered, and the crew echoes her position. Captain Keeney's point of view is understandable after the discovery of the whales.

*5. *Wiser decision for Captain Keeney*   The tragedy may be that Captain Keeney cannot win either way. If he gives in to his wife's needs, his self-esteem may suffer irreparable damage, given its dependence on a successful voyage's reinforcing his reputation. If he ignores his wife's needs, which, in the end, he does, he must live with the responsibility for her mental state.

*6. *Ability of characters to control their fate*   The power of the play resides in O'Neill's substitution of human psychology for what was considered fate by the Greeks. The characters are limited by their personalities. Those who can be flexible and adaptable fare much better than those who are either obsessed (Captain Keeney) or who react passively to their experiences (Mrs. Keeney).

7. *Seamen's reaction to Captain's decision*   Given their financial stake in a successful voyage, the seamen will support Captain Keeney once the whales are in sight.

8. *Themes*   Themes include: (a) a person's personality determines his or her fate; (b) doing everything in moderation (flexibility, modest goals) creates a generally happier life.

ANALYZING LITERARY TECHNIQUE: POSSIBLE ANSWERS

1. *Function of Ben and Steward*   The conversation between Ben and the Steward provides the exposition, revealing the underlying situation as the play opens, including the problem of finding whales and its effect on the attitudes of all onboard ship—the crew, Mrs. Keeney, and Captain Keeney.

2. *Foreshadowing*   A source of *Ile's* power resides in the inevitability of the drama. One example of foreshadowing occurs when, as part of the exposition, Ben and the Steward characterize Captain Keeney and Mrs. Keeney. It is clear what will happen if the Captain continues the whaling expedition.

*3. *Fate*   Fate takes two forms: (a) the force in life that supplies whales after the Captain has agreed to return home; (b) the force within the Captain that programs him to react to life's situations as he does. The whales are the catalyst for the tragedy, which Captain Keeney brings upon himself.

4. *Connection between setting and tone*   The setting of the action—at sea in the high Arctic, with its isolation, impenetrable ice, and gray skies—creates a tone of depression, frustration, and mounting hysteria.

5. *Crisis and climax*   The crisis occurs when Captain Keeney decides to pursue the clear passage northward, regardless of the effect of his action on his wife. The cli-

max occurs when Mrs. Keeney loses her mind. It is intensified by the Captain's denial of the reality of her condition, a denial made necessary by the fact that his actions were the precipitating factor.

*6. *Captain Keeney as a tragic figure*   Captain Keeney is compelled by his nature to act in such a way that he causes the destruction of Mrs. Keeney. His excellence *(aretē)* is his expertise as a whaling captain; he always returns from his voyages with a full load of oil. His excessive pride in his accomplishments *(hubris)* leads him to take rash action *(atē)*, in that he continues to pursue whales in spite of the risk to his wife. Retribution *(nemesis)* occurs in the form of Mrs. Keeney's insanity. Captain Keeney knows what form the retribution will take before he makes the critical decision, but he denies both the possibility and the reality, and he shows no remorse.

*7. *Paradox*   Paradoxes include: (*a*) Single-minded devotion to the immediate goal of achieving financial success can prevent people from realizing their ultimate goal of improving their lives.

(*b*) People may base their attitudes and behavior on how they think others view them, when, in reality, others view them quite differently or may not think about them at all.

(*c*) A person whose emotional needs are not being met can be desperately unhappy despite his or her economic security.

(*d*) A person's greatest strength is often that person's greatest weakness as well.

8. *Symbolism*   The world of the sea symbolizes the uncaring, hostile, or absurd universe in which human beings live. Its concealment and disclosure of whales motivates Captain Kenney's behavior, which, in turn, causes Mrs. Keeney's depression and madness.

9. *Repetition*   Repetition emphasizes the characterization of Captain Keeney ("I got to git the ile!") and Mrs. Keeney ("Take me home . . . I can't bear it. . . . I'll go mad"). It also emphasizes the sense of inevitability (through foreshadowing and tone), thus enhancing *Ile*'s dramatic power.

WRITING ABOUT LITERATURE

1. *Expository analysis of Captain Keeney as a tragic figure*   Call students' attention to the directions in the textbook assignment with regard to content. (See **U.P.** questions 1–6, and **A.L.T.** questions 3, 6, and 7 above.)

2. *Creative writing: a dialogue between another captain and his wife*   Students should focus on the issue of one's responsibility to oneself and to others, on the roles of love and career in marriage, and on the attitudes of husband and wife toward these issues. **(PLJ)**

FURTHER READING

O'Neill, Eugene, *The Great God Brown; Mourning Becomes Electra; The Iceman Cometh; Long Day's Journey Into Night.*

Cat in the Rain

ERNEST HEMINGWAY

INTRODUCING THE STORY

"Cat in the Rain" is an appealing story that is typical of Hemingway's work. The wife, looking out a hotel window on a rainy afternoon in Italy, sees a cat out in the rain and wishes to make it hers. She is feeling lonely, sad, and dissatisfied with her life. Seeing the cat, she identifies with it and welcomes the opportunity to give it the home that she herself longs to have. The conscientious hotel-keeper, sensing her feelings about the cat and understanding its importance to her, not only sends a maid to accompany her on her search but finds a cat to give her when the cat in the rain has disappeared. Meanwhile, the husband, George, well-meaning as he is, does not recognize his wife's need for something to love and care for; his world is complete as it is.

Thus, the hotel-keeper and the wife are the sensitive Hemingway hero-types. They are aware of an impersonal and uncaring universe, and they are determined to live by a personal code that provides meaning in spite of it. Hemingway writes in *For Whom the Bell Tolls,* "Stay with what you believe now. Don't get cynical. . . . Each one does what he can. You can do nothing for yourself but perhaps you can do something for another." The wife's and the hotel-keeper's decency, compassion, and involvement with others buttress them against feelings of isolation, estrangement, and loneliness. In contrast, George represents the insensitive majority, those who do not pay serious attention to the emotional needs and suffering of others in their presence.

Hemingway is a realist in his attention to selective detail and a symbolist in his desire to use details in orders to evoke an emotional response. His stories are designed to convey the essence of a particular experience, to provide a type of Joycean epiphany. Thus, they omit any extraneous detail and mean more than they say. Hemingway conveys tone through setting and repetition of key words in the dialogue. A rainy afternoon in a foreign country is conducive to feelings of loneliness and longing, feelings conveyed through the repeated use of "I want." The power of the story resides in the implied connection between the miniworld of the hotel room and the larger world beyond it. The cat in the rain bridges both worlds, providing love and purpose for the wife in a world where individuals must create their own values and ultimate sources of personal satisfaction and pride.

PLJ: To what extent, if any, does weather affect your mood? Give examples. To what extent, if any, do those closest to you understand your feelings? Give examples.

Literary Terms: contrast, epiphany, irony, realism, repetition, symbolist, theme, tone

COMPREHENSION QUESTIONS

1. Where are the two Americans? (hotel in Italy)
2. Why does the wife want a cat? (to pet and love it)

3. What is George's attitude? (He is indifferent to his wife's feelings. He thinks she is fine with or without the cat.)
4. What does the hotel-keeper do? (sends maid with umbrella; later sends maid with cat)

UNDERSTANDING THE STORY: POSSIBLE ANSWERS

1. *Connection between wife's complaints and desire for cat*   The cat symbolizes the wife's place in the universe: Both are homeless and lonely in an uncaring world. Her complaints reveal aspects of herself and her life with which she is dissatisfied. While she may not be able to change them, if she can acquire a cat, she will provide a home for it. She will then have something she wants that will satisfy her desire to love and care for another, and be loved in return.

2. *What George's attitude reveals about their relationship*   George's attitude reveals that he has no understanding of his wife's needs and feelings.

3. *George's response to wife's complaints*   George is satisfied with living in hotels and not being tied down. He is irritated by his wife's desire for more stability, represented by her desire to grow out her hair, to have her own table, and to have a cat.

4. *Significance of cat*   The hotel-keeper makes the wife feel important and respected. By finding the cat for her, he affirms her value in a way that her husband does not.

5. *Theme*   Helping others is an effective way to help oneself. The hotel-keeper gets satisfaction from doing his job well, and this includes taking a personal interest in his guests and looking after their needs and interests. The wife will find meaning in life by attending to the needs of a pet, and, in return, the cat will return her affection and attention.

ANALYZING LITERARY TECHNIQUE: POSSIBLE ANSWERS

1. *Function of rain*   Rain sets the tone of the story. It provides the psychological landscape, both affecting and reflecting the wife's emotions. The day is gray and wet, and the wife is depressed.

2. *Significance of only two Americans*   Their being the only two Americans reinforces the story's sense of isolation. George and his wife have no one else with whom to talk or to be. This makes the hotel-keeper's interest and involvement significant for the wife.

3. *Situational irony*   It is ironic that the hotel-keeper is more sensitive to the wife's needs than George is. This dramatizes the inherent separateness and loneliness of the individual, even among acquaintances, friends, and relatives. George's lack of emotional support drives his wife to find other sources of satisfaction and support.

4. *Style*   Hemingway omits background information about the American couple: the wife's name; why they are in Italy; and most details about their appearance, their personalities, and their marriage. The lack of extraneous detail focuses the reader's attention on the point of the story (the need to create personal values and meaning in an uncaring universe) and gives it universality.

*5. *Repetition*   Examples of repetition include: (*a*) the repeated emphasis on rain, which creates mood and establishes a reason for strangers to relate to one another; (*b*) the wife's repeated expression of a liking for the hotel-keeper, which emphasizes his character and their sympathetic relationship; (*c*) the wife's repetition of "want," which emphasizes the depth of her emotional needs.

6. *Contrast*   One contrast is between the hotel-keeper and George. The wife likes the hotel-keeper because of his serious attitude toward his job, which is reflected in his attitude toward complaints and in his desire to serve his guests, and because of his dignity. The contrast between the hotel-keeper and George accentuates the difference between the sensitive Hemingway heroes (hotel-keeper and the wife) who are aware of an impersonal and uncaring universe and are determined to live by a personal code that provides meaning in spite of it, and the insensitive majority (George), who either do not see or do not care about the emotional needs and suffering of others in their presence.

A second important contrast is between the life the couple is leading—rootless, unsettled, isolated—and the life the wife wants to lead—with a home, long hair that requires time and attention, and a cat.

7. *Title*   "Cat in the Rain" accentuates the problem (loneliness in an uncaring and inhospitable universe) and a way of solving the problem (establishing personal, nurturing relationships).

WRITING ABOUT LITERATURE

1. *Expository analysis of repetition*   Call students' attention to the directions in the textbook assignment with regard to content and organization. (See **A.L.T.** question 5.)

2. *Creative writing: The story from the hotel-keeper's or George's point of view*   Call students' attention to the suggestions in the textbook assignment. **(PLJ)**

FURTHER READING

Hemingway, Ernest, *The Old Man and the Sea;* "The Killers"; "The Snows of Kilimanjaro"; "Hills Like White Elephants"; "A Clean, Well-Lighted Place"; "In Another Country"; "The Short Happy Life of Francis Macomber."

Mother to Son
LANGSTON HUGHES

INTRODUCING THE POEM

"Mother to Son" is a mother's exhortation to her son to follow her example of effort and courage. It is clear from her message that the mother possesses dignity and pride despite her difficult life and that she cares about how the son she loves will choose to lead his life.

Hughes characterizes the mother through her speech patterns as well as by the nature of her advice. His use of free verse enables him to tell her situation as it is, in her own language, and to achieve emphasis through the use of movement and pauses in the structure of her sentences.

Hughes achieves power and poignancy through the symbol of the stairway, part of the urban dweller's apartment life and a necessary way of traveling from one location to another. The stairway lends itself to being treated as an extended metaphor, where, like life itself, it is not what one wishes it to be, and difficulties on its steps represent real difficulties on the journey of life.

PLJ: A popular saying states, "When the going gets tough, the tough get going." To what extent do challenges excite you, and to what extent do you find them discouraging? Explain your point of view.

Literary Terms: apostrophe, characterization, connotative language, contrast, figurative language, free verse, metaphor, symbol, theme

COMPREHENSION QUESTIONS

1. What type of life has the mother had? (difficult)
2. What is the mother's attitude toward life? (keep aiming high)
3. What advice does she give her son? (keep trying to reach goals)
4. What symbol does Hughes use to represent the mother's life? (a stairway)
5. What is Hughes's metaphor for an easy life? (a crystal stair)

UNDERSTANDING THE POEM: POSSIBLE ANSWERS

1. *Identity of mother*   (a) It is clear from her use of English that the mother's knowledge is primarily from hard life experiences, rather than from traditional education.

     (b) The nature of the mother's life is important because it explains her goal of wanting to improve the life of her family and herself. It also explains her use of stairs as a metaphor. Presumably, living in an inner-city apartment building, she would literally have climbed stairs that are in the condition she describes in the poem.
2. *Why mother describes her life to son*   The mother wants the son to know that it is possible to succeed in spite of the many obstacles in their lives and that he should follow her example and keep aiming to achieve his goals.
3. *Mother's character*   (a) Her description of continuing to climb the stairway of life despite every type of obstacle, often accompanied by physical pain and psychological discomfort, reveals her to be a woman of dignity, courage, and perseverance.

     (b) Her desire to communicate her values to her son reveals her to be loving and supportive, with high expectations for the son as well as for herself.
*4. *Themes*   (a) A motivated person can overcome many serious obstacles; (b) if at first

you don't succeed, try again and again; (*c*) parents can set good examples for their children; (*d*) dignity, courage, and perseverance do not depend on economic status.

ANALYZING LITERARY TECHNIQUE: POSSIBLE ANSWERS

*1. *Stairway as symbol*   Life moves from youth to old age, and a stairway is one way of moving from one place to another. It is particularly appropriate here because it is an inherent part of apartment living in most urban neighborhoods, and in the mother's neighborhood, one could expect that the stairway would be in poor condition. One walks down stairs as often as one climbs up; the mother's climb up the stairs rather than down them symbolizes her efforts to improve her life.

*2. *Stairway as extended metaphor*   Students' responses will vary. Some possible answers include:

(*a*) Tacks and splinters: racial prejudice in the form of slurs, discrimination, and injustice.

(*b*) Boards torn up: obstacles to achievement based on racial discrimination, lack of education, or lack of money.

(*c*) No carpet: difficult tasks with nothing to ease them.

(*d*) Landings: brief periods when life is easier.

(*e*) Turning corners: a new stage in the progress toward old goals.

(*f*) Being in the dark: being uncertain of the future—unsure of how to achieve one's goals, and unsure of success.

3. *Apostrophe*   Hughes's use of apostrophe gives the impression that the son is present and is listening to the mother's advice. Thus, the mother's communication is particular (addressed to a real person) and immediate (some type of response will be forthcoming).

4. *Techniques for characterizing mother*   Hughes characterizes the mother by (*a*) what she says—her desire to communicate her values to her son; (*b*) what she does—her continuing to climb the stairway of life despite every type of obstacle, and even though she is often in physical pain and psychological discomfort; and (*c*) how she says it—the mother's use of English. (See **U.P.** question 3 above for what each of these techniques reveals.)

5. *Advantage of free verse*   Free verse gives Hughes the freedom to let the mother speak in her own style and, therefore, convey who she is and how she lives her life. The structure of her sentences, with their movement and their pauses, conveys the progress of her life and emphasizes the low points ("tacks," "splinters," "boards torn up," and, particularly, "Bare").

WRITING ABOUT LITERATURE

1. *Expository writing: an essay analyzing the extended metaphor*   Call students' attention to the directions in the textbook. (See **U.P.** question 4, and **A.L.T.** questions 1 and 2 above.)

2. *Creative writing: response from son to mother*   Call students' attention to the directions in the textbook assignment. Students can choose to write a poem or a letter. **(PLJ)**

FURTHER READING

Hughes, Langston, *Selected Poems; The Best of Simple.*

A Worn Path

EUDORA WELTY

INTRODUCING THE STORY

"A Worn Path" is the story of an African-American woman, Phoenix Jackson, who undertakes an arduous journey on foot in order to procure medicine for her grandson, as she always does whenever he needs it. Phoenix is the most humane of humans, at one with herself and with the universe. She expects from others the respect with which she herself regards the living world, and she usually receives it.

On one level, "A Worn Path" is the story of an old woman's love for her grandchild, and her devotion is dramatized by how she experiences her journey and the gift she buys for him at the end. No obstacle can deter her, neither the infirmities of old age nor the vicissitudes of nature, and no personal sacrifice is too great.

On another level, "A Worn Path" is an affirmation of life despite all its obstacles. In the course of her journey, Phoenix experiences a series of anticipated and unexpected trials, all of which she accepts as a part of life. Although time has attacked her body, her spirit refuses to be daunted. Beyond Phoenix's acceptance of life and her ability to endure its trials is her joy of simply being alive. She loves having one more day in which to enjoy the sights, sounds, smells, and feel of the universe. The story ends with a symbolic affirmation of life as Phoenix goes off to spend her two precious nickels on a paper windmill (pinwheel) for her grandson. She will hold it high all the way home, and the reader anticipates her enjoyment of its color and movement despite her clouded vision.

Opinions differ as to whether Phoenix's grandson is still alive. Those who advocate his death cite the following details. Once Phoenix enters the doctor's office, her personality becomes more complex. She has had no trouble responding to the people she has met on her journey, but now she appears to be deaf to questions about her grandson's health. She has come for medicine to relieve life-threatening symptoms that would have killed him before she returned home. Although he swallowed lye two to three years ago, he has not recovered, and the doctor does not ask to examine him. Phoenix describes him as an infant rather than as a young child. Finally, her statement that they are all alone in the world reveals her need to deny his death and create the illusion of his life.

For those readers who decide that Phoenix's grandson is dead, this dimension intensifies the power of the story and its statement about the human condition. Phoenix, true to the legendary bird that is reborn out of its own ashes, keeps herself alive by keeping her grandson alive. As long as she can continue to make herself believe that he lives, her life will contain love, companionship, and purpose.

Welty addresses the question of Phoenix's grandson in her essay, "Is Phoenix Jackson's Grandson Really Dead?" (*The Eye of the Story: Selected Essays and Reviews*) because it is the most frequent question she is asked by students and teachers. In her opinion, it does not matter and the reader is free to choose. The story is told from Phoenix's point of view, and to her, he is alive. Her journey is the focal point of the story, and the possibility that Phoenix would continue to make the journey even if her grandson were dead is present in her love for him, in her devotion to her task of caring for him, and in her hope for his continued life and well-being. Welty states in another interview *(Listen to the Voices)*, "It doesn't bother me one bit if someone interprets something in a different way . . . because you try to make it (the story) full of suggestions, not just one."

PLJ: Have you ever been lonely? If so, what did you do about it? Do you know any older people who are lonely? What do they do about it?

Literary Terms: characterization, humor, setting, symbolism, tone

COMPREHENSION QUESTIONS

1. Describe Phoenix Jackson. (old African-American woman, red rag tied on her head)
2. What is she doing? (walking a long way through the country into town)
3. Name one of her difficulties. (difficulty seeing, walks with cane, bush catches dress, crawls through barbed-wire fence, crosses stream on log, knocked down by dog)
4. What is her goal? (medicine for grandson)
5. What is unusual about her goal? (Phoenix's grandson may be dead.)

UNDERSTANDING THE STORY: POSSIBLE ANSWERS

1. *Factors compelling Phoenix's journey*   Phoenix makes the journey to procure medicine for her grandson. Her need to have someone to care for, a reason for staying alive and living a life that has purpose and meaning, motivates her.
*2. *Purpose of Phoenix's adventures*   Phoenix's adventures and her running conversation with the landscape define her character. They reveal her dignity (tied shoelaces; an untorn dress), pride (falling into the ditch with humor), determination (crossing a creek on a log; crawling through a barbed-wire fence), courage (facing the ghost in the cornfield), cleverness (distracting the young man from the coin she wants), self-knowledge (recognizing her "theft" of the coin), sense of humor

(greeting the white man from the ditch; laughing about the scarecrow), and unselfish purpose (coping with the obstacles of this journey in order to procure medicine for her grandson). Her determination, courage, and unselfish purpose make her a heroic figure.

3. *Significance of cake and scarecrow*   The episodes of the cake and the scarecrow reveal that Phoenix's mind sometimes wanders, and that she sometimes has trouble remembering where she is and what is happening. They also reveal her ability to return to reality, as when she reaches out and touches the "ghost," only to find it a scarecrow. Phoenix's ability to laugh at herself reveals her still to be mentally sharp in many ways. It also reveals her ability to stand apart from herself and to see herself as someone else might view her.

4. *Meeting with the hunter*   The young hunter is at best insensitive and at worst threatening to Phoenix. His "What are you doing there?" is unfeeling, considering that she is lying on the ground because she was knocked over by his dog. His admonition to her to return home might be interpreted as well-meaning, but it indicates that he does not understand that she could have a serious purpose for being so far away from home; his remark about "old colored people" and Santa Claus is a derogatory stereotype. His question about her age is rude. Finally, his pointing the gun at Phoenix is a genuine threat, something she acknowledges.

    The meeting is an important one, revealing more of Phoenix's character and hinting at the type of treatment she will receive from the attendant in the doctor's office.

5. *Changes in Phoenix's behavior at the doctor's office*   Phoenix becomes stiff and silent, instead of relaxed and talkative. She develops a nervous twitch and appears to be deaf. Fatigue appears to be an insufficient answer, given the remainder of the story. It is possible that Phoenix is close to being consciously aware of her grandson's true state, and these changes reflect that strain.

6. *Attitudes of attendant, nurse, and doctor*   The attitudes of those who work in the doctor's office reveal levels of sensitivity and knowledge. The attendant does not know Phoenix and treats her like a stranger. The nurse knows her and is gentle and considerate. The doctor knows why Phoenix keeps returning for the medicine, which is why he permits Phoenix to have it without wishing to examine her grandson.

7. *Phoenix's grandson: dead or alive?*   Student opinion will probably differ as to whether Phoenix's grandson is dead or alive. Those who think he is alive will cite Phoenix's determination to succeed in her journey, her general ability to distinguish between fantasy and reality, her ease in acquiring the medicine from the doctor, and her purchase of the pinwheel. Those who think he is dead will cite the relationship between the nature of his symptoms and the length of Phoenix's journey for medicine, the nurse's surprise that the boy's condition has not changed, the doctor's willingness to supply medicine without examining the boy or talking with Phoenix, and Phoenix's need to believe in her grandson's continued life.

8. *Welty's attitude toward Phoenix*   Welty is filled with sympathy and compassion for Phoenix. Evidence for this includes: the kind of person she reveals Phoenix to be

during the journey; Phoenix's handling of the scene in the doctor's office; and Phoenix's intended purchase and treatment of the paper windmill.

ANALYZING LITERARY TECHNIQUE: POSSIBLE ANSWERS

1. *Technique of gradual revelation*   Withholding the fact that it is near Christmas time and the purpose of Phoenix's journey permit the reader to concentrate on Phoenix's character as the challenges of the journey reveal it. Withholding facts about the illness of Phoenix's grandson enables the reader to see numerous examples of Phoenix's mental health before it becomes necessary to examine her behavior in terms of her grandson's true condition.
2. *Phoenix*   The phoenix is a legendary bird that every 500 years builds a pyre, burns itself to ashes, and then emerges alive and renewed to live again. Phoenix renews her life by living for her grandson and meeting all the challenges in her life. Her grandson is also a phoenix symbol in that, in his grandmother's mind, he has emerged alive from death (survived his life-threatening symptoms).
3. *Pinwheel as symbol*   The pinwheel symbolizes Phoenix's enjoyment of life, through its movement, color, and design. She does more than endure and persevere.
4. *Title as symbol*   "A Worn Path" emphasizes the repeated, ritual nature of Phoenix's journey and focuses on the journey rather than on its purpose. It symbolizes the nature of human life—a journey with trials, failures, and accomplishments—and the personality traits necessary to make the journey successfully.
5. *Welty's style*   Welty's style makes the story read like a folktale, giving it an oral quality. The simple and direct sentences reflect Phoenix's personality and her relationship with the world around her.

WRITING ABOUT LITERATURE

1. *Expository analysis of Phoenix as a heroic figure*   Call students' attention to the directions in the textbook assignment with regard to content and organization. Remind them that both direct quotations and their own ideas are important (See **U.S.** question 2 above.)
2. *Creative writing: reports from two different points of view*   Call students' attention to the directions in the textbook assignment. Remind them to focus on an analysis of Phoenix and her grandson. **(PLJ)**

FURTHER READING

Welty, Eudora, *The Collected Stories of Eudora Welty.*

Come Dance with Me in Ireland

SHIRLEY JACKSON

INTRODUCING THE STORY

"Come Dance with Me in Ireland" dramatizes the subtle ways in which people with good intentions can mistreat others whom they consider to be inferior to themselves. Mrs. Archer shows that she thinks Mr. O'Flaherty is inferior by where she lets him sit and how she sets the table. Mrs. Corn treats him as a drunkard, being unable to view him as a human being who is old and poor. Kathy Valentine treats him as a girl-scout project. She assumes that he is starving, enjoys giving him what she thinks "these people" need and like, and then expects that he will be appreciative. Avoiding any form of authorial intrusion, Jackson reveals the women's underlying prejudices through their ordinary conversation and behavior.

At the end of the story, Mr. O'Flaherty asserts himself. He may be poor, but he knew Yeats. His inherent self-esteem and dignity push aside his polite demeanor, and he criticizes the women for their patronizing treatment of him. Like all other human beings, Mr. O'Flaherty needs more than food; he needs respect. His request: "Come out of charity, come dance with me in Ireland," can be interpreted as his desire for the women to put themselves into his shoes, to appreciate his former happiness, and to understand his present situation. His own experience testifies to the fact that life takes ironic twists, and he takes comfort in the knowledge that the passage of time will hold its own surprises for his hostesses.

PLJ: How do you treat people who are obviously much wealthier or poorer than you are? To what extent, if any, do you treat them differently?

Literary Terms: allusion, characterization, contrast, irony, paradox, satire, symbol, theme, tone

COMPREHENSION QUESTIONS

1. Why does Mr. O'Flaherty come to Mrs. Archer's door? (to sell shoelaces)
2. Why does Mrs. Archer bring him inside? (fears he is ill)
3. What does Mrs. Archer do for Mr. O'Flaherty? (feeds him eggs and coffee)
4. How does Mr. O'Flaherty feel about Mrs. Archer's behavior? (thinks it is condescending)
5. How does Mr. O'Flaherty feel about Mrs. Corn? Why? (hates her because she treats him as if he were drunk)

UNDERSTANDING THE STORY:
POSSIBLE ANSWERS

1. *What motivates Mrs. Archer's behavior toward Mr. O'Flaherty?*   Mrs. Archer is concerned about his well-being, but she feels uncomfortable having a type of bum in her house.

2. *Aspects of Mrs. Archer's behavior Mr. O'Flaherty finds objectionable*   Mr. O'Flaherty dislikes receiving poor sherry in a kitchen glass, a paper-bag placemat, and lunch leftovers. He recognizes that Mrs. Archer's hospitality is halfhearted, and he resents being patronized.

3. *Narrator's attitude toward the women*   The narrator's attitude is critical; her tone is satiric. Her choice of dialogue reveals stereotyping—prejudice based on fear of the poor stranger.

4. *Theme*   Themes include: (*a*) Do unto others as you would have them do unto you; (*b*) respect all human beings as members of the same human family; (*c*) you can't judge a book by the cover.

5. *Application to life in your community*   Students may discuss such topics as fear of strangers and courtesy toward salespeople.

ANALYZING LITERARY TECHNIQUE:
POSSIBLE ANSWERS

1. *How Jackson conveys attitudes of Mrs. Archer and friends*   The dialogue and actions of Mrs. Archer and her friends, and the reasons they express for their actions, reveal their attitudes.

2. *How Jackson individualizes characters*   Each speaks with a distinctive voice: (*a*) Mrs. Archer is unsure about what to do and how to do it; (*b*) Miss Valentine takes charge—she views the three women as girl scouts who are helping a starving man. He is to call them by their surnames, while they call him by his first name; (*c*) Mrs. Corn sees Mrs. O'Flaherty as a drunkard, undeserving of their aid.

3. *How Jackson characterizes Mr. O'Flaherty*   Mr. O'Flaherty's speech and manner reveal his background. His English is correct, and his manner is polite until the end, when he speaks out.

4. *Allusion*   Mr. O'Flaherty's allusion to Yeats reveals Mr. O'Flaherty to be a person of education and distinction. His allusion to Yeats's poem reflects a love of fine poetry, and asserts his own dignity and worth. The importance of the allusion is highlighted by the women's ignorance of who Yeats is.

5. *Title*   Mr. O'Flaherty uses the quotation after he states that he has known Yeats. The allusion to Yeats's poetry symbolizes Mr. O'Flaherty's real persona. He is probably well educated and may have been active, along with Yeats, in the Irish Cultural Revival. The quotation is his way of asking the women to put themselves into his shoes in order to appreciate the richness of his former life and understand his present situation.

*6. *Contrast*   Contrasts include: (*a*) youth vs. age; (*b*) native-born vs. immigrant;

(*c*) financially secure vs. poor; and (*d*) ill-educated vs. better educated. Jackson contrasts the world of a "have-not" with the world of the "haves," revealing, with dramatic irony, the paradox that the "have-nots" may have important possessions that the "haves" lack. Mr. O'Flaherty possesses education, culture, and sophistication. All that the woman appear to possess is financial security.

7. *Irony* Irony gives the story its power. Mr. O'Flaherty's statement, "We are of two different worlds," is an example of verbal irony in that it means something different to the different parties. To Mr. O'Flaherty, his is the better world, containing an acquaintance with Yeats, knowledge of literature and fine wine, and respect of one person for another. He considers the women's world to be one of superficial postures and shallow values. Mrs. Archer and her friends view their world as the better one because they have the money to buy things. They feel superior to him and treat him in a condescending manner.

WRITING ABOUT LITERATURE

1. *Expository analysis of contrast: Mrs. Archer's world vs. Mr. O'Flaherty's* Call students' attention to the directions in the textbook assignment with regard to content. (See **A.L.T.** question 6 above.)
2. *Creative writing: Mr. O'Flaherty entertains Mrs. Archer and friends at his home* Call students' attention to the directions and to the questions suggested in the textbook assignment. **(PLJ)**

FURTHER READING

Jackson, Shirley, *Life Among the Savages; The Lottery; Raising Demons* (all collections of short stories).

Day of the Butterfly
ALICE MUNRO

INTRODUCING THE STORY

"Day of the Butterfly" is the poignant story of the fragile friendship between two girls, Helen, the sensitive insider, and Myra Sayla, an outsider. With an eye for revealing detail, Munro vividly recalls the world of sixth-grade girls, in which conformity reigns. Its rule is so tyrannical that even the most sensitive girls, like Helen, often feel forced to be cruel to outsiders by ignoring them. They lack the courage to be kind for fear of incurring ridicule and isolation from their group.

Like a shadow in the background is the story of Myra's six-year-old brother, whose need for her makes her different from the other girls. He, too, suffers from the rule of conformity among first-grade and older boys. In fact, the power of this story emanates from its ability to remind readers of the ways in which conformity rules their own lives and the price that they, too, pay for social acceptance.

Helen narrates this story years after its occurrence. Her distance from her subject enables her to be selective in the incidents and details that she presents, thus creating a story that moves powerfully to its conclusion without distracting extraneous details. Her distance from her younger self enables her to be objective in confronting her conflicting attitudes and emotions in a difficult social situation.

PLJ: To what extent, if any, is it important to you to be like your friends in the way that you dress, speak, and act? To what extent, if any, do you try to be independent of the control of others?

Literary Terms: characterization, conflict, narrative perspective, paradox, theme

COMPREHENSION QUESTIONS

1. What is Myra Sayla's problem? (needs to care for younger brother in school)
2. Why do the sixth-graders know Jimmy Sayla? (enters their classroom when he needs Myra's help)
3. What does Jimmy do at recess? (stays inside if being punished; or stays in separate area with Myra)
4. How is Jimmy treated by the other boys? (beaten up)
5. What does Miss Darling ask the sixth-grade girls to do? (be nice to Myra)
6. What is Helen's position in the group? (accepted by group but still somewhat of an outsider since she lives on a farm)
7. What memorable event happens on Helen's walk with Myra? (Myra finds a butterfly brooch in the Cracker Jack; Helen gives it to her as a gift.)
8. Why is Myra not in school? (in hospital with leukemia)
9. What suggestion of Miss Darling's is accepted? (celebrate Myra's birthday early in hospital)
10. What important event occurs at the end of the girls' visit with Myra? (Myra gives Helen one of the best birthday gifts.)

UNDERSTANDING THE STORY: POSSIBLE ANSWERS

*1. *Conflict* The conflict occurs within Helen, rather than between Helen and her group or Helen and Myra, and involves whether or not to be nice to Myra. Helen feels ambivalent: Her instincts to be kind and friendly to an outsider confront her fears that her group will ridicule her or punish her by rejecting her. Helen's inner conflict is intensified by her perception of the tenuous nature of her own position in the group as a farm girl rather than a town girl.

*2. *Relationship between Jimmy Sayla's problem and Myra's treatment*   The group operates under the principle of contamination by association. Jimmy's bathroom problem contaminates Myra and makes her unacceptable to the group. Like Myra, Jimmy is also an outsider, and he is persecuted by the other boys at recess. He has learned that if he misbehaves, he will be punished by being kept inside at recess; consequently, he misbehaves.

*3. *Why Jimmy and Myra are "uncommunicative"*   Jimmy and Myra are "meekly, cryptically uncommunicative" in order to have as little to do with the other children as possible. They try to do nothing that will call attention to themselves for fear of being tormented when they are noticed. Being ignored is the best treatment that they can expect in school.

 4. *Miss Darling's role in Myra's life*   Some students may feel that it would have been kinder to Myra to leave her alone, and that to ask the girls to be nice to her was, in fact, to invite their insincere, callous, and even cruel behavior toward her. Others may feel that Myra's school experience was so painful that Miss Darling was obligated, as a caring teacher, to do her best to try to inspire the girls to be more kind.

*5. *Danger Helen senses about her school life*   Because Helen lives on a farm and cannot go home for lunch, she must dress differently from the town girls and bring a box lunch. Her situation causes a conflict. Being different from the other girls, Helen is more sensitive to Myra's feelings and her plight. However, being different herself, she runs the risk of being socially rejected and, therefore, is less likely to take other social risks, such as being friendly to an outcast.

*6. *Myra's birthday*   Miss Darling wants Myra to have a birthday party before she dies, and she probably will not live until July. The party becomes fashionable because Miss Darling will let only a select group of students go to the party. Gladys can take her desired role as leader, since she can impress her peers with special knowledge (her aunt is a nurse).

*7. *Myra's gift to Helen*   Myra reconfirms their friendship by giving a gift in return for the butterfly brooch. At first, Myra's gift is a source of danger for Helen, in that her acceptance of it implies a friendship with Myra that could be socially disastrous for Helen.

   The intrusion of the real world outside the hospital reminds Helen that she will not become Myra's friend and that she has misled her by permitting their exchange of gifts. Thus, Helen frees herself from the danger that Myra's gift promises.

*8. *Myra's reactions to party*   During the course of the party, Myra changes from being suspicious of a new experience that might disappoint her to being captivated by the event. Helen notices Myra's small, private smile and her feeling of pride. However, the last lines of the story suggest that Myra, having been disappointed so often by her peer group, has permanently walled herself off from the others in order to protect herself. If this is true, shortly after her party she will have forgotten about her gift to Helen and the implications of a friendship between them.

   The butterfly brooch and the birthday party may have been the highpoints of Myra's short life, since Helen's misgivings have been private.

ANALYZING LITERARY TECHNIQUE: POSSIBLE ANSWERS

1. *Setting*   The setting, an elementary school in the recent past, makes the story believable. Myra's status as an outsider is threatening to Helen, who must decide whether to risk her own status in order to be Myra's friend. The age of the girls (about twelve years) is one during which actions and feelings can take on great significance for future behavior. It is believable that Helen could remember with such detail and emotion experiences that occurred at that age.

2. *Butterfly as symbol*   The butterfly symbolizes friendship, a gesture of kindness made by Helen and accepted by Myra. Helen's uncertainty about the ramifications of offering friendship to Myra is emphasized by her relief that Myra does not actually wear the butterfly brooch, thus preventing any questions and explanations about their relationship.

   The butterfly is a suggestive symbol, in that butterflies, like Helen's friendship for Myra, are ephemeral.

3. *Narrative perspective*   Helen, as an adult, narrates this story from her own youth. She is the center of consciousness, so that the reader never knows the thoughts of another character. Her distance from her subject enables her to be selective in the incidents and details that she presents, avoiding extraneous details that would distract readers' attention from her point. Helen's distance from her younger self enables her to be objective in confronting her conflicting attitudes and emotions in a difficult social situation.

4. *Helen as reliable narrator*   Helen's language and insights reveal her to be an adult. Her acknowledgment of her internal conflict, arising from her feeling of vulnerability in her social group, presents her to the reader as being very human; she makes no effort to cause the reader to view her behavior as better than it is.

*5. *Paradox*   It is paradoxical that good people (like Helen) can knowingly be callous and cruel.

WRITING ABOUT LITERATURE

1. *Expository writing: an essay analyzing what Munro reveals about human nature*   Call students' attention to the directions in the textbook assignment. Helen: A person who feels insecure about her or his acceptance in a group will be careful to conform to the group's expectations. Myra: An outsider develops defensive strategies designed to protect her or him from being hurt by the group. Gladys: The leader of a group knows what personal qualities have earned her or him that position and uses ridicule against anyone who threatens that authority and control. Miss Darling: A well-intentioned but unrealistic authority figure can do more harm than good. (See **U.S.** questions 1–3 and 5–8 above.)

2. *Creative writing: a different ending*   Call students' attention to the assignment in the textbook. **(PLJ)**

FURTHER READING

Munro, Alice, *Dance of the Happy Shades; The Progress of Love; Who Do You Think You Are?; Friend of My Youth.*

Roselily
ALICE WALKER

INTRODUCING THE STORY

"Roselily" is the poignant story of an African-American woman who is marrying a man in order to lead a new life. Roselily is leaving rural Mississippi, where she has lived the exploitive life of the rural black woman in the Deep South. She has given birth to four children by four different fathers, none of whom married her. Economics has dictated her need to work, and lack of education and opportunity have led her to work in a sewing plant, a job she is anxious to leave. For her children and herself, she wants respect, and she wants a future. She wants freedom to find and to be herself, and she want to be loved.

Part of the story's power resides in Roselily's need to choose between two unattractive alternatives, either to continue her life in Mississippi or to marry and move to Chicago. To remain is to relinquish her dreams of self-fulfillment and a better life for her children; to leave is to take great risks. Her husband is a Black Muslim. His religion differs from hers, and his values differ from hers. He is taking her to Chicago, far away from the only life she has ever known. She worries about being ignorant, wrong, and backward in her new environment. Her husband loves her, but he appears to be insensitive to her emotional needs. She may be exchanging one form of subjugation and tyranny (that of society) for another (that of a domineering husband)—but this time, she will be a stranger in the strange land of opportunity.

Walker's narrative technique enhances the power of the story. By presenting Roselily's stream of consciousness as she hears each part of the marriage ceremony, Walker juxtaposes Roselily's past and future with her present. While her life parades through her mind and she worries about how successfully she will be able to cope with her future, the marriage ceremony is moving forward and that future is becoming a reality.

PLJ: How do you feel about the prospect of change in your life, such as moving or changing schools? If you were to move, would you rather live in or near a small town or in a big city? List some of the advantages and disadvantages of each location.

Literary Terms: characterization, contrast, figurative language, interior monologue, irony, narrative perspective, psychological realism, stream of consciousness, symbolism, theme, third-person limited omniscience

COMPREHENSION QUESTIONS

1. What is occurring in Roselily's life? (being married)
2. What is different about Roselily's husband? (religion; Chicago; joyless)
3. What does Roselily want in life? (love, respect)
4. What is Roselily concerned about? (life of son; marriage; future)
5. How does Roselily feel about what is happening? (ambivalent; curious, yet reluctant)

UNDERSTANDING THE STORY: POSSIBLE ANSWERS

*1. *Roselily like cotton*   In the course of her life, Roselily has been treated more like a commodity than a human being. Now, she is "selling" herself for the best price, for a new and what she hopes will be a better life. Just as cotton cannot be cleaned completely, so Roselily cannot be separated completely from her past life-experiences, her memories and ingrained attitudes and behavior ("dry leaves and twigs").

2. *Roselily's husband's attitude toward marriage*   Roselily's husband supports the institution of marriage, but not the particular religious ceremony. His religion is different (Black Muslim).

3. *Weakness of father of Roselily's fourth child*   That father did not stand by Roselily. He loved her enough to father her child and live with her through her pregnancy, but not enough to leave his wife and marry her. He was ashamed to bring her into his Northern life, believing that she could not master the skills he valued, and he had no wish to adapt to her Southern life. Rearing their child at his home in the North, he does not have the courage to communicate about its well-being. He also may not have the courage to let that child know its real mother.

*4. *Importance of roots to Roselily*   Roselily recognizes her ties to her past: her mother, her father, and her grandparents. She views herself as a totality that includes her past as well as her present and her future.

*5. *Why Roselily is marrying*   Roselily's life is a closed book as long as she remains at home in Mississippi. She wants love, respect, opportunity for self-fulfillment, and a better life for her children. By marrying and moving to Chicago, she has more to gain than to lose. This marriage will remove her from her life in the rural South, where she must work at a job she dislikes, rear her children alone, and expect that the future for herself and her children will simply mirror the past. Even if her marriage fails, more job opportunities and a greater variety of people are available to her.

*6. *Chicago not be a new experience for Roselily*   Roselily's marriage and the Chicago experience may disappoint her. She may not find the happiness she seeks. Ironically, she may have no more control over her life in Chicago than she did in Mississippi. Her decisions in her old life were determined by economic necessity. Her decisions in her new life may be determined by her husband, and she may simply be substituting one type of constraint for another.

*7. *Roselily's view of the preacher*   The preacher represents acceptance of things as they are. His religion teaches him to advise turning the other cheek rather than striking out. Therefore, in Roselily's hopes and attempts to improve herself and her situation, he not only is of no help, but he appears to be critical of her hopes and attempts.

*8. *Why Roselily feels wrong*   In the end, Roselily feels inadequate for the challenges she faces in her new life, and therefore she is afraid of what she has done. The risks are real. Her husband has different values, and their marriage may not survive these differences. Each of them seems to see the other more as an object or symbol than as a particular individual. For Roselily, her husband is the ticket to a better life. She has not thought about the nature of his personality, just about acquiring freedom and opportunity. For her husband, Roselily is someone to love and to rescue from the clutches of the past. He appears to have more understanding of her condition than he does of her psychological being. Roselily may not be able to adapt to ways so different from those she has known. She may feel isolated and estranged, and she may be homesick for the comfort of the customary path. Her husband may not be able to understand her feelings, and therefore, may not be able to give her the emotional support that she needs.

*9. *Characterization of Roselily*   Roselily is courageous in that she is marrying a city man who has different values, and she is leaving home to start a new life in a distant city. She has also given one of her children to his father so that that child can have greater opportunities.

ANALYZING LITERARY TECHNIQUE: POSSIBLE ANSWERS

1. *Narrative perspective; psychological realism*   Because the story is told through Roselily's thoughts, the reader gains intimate knowledge of Roselily's situation and is able to sympathize with her. The story is organized around the minister's words of the marriage ceremony. To Roselily, each group of words suggests thoughts of her past and her future. This narrative technique imitates the working of the human mind, and it is very appropriate given the circumstances (a wedding) and Roselily's particular situation (leaving one life for a new and different one). Thus, it is very effective.

2. *Relationship between marriage ceremony and Roselily's thoughts*   The contrast between the preacher's words and Roselily's thoughts dramatizes the contrast between the world in which she has been living (that of a single woman in the rural South) and the precarious nature of her new marriage. The marriage is juxtaposed with images of ropes and chains, a new union with children born of previous relationships, the formality of objection with the real problems of the demands of her husband's religion, their life together with her separation and isolation in the home, and the invitation to speak out with her being so impatient to escape that she never asked enough questions.

3. *Contrast*   Walker contrasts: (*a*) the South and the North; (*b*) country and city; (*c*) old and new; and (*d*) the male and female view of women. The contrasts accentuate the tremendous change that is about to occur in Roselily's life, enabling the reader to identify with her ambivalent feelings of anticipation and regret. With all its shortcomings, Roselily feels an affection for the unsophisticated life in the South, which has been the only type of life she has ever known.

*4. *Symbolism*   Examples of symbols of constraint include: (*a*) ropes, (*b*) chains, (*c*) handcuffs, (*d*) religion, (*e*) yoke, (*f*) trapped rat, and (*g*) quicksand. Roselily desires freedom from the constraints of a society that limits her potential, and she thinks of the factors that have obstructed and will obstruct her opportunity to achieve self-fulfillment.

WRITING ABOUT LITERATURE

1. *Expository writing: analysis of symbols of constraint and their function*   Call students' attention to the directions in the textbook assignment. Remind them to incorporate direct quotations into their analysis. (See **U.S.** question 7, and **A.L.T.** question 4 above.)

2. *Expository writing: character sketch of Roselily*   Call students' attention to the directions in the textbook assignment. Remind them of the importance of direct quotations. (See **U.S.** questions 1 and 4–9 above.)

3. *Creative writing: a letter from Roselily describing her new life*   Roselily may have either a negative or a positive experience. She may be accepted or rejected by her husband's friends. She may adapt to city life, or she may prefer the unsophisticated life of her Southern community. She and her husband may or may not have a satisfying marriage in that they may or may not understand and support each other. **(PLJ)**

FURTHER READING

Walker, Alice, *Good Night, Willie Lee, I'll See You in the Morning: Poems; Revolutionary Petunias and Other Poems; The Color Purple; In Love and Trouble.*

Great Britain

The Tempest

WILLIAM SHAKESPEARE

INTRODUCING THE PLAY

The Tempest is a fairy tale complete with love, intrigue, magic, and comedy. It celebrates love, freedom, reconcilation, and the wonder of life. In Shakespeare's view, nothing substitutes for the rich experience of living in the real, although imperfect, world. Thus, Prospero exchanges his power (his magic wand and Ariel) and his island paradise for the complexities, challenges, and excitement of court life in Milan.

The Tempest reveals that whether civilized or savage, and regardless of social status, people share the same need for self-esteem and power. Thus, Prospero enslaves Ariel and Caliban. Sebastian and Antonio would murder for political gain. Moreover, even the commoners exhibit political ambition: Stephano and Trinculo plot with Caliban to murder Prospero and usurp his power.

While all human beings share the same basic nature, *The Tempest* reflects a view, widely held in Shakespeare's day, that those who are "civilized" are superior to those who are not. Civilized people can be either kind, sensitive, and unselfish, or cruel, callous, and self-centered. Regardless of their faults, they are superior to uncivilized people in that they possess the potential capability to know and judge themselves, to feel remorse, and to restrain their evil impulses and improve their behavior. However, despite their potential, their inner virtue may not be strong enough to triumph over their ignoble inclinations. Thus, at the end of the play, Prospero and Alonso have become better human beings, but Antonio and Sebastian have not.

Prospero loves and values the real world, which is neither unusually "brave" nor "new." He uses his special powers not only to restore the natural order but to try to teach his enemies important lessons. Yet once he has done his best to change their attitudes and behavior, he accepts their limitations and forgives them. Prospero recognizes and accepts that Antonio and Sebastian, as well as Stephano and Trinculo, are self-centered, governed more by personal consequences than by ideals.

Prospero believes that idealizing aboriginal people ignores reality. He has tried his best with Caliban, but Caliban cannot conquer his passions and develop beyond a partly civilized veneer; the noble savage is, in Prospero's view, doomed to be crippled by his own insurmountable limitations. At best, Caliban's impulsive, amoral behavior can teach others about their own inner nature and the advantages of being civilized.

However, Prospero does not understand that Caliban finds no value in being civilized. Caliban is accustomed to being free to act in whatever way will gratify his desires. Once civilization, in the form of Prospero and Miranda, invades the island, Caliban loses his independence and his power. From his point of view, civilization has robbed him of his identity and self-esteem, and it has denied him Miranda. Therefore, Caliban has reason to present his worst side in *The Tempest*. He was better off before Prospero brought civilization to the island.

BACKGROUND INFORMATION

The Tempest is probably the last play that Shakespeare wrote. Some scholars see a connection between Prospero, who breaks his wand and leaves his magic at the end of the play, and Shakespeare, who, with this play, leaves the theater. *The Tempest* is the first play presented in the First Folio, where it contains unusually good detail as to acts and scenes and stage directions. About a year after its initial performance in November 1611, Shakespeare added the masque (Act IV, Scene i) for a performance for King James I as part of the wedding festivities for Princess Elizabeth. During Shakespeare's time, social values dictated that, for the sake of propriety, only males could appear on stage. Consequently, boys and young men performed all female roles.

The plot of *The Tempest* is clearly original. However, Shakespeare adapted some ideas from folktales and other ideas from contemporary writings, classical literature, and Italian commedia del l'arte theater. The opening storm and shipwreck (Act I, Scene i) reflect William Strachey's amazing account (published as *True Reportory* in 1610) of the wreck of the *Sea-Adventure* in a terrible storm off Bermuda in 1609. The ship had been part of an expedition to settle Virginia, and everyone on it was thought to have died. A year after the wreck, survivors suddenly appeared in England with amazing testimonies of how an island previously thought to be inhabited by devils and avoided by sailors was, in fact, a paradise.

The discussion of Dido and Aeneas (Act II, Scene i) refers to Books I–VI of Virgil's *Aeneid*. Gonzalo's depiction of the ideal society (Act II, Scene i) accurately reflects Michel de Montaigne's essay "On Cannibals" (written in 1580, translated in 1603, and depicting the American Indian as a "noble savage"). Prospero's farewell to his art (Act V, Scene i), is a paraphrase of one of Medea's speeches in a 1567 English translation of Ovid's *Metamorphoses*. The antics of Stephano, Trinculo, and Caliban reflect those of the clever servants in commedia del l'arte plays, performed in London by visiting Italian troupes.

PLJ: What is the advantage in treating others as you wish they would treat you? Why is it often difficult to do this? What is the appeal of being in the position of ruling other people? What disadvantages accompany being the authority figure?

Literary Terms: characterization, climax, comedy, contrast, epilogue, farce, foreshadowing, irony, masque, pastoral, plot, romance, soliloquy, subplot, symbol, theme, tragedy, tragicomedy

COMPREHENSION QUESTIONS

1. (I.i.)   What is unusual about both the tempest and the shipwreck? (Neither is natural; Prospero had Ariel cause them in order to bring his enemies to his island.)
2. (I.ii.)   Who does Prospero tell Miranda he really is? (Duke of Milan)
3. (I.ii.)   What did Antonio do to his brother Prospero? (took over Prospero's kingdom, which he was ruling in Prospero's name)
4. (I.ii.)   What role did Alonso, King of Naples, play? (His army removed Prospero and Miranda, took them out to sea, and left them in a small boat to die.)

5. (I.ii.)   What role did Gonzalo play? (He provided Prospero and Miranda with food, clothes, and Prospero's prized books.)

6. (I.ii.)   Who is Ariel, and what is his role in Act I? (Ariel is a nonhuman air-spirit, who is Prospero's slave and servant. He causes the tempest and wreck as Prospero has directed.)

7. (I.ii.)   Who is Sycrorax? What is Sycorax's connection with Caliban and Ariel? (Sycorax is a witch and Caliban's mother. She imprisoned Ariel in a tree when he would not obey her.)

8. (I.ii.)   How does Prospero treat Ferdinand? Why? (Prospero punishes Ferdinand with tasks in order to test his love for Miranda.)

9. (II.i.)   What plan do Sebastian and Antonio make? (to kill Alonso and Gonzalo)

10. (II.ii.)   What does Stephano initially want to do with Caliban? What does he want to do with him later? (He initially wants to sell Caliban in Naples. He later wants to rule the island with Caliban as his subject.)

11. (III.i.)   Prospero has two reasons for wrecking the ship. Which goal is accomplished first? (the goal of finding a suitable husband for Miranda)

12. (III.ii.)   What two things does Caliban advise Stephano to do to Prospero? (burn Prospero's books, and kill him while he is asleep)

13. (III.iii.)   What does Ariel tell Alonso, Sebastian, and Antonio after he removes the banquet? (They are three sinners who must repent and lead good lives in order to avoid further suffering.)

14. (IV.i.)   What double purpose does the playlet (masque) serve? (Juno and Ceres bless the marriage of Ferdinand and Miranda; the playlet impresses Ferdinand, who sees Prospero as a gifted magician.)

15. (V.i.)   Why does Prospero release his three enemies? (Ariel leads Prospero to believe that they have become penitent. His reason rules his passion, and he gives up vengeance.)

UNDERSTANDING THE PLAY: POSSIBLE ANSWERS

*1. (I.ii) *What first two scenes reveal about Prospero*   Prospero, the true Duke of Milan, has the magical ability to control nature and nature spirits. The audience also learns the history of Prospero and Miranda's arrival on the island.

2. (I.ii) *Characterization of Miranda*   Miranda is civilized but innocent; she has compassion for the shipwrecked victims.

3. (I.ii) *Prospero's fairness in enslaving Ariel*   It is never fair to enslave someone. However, Prospero made a bargain with Ariel, freeing Ariel from the tree in return for a period of enslavement, and Prospero does not mistreat him.

4. (I.ii) *Prospero's wisdom in enslaving Caliban*   From Prospero's point of view, it was probably wise to enslave Caliban because he is a physical danger to Miranda. Caliban is the son of both a devil and a witch, so he feels free to act in evil ways. Prospero first tried to civilize Caliban but was unsuccessful.

5. (I.ii) *Caliban's curse on Prospero and Miranda (lines 321–24)*   Caliban curses Prospero and Miranda with physical discomfort. He invokes destructive natural forces (dew, wind). His curse reveals his connection with the forces of the earth and nature.

*6. (I.ii) *Justification for Caliban's feelings*   Shakespeare primarily tells this story from Prospero's point of view. From Caliban's point of view, Prospero has invaded Caliban's island and has made Caliban his subject. Moreover, after a period of treating him humanely, Prospero has enslaved him. Therefore, in Caliban's view, civilization is a disaster. It has brought him loss of individual freedom and has created both new expectations and the frustration of disappointed hopes. Thus, he tells Miranda that he can best use their language to curse, for it expresses his feelings about them and their culture. Caliban obeys Prospero because Prospero's magic is too strong for him to fight.

7. (I.ii) *Prospero's test of Ferdinand*   Prospero wants to be certain that Ferdinand values Miranda and that he will be worthy of her. Ferdinand's response reveals that he is a worthy mate for Miranda. He is willing to do whatever Prospero requires of him.

8. (II.i) *Nature of island (lines 34–66)*   Reality is relative: Gonzalo sees beauty and miracle; others see the catastrophe of shipwreck.

9. (II.i) *Gonzalo's plans (lines 141–61)*   Gonzalo's plans for ruling the island are an ironic commentary on the nature of contemporary civilization. They reveal that the world in which Gonzalo lives is far from ideal. It contains poverty, treason, and felony. However, it also contains such positive aspects as learning, trade, and industry.

*10. (II.ii) *Why Caliban serves Stephano*   Caliban believes that Stephano's liquor is celestial and that Stephano is a wondrous god or man who has dropped from heaven. Caliban expects to regain his freedom under Stephano's rule. He intends to serve Stephano well by showing him how to take advantage of the island's fertility.

11. (III.ii) *Caliban's attitude toward books*   Caliban recognizes that without books Prospero would be an ordinary man rather than a magician, and uncivilized rather than civilized.

12. (III.iii) *Reactions to Ariel's condemnation (lines 53–82)*   Gonzalo is an honorable person, and Ariel does not condemn him. He sees and hears nothing. Alonso recognizes his crime and feels remorse. Sebastian and Antonio are unrepentant and remain aggressive. Discovery does not change their personalities.

*13. (IV.i) *Nature of characters in masque (lines 148–58)*   Prospero compares the characters in the masque to aspects of the real world. He states that everything is ephemeral. All life, every structure that human beings have built, and the earth itself will fade away. Prospero's magic is equated with the magic of life.

*14. (V.i) *Why Prospero gives up magic*   Prospero gives up his magic because he has accomplished his goals of avenging the past and securing Miranda's future. He is ready to return to the complexities of the civilized world and the responsibility of being the Duke of Milan.

15. (V.i) *"Goodly creatures"* and *"beauteous mankind"* *(lines 181–84)* Shakespeare probably expected these lines to provoke laughter. Miranda's experience of other people has been so limited that she lacks sophistication. Her father and Ferdinand are the only civilized people she has seen, and although she claimed to listen to her father's tale, it hasn't left a mark upon her innocence. Her comment provides an ironic commentary on civilization in the real world, where people are capable of treachery as well as kindness. Prospero recognizes her innocence and responds to her joyful discovery of a "brave new world" by replying "'Tis new to thee."

16. (V.i) *Prospero's wisdom in releasing court group* Prospero is wise only if the court group has learned its lesson and if Antonio and Sebastian are truly penitent. He is aware of their nature and will watch their behavior, but he is still taking a risk.

17. (V.i) *What Caliban learns from his experience (lines 292–95)* Caliban criticizes himself for viewing the drunken Stephano as a god. He has learned to be careful of whom he admires.

18. *Why Prospero chooses to leave island and magic* Prospero prefers the complexity, interest, and challenge of an imperfect civilization to the boredom and sterility of the island. His decision reflects his love of the real world, despite its problems.

19. *Themes* Themes include: (*a*) One should change what one can, accept what one cannot change, and be wise enough to know the difference between the two; (*b*) People must take risks when they attempt to improve their lives; (*c*) Life includes humor and tragedy, and one's perception of reality is relative. One can choose to emphasize the wonder and the beauty or the problems; (*d*) Love, freedom, and the wonder of the universe make life worthwhile despite its problems; (*e*) Reason should rule passion; (*f*) Reconciliation is more important than revenge.

ANALYZING LITERARY TECHNIQUE: POSSIBLE ANSWERS

1. *Structure of play* *(*a*) *Opening shipwreck* Beginning with storm and shipwreck dramatizes danger, terror, and disorder. Ironically, the shipwreck is an illusion: All is actually safe and sound. The storm and wreck reveal Prospero's power and Ariel's ability. The initial contrast of appearance (illusion) and reality foreshadows similar situations later in the play. Moreover, by beginning with the shipwreck, Shakespeare is able to make the action progress from a state of disorder to one of order and harmony.

(*b*) *Choice of exposition instead of drama* Dramatizing Prospero's earlier political situation in Milan as present events would emphasize ambition, intrigue, and treachery and would make the play a tragedy. In contrast, by treating these past events as exposition, Shakespeare emphasizes reconciliation. Prospero switches from vengeance to forgiveness, giving the play a benevolent tone.

(*c*) *Pattern of quest, trial, and knowledge* The repetition of this pattern helps to unify the plot. Some examples of the pattern include:

(*1*) Ferdinand searches for Miranda; he earns her by accomplishing Prospero's tasks; and their marriage is blessed in the masque.

(*2*) The members of the court group search for Ferdinand, wander throughout the island, and confront their inner natures in the banquet scene.

(*3*) Stephano, Trinculo, and Caliban search for Prospero, fall into the horsepond and are hunted by dog-spirits, and learn reality through the experience of being distracted by Prospero's clothes.

*(*d*) *Climax*   The climax for Prospero and the court group occurs when Ariel, as a harpy, confronts the court group as sinners and tells them what they must do to repent. The climax for Ferdinand and Miranda occurs when they reveal their love for each other. The climax for Stephano, Trinculo, and Caliban occurs when, as a cohesive group, they decide to murder Prospero. The fact that the climax of the action for the three groups of characters occurs in the same act intensifies the power of that act.

*(*e*) *Relation of subplot to plot*   The subplot contributes the humor of low comedy, and it also amplifies and adds an ironic twist to one of the themes of the play. It is an ironic commentary on the negative aspects of civilization that Stephano and Trinculo, despite their low social status, have the same type of murderous ambition and immorality as Antonio and Sebastian in the court group.

(*f*) *Unities of time and place*   Unity of time and place creates greater immediacy and compression of action. The play has a tighter focus, and the audience is more involved.

(*g*) *Epilogue*   The epilogue reinforces the themes of reconciliation and liberty, in that Prospero asks for both pardon and his freedom, just as he has pardoned his enemies and freed them and Ariel.

2. *Function of characters* (*a*) *Prospero*   Prospero functions as Shakespeare's director of the play, and thus it becomes his play. He controls the complete environment, both the natural elements and the human forces. It is possible that Prospero's attitude toward his magic, his reconciliation with his old enemies, and his view of life may represent Shakespeare's attitudes at this time in his own life, when he was preparing to retire from the theater.

*(*b*) *Ariel*   Ariel is a usually invisible air spirit who possesses great intelligence but lacks important human emotions. For example, Ariel calls the court group "men of sin" and tells Prospero that their remorse would make him pity them if he were human, which he is not. Ariel's role is to make the magical events of the play occur. While Prospero tells Ariel what to do, Ariel devises how to do it.

(*c*) *Caliban*   Caliban is a creature of the earth and a type of "noble savage." Being an aspect of nature that refuses to become civilized, he is at once monstrous and human, disgusting and noble. Before Prospero arrived, Caliban was the king of the island, and Shakespeare gives him the ability to appreciate the beauties of nature and to speak about them with eloquence.

Explorers and settlers of the lands outside Europe often viewed the aboriginal peoples they encountered, who were not Christian, as being possessed by the devil. Consequently, it is not surprising that Caliban has a devil for a father and a witch for a mother. In Act IV, Scene i, Prospero describes Caliban as "a born devil on whose nature /Nurture can never stick" (lines 188–89). However, Caliban may choose to reject civilization because he was better off without it. In the form of Prospero, civilization has enslaved him. In Act V, Scene i, Caliban shows some ability to judge himself and to learn from experience. He criticizes himself for having worshipped Stephano and says, "I'll be wise hereafter,/ And seek for grace" (lines 292–93).

(d) *Ferdinand and Miranda*   Ferdinand and Miranda represent the innocence and idealism of youth and, therefore, hope for the future. They are honest, unselfish, and good.

(e) *The court group*   Gonzalo is the honorable idealist. He provided for Prospero in Prospero's time of need, and his vision of the island addresses the ills that are inherent in contemporary society, thereby revealing them.

Alonso represents those in society whose inner virtue is strong enough to conquer their evil inclinations. He reveals the capacity to know and judge himself, to feel remorse, and to become a better human being.

Sebastian and Antonio represent those in society who permit their self-interest and lust for power to ignore ethical and humanitarian concerns. Both men appear to withstand Ariel's condemnation without remorse and, therefore, are not to be trusted.

In Act II, Scene i, Francisco tells the court group that he saw Ferdinand swim successfully to the island, thus foreshadowing Alonso's recovery of his lost son.

3. *Dramatic techniques*   *(a) *High comedy and low comedy*   An example of high comedy occurs in Act II, Scene i. The humor is verbal, involving word-play, and appeals to an educated audience. An example of low comedy, occurs in Act II, Scene ii. It is active, involves slapstick humor, and appeals to everyone, especially an uneducated audience. By including both types of comedy, Shakespeare includes something for everyone in the audience.

*(b) *Dramatic irony*   Dramatic irony often functions as a source of humor. In Act II, Scene ii, Stephano misjudges Caliban because he does not see that Trinculo is hiding beneath Caliban's coat. In Act III, Scene ii, when Ariel, who is invisible, speaks, Trinculo is blamed for it.

4. *Motifs (a) Sleep*   Sleep determines what does and does not occur. In Act I, Scene ii, it permits Ariel to enter visibly and communicate with Prospero, and it also removes the crew of the ship from an active role in the plot. In Act II, Scene i, it permits the court group to plan a murder. (The plan is foiled by Ariel, who awakens Gonzalo and Alonso, the intended victims.)

(b) *Dream*   Shakespeare uses dreams to reveal the evanescent nature of reality. In Act I, Scene i, Miranda remembers her early years in Milan as if that part of her life were a dream. In Act IV, Scene i, Prospero explains how the nature of reality is actually no more permanent than the nature of theater, and he tells Ferdinand that "We are such stuff/ As dreams are made on" (lines 156–57). In Act V, Scene i, the recently awakened Boatswain, upon finding his boat, crew, and passengers restored, wonders whether he is living in the world of reality or in the world of dream.

*(c) *Effect of illusion on reality*   The illusory shipwreck brings all of Prospero's enemies to his island in such a way that he can be in control. They are unaware of his presence and identity, and they are at his mercy.

The illusory banquet terrifies Prospero's enemies into coming to grips with their crimes. Ariel appears as a harpy and accuses the court group, explains the expiation, and permits them to learn their lessons without hurting anyone. This permits Prospero to forgive them and reconciliation to occur.

The separation of Alonso and Ferdinand, during which each thinks that the other has drowned, permits Ferdinand to meet and fall in love with Miranda, and to pass Prospero's tests independent of his father's judgment and without knowing Prospero's true identity. It also permits Alonso to learn through suffering, so that he becomes genuinely penitent about his role in Antonio's usurpation of Prospero's dukedom.

Prospero's talents as a magician, combined with his use of Ariel's talents, cause the events that bring about his eventual reconciliation with his old enemies and that enable him to return to his rightful place in the civilized world.

*(d) *Transformations*   Each of the transformations in the play involves something's changing from bad to "wonderful." The transformation from threatening and tempestuous seas to merciful and calm seas reinforces the theme that order exists in nature. The transformation from treachery to reconciliation reinforces the themes that reason should rule passion and that reconciliation is more important than revenge. The transformation of Prospero from a magician on an isolated island to the restored Duke of Milan reinforces the theme that order exists in society. The transformation of Miranda from the daughter of a magician to the daughter of the Duke of Milan and wife of the heir to the kingdom of Naples reinforces the theme that life includes wonder and beauty. Finally, the transformation of Alonso reinforces the theme that civilized people are capable of improving their attitudes and behavior.

(e) *Sound*   Threatening sounds reveal the universe in disorder. They include those of the storm that surrounds the shipwreck in Act I, Scenes i and ii; the sounds of the beasts that Sebastian describes in Act II, Scene i, as a rationalization for his imminent use of his weapon; and the storm-like sounds that awaken the sleeping Boatswain and crew in Act V, Scene i.

Harmonious sounds reveal the order in the universe and the beauty of nature. Ariel plays solemn music in Act II, Scene i, in order to awaken Gonzalo, and again in Act III, Scene iii, to accompany the banquet scene. In Act III, Scene ii, Caliban tells Stephano and Trinculo that "the isle is full of noises, / Sounds and sweet airs that give delight and hurt not" (lines 126–27).

5. *Language*   (a) *Sea imagery*   Caliban is often referred to as a fish, as a way of calling attention to his nonhuman nature. For example, in Act II, Scene ii, Trinculo decides that Caliban is a fish because of his smell. In Act V, Scene i, Antonio refers to Caliban as a "plain fish and no doubt marketable" (line 265).

In Act V, Scene i, understanding or reason swells as a tide to wash away what is foul and muddy. The sea, which was threatening in Act I, Scene i, is merciful and calm in Act V, Scene i, reflecting the resolution of Prospero's conflict and the reconciliation that has occurred at the end of the play.

(b) *Use of poetry and prose*   With the exception of Stephano, Trinculo, and occasionally Caliban (when he is conversing with them), the characters speak in poetic form. This is consistent with their status: Most are aristocrats; Ariel is an air-spirit; and Caliban is the natural lord of the island. Caliban is as eloquent about the life of nature as Prospero is about the nature of life. The prose style of Stephano and Trinculo betrays their low social status and their common values.

WRITING ABOUT LITERATURE

1. *Expository analysis of function of subplot*   Call students' attention to the directions in the textbook assignment with regard to content. Remind them of the importance of using direct quotations to support their ideas. (See **U.P.** questions 6 and 10, and **A.L.T.** questions 1.d, 1.e, 3.a, and 3.b above.)
2. *Expository analysis of illusion and reality*   Call students' attention to the directions in the textbook assignment with regard to content. Remind them of the importance of using direct quotations to support their analysis. (See **U.P.**. questions 1 and 13, and **A.L.T.** questions 1.a, 2.b, 4.c, and 4.d above.)
3. *Expository analysis of transformations*   Call students' attention to the directions in the textbook assignment with regard to content. (See **A.L.T.** question 3.d above).
4. *Creative writing: Miranda's story from a modern point of view*   Call students' attention to the directions in the textbook assignment with regard to content. Remind them to use dialogue to reveal Miranda's personality, ideas, and values.
5. *Creative writing: Ariel's or Caliban's life after Prospero leaves*   Call students' attention to the directions and questions suggested in the textbook assignment. Remind them that they can choose between Ariel and Caliban.

FURTHER READING

Shakespeare, William, *As You Like It; Romeo and Juliet; A Midsummer Night's Dream; Twelfth Night; The Taming of the Shrew; The Winter's Tale; Hamlet; Macbeth; King Lear; Julius Caesar; Richard III; Henry IV (Part 1).*

On His Blindness
JOHN MILTON

INTRODUCING THE POEM

Milton's sonnet ''On His Blindness'' reveals the thoughts of a man who, having become blind at the age of 43, and with half his life still to be lived, fears that his blindness will prevent him from writing his major creative work. A man of strong religious and political convictions and poetic genius, for over ten years he has used words to fight for religious, civil, and personal freedom. Now, he muses on how a blind poet can serve God. He remembers the parable of the talents (Matthew 25: 14–30), where the servant is punished for not using his gift profitably, by being cast "into the outer darkness." Milton asks, "Doth God exact day-labor, light denied?" He decides that God's work will get done, and that the best way he can serve is to bear his circumstances patiently: God accepts those who "only stand and wait." Milton therefore decides that he can accept his affliction.

Contrast is a major technique that Milton uses in the poem. The first eight lines (the octave) pose the critical question of how Milton can continue to serve God, and the last six lines (the sestet) respond with the fact that God will accept him for patiently bearing his affliction. His acceptance of his situation is the climax of the poem.

This is a summary of the parable of the talents in Matthew: Before leaving on a long journey, a master leaves his wealth, in the form of talents (units of weight equal to an amount of money), with his servants. The first and second servants use their talents in trade and double their value; the third buries the one talent that he was given. When the master returns and calls his servants to account, he is overjoyed with the behavior of his first two servants. The third servant explains that he was afraid of how the master had acquired the talent, so, instead of using it, he simply saved it for the master's return. His master punishes him by casting him out of the household and by giving his talent to the wealthiest servant.

PLJ: What do you value about your physical and mental abilities? How would you react if you lost one of your faculties? What emotions would you feel? What questions would you ask? What could help you accept your situation?

Literary Terms: allusion, contrast, irony, parable, paradox, personification, sonnet, theme, tone

COMPREHENSION QUESTIONS

1. When in his life did Milton become blind? (middle age)
2. What does Milton think it is "death to hide"? (one's gifts or abilities)
3. What question does Milton ask? (Does God expect a person who cannot see to perform work that requires vision?)
4. Why doesn't God need either "man's work or his own gifts"? (God's work in the world will be performed no matter what.)
5. How do those in the last line of the poem serve God? (simply stand and wait)

UNDERSTANDING THE POEM:
POSSIBLE ANSWERS

*1. *Milton's internal conflict* Milton is accustomed to using his poetic gifts to serve God. With the loss of his vision, he doesn't know how he will manage what he feels is his responsibility.

2. *Two meanings of talent* First, *talent* means a person's natural gifts, often a creative ability. Second, *talent* means an ancient monetary unit of gold or silver. Thus, the word has both a connotative and denotative meaning.

*3. *Milton's goal* Milton considered his one talent to be his poetic genius. His major goal has been to write a great English epic. At this early stage in his blindness, he cannot imagine how it will be possible to do it.

4. *God's "mild yoke" (line 11)* A yoke is a harness for some type of work or servitude, as oxen are yoked to pull a plow. God's "yoke," requiring human beings to serve as they are called by God, is considered light.

*5. *Patience's reply* Patience's reply means that God knows Milton's circumstances and will be pleased by Milton's patient acceptance of God's will. Like many Puritans and others in the seventeenth century, Milton believed that God would provide direct guidance in his life, telling him what he was to do. Milton's service is to wait and learn what his responsibilities will be.

*6. *Theme* (*a*) There are many ways to serve God; (*b*) Those who merely persevere also serve God.

ANALYZING LITERARY TECHNIQUE: POSSIBLE ANSWERS

*1. *Contrast* Contrast is an important technique in the poem. It is evident in the poem's structure: The first eight lines pose the critical question of how Milton can continue to serve God, and the last six lines respond with the fact that God will accept him for patiently bearing his affliction.

Thematically, the contrast between "my light is spent" (line 1) and "this dark world" (line 2) emphasizes what Milton has lost in losing his eyesight. The contrast between "at his bidding speed . . . without rest" (lines 12–13) and "serve who only stand and wait" (line 14) emphasizes the idea that God accepts equally all kinds of service.

2. *Allusion* Milton's allusion to the parable of the talents enriches his concern about his inability to serve God now that he is blind. The parable makes it clear that God expects people to use their gifts, whatever those gifts may be.

*3. *Personification* Milton personifies Patience in order to emphasize the importance of that quality.

*4. *Tone* The tone of the poem changes from one of concern about the effect of his blindness on Milton's life (the question in the octave) to one of acceptance and resignation (the reply in the sestet).

*5. *Paradox* It is paradoxical that a blind man can serve God, and that those who "stand and wait" can serve God. One might have thought that the only way to serve God would be to do important good deeds.

WRITING ABOUT LITERATURE

1. *Expository writing: an analysis of Milton's use of Petrarchan sonnet form* Call students' attention to the directions in the textbook assignment. You may want to

provide students with other examples of both Petrarchan and Shakespearean sonnets. Sonnet 32 by Elizabeth Barrett Browning, also included in the text, is another Petrarchan sonnet. Sonnets by William Shakespeare that may interest students include Sonnets 30 (''When to the sessions of sweet silent thought''), 44 (''They that have power to hurt and will do none''), 66 (''Let me not to the marriage of true minds''), and 80 (''My mistress' eyes are nothing like the sun''). (See **U.P.** questions 1, 3, 5, and 6, and **A.L.T.** questions 1, and 3–5 above.)

2. *Creative writing: a tribute to physical or mental abilities*   Call students' attention to the directions in the textbook assignment. Encourage them to think carefully about what they consider an ''ability.'' Many students may—like Milton in the first part of the sonnet—have a stereotyped idea about what it means to have or to lose certain faculties. Remind them to include particular examples and to use words that paint pictures. **(PLJ)**

FURTHER READING

Milton, John, ''To Cyriack Skinner''; ''Lycidas''; *Paradise Lost*.

My Heart Leaps Up

WILLIAM WORDSWORTH

INTRODUCING THE POEM

''My Heart Leaps Up'' is a celebration of Wordsworth's joyful appreciation of nature. He is delighted that he is able to perceive and appreciate the natural world with the mind of a child, open to nature's wonder and beauty. This faculty for appreciation (''natural piety'') is so important that he would die rather than lose it.

Wordworth's style achieves his goal: the union of imagination with simple means of expression. Wordsworth believed adults should attempt to retain the attitudes toward nature that they had as children, namely, a sense of wonder and an appreciation of beauty. He conveys this complex philosophical idea through the use of paradox (''The Child is father of the Man''), and he expresses the joy of nature through his metaphorical use of a verb (''leaps'').

The theme of the poem, appreciation of nature, is important to all human beings. Beauty often surrounds people in small, apparently insignificant forms. Such beauty is easily missed by those who get lost in the larger events of their lives. Yet, for those who remember to look outside themselves, appreciation of the various facets of nature enhances the experience of living. It provides a touch of beauty in what is often a highly pressured or drab environment.

PLJ: What role does an appreciation of nature play in your life? Have you always reacted to nature in the way that you do now? To what extent, if any, has any sight or experience in nature from your childhood had an effect on your later life?

Literary Terms: metaphor, paradox, repetition, theme

COMPREHENSION QUESTIONS

1. What does Wordworth love to behold? (nature, represented by the rainbow)
2. About how old is the poet when he writes this poem? (middle-aged)
3. What unusual statement does the poet make? (The child is father of the man.)

UNDERSTANDING THE POEM: POSSIBLE ANSWERS

1. *Important*   An appreciation of nature is most important. It is especially important to retain a childlike sense of wonder about nature.
*2. *"Child is father of the man" (line 7)*   An adult is a child grown up. A person's child-hood experiences determine to a considerable extent how he or she reacts to later life-experiences. Wordsworth applies this relationship to the appreciation of nature.
3. *Natural piety*   *Piety* means faithful devotion. "Natural piety" means faithful de-votion to nature.
4. *Theme*   The appreciation of nature is a critically important aspect of one's life. A goal in life should be to preserve the view of the natural universe that one had as a child.

ANALYZING LITERARY TECHNIQUE: POSSIBLE ANSWERS

*1. *Paradox*   "The Child is father of the Man" is the opposite of the usual way in which people think about the parent-child relationship. This formulation of the relationship reveals the unity within each person from childhood to old age and implies a cause-and-effect relationship between early life-experiences and later reactions to life-experiences. Just as a parent teaches a child, it is possible to view the child as the teacher of the adult. The child views the world as a new and delightful experience, one that is filled with wondrous sights and events. Those who retain their appreciation of the wonder and beauty of the natural environment (and of life itself) lead far richer lives.
2. *Poem in terms of Wordsworth's goals (See textbook Introduction)*   The poem is a fine example of Wordsworth's goals. His subject is his powerful emotional reaction to na-ture, which he expresses in terms of his heart's leaping joyfully upon seeing a rainbow. He also achieves remarkable success in using common language to describe a common sight in a way that expresses the spiritual relationship between human beings and nature. Except for the opening metaphor, Wordsworth avoids figurative language.

   In addition, the paradox ("Child is father of the Man") conveys a complex rela-tionship in graphically simple terms. Wordsworth even avoids adjectives and adverbs. The result is a philosophical theme that is presented in an extremely simple and uncluttered form.

3. *Metaphor*   The verb *leaps* is effective in that it conveys life, vitality, excitement, and enjoyment. Animals leap with vitality; people leap with joy. Wordworth's leaping heart signifies his joyful reaction to the beauty in nature.

4. *Capitalization*   The capitalization of "Child" and "Man" accomplishes two goals simultaneously: Wordsworth emphasizes both words and their meanings, and their meanings expand to represent all children and all adults.

5. *Repetition*   The repetition of *so* expresses the continuity of Wordsworth's feelings throughout his three stages of life.

6. *Comparison between Wordsworth's attitude expressed in quote from a sonnet (See textbook Introduction) and in "My Heart. . ."*   The question is whether people are able to retain their childlike appreciation of nature, or whether they are inevitably condemned by the experiences of living to lose their ability to respond to their environment with an immediate sense of wonder and joy. Opinion will depend on each student's personality and experiences.

WRITING ABOUT LITERATURE

1. *Expository writing: an essay on the paradox of the child's being the parent of the adult*   Call students' attention to the guide questions in the textbook assignment. Remind them to support their ideas with specific examples. (See **U.P.** question 2, and **A.L.T.** question 1 above.) (**PLJ**)

2. *Creative writing: a memorable experience in nature*   Remind students that they can choose to express their thoughts in either prose or poetry. Also remind them to choose words that will help others see the sight or feel the experience.

FURTHER READING

Wordsworth, William, "The Daffodils"; "To the Cuckoo"; "The Solitary Reaper"; "Lucy"; "The World Is Too Much with Us"; "Ode: Intimations of Immortality from Recollections of Early Childhood."

Sonnet 32

ELIZABETH BARRETT BROWNING

INTRODUCING THE POEM

Sonnet 32 is particularly appealing in that Barrett eloquently expresses doubts that are common to many people before they make a lasting emotional commitment. She finds it ironic that Browning has chosen to love her when he surely can find a younger, healthier, and more attractive woman. She wonders whether he is acting so quickly that he will soon be sorry. By the end of the poem, she has accepted Browning's judgment, believing that his love has made her the person that he loves and that it is possible for two "great souls" to overcome physical imperfections and to unite with confidence.

The poem is based on the paradox that one who loves can make a plain-looking loved one beautiful, or in the central image of the poem, a master musician can produce perfect music using an old, out-of-tune, and mostly obsolete instrument. Barrett uses the simile of "an out-of-tune/Worn viol" (lines 7–8) to describe herself and the metaphor of "a good singer" (line 8) to describe Browning. At the end of the poem, Barrett unites the contrasting musical strands, stating that "master-hands" can bring forth "perfect strains" from "instruments defaced," and that "great souls, at one stroke, may do and dote" (lines 12–14).

Contrast is a major technique in the poem, in that it establishes the disparity between the speaker's view of herself and the lover's view of her. Barrett carries the contrast through the first eleven lines of the poem. The end of the contrasts in the last lines of the poem marks the speaker's acceptance of her lover's point of view. Her changed attitude is the climax of the poem.

PLJ: Have you ever felt unworthy of the love of someone whom you admire, or have you known someone who felt unworthy of your affection and attention? What caused you or the other person to feel inadequate?

Literary Terms: alliteration, climax, contrast, figurative language, irony, metaphor, paradox, rhyme, simile, sonnet, tone

COMPREHENSION QUESTIONS

1. What bothers the speaker about her lover's oath? (made too quickly)
2. What does the speaker expect might happen? (Her lover will be sorry and change his mind.)
3. To what does the speaker compare herself? (an old, out-of-tune, defaced viol)
4. What does the speaker conclude about her attitude? (It wrongs her lover.)
5. What is the tone of the conclusion? (optimistic)

UNDERSTANDING THE POEM: POSSIBLE ANSWERS

1. *Speaker's doubts* The speaker believes that she is too unattractive, worn, and out of date for him.
2. *Speaker's reluctance to accept love* The speaker is concerned that her lover has fallen in love too quickly and that he will soon tire of her or find her lacking in qualities that are important to him. If this happens, she will be hurt.
3. *How speaker's attitude wrongs her lover* The speaker decides that her lover loves

what he sees in her rather than what she sees in herself. She recognizes that what he sees is also part of herself, so she can trust his love.

4. *Speaker's conclusion*   The speaker concludes that two mature people who are right for each other may know it soon and with certainty.

5. *Importance of effort in a relationship*   The critical ingredient in a relationship is the attitude of both partners (the "greatness" of their souls) and the quality of their love, rather than superficial details such as physical appearance, age, or length of acquaintance.

ANALYZING LITERARY TECHNIQUE: POSSIBLE ANSWERS

*1. *Contrast*   Contrast establishes the disparity between the speaker's view of herself and her lover's view of her. Barrett carries the contrast through the first twelve lines of the poem. Examples include: (*a*) the constant sun vs. the inconstant moon (lines 1–2); (*b*) "thine oath / To love me" vs. "slacken bonds of love" (lines 1–3); (*c*) "quick-loving" vs. "quickly loathe" (line 5); (*d*) "out-of-tune / Worn viol" vs. "good singer" (lines 7–8); (*e*) "snatched in haste" vs. "laid down at the first ill-sounding note" (lines 9–10); (*f*) "did not wrong myself" vs. "placed / A wrong on thee" (lines 11–12); (*g*) "perfect strains" vs. "instruments defaced" (lines 12–13).

*2. *Extended metaphor*   Barrett uses the simile of an out-of-tune viol to describe herself and her relationship to Browning, whom she describes metaphorically as "a good singer." The extended metaphor built on these figures of speech symbolizes the details of her view of their relationship. Examples include: (*a*) the singer would "spoil his song" with the "out-of-tune / Worn viol" (lines 7–9); (*b*) an instrument "snatched in haste, / Is laid down at the first ill-sounding note" (lines 9–10); (*c*) "perfect strains may float / 'Neath master-hands, from instruments defaced" (lines 12–13); (*d*) "great souls, at one stroke" (line 14).

3. *Relationship of climax to sonnet structure*   The climax occurs at the end of the sonnet, in the last sentence (the last three lines). It presents a change of attitude, one that unites the contrasting strands of the rest of the poem. The speaker decides that "master-hands" can bring forth "perfect strains" from "instruments defaced," and "great souls, at one stroke, may do and dote."

4. *Relationship of tone to sonnet structure*   The tone changes from one of skepticism to one of confidence, with skepticism being the tone of the first ten lines, and confidence taking over the remaining four lines.

*5. *Consonance, assonance, and rhyme*   The sound devices help to unify the poem. Together, they make the lines read smoothly and musically, thus reinforcing the poem's central musical metaphor. Examples include: (*a*) Repeated open consonants and spirants (*f, l, m, n, s,* and *r* sounds) give the lines a rolling, flowing sound; (*b*) Repeated vowel sounds, especially long vowels ("the sun rose on thine oath / To love me, I looked forward to the moon" [lines 1–2]) add to the musical softness of the poem; (*c*) The use of near rhyme (oath/troth/loathe/wroth, moon/soon/one/tune) softens the chiming, singsong effect of repeated perfect rhyme.

WRITING ABOUT LITERATURE

1. *Expository writing: an analysis of figurative language*   Call students' attention to the directions in the textbook assignment. Remind them to use direct quotations from the poem. (See **A.L.T.** questions 1, 2, and 5 above.)
2. *Creative writing: a response from the lover*   Remind students that they can choose the form of their responses.

FURTHER READING

Browning, Elizabeth Barrett, *Sonnets from the Portuguese; Aurora Leigh*.

The Old Stoic
EMILY BRONTË

INTRODUCING THE POEM

Emily Brontë's eloquent, personal plea for freedom and the courage to endure all trials reveals the values that sustained her to the day of her death. In her poem, as in her life, she rejects the goals that many people value: love, wealth, and fame. Brontë's creed is confirmed in the "Biographical Notice of Ellis and Acton Bell," included in the second edition of *Wuthering Heights*, where Currer Bell (Charlotte Brontë) describes Emily Brontë's nature, the lack of recognition for her poetry and her novel, and how she faced the ravaging effects of tuberculosis. Her creed is also confirmed by how she chose to live her life, walking in solitude on the moors that sustained her, seeking only the company of her sisters, and persevering in her writing despite its unfavorable reception.

Stoicism dates from c. 300 B.C. and the Greek philosopher Zeno. Stoicism states that it is the obligation of human beings to reject the appeals of pleasure and, instead, to devote their lives to good works and to accept their fate with courage. Brontë's wish for the courage to endure and her rejection of love, wealth, and fame reveal the indifference to pain and pleasure that characterizes the stoic. However, she substitutes her passion for liberty for the stoic's commitment to duty.

Part of the poem's appeal is its musical quality. Brontë achieves this through her choices of rhythm (iambic tetrameter, alternating with iambic trimeter) and rhyme.

PLJ: What do you need in order to have a happy life? What would you sacrifice in life in order to have what you value?

Literary Terms: connotative language, contrast, lyric, metaphor, rhythm

COMPREHENSION QUESTIONS

1. What does the speaker value lightly? (riches)
2. What does the speaker scorn? (love)
3. What dream has vanished? (desire for fame)
4. For what does the speaker pray? (to keep her heart; to be free)
5. What does the speaker want through life and death? (a free soul; courage to endure)

UNDERSTANDING THE POEM: POSSIBLE ANSWERS

1. *Values of speaker*   The speaker values liberty more than anything else—more than wealth, love, and fame.
2. *What else poem reveals about speaker*   The poem also reveals that the speaker is aging, which suggests that the speaker's stoicism comes of experience and perhaps of disappointments. The speaker is concerned about maintaining her integrity even beyond the grave.

ANALYZING LITERARY TECHNIQUE: POSSIBLE ANSWERS

*1. *Contrast*   The speaker emphasizes the importance of liberty by comparing her passion for liberty with her rejection of the love, wealth, and fame that most people value.
2. *"Chainless soul" (line 11)*   The metaphor of a "chainless soul" in the last stanza creates a visual picture of a free spirit, both in life and death. This is the liberty that the speaker passionately values. She prays for it in the second stanza, having stated in the first stanza that she has no interest in any other aspect of life.
3. *Ballad meter and rhyme scheme*   The seven-stress lines of ballad meter or hymn meter (iambic tetrameter alternating with iambic trimeter) combine with the regular, *abab* rhyme scheme to give the poem a soothing, musical quality. Ballad or hymn meter connects the poem with traditional, oral forms of poetry. It contributes to the poem's simplicity and directness.
4. *Connotative language*   Bronte's use of connotative language gives the poem its power. "Laugh to scorn" (line 2) reveals the ease with which the speaker dismisses love from her life. "A dream / That vanished" (lines 3–4) conveys the transitory nature of the speaker's wish for fame. "Liberty" (line 8), by not being more specific, becomes personal to each reader, being open to individual interpretation. "Give me" (line 8) combines the directness of the command with the passion of "I want. " "I implore" (line 10) conveys great depth of feeling.
5. *Lyric poem*   This is a lyric poem in that the poet is expressing personal feelings in a form that is short, complete in itself, and musical in quality.

WRITING ABOUT LITERATURE

1. *Expository writing: an analysis of Brontë's use of contrast*   Remind students to support their ideas with direct quotations. (See **A.L.T**. question 1 above.)
2. *Creative writing: how did the speaker become a stoic?*   Remind students that they are free to choose both the content and the form of this work. Students may wish to experiment with ballad meter, a fairly easy-to-write poetic form. **(PLJ)**

FURTHER READING

Brontë, Emily, "Remembrance"; "No Coward Soul Is Mine"; "The Prisoner"; *Wuthering Heights*.

Goblin Market
CHRISTINA ROSSETTI

INTRODUCING THE POEM

"Goblin Market" operates on two levels. On the surface, it is the delightful and heroic story of the triumph of love over adversity. Lizzie's love for her sister Laura is so great that, after Laura has been poisoned by eating the tempting and forbidden goblin-fruit, Lizzie conquers her fears and subjects herself to the powers of the evil goblins to save Laura's life. By courageously withstanding temptation and stoically enduring the goblins' taunts and abuse, she returns with the antidote for the poison.

Beneath the surface, "Goblin Market" is the story of the triumph of self-control over temptation. Woven into its texture are two biblical themes. The first, from Genesis, involves the loss of innocence by succumbing to the temptation to eat forbidden fruit. The second, from the New Testament, involves the Christlike salvation of a sinner through love and suffering.

Also woven into the texture of "Goblin Market" are interesting psychological themes. The sisters share all of life's experiences, with one critical exception. Laura functions as Lizzie's Shadow or doppelgänger in that she represents Lizzie's unrestrained self, the part of Lizzie that is willing to be curious and to experiment despite the risks. In contrast, Lizzie "thrust a dimpled finger / In each ear, shut eyes and ran" from the goblin men (lines 67–68). Thus, the relationship between Lizzie and Laura can be viewed as symbolizing an internal conflict within one person between two diametrically opposed inclinations, those that are rational and viewed by the self as "good" and those that are irrational and viewed by the self as "evil."

Using the terminology of Albert Guerard, it is possible to view "Goblin Market" as the soul-satisfying "solitary spiritual journey" or "night journey" of a person who is dealing with an inner conflict between these inclinations. Her Lizzie-self first abdicates; she runs in fear from the goblin men's temptations and lets her Laura-self indulge her curiosity and experience the disastrous, tempting fruits. Then, her Lizzie-self musters her courage and proves that she possesses the qualities necessary to save her Laura-self by confronting the goblin men's temptations and resisting them. As a result, her Lizzie-self can triumphantly claim a double victory. She has saved the life of her Laura-self and has proved that her Lizzie-self no longer needs to fear temptation. Thus, through the night journey, the person who has been experiencing the inner conflict heals herself of her internal division and emerges as an integrated personality.

The plot, character development, and thematic material of "Goblin Market" reveal the poem to be similar to an allegory in that it can be understood on two levels, with a simple narrative on the surface and a moral meaning beneath the literal one. Lizzie's actions on Laura's behalf reveal the power of a person's love to support and enrich the life of a loved one. The goblin's fruits reveal two paradoxes: First, evil (their fruit) can appear to be attractive and benign; second, actions that are pleasurable can also lead to corruption and death. Finally, as Lizzie learns, one can combat evil only by confronting it; ignoring it simply perpetuates it.

"Goblin Market," with its rhythms, rhymes, and repetitions, asks to be read aloud. Its lists of details regarding tempting fruits and evil goblin men enrich the imagination. However, the stylistic highlight may be Rossetti's technique of emphasizing each significant dramatic point in the story by means of a series of remarkable similes.

PLJ: To what extent, if any, do you consider present pleasure to be worth the possibility of future pain? If you are a person who avoids temptation, what methods do you use to achieve this goal? Do you find that it is better for you to avoid the tempting situation or to confront it?

Literary Terms: allegory, alliteration, conflict, connotative language, contrast, doppelgänger, fairy tale, figurative language, foreshadowing, irony, metaphor, narrative, night journey, onomatopoeia, paradox, parallelism, repetition, rhyme, Shadow, simile, symbol, theme

COMPREHENSION QUESTIONS

1. To whom do the goblin men call? (young women and girls)
2. When do the goblin men sell their wares? (morning and evening)
3. What do the goblin men sell? (fruit)
4. What is Laura's attitude toward the goblin men? (curious)
5. What is Lizzie's attitude toward the goblin men? (fearful)
6. Who is Jeanie? (girl who ate goblin-fruit and died)
7. What is unusual about the cost of goblin fruit? (money not accepted; payment must be something from oneself)
8. What does Laura do? (eats goblin-fruit and begins to die)
9. How does Lizzie respond? (brings goblin-fruit juice to Laura and cures her)
10. What is the concluding idea in the poem? (A sister is the best friend.)

UNDERSTANDING THE POEM: POSSIBLE ANSWERS

1. *Goblin men's customers*   The goblin men are only interested in corrupting innocence. Thus, they have no interest in women who have eaten their fruits, or in married women.

2. *Goblin men's charge for wares*   The goblin men do not sell their fruit for financial gain. Their payment is corruption. When Laura pays with a lock of hair and a tear (lines 126–27), she is literally and symbolically paying a personal price for choosing evil. She is losing not only part of herself in terms of her hair, but part of herself in terms of her innocence.

3. *Jeanie's fate*   Before Laura consorts with the goblin men, she knows Jeanie's fate as well as Lizzie does. Laura simply disregards all prior knowledge and experience in order to act as she chooses, without concern for the consequences. She has become blind to the reality that the goblin men are evil and deaf to her conscience and Lizzie's admonitions.

4. *Lizzie's inner conflict and its resolution*   Lizzie, who has chosen never "to listen and look" for goblin men, must choose between her fear for her own personal safety and her love for her sister. Her love for Laura gives her the courage to suppress her fears and seek the goblin men.

*5. *Lizzie's courage and heroism*   Lizzie's initial courage is supported by her determination not to let the goblin men's evil contaminate her. She keeps the image of Jeanie at the forefront of her mind in order to resist the goblin men's efforts to tempt her. She keeps the image of Laura at the forefront of her mind in order to be able to tolerate the goblin men's physical abuse.

   Lizzie, who has earlier trained herself not to see and not to look at what is tempting but evil, now summons the ability not to feel the assault of evil against her person. Her motivation and self-discipline enable her passively and stoically to submit to the goblin men's tortures until they give up. Lizzie's heroic qualities include (*a*) her purpose in confronting evil, which is for the benefit of someone other than herself; (*b*) her courage; (*c*) her determination; (*d*) her perseverance; and (*e*) her stoical suffering.

6. *Nature of goblin-fruit*   Rossetti's treatment of the goblin-fruit implies that what is a poison or an antidote is determined by the intentions of the person who is using it. The goblin men's evil purpose contaminates their fruits, and Lizzie's purpose transforms the nature of the fruit from one of evil to one of healing.

7. *Nature of evil*   (*a*) Evil can appear in the guise of something harmless or good (delicious goblin-fruit). (*b*) Actions that are enjoyable can lead to corruption and death (eating goblin-fruit). (*c*) Evil intent can corrupt what would otherwise be good (the goblin men's contamination of the fruit). (*d*) Anyone who disregards rational thought, indulges emotion, and lives without moral restraint consorts with evil (Laura's loss of innocence by meeting with the goblin men and eating their fruit).

*8. *Themes*   (*a*) Evil can appear disguised as attractive and benign. (*b*) A person can combat evil only by confronting it. (*c*) Evil intent can corrupt what would otherwise be good. (*d*) Heroic behavior involves taking personal risks and suffering for the good of someone else. (*e*) To give in to temptation is to risk hurting oneself.

ANALYZING LITERARY TECHNIQUE: POSSIBLE ANSWERS

*1. *Goblin men*   The goblin men and their fruit symbolize whatever temptations in society lead to behavior that is either self-destructive or harmful to others. Examples include smoking, alcohol abuse, drug abuse, and promiscuous or irresponsible sexual activity.

*2. *Fairy tale*   Like a fairy tale, "Goblin Market" contains a heroic confrontation with evil, supernatural figures (goblin men), and a symbolic relationship to human experience. However, the moral focus of the symbolic relationship in "Goblin Market" (note its many moral themes) is characteristic of allegory.

 3. *Night journey*   Both Laura and Lizzie experience night journeys. Laura's night journey is negative, causing her to lose her innocence and to begin wasting away. Lizzie's night journey is positive. By courageously confronting the temptations that she has fearfully avoided, Lizzie proves to herself that she no longer needs to fear them because she is strong enough to resist them. (Her concern for her sister motivates her to overcome her fears.)

 4. *Foreshadowing*   Jeanie's story foreshadows what will happen to Laura if Lizzie does not intervene and save her.

*5. *Sound devices*   The effect of this poem depends largely on sound devices. Rossetti employs an irregular metrical and rhyme scheme. While lines usually have four stresses, some lines have three and others have only two. The poem is not arranged into couplets or quatrains—any number or combination of lines can rhyme, and sometimes rhyme is only suggested, as in the lists of fruits. The irregular meter and rhyme scheme contributes to the poem's fairy-tale-like effect and creates a singsong quality characteristic of children's rhymes. The poem is very pleasing when read aloud.

   Some examples of specific sound devices include: (*a*) Alliteration: "Crouching close together / In the cooling weather, / With clasping arms and cautioning lips" (lines 37–39); "Plums on their twigs; / Pluck them and suck them,— /Pomegranates, figs" (lines 360–62); "Kicked and knocked her, / Mauled and mocked her" (lines 428–29).

   (*b*) Assonance: "Do you not remember Jeanie, / How she met them in the moonlight, / Took their gifts both choice and many" (lines 147–49); "Poor Laura could not hear; / Longed to buy fruit to comfort her, / But feared to pay too dear" (lines 309–11).

   (*c*) Onomatopoeia: "She heard a voice like voice of doves / Cooing all together" (lines 77–78); "Puffing and blowing, / Chuckling, clapping, crowing, / Clucking and gobbling" (lines 334–36).

   (*d*) Repetition: "Come buy, come buy" (throughout the poem); lists of goblin-fruit (such as lines 5–15); descriptions of goblin men (such as lines 71–76); chains of similes, especially to describe Laura and Lizzie (such as lines 82–86). (See also question 6 below.)

*6. *Figurative language*   Rossetti employs chains of images for dramatic effect to highlight significant points in the narrative: (*a*) ''Like a rush-imbedded swan . . . last restraint is gone'' (lines 82–86) conveys the dangerous extent of Laura's curiosity; (*b*) ''Sweeter than honey . . . flowed that juice'' (lines 129–31) conveys the delicious nature of goblin-fruit; (*c*) ''Like two pigeons in one nest . . . gold for awful kings'' (lines 185–91) conveys the close relationship between the two sisters; (*d*) ''Like a lily in a flood . . . tug her standard down'' (lines 409–21) conveys Lizzie's determined and courageous stand against the assaults of the goblin men; (*e*) ''Her locks streamed like the torch . . . flag when armies run'' (lines 500–506) conveys the power of the antidote to invade Laura's body; and (*f*) ''Like the watchtower of a town . . . She fell at last'' (lines 514–21) conveys the great battle between the antidote and the poison in Laura's system.

WRITING ABOUT LITERATURE

1. *Expository writing: a character sketch of Lizzie as a hero*   Call students' attention to the directions in the textbook assignment. (See **U.P.** question 5 above.)
2. *Expository writing: an analysis of Rossetti's treatment of a particular theme*   Call students' attention to the directions in the textbook assignment. Remind them to use direct quotations to support their ideas. (See **U.P.** question 8, and **A.L.T.** question 1 above).
3. *Creative writing: A fairy tale narrative*   Call students' attention to the directions in the textbook assignment. Remind them of their choices with regard to content, style, and form. (See **U.P.** question 8, and **A.L.T.** questions 1, 2, 5, and 6 above.) **(PLJ)**

FURTHER READING

Rossetti, Christina, ''A Birthday''; ''Echo''; ''Uphill''; ''When I Am Dead, My Dearest''; ''In an Artist's Studio''; ''Remember.''

An Outpost of Progress

JOSEPH CONRAD

INTRODUCING THE STORY

''An Outpost of Progress'' is an adventure story about the fate of two ordinary Belgians who become ivory traders in central Africa. On one level, the story is a bitter indictment of colonialism and the slave trade. Kayerts and Carlier are typical of the white traders who entered central Africa under Belgian rule. Ostensibly bringing the fruits of civilization with them, they, in fact, both destroy and are destroyed by the environment in which they find themselves. Like many men whom Conrad observed on his own Congo journey, they exploit the natives for their own financial gain. Without civil law and public opinion to guide their behavior, they lack the inner resources to behave honorably and responsibly.

On a deeper level, Conrad's tale reveals the dual nature of human beings. What Conrad will call the "heart of darkness," G. H. Schubert, in *The Symbolism of Dreams* (1814) calls the doppelgänger, referring to a second, passionate self that haunts the rational self. Carl Jung calls this subconscious self the Shadow, and describes it as "a living part of the personality" that "personifies everything that the subject refuses to acknowledge about himself and yet is always thrusting itself upon him directly or indirectly." Jung also explains that "to become conscious of it involves recognizing the dark aspects of the personality as present and real," which a person usually does through dreams. In literature, the process by which this discovery occurs has become known as the "night journey." Albert Guerard, in discussing Conrad's works, describes it as "an essentially solitary journey involving profound spiritual change in the voyager" and explains that the particular experience and the nature of the psychological change vary with each voyager.

Conrad specifically reveals how the civilized veneer falls away from people who, when their survival is threatened, lack internalized moral values to sustain their humanity. With no understanding of the consequences, Kayerts and Carlier move from untidiness, to total laziness, to accepting immoral behavior in Makola, to joining Makola in that behavior. In time, they not only blindly aid Makola's barter of their workers for ivory, but they accept the ivory even though it was obtained by selling human beings into slavery. With this deed, they forfeit their souls. Although they are not consciously aware of it, their behavior is now being governed by their basest instincts.

When Kayerts realizes that he has murdered his unarmed friend, his attempt to rationalize his behavior ultimately fails, and he must acknowledge the reality of his dark inner self. His recognition of his doppelgänger or Shadow marks the culmination of his night journey. He is already filled with self-hatred, and the arrival of the delayed supply boat, bringing with it the judgment of society, is more than he can tolerate. He commits suicide. The captain finds Kayerts hanged and with his swollen tongue extended, which may symbolize the dead man's disdain for a civilized culture that had failed him in his time of need.

Makola may be the most interesting character in that he is a civilized African native who has also become completely amoral in this isolated environment. He, too, lacks the inner convictions that would enable him to be a man of honor. Not only does he despise and manipulate Kayerts and Carlier because they are white traders, but he also is willing to sell the station's African workers into slavery to obtain ivory. When Conrad says that Makola "cherished in his innermost heart the worship of evil spirits," he has more in mind than local tribal deities.

In "An Outpost of Progress," Conrad moves from one form of literary realism to another. For most of the tale, he achieves realism in a traditional manner by having most of the story controlled by an omniscient, impersonal narrator. However, once Carlier threatens to show Kayerts who is the master, even if it means killing him, Conrad switches to a realism that is psychologically oriented. With Kayerts's response to Carlier, the narrative perspective is limited to Kayerts's perceptions. As an effective bridge between the two kinds of narration, Conrad chooses to remain with the third-person form rather than to switch to the first-person form.

A particularly important factor in "An Outpost of Progress," as in Conrad's other works, is the relationship of the setting to the plot and the theme. It is Kayerts and Carlier's physical, social, and emotional isolation in the Congo jungle that leads them to discard their civilized veneer and surrender to their basest instincts. Consequently, Conrad depicts that environment with special care so as to convey the debilitating intensity of the sun, the dark density of the forest with its mysterious hidden noises and rhythms, and the shroudlike blanket of fog that covers the dead.

Note: The word *nigger,* conventional in Conrad's time, has been changed to *native* without damage to the meaning of the story.

PLJ: To what extent, if any, would you lead a different kind of life if you were alone, and if no one cared what you did or did not do? What values would you keep? What values would you discard?

Literary Terms: characterization, doppelgänger, existentialism, foreshadowing, impressionism, interior monologue, irony, limited omniscience, modernism, narrative perspective, night journey, setting, Shadow, symbol, theme, unreliable narrator

COMPREHENSION QUESTIONS

1. How does Makola feel about Kayerts and Carlier? (despises them)
2. What happened to the first chief of the station? (died of fever)
3. What is Kayerts and Carlier's job? (managing ivory trade and the trading station itself)
4. What is the major problem of this station? (isolated; not profitable)
5. What makes Kayerts and Carlier like each other? (fear of being alone)
6. What does Gobila do for Kayerts and Carlier? (gives them friendship and food)
7. What ends their relationship with Gobila? (They aid Makola in selling his tribe into slavery in return for ivory.)
8. What do Kayerts and Carlier argue about at the end? (sugar for coffee)
9. How does this argument end? (Kayerts murders Carlier.)
10. What does the Director find upon his arrival? (Kayerts has hanged himself.)

UNDERSTANDING THE STORY: POSSIBLE ANSWERS

*1. *Incapability of Kayerts and Carlier*   Both Kayerts and Carlier are incapable of independent thought and action. Without supervision, they resort to indolence. Their lack of commitment and their laziness contribute to their eventual moral decay.

2. *Courage and principles belong to the crowd; contact with primitive nature brings trouble to heart* Many people permit their values and behavior to be governed by society. When contact with primitive forces touches a person's inner core, and that core is hollow, it initiates a re-examination of values. That person's intellect and honor may then be surrendered to his or her uninhibited passions. The situation is dangerous in that neither the exterior controls of group opinion and law, nor strong internal resources, exist to prevent that person's loss of civilized veneer and to control his or her immoral behavior.
3. *Gobila's ideas and attitudes* Gobila's misunderstanding and misperception of the white ivory traders parallels their misunderstanding and misperception of the native Africans. A cultural chasm exists between them.
*4. *Makola as Henry Price* Makola demonstrates how the supposedly admirable goal of "civilizing" African natives can be misguided. Makola's identification with European customs and accomplishments suggests that isolation corrupts African natives just as it does white Europeans. Despite Makola's "civilized" veneer, he lacks moral values, and he uses others as objects to fulfill his own desires. Additionally, the white Europeans despise his aspirations, treating him no differently than they treat the other African natives.
*5. *Makola's discomfort and uncommunicativeness* Makola doesn't want Kayerts and Carlier to learn the nature of his dealings with the armed men. He despises the agents, and he manipulates them for his own ends. Therefore, he implants the fear of their own deaths and raises the question in Kayerts's mind of the cause of the first agent's death.
*6. *Kayerts and Carlier's responsibility for slave trade* Kayerts and Carlier let Makola manipulate them. They try to avoid being suspicious; they condemn Makola's behavior without making any effort to restrain him; and finally, they rationalize their acceptance of Makola's ivory as the "Company's ivory."

   As a result, Kayerts and Carlier lose all restraint and all vestiges of civilized values. They become increasingly vulnerable to moral decay in the absence of any internal or external controls.
*7. *Cause of fight* On the surface, the rules about the use of sugar cause the fight between Kayerts and Carlier. The underlying causes of the fight are their loss of self-respect, their loss of respect for others, and their loss of respect for authority and rules.

   Kayerts and Carlier have changed psychologically beyond recognition. They do not realize who they themselves are, and they do not recognize who the other has become. As can be true of other human beings, when Kayerts and Carlier do not acknowledge the doppelgänger or Shadow that is part of their personality, they become vulnerable to its control of their behavior. Once the Shadow or doppelgänger controls a person's behavior, that person is capable of anything and everything. Thus, Kayerts is able to shoot an unarmed man who had been his friend.
*8. *Role of fear* (a) Kayerts and Carlier fear death from the dangers of the sun and illness because that is their impression of how the first station manager died.

(*b*) Makola threatens Kayerts and Carlier with the death of the first station manager, and thus continues to instill fear of the sun and fever in them in order to be able to control them. (*c*) By the end of the story, Kayerts and Carlier have become so different, and, therefore, so afraid of each other, that Carlier is able to threaten to shoot Kayerts, and Kayerts is able to kill Carlier without noticing that Carlier is unarmed.

*9. *Kayerts's attitude toward death and life*   Before Kayerts kills Carlier, Kayerts is aware that he has lost his moral bearings. He realizes that he has lost his relationship with his only friend. While he can still choose to behave courteously today, he has lost his confidence in tomorrow, and he fears for his survival. Human life, including his own, has lost its value. Therefore, he advocates amorality as a value.

After he murders Carlier, Kayerts's fear of his own death and his horror of his deed combine to make him oblivious of his murder of Carlier.

*10. *Effect of Makola's comment about Carlier and fever on Kayerts*   Makola makes Kayerts question the real cause of the first agent's death. Makola's apparent knowledge and his complete control of the situation cause Kayerts to fear Makola.

*11. *Why Kayerts commits suicide*   Kayerts commits suicide because he can no longer live with himself, and he cannot live in society. He cannot tolerate being judged and condemned for what he has become.

12. *Theme*   The primary theme is know thyself: It is important to have strong, internalized values so that one can be true to oneself when faced with competing values or the absence of external values.

ANALYZING LITERARY TECHNIQUE: POSSIBLE ANSWERS

1. *Relationship between setting and plot*   Kayerts and Carlier's physical, social, and emotional isolation from civilization leads them to discard their civilized veneer. Conrad depicts the debilitating intensity of the sun, the dark density of the forest with its mysterious hidden noises and rhythms, and the shroudlike blanket of fog that covers the dead so as to convey how the location in which Kayerts and Carlier live and work erodes their attitudes and behavior.

2. *Significance of title*   The title is ironic. The outpost has been established in the name of civilization and progress, but it is an outpost of regressive, uncivilized behavior and values that have disintegrated. Conrad finds that these ''pioneers of trade and progress'' do nothing except harm natives and themselves.

*3. *Makola's role*   Makola's behavior reveals that isolation affects both whites and African natives in the same way. Makola encourages the greed of the agents and helps to destroy their principles and themselves.

4. *Foreshadowing*   Some examples include: (*a*) The untidiness of the agents foreshadows their later laziness, lack of discipline, and lack of self-restraint. (*b*) The

phrase "more white men to play with" foreshadows that Makola will encourage the agents' greed and their self-destruction. (*c*) The incident where Carlier replants the cross and hangs on it to test it foreshadows Kayerts's use of it to commit suicide. (*d*) The act in which the agents load their revolvers in preparation to cope with "bad men" foreshadows the argument in which Carlier threatens to shoot Kayerts and Kayerts uses his gun to kill Carlier.

5. *Crisis and climax*   The crisis in the story is the point where Kayerts and Carlier accept the ivory that Makola acquired by selling Gobila's people into slavery. The immediate result of the action is the loss of Gobila's help, which, in turn, increases their fears for their safety and their survival. The climax, Kayerts's murder of Carlier, is directly related to these fears, given the disintegration of their personalities and their relationship, and given the scarcity of their provisions.

*6. *Narrative perspective*   Once Carlier threatens to shoot Kayerts, the omniscient narrative perspective ends. While the narrative stays in the third person, the remainder of Kayerts's experiences are told exclusively from Kayerts's limited point of view. The change creates suspense because the reader must rely on a narrator who does not understand everything and is unreliable. It creates immediacy because the reader experiences Kayerts's perceptions directly.

*7. *Kayerts's night journey*   The climax of Kayerts's rule by his doppelgänger or Shadow is his murder of Carlier, who is unarmed. When Kayerts realizes that he has murdered his unarmed friend, his attempt to rationalize his behavior ultimately fails, and he must acknowledge the reality of his dark inner self. This recognition marks the culmination of his night journey. Being unable to tolerate the person he has become, and unable to face society and take responsibility for his actions, Kayerts commits suicide.

WRITING ABOUT LITERATURE

1. *Expository analysis of the role of fear*   Call students' attention to the directions in the textbook assignment. (See **U.S.** question 8 above.) **(PLJ)**
2. *Expository analysis of Kayerts's progressive psychological disintegration*   Call students' attention to the directions in the textbook assignment with regard to prewriting and to content. (See **U.S.** questions 1 and 6–11, and **A.L.T.** questions 6 and 7 above.)
3. *Creative writing: Makola's point of view*   Call students' attention to the directions and suggested questions in the textbook assignment. (See **U.S.** questions 4 and 5, and **A.L.T.** question 3 above.)

FURTHER READING

Conrad, Joseph, "Heart of Darkness"; "The Lagoon"; "The Secret Sharer"; *Lord Jim*; "The Nigger of the *Narcissus*."

The Lake Isle of Innisfree

WILLIAM BUTLER YEATS

INTRODUCING THE STORY

"The Lake Isle of Innisfree" masterfully conveys Yeats's love and nostalgia for the Irish countryside in which he spent his childhood. In a captivating rhythm that begs to be read aloud, he paints a word picture of a beautiful pastoral scene: a simple cabin on a small island where the only noises are the lake water's lapping the shore, birds, crickets, and bees. His depiction of the simple beauties of nature in lovely summer weather connote a sense of luxuriant peace, a tonic for the poet, now an adult city-dweller who lives in a crowded, noisy, and drab environment. The lazy, hypnotic feeling of the poem is conveyed by its style as well as its content. The rhythm sings soothingly, and repeated words give a sense of familiarity and emphasis. Rhyme and aliteration, with consonant sounds from the first half of a line repeated in the second half, provide a sense of continuity and further enhance the poem's musical quality.

The Symbolist influence in the poem is revealed in Yeats's ability to make his picture of Innisfree reflect and communicate his emotional yearning. On a symbolic level, the pastoral details symbolize the sense of inner peace, tranquility, freedom, and ease that the idea of Innisfree creates.

The poem also has many romantic qualities, such as Yeats's focus on his own state of mind, his feeling of nostalgia for a simpler life, his emphasis on the sensuous elements of nature, and his lyrical style.

PLJ: Have you ever been to a place to which you would love to return? List the details about the place that appeal to you. If you are fond of your home, you may use it as an example.

Literary Terms: alliteration, contrast, figurative language, repetition, rhyme, rhythm, setting, tone

COMPREHENSION QUESTIONS

1. What is the first thing that the speaker will do on Innisfree? (build a cabin)
2. What appeals to the speaker about Innisfree? (peace; beauty of nature; solitude)
3. Who will live on Innisfree with the speaker? (no one)
4. Where does the speaker hear the lake water's lapping? (deep in his heart, or echoed in his heartbeats)
5. Where is the speaker when he narrates this poem? (in the city; on a road or sidewalk)

UNDERSTANDING THE POEM: POSSIBLE ANSWERS

1. *Why thoughts of Innisfree?*   The speaker thinks of Innisfree because he is living in the city; streets and sidewalks remind him of the opposite, the country and nature.

2. *What thoughts of Innisfree reveal about current life*   The speaker's thoughts of Innisfree reveal that he prefers the island to the city. He misses all of the qualities that he associates with Innisfree: solitude, nature, peace, simplicity of living, and a quiet environment.

ANALYZING LITERARY TECHNIQUE: POSSIBLE ANSWERS

1. *Contrast*   The fact that the speaker thinks of Innisfree when he is standing on roads and pavements implies that it is the contrast between the two environments that makes him long for the country when he is in the city. Therefore, the detailed description of Innisfree implies a series of opposites with respect to the environment in which the speaker finds himself.

*2. *Tone*   The tone is one of tranquility, conveyed by the sights and sounds of Innisfree and also conveyed by the poetic techniques of rhythm, rhyme, alliteration, and repetition.

*3. *Figurative language*   (*a*) "Bee-loud" (line 4) cleverly describes the quiet noise level of the island; (*b*) "peace comes dropping slow" (line 5) conveys a mood of languor and, in a way, alludes to the movement of honey procured from the beehive and therefore contributes unity to the poem; (*c*) "veils of the morning" (line 6) conveys the atmosphere of early morning mist, which complements the atmospheres described as the "glimmer" of midnight and the "purple glow" of noon (line 7).

*4. *Sound devices*   Rhythm, repetition, alliteration, and rhyme help to unify the poem. The poem begs to be recited aloud because of its musical appeal. The rhythm is musical, and sounds musically connect with each other through repeated words ("arise and go"; "dropping"; "hear"), repeated consonants ("have," "hive," "honey"; "glimmer," "glow"; "lake," "lapping," "low"), and rhyme (*abab*).

WRITING ABOUT LITERATURE

1. *Expository writing: an analysis of the poem as romantic*   Although romanticism was no longer in vogue, the poem reflects many romantic qualities: (*a*) the speaker's emphasis on his own emotions (longing); (*b*) his view that civilization is a burden (implied in the contrast between the city streets and the preferable world of nature); (*c*) his feeling of nostalgia for a simpler place (solitary living on an

island in a country lake); (*d*) his emphasis on nature (beans, bees, birds, and atmosphere); (*e*) his emphasis on the sensuous elements of nature (sights and sounds); and (*f*) the lyrical, more relaxed structure of the poem (its rhythm and arrangement of sounds). (See **A.L.T.** questions 2–4 above.)

2. *Creative writing: description of a favorite place*   Call students' attention to the directions in the textbook assignment. Remind them that they can use their imagination and that details are important. Some students may wish to write in verse. **(PLJ)**

FURTHER READING

Yeats, William Butler, "An Irish Airman Forsees His Death"; "An Acre of Grass"; "A Coat"; "The Wild Swans at Coole"; "Sailing to Byzantium"; "Among School Children"; "The Second Coming."

Araby

JAMES JOYCE

INTRODUCING THE STORY

A bazaar is the focal point for this story about the loss of a young boy's childish innocence. In just a few pages, Joyce takes the reader from the beginning to the end of the boy's short but intense infatuation with his friend's older sister. In the process, the story conveys the feelings of outsiders, those who are unwilling or unable to share their deepest feelings and experiences. In the end, "Araby" is more than a jolting initiation that reveals the pain that often accompanies personal growth. It suggests all experiences in which reality is disappointingly different from one's hopes and dreams.

Joyce chooses the narrative perspective of an older narrator, a narrator who remembers a painful experience, reconstructs it selectively step by step, and then enhances its significance by alluding to religious images. The wording and structure of each sentence have been so painstakingly crafted that every aspect of the story is more than it initially appears to be.

An important characteristic of Joyce's style is his use of the "epiphany." The term means "showing forth"; the Christian feast of the Epiphany marks "the divine made visible to human eyes," and commemorates the infant Jesus' revelation to the Magi as the Christ. In *Stephen Hero*, Stephen explains an epiphany as "the most delicate and evanescent of moments," in which, in an insignificant event, the observer intuits "a sudden spiritual manifestation, whether in the vulgarity of speech or of gesture or in a memorable phase of the mind itself."

At the end of "Araby," the trivial conversation between the young lady and the two young men at the bazaar is the ordinary event that provides an epiphany for the young boy. His romantic concept of the sacred nature of love abruptly collapses before the harsh reality of casual and common flirting. The bazaar, that place of "Eastern enchantment," becomes a place of total disillusionment. The boy now feels that his behavior has been ridiculous, and realizing that his childish illusions have no basis in the real world, he is engulfed by anguish and anger.

PLJ: Have you ever been infatuated with someone? How did your infatuation begin? Was the object of your admiration aware of your feelings? How were you treated, and how did you feel about it? How did your infatuation end? What were your final feelings? Was this a memorable experience? Why?

Literary Terms: allusion, contrast, epiphany, figurative language, foreshadowing, imagery, narrative perspective, symbolism

COMPREHENSION QUESTIONS

1. What is Araby? (a bazaar; a fair for the sale of goods for charity)
2. Why does the boy go to Araby? (to buy a gift for his friend's sister on whom he has a crush)
3. Why isn't he successful? (arrives so late that most stalls are closed)
4. What emotions does he feel at the end of the story? (anguish; anger)
5. What causes him to feel this way? (overhears a conversation that makes him feel young and foolish about his crush)

UNDERSTANDING THE STORY: POSSIBLE ANSWERS

*1. *Effect of conversation on the boy*   The boy becomes conscious of his age as a barrier, making him an outsider. The trivial banter between the young woman and the young men makes him aware that he has idealized his feelings and his relationship.
*2. *Anguish, anger, and significance*   The boy suffers from the end of his infatuation, and he experiences both the loss of his great love (the particular girl) and the loss of his idealized view of love in general. He is embarrassed by his naiveté and is angry at himself for being so foolish. He is also angry at life for being so different from his dreams. He remembers the experience because of its importance in his life. His fall from illusion into reality causes such great anguish and anger that he is no longer the same person.
*3. *Initiation, rite of passage, and loss of innocence*   The narrator's use of religious symbolism and the boy's anguish and anger reveal that this experience had the significance of a rite of passage in the boy's life. He is now a more mature person, in that he knows more about himself and the world in which he lives.

ANALYZING LITERARY TECHNIQUE:
POSSIBLE ANSWERS

1. *Narrative perspective*   Joyce uses the perspective of an older person, who is relating an experience from his childhood. A younger person probably would choose different details and express them in simpler language. A much older person might have outgrown his interest in the significance of the experience. By relating the experience in retrospect, the narrator can exercise a selective memory and omit all extraneous details. He can also use language and sentence structures that are complex, and he can add religious imagery to his rendition of the experience.

*2. *Religious allusions and symbolism*   Religious allusions symbolize the nature and intensity of the boy's feelings. The words, *litanies, chalice, prayers, praises*, and *adoration* reveal the pure and sacred nature of his love. Then, his visit to Araby destroys his illusions of the sacred. The silence in the hall, like a "church after a service," the "counting of money," and the "fall of coins onto a salver" all symbolize the secular world of Araby and the foolishness of his love. Like Jesus, who angrily drove the merchants and moneychangers out of the temple, the boy is appalled and repelled by those who destroy what he has considered to be sacred.

*3. *Foreshadowing*   Examples of foreshadowing include: (*a*) The disparity in the ages of Mangan's sister and the boy; (*b*) the late arrival of the boy's uncle; (*c*) the boy's ride to Araby on a deserted train; (*d*) the dark, silent hall in which the bazaar is being held; and (*e*) the lone remaining seller's lack of interest in a boy of his age. All of these examples foreshadow the inevitable double failure of the boy's expedition and his romantic expectations.

*4. *Purpose of boy's late arrival*   The late hour means that most stalls will be closed, fewer people will be present, and there will be no distractions to ameliorate the boy's uncomfortable situation. Single details stand out: the commercial aspect of the bazaar; the meager choice of gifts; and the older girl's attitude toward the boy.

*5. *Contrast*   Joyce constructs this story on the gap that exists between the boy's illusions and the reality of his world.

(*a*) The dull houses on North Richmond Street, where the boy lives, contrast with the color and excitement of the Araby bazaar, which, in turn, contrasts with the dark, empty real bazaar that he finds upon his late arrival.

(*b*) The young age of the boy contrasts with the older age of Mangan's sister and foreshadows the collapse of his romantic illusions about a relationship between the two of them.

(*c*) The boy's romantic and religious conceptions of love contrast with the silly behavior of the young lady with the young gentlemen at the bazaar and cause the boy's illusions about love to collapse.

6. *Epiphany*   The trivial conversation between the young lady and the two young men at the bazaar is the ordinary event that provides an epiphany for the young boy. His romantic concept of the sacred nature of love abruptly collapses before the harsh reality of casual and common flirting. He now feels that his behavior has

been ridiculous, and realizing that his childish illusions have no basis in the real world, he is engulfed by anguish and anger.

WRITING ABOUT LITERATURE

1. *Expository theme on the quotation from* The Irish Times   Call students' attention to the poem and the directions in the textbook assignment. Remind them that it is important to explain the relevance of the quotations that they choose because it is their own ideas that make their essay unique. (See **U.S.** questions 1–3, and **A.L.T.** questions 2–5 above.)
2. *Expository analysis of contrast*   Call students' attention to the directions and suggestion in the textbook assignment with regard to content and organization. (See **A.L.T.** question 5 above.)
3. *Creative writing: retelling the story from the boy's point of view*   Call students' attention to the directions and suggestions in the textbook assignment. Remind them to write with the eyes, ears, and interest of a young boy. Consequently, their choice of details, language, and sentence structure should all be appropriate. (**PLJ**)

FURTHER READING

Joyce, James, *Dubliners*: "Eveline" and "The Dead"; *Stephen Hero; A Portrait of the Artist as a Young Man.*

The Hollow Men
T. S. ELIOT

INTRODUCING THE POEM

Written shortly after the end of World War I and prior to Eliot's conversion to Anglo-Catholicism, "The Hollow Men" is a psychological portrait of the modern age. Although it is Eliot's most pessimistic poem, its striking images and its rhythms make it among the most memorable of his works.

With lives that are devoid of meaning, the "hollow men" have ceased to exist in any creative sense. They live in a sterile world, a dead land of cactus plants and stone images in a valley of dying stars. Eliot may be describing the world after a great war, or he may simply be referring to the world of bustling technology that moves through time like a mindless robot. Either way, in this "waste land," whatever has bound human beings to one another and has provided meaning in life no longer exists. The "hollow men" have no past, no future, and a dismal present. They despair because they are paralyzed, or they are paralyzed because they despair. Either way, they symbolize passivity, sterility, and wasted life. Their world ends "not with a bang but a whimper." Eliot invites readers to see their own reflection in his mirror by using the word "we" in the opening lines of the poem: "*We* are the hollow men / *We* are the stuffed men . . ."

Eliot was interested in Jungian psychology. The "hollow men" may allude to Jung's Shadow, that inherent part of each person's personality that "personifies everything that the subject refuses to acknowledge about himself and yet is always thrusting itself upon him directly or indirectly." According to Jung, "to become conscious of it involves recognizing the dark aspects of the personality as present and real."

The possibility of this interpretation is confirmed by Eliot's use of the epigraph about Kurtz from Conrad's "Heart of Darkness." Mr. Kurtz, a civilized, educated man, enters the heart of Africa in order to collect ivory from the natives. His sojourn among them, far from the laws and customs that govern civilized peoples, destroys his civilized veneer and releases the primitive nature that exists beneath the civilized one. As he dies, he thinks about his deeds among the natives, recognizes the darkness that inhabits his own soul, and exclaims, "The horror! The horror!"

Conrad believed that everyone harbors the capacity to lose self-restraint and to be evil, and that only by looking deep within themselves and recognizing this potential can people hope to control their actions, for people cannot deal with problems that they cannot acknowledge. Eliot's choice of this epigraph implies that the "hollow men" need to look within themselves, acknowledge the emptiness of their values, and then, presumably, muster the courage to make the changes necessary in order to revitalize themselves. The power of the allusion to Kurtz resides in the contrast between his self-knowledge and the "hollow men's" self-deception.

Like the Symbolists, Eliot wants readers to enter the world of the poem prepared for the unusual and the unexpected and prepared to feel more than they can logically understand. In "The Hollow Men" as in other poems, Eliot places familiar words in new contexts in order to express new ideas and emotions. The allusions he uses gain intense emotional power by emphasizing contrast rather than similarity. He deliberately juxtaposes symbols, verbal styles, emotions, past and present, and thought with action in a way that defies conventional logic but that is consistent with the world within the poem. Finally, he repeats phrases or sentences to intensify the emotional content of the poem and unify it.

PLJ: What might lead a poet to describe human beings as "hollow"? What type of world do you think hollow people would inhabit? To what extent, if any, do you view any people alive today as being hollow? Why?

Literary Terms: allusion, characterization, connotative language, contrast, epigraph, figurative language, Imagist, lyric, metaphor, oxymoron, paradox, parallelism, repetition, rhythm, Shadow, simile, Symbolist, theme

COMPREHENSION QUESTIONS

1. (I) What adjectives does Eliot use to describe his characters? (hollow, stuffed)
2. (II) How does the poet feel about death's dream kingdom? (afraid of it; wishes to avoid it)

3. (III) What adjectives does Eliot use to describe the land of the "hollow men"? (dead; cactus; stone images)
4. (IV) What adjective describes his characters? (sightless: "no eyes here")
5. (V) To what children's singing game does Eliot allude? (Here we go 'round the mulberry bush.)
6. (V) To what prayer does Eliot allude? (the Lord's Prayer)

UNDERSTANDING THE POEM: POSSIBLE ANSWERS

1. *(I) "Hollow"*   "Hollow" epitomizes emptiness, and the word even sounds empty. The men are hollow because they live without values or beliefs, without thinking, feeling, or acting in any significant way.

*2. *(I) Shape without form . . . gesture without motion*   The description may suggest a ghost. Like the "hollow men" and the scarecrows, its form is human, but it is dead. The image creates a strong contrast between appearance and reality, and it functions as a strikingly effective characterization of the "hollow men."

*3. (I, II) *"Death's other Kingdom" (line 14); "death's dream kingdom" (line 20)*
    (a) "Death's other Kingdom" is possibly the kingdom of the dead who have died as compared with the kingdom of the dead "hollow men," who are still alive.
    (b) "Death's dream kingdom" possibly also refers to the kingdom of the dead who have died. It is better than the land of the living dead in that the sun shines, the trees live, the wind sings, and voices are perceptible (not quiet and meaningless whispers). It is worse because it is the land of eternal death, inescapable, unchangeable, and final. (The speaker does not want to die.)

4. (III) *Stone images (lines 41–43)*   It is possible that the "stone images" are modern buildings, houses of worship, or other material creations of the "hollow men." The "hollow men" are the living dead who live in a dead land. They live among the wonders of modern technology, and they worship the gods of wealth and material possessions. These materialistic values have replaced the spiritual values, such as love, kindness, sympathy, and generosity. In section III, Eliot also states, "At the hour when we are / Trembling with tenderness / Lips that would kiss / Form prayers to broken stone" (lines 48–51).

5. (IV) *"Lost kingdoms" (line 56)*   According to Eliot, the people of the modern age have lost both the kingdom of the living and the kingdom of faith. The kingdom of the living has become the "hollow men's" dead, cactus land. The kingdom of faith lies beyond the "hollow men's" reach. The Shadow that controls their lives, blinding and paralyzing them, is the side of themselves that they do not acknowledge. They must dispel that Shadow before they can truly live, and they can do this only by recognizing its existence and thus its nature.

6. (V) *"Life is very long" (line 83)*   The fact that "life is very long" provides the only hopeful note: the possibility of change for the better. Yet, at the end of the

poem, even that hope is cut short by the paralysis that exists because of lack of self-knowledge. Length of life does not insure change.

7. (I,V) *Connection between "Remember us . . . As the hollow . . . stuffed men" (lines 15–18) and "This is the way the world ends / Not with a bang but a whimper" (lines 97–98)* The "hollow men" are passive, not aggressive. A "lost" soul may act out in some counterproductive way; the "hollow men" do not act out at all.

8. *Themes* Themes include: (*a*) People must recognize what they have become in order to change who they are; (*b*) It is possible to be alive and yet lead such a sterile life that one is figuratively dead.

ANALYZING LITERARY TECHNIQUE
POSSIBLE ANSWERS

1. *"Stuffed men" (line 2)* "Stuffed men" is an appropriate metaphor for modern men and women because scarecrows cannot think, talk, act, or relate to others. The metaphor suggests immobility and inaction rather than vitality.

*2. *Vision imagery* The "hollow men" lack the ability to see clearly, "With direct eyes" (line 14). The "hollow men" are either empty or are in disguise (lines 31–36), so that even one who looks "With direct eyes" could not see them properly. Also, the "hollow men" lack the ability to see: "The eyes are not here / There are no eyes here" (lines 52–53); "We grope together" (line 58); "Sightless, unless / The eyes reappear" (lines 61–62). The vision imagery supports the poem's theme of inability and inaction.

*3. *Allusion to "Here we go 'round the mulberry bush"* The mulberry bush symbolizes a fertile environment, while the prickly pear symbolizes the environment of the desert. Eliot's substitution of the prickly pear cactus for the traditional mulberry bush creates a contrast between the environment of the "hollow men" and readers' views of their own environment. It is a terrifying reminder of how people can become accustomed to whatever type of lives they lead.

The allusion to a children's song is also effective because children lack adult sophistication. They are not blind to the fact that they live in a sterile world, and their acceptance of their world is frightening. The tone of the second verse of the dance is in striking contrast to the tone of the first verse, the second being as depressing as the first is cheerful. Having the children sing these lines increases the power of the poem's chilling prediction about the end of the world.

*4. *Mistah Kurtz* The power of the allusion rests in the contrast between Mr. Kurtz's self-knowledge and the "hollow men's" self-deception. Conrad believed that everyone has the capacity to lose self-control and to be evil, and that only by looking deep within themselves and recognizing this potential can people hope to control their actions. Eliot's use of this epigraph implies that the "hollow men" need to look within themselves and learn from the emptiness that they find there.

*5. *Guy Fawkes*   The power of this allusion rests in the similarity between the fun of a holiday that marks a very serious event in English history and the "hollow men" who are without form, color, and movement. The modern effigies of Fawkes have become detached from the roots that made him significant. The shell of the effigy mocks the original man, who had conviction and purpose and acted upon both. The "hollow men" are figurative effigies (or scarecrows) of what they, too, once were, in that people in the past lived with convictions and purpose.

*6. *Figurative language*   Eliot uses oxymorons ("Shape without form . . . gesture without motion" [lines 11–12]), similes ("rats' feet over broken glass" [line 9]), metaphors ("stuffed men" [line 2]), and allusions (Kurtz, Fawkes, the mulberry bush) to compare objects and ideas no one had ever thought to combine. His allusions gain intense emotional power by emphasizing contrast rather than similarity (Kurtz, the mulberry bush). He deliberately juxtaposes one symbol with another (the prickly pear and mulberry bush), one verbal style with another (the Lord's Prayer and the children's singing game), one emotion with another ("Lips that would kiss / Form prayers to broken stone" [line 50–51]), the past with the present (Guy Fawkes), and thought with action (the Shadow and the Lord's Prayer with the children's ring dance) in a way that defies conventional logic but that is consistent with the world within the poem. An equally great contrast exists between the poem's aural appeal and its somber subject matter.

7. *Sound devices*   Repetition, parallelism, and rhythm reinforce the incantatory quality of the poem, a quality that is also reinforced by the children's rhyme and lines from the Lord's Prayer. Eliot repeats phrases or sentences to reinforce the poem's meaning, to intensify its emotional content, and to unify it.

WRITING ABOUT LITERATURE

1. *Expository analysis of contrast*   Call students' attention to the directions in the textbook assignment with regard to content and organization. (See **U.P.** questions 2 and 3, and **A.L.T.** questions 2–6 above.)

2. *Expository analysis of poem's relation to Jung's Shadow*   When Eliot states that the "hollow men" have no eyes and are "Sightless, unless / The eyes reappear . . . The hope only / Of empty men" (lines 61–67), he is expressing the idea that the "hollow men" are blind to the type of people that they have become (their sterile Shadow-selves), and that their only hope for improving the quality of their lives is to look within themselves and acknowledge the emptiness of their values. If self-knowledge replaces self-deception, they might be able to muster the courage necessary to revitalize themselves. However, the poem's ending makes this possibility seem unlikely.

    Call students' attention to the questions in the textbook assignment. (See **A.L.T.** question 2 above.)

3. *Creative writing: theme on whether or not modern people are "hollow"* Call students' attention to the directions in the textbook assignment. (**PLJ**)

FURTHER READING

Eliot, T. S. "The Love Song of J. Alfred Prufrock"; *Murder in the Cathedral.*

The Fly

KATHERINE MANSFIELD

INTRODUCING THE STORY

"The Fly" is a fine example of how an apparently minor incident can illuminate a character's fundamental personality. The story is a character sketch of a man, significantly known only as "the boss." He is visited by an old friend and associate, Mr. Woodifield, who refers to their respective sons, both of whom were killed six years earlier in World War I. Later, in coping with memories of his son, the boss tortures a fly to death, revealing his basic personality and confirming earlier hints that he is more complex than he appears.

Every word in this story, sounding natural and casual in its place, proves to have far-reaching significance. Mr. Woodifield's thought that "We cling to our last pleasures as the tree clings to its last leaves," provides one of the themes; the description of the photograph of the boss's son introduces the question of his personality; and Mr. Woodifield's memory lapse foreshadows the boss's later, related, memory lapse.

Jung defines the Shadow as "a living part of the personality" that "personifies everything that the subject refuses to acknowledge about himself and yet is always thrusting itself upon him directly or indirectly." Just as a bully conceals a Shadow who is a coward, a boss conceals a Shadow who is a wimp. Thus, the boss in "The Fly" always feels compelled to overcompensate for his fear of his weak Shadow-self by taking total control of himself and others. His fear of his own weakness also makes him intolerant of weakness in anyone or anything else, including Mr. Woodifield, his son, and the fly.

The boss handles weakness in others by giving them challenges they need strength to master. He insists that Mr. Woodifield drink straight whiskey, and he challenges the fly to overcome ink blots. Unfortunately, the boss's fear of weakness is so strong that the challenges he creates for others may be too great for them. Recognizing that the fly's efforts have become timid and weak, he nevertheless is compelled to give it the challenge that kills it. Thus, his behavior contains both sadistic and tragic qualities.

The power of the story resides in what the boss's treatment of the fly and his reaction to its death reveal about him and his son. James Joyce would call this incident an epiphany, a sudden moment of illumination that reveals the boss's true character and destroys the veil of illusion that has concealed the private man beneath the public image. Memories of his enjoyment of his son's success in learning the family business lead the boss to treat the fly as he does, and in the process, he unconsciously re-creates the pattern of his son's life and death. Thus, as the fly copes with its challenges, the boss enjoys its successes with the same pleasure that he watched those of his son, and when it dies, his "grinding feeling of wretchedness" frightens him into disconnecting his memory of both the emotion and all that produced it.

The boss does not usually permit himself to think about his son's death because it destroys the principle that governs his own life, namely, that those who are strong enough can overcome any adversity, even the possibility of death. His torture of the fly is an experiment which, on a symbolic level, re-creates his son's life and death under circumstances over which he has complete control. When the fly's death confirms the destruction of the principle that is crucial to his own life, the boss finds that, once again, both this knowledge and his emotional response to it are so frightening that he must immediately forget them.

On a different level, "The Fly" also presents two ways of handling the death of a loved one. Mr. Woodifield mourns the loss of his son and proceeds to live as meaningful a life as his poor health will permit. In contrast, once the boss's son dies, the boss lives on only as a mechanical being. Health, financial success, and remaining family mean nothing to him. His son was an extension of himself, and that death killed his own interest in life.

PLJ: Have you ever had a goal that, due to circumstances beyond your control, you could not achieve? How did you react? In the end, to what extent, if any, did you come to accept the situation?

Literary Terms: characterization, epiphany, foreshadowing, narrative perspective, paradox, psychological realism, Shadow, theme, tone

COMPREHENSION QUESTIONS

1. What important topic does the guest mention? (grave of boss's son)
2. How does the host react? (appears not to care; left alone, can't cry)
3. What happens to the fly? (boss tortures it to death)
4. Name two characters who lack proper names. (boss, his son)

UNDERSTANDING THE STORY: POSSIBLE ANSWERS

*1. *Boss's lack of proper name*   The constant use of the boss's title, rather than his name, reveals who the boss is and how he functions in interpersonal relationships. The need always to be "boss" reveals his fear of weakness in himself and his inability to tolerate it in others.

    The boss's behavior, consistent with his title, reflects his overwhelming need to control himself and others, including his response to Woodifield in the opening scene, the nature of his thoughts about his son and his son's death, and his treatment of the fly in the closing scene.

*2. *Why the boss keeps photo*   The boss may keep this photo on his desk, even if he doesn't like it, because it makes a good public impression. The boss can appear to be proud to have had a son who gave his life for his country and, thus, died a heroic death. This is consistent with the boss's interest in redecorating his office and his absolute control over his emotions in public. Maintaining appearances is very likely second only to maintaining control, and, in fact, is a way of exercising control.

The photograph of the boy also reminds the boss that his own life no longer has a purpose, since his sole interest was to pass on his business to his son, and his son is dead.

*3. *Why the boss never uses son's name*   Calling his son "the boy" creates an emotional distance from him, almost as if he is not the boss's son. Distance relieves the pain. Memories of his son call forth memories of his death. His son's death reminds him that, just as he had no control over his son's death, he will have no control over his own death, and with him, control is the most important factor in life.

*4. *Why the boss has not seen son's grave*   The boss has the financial ability but not the motivation to see the grave. His decision reflects a form of denial, his inability to deal with the reality of his son's death and the effect of that loss on his life. His son's death is a reminder of his inability to control mortality, including his own.

*5. *Why the boss can't cry*   With time, the boss has been able to bury his emotions in an area of his psyche where he can no longer feel them. However, although he cannot summon them, they still exist, and they erupt when the fly dies. Part of anyone's reaction to anything is a response to the questions "How does this affect my life? What will happen to me?" The boss's tears reflected his response to these questions. The death of his son, who was an extension of himself, was an excruciatingly personal loss. That death also devastated the principle by which the boss lived, that strength overcomes all adversity.

*6. *Why boss tortures fly to death*   The experience provides an acceptable outlet for great anger and frustration: anger at his son's death and, consequently, the loss of his own dreams, and frustration at his own inability to control what was most important to him in life (his son's life). His method of killing the fly enables him to examine the process of life and death under circumstances that he controls.

The boss admires the fly's heroic efforts and is not consciously aware that his challenges are torturing it to death. However, when it dies, he feels wretched because he subconsciously realizes that his treatment of the fly has reproduced the pattern of his son's life and death and of his own, as well. The boss has constructed his life on the principle that those who are strong enough can overcome any adversity, even death. The fly's death reinforces the message of his son's death, that no one can control important aspects of life.

7. *Themes*   Themes include: (*a*) a person's actions reveal aspects of that person's character; (*b*) people who feel unbearable emotions may conceal them from themselves and others.

ANALYZING LITERARY TECHNIQUE: POSSIBLE ANSWERS

1. *Function of Woodifield*   Woodifield's major function is to evoke the boss's memories of his son. Woodifield contrasts with the boss in the lack of control Woodifield exercises over his life, and Woodifield's behavior elicits the boss's response to weakness in others. Woodifield also contrasts with the boss in their respective attitudes toward the death of their sons. Woodifield accepts the death and continues to appreciate all the good in life. The quality of the boss's life died with his son, whom the boss viewed as an extension of himself.

*2. *Photo of boss's son as symbol*   The difference between the son's photograph and the boss's memory of his son reveals the difference between reality (the photo) and illusion (the boss's memories). The "grave-looking" photo of a "cold, even stern-looking" youth depicts the real son as a young adult, possibly unhappy, and possibly a victim of his father's need to control everything and everyone connected with his own life. In order to be sure that his son became strong, the boss may have given him overwhelming challenges just as he did with the fly. The boss cannot acknowledge the true nature of either his son or himself. He lives with illusions of both that he has created to satisfy his own needs.

*3. *Fly as symbol*   The fly symbolizes the boss's own life-experience in that, like the fly, the boss is subject to forces beyond his control. (He had no power to control his son's death.)

   The fly also symbolizes the boss's son in that the boss challenges both to be successful, enjoys their successes, and then finds that their abilities cannot prevent them from being killed by forces beyond their control. The boss challenges both to be as strong as they can because the boss's fear of his own inner weakness makes him intolerant of weakness in anyone associated with him. The boss's torture of the fly is a re-creation of his son's life and death. The fly's death confirms what his son's death taught him about life, and the boss is so distressed and frightened by this knowledge that he does not permit himself to remember it or anything connected with it.

*4. *Role of memory*   Both Woodifield and the boss forget an emotionally unpleasant subject, the death of their respective sons in WW I. For the boss, this includes the memories of his son that led to his torture of the fly and the manner in which the fly died. The boss's son's death so devastated the governing principle by which the boss lives that, in order to continue to live by it, he cannot permit himself to remember anything that causes him to question the validity of the principle.

5. *Psychological realism*   Mansfield creates a limited but effective form of psychological realism with a narrative perspective that uses a third-person narrator who makes the boss the center of consciousness. This technique enables the reader to enter the boss's mind and gain access to whatever thoughts and feelings he permits himself without forcing the author to sacrifice the objective descriptions that the boss would not use.

*6. *Epiphany*   The scene in which the boss tortures the fly to death is an epiphany in that, in Joycean terms, it is an insignificant event that suddenly reveals the boss's essential nature. He has lived his life according to the principle that those who are strong enough can overcome any adversity, even the possibility of death. His torture of the fly is an experiment which, on a symbolic level, re-creates his son's life and death under circumstances over which the boss has complete control. The fly's death, like the death of the boss's son, confirms the faulty nature of the boss's guiding principles. Consequently, the boss is first distressed, and then his fright causes him to "forget" the incident.

*7. *Paradox*   Paradoxes include: (*a*) People act as if they live in a universe that is comprehensible and predictable, whereas, in reality, the universe may be irrational and unpredictable; (*b*) The most powerful human being is unable to control many aspects of his or her own life, such as death.

WRITING ABOUT LITERATURE

1. *Expository essay: appropriate choice of name "boss" for main character*   Call students' attention to the directions in the textbook assignment. Remind them to use direct quotations to support their ideas. (See **U.S.** question 1 above.) (**PLJ**)
2. *Expository essay applying Woodifield's thought (pleasures/leaves) to theme*   Call students' attention to the directions in the textbook assignment with regard to content. Remind them of the importance of using direct quotations to support their ideas. (See **U.S.** questions 2–6, and **A.L.T.** questions 2–4 and 6 above.)
3. *Creative writing: point of view of boss's son*   Call students' attention to the choices suggested in the textbook assignment. (**PLJ**)

FURTHER READING

Mansfield, Katherine, *Bliss; The Dove's Nest; The Garden Party; Something Childish.*

Part Three: Selected Bibliography

The Mediterranean
General
Bye, Charles Rowan. *Ancient Greek Literature and Society.* New York: Doubleday/Anchor, 1975. (Sappho and Sophocles)

Dudley, D.R., Ed. *The Penguin Companion to Literature. Vol. 4: Classical and Byzantine.* New York: Penguin, 1969.

Hadas, Moses. *A History of Greek Literature.* New York: Columbia UP, 1965. (Sappho and Sophocles)

Howatson, M.C., Ed. *The Oxford Companion to Classical Literature.* 2nd ed. New York: Oxford UP, 1989.

Rimanelli, Giose and Kenneth J. Atchity, Eds. *Italian Literature: Roots and Branches.* New Haven: Yale UP, 1976.

Akhenaton
Breasted, James Henry. *The Dawn of Conscience.* New York: Scribner's, 1976.

Budge, E.A. Wallis. *Egyptian Religion.* New York: Penguin, 1988.

——. *The Gods of the Egyptians or Studies in Egyptian Mythology.* 2 vols. New York: Dover, 1969.

Pritchard, James B. *Ancient Near Eastern Texts Relating to the Old Testament.* 3rd ed. with Supplement. Princeton: Princeton UP, 1969.

David
Alter, Robert and Frank Kermode, Eds. *The Literary Guide to the Bible.* Cambridge: Harvard UP, 1987.

Frye, Northrop. *The Great Code: The Bible and Literature.* San Diego: Harcourt, 1983.

Sandmel, Samuel. *The Hebrew Scriptures: An Introduction to Their Literature and Religious Ideas.* New York: Oxford UP, 1978.

Schneidau, Herbert N. *Sacred Discontent: The Bible and Western Tradition.* Berkeley: U of California P, 1976.

Sappho
Campbell, David A., Ed. *Greek Lyric, Vol. 1: Sappho and Alcaeus.* Cambridge: Harvard UP, 1990.

Dover, Kenneth J., Ed. *Ancient Greek Literature.* New York: Oxford UP, 1980.

Lattimore, Richmond, Ed. and Trans. *Greek Lyrics.* rev. ed. Chicago: U of Chicago P, 1960.

——. *Sappho.* Chicago: U of Chicago P, 1970.

Sophocles
Bloom, Harold, Ed. *Sophocles.* New York: Chelsea House, 1990. (Critical essays)

Kaufman, Walter. *Tragedy and Philosophy.* Princeton: Princeton UP, 1968.

Kitto, Humphrey D. *Greek Tragedy, A Literary Study.* 3rd rev. ed. New York: Routledge, 1966.

Knox, Bernard M.W. *The Heroic Temper: Studies in Sophoclean Tragedy.* Berkeley: U of California P, 1965.

——. Introduction. *The Three Theban Plays.* New York: Viking, 1982.

——. *Word & Action: Essays on the Ancient Theater.* Baltimore: Johns Hopkins UP, 1980.

Vickers, Brian. *Towards Greek Tragedy: Drama, Myth, Society.* London: Longman, 1973.

Dante Alighieri
Bergin, Thomas G. *A Diversity of Dante.* New Brunswick, NJ: Rutgers UP, 1969.

Bloom, Harold, Ed. *Dante.* New York: Chelsea House, 1986. (Critical essays)

Freccero, John. *Dante: The Poetics of Conversion.* Cambridge: Harvard UP, 1988.

Haller, Robert S., Ed. *Literary Criticism of Dante Alighieri.* Lincoln: U of Nebraska P, 1974.

O'Donoghue, Bernard. *The Courtly Love Tradition*. Manchester, Eng.: Manchester UP, 1982.
Quinones, Ricardo J. *Dante*. Boston: G.K. Hall, 1985.

Luigi Pirandello
Bloom, Harold, Ed. *Luigi Pirandello*. New York: Chelsea House, 1989. (Critical essays)
Cambon, Glauco, Ed. *Pirandello: A Collection of Critical Essays*. New York: Prentice, 1967.
Starkie, Walter. *Luigi Pirandello, 1867–1936*. Berkeley: U of California P, 1965.

S.Y. Agnon
Band, Arnold J. *Nostalgia and Nightmare: A Study in the Fiction of S.Y. Agnon*. Berkeley: U of California
    P, 1968.
Fisch, Harold. *S.Y. Agnon*. New York: Ungar, 1975.

Federico García Lorca
Campbell, Roy. *Lorca: An Appreciation of His Poetry*. New York: Haskell House, 1971.
Duran, Manuel, Ed. *García Lorca: A Collection of Critical Essays*. Englewood Cliffs: Prentice, 1962.
Gershator, David, Ed. and Trans. *Federico García Lorca: Selected Letters*. New York: New Directions,
    1984.
Gibson, Ian. *Federico García Lorca: A Life*. New York: Pantheon, 1989.

Continental Europe
General

Bloom, Harold, Ed. *German Poetry: The Renaissance Through 1915*. New York: Chelsea House, 1990.
    (Critical essays)
Brée, Germaine. *Twentieth Century French Literature: 1920–1970*. Trans. Louise Guiney. Chicago: U of
    Chicago P, 1983. (Sartre and Camus)
Friedman, Maurice. *Problematic Rebel*. Chicago: U of Chicago P, 1970. (Dostoyevski, Kafka, Camus)
Glicksberg, Charles I. *The Tragic Vision in Twentieth-Century Literature*. Carbondale: Southern Illinois
    UP, 1963. (Kafka, Camus, Sartre)
Quennell, Peter and Tore Zetterholm, Eds. *An Illustrated Companion to World Literature*. London: Orbis,
    1986.
Seymour-Smith, Martin, Ed. *The New Guide to Modern World Literature*. New York: Peter Bedrick
    Books, 1985.
Simmons, Ernest J. *Introduction to Russian Realism: Pushkin, Gogol, Dostoyevski, Tolstoi, Chekhov,
    Sholokhov*. Bloomington: Indiana UP, 1965.

Hans Christian Andersen
Conroy, Patricia L. and Sven H. Rossel, Eds. and Trans. *The Diaries of Hans Christian Andersen*. Seattle:
    U of Washington P, 1991.
———. Introduction. *Tales and Stories by Hans Christian Andersen*. Seattle: U of Washington P, 1980.

Fyodor Dostoyevski
Bloom, Harold, Ed. *Fyodor Dostoyevski*. New York: Chelsea House, 1989. (Critical essays)
Dostoyevsky, Anna. *Dostoyevsky: Reminiscences*. Trans. Beatrice Stillman. New York: Liveright, 1975.
Frank, Joseph. *Dostoyevsky: The Seeds of Revolt, 1821–1849*. Princeton: Princeton UP, 1976.
———. *Dostoyevsky: The Years of Ordeal, 1850–1859*. Princeton: Princeton UP, 1986.
———. *Through the Russian Prism: Essays on Literature and Culture*. Princeton: Princeton UP, 1990.
Jackson, Robert L. *The Art of Dostoyevsky: Deliriums and Nocturnes*. Princeton: Princeton UP, 1981.
Mochulsky, Konstantin. *Dostoyevsky: His Life and Work*. Trans. Michael Minihan. Princeton: Princeton
    UP, 1967.
Schuster, M. Lincoln, Ed. *A Treasury of the World's Great Letters: From Alexander the Great to Thomas
    Mann*. New York: Simon & Schuster, 1968.
Wellek, René, Ed. *A Collection of Critical Essays*. Englewood Cliffs: Prentice, 1962.

Henrik Ibsen

Fjelde, Rolf, Ed. *Ibsen: A Collection of Critical Essays*. Englewood Cliffs: Prentice, 1965.
Gray, Ronald D. *Ibsen: A Dissenting View*. Cambridge, Eng.: Cambridge UP, 1980.
McFarlane, James W. *Ibsen and Meaning: Studies, Essays, and Prefaces, 1953-1987*. Chester Springs,
　　PA: Dufour Editions, 1989.
Meyer, Michael. *Ibsen: A Biography*. New York: Penguin, 1985.
Rose, Henry. *Henrik Ibsen: Poet, Mystic & Moralist*. New York: Haskell House, 1972.

Leo Tolstoy

Bloom, Harold, Ed. *Leo Tolstoy*. New York: Chelsea House, 1986. (Critical essays)
Christian, R.F., Ed. and Trans. *Tolstoy's Diaries*. 2 vols. New York: Macmillan, 1985.
——. *Tolstoy's Letters*. 2 vols. New York: Scribner's, 1978.
Matlaw, Ralph E., Ed. *Tolstoy: A Collection of Critical Essays*. Englewood Cliffs: Prentice, 1967.
Rowe, William W. *Leo Tolstoy*. Boston: Hall, 1986.
Simmons, Ernest J. *Introduction to Tolstoy's Writings*. Chicago: U. of Chicago P, 1969.
Wasiolek, Edward. *Critical Essays on Tolstoy*. Boston: Hall, 1986.

Selma Lagerlöf

Gustafson, Alrik. *A History of Swedish Literature*. Minneapolis: U of Minnesota P, 1961.
——. *Six Scandinavian Novelists*. Princeton: Princeton UP, 1940.

Anton Chekhov

Chekhov, Anton. *Short Stories*. Critical Edition. Ed. Ralph E. Matlaw. New York: Norton, 1979.
Hellman, Lillian, Ed. *The Selected Letters of Anton Chekhov*. Trans. Sidonie K. Lederer. New York:
　　Farrar, 1984.
Jackson, Robert L., Ed. *Chekhov: A Collection of Critical Essays*. Englewood Cliffs: Prentice, 1967.
Karlinsky, Simon and Michael Heim, Eds. and Trans. *Anton Chekhov's Life and Thought: Selected Letters
　　and Commentary*. Berkeley: U of California P, 1976.
Pritchett, V.S. *Chekhov: A Spirit Set Free*. New York: Random, 1988.
Simmons, Ernest J. *Chekhov: A Biography*. Chicago: U of Chicago P, 1970.
Troyat, Henri. *Chekhov*. Trans. Michael Heim. New York: Fawcett, 1988.

Colette

Cottrell, Robert D. *Colette*. New York: Ungar, 1974.
Lottman, Herbert R. *Colette: A Life*. Boston: Little Brown, 1991.
Phelps, Robert. *Belles Saisons: A Colette Scrapbook*. New York: Farrar, 1978.
——, Ed. *Earthly Paradise: An Autobiography of Colette Drawn from Her Lifetime Writings*. Trans.
　　Herma Briffault. New York: Farrar, 1966.
——, Ed. *Letters from Colette*. New York: Farrar, 1980.

Rainer Maria Rilke

Rilke, Rainer Maria. *Letters to a Young Poet*. Trans. Stephen Mitchell. New York: Random, 1986.
Peters, H. Frederic. *Rainer Maria Rilke: Masks and the Man*. Staten Island, NY: Gordian Press, 1977.
Rose, William and G. Craig Houston, Eds. *Rainer Maria Rilke: Aspects of His Mind and Poetry*. Staten
　　Island, NY: Gordian Press, 1970.

Franz Kafka

Bloom, Harold, Ed. *Franz Kafka*. New York: Chelsea House, 1986. (Critical essays)

Brod, Max. *Franz Kafka: A Biography*. New York: Schocken Books, 1963.

——, Ed. *The Diaries of Franz Kafka: 1910–1913*. Trans. Joseph Kresh. New York: Schocken Books, 1987.

——, Ed. *The Diaries of Franz Kafka: 1914–1923*. Trans. Martin Greenberg. New York: Schocken Books, 1987.

Emrich, W. *Franz Kafka: A Critical Study of His Writings*. Trans. Sheema Zeben Buehne. New York: Ungar, 1968.

Flores, Angel. *The Problem of the Judgment: Eleven Approaches to Kafka's Story*. Staten Island, NY: Gordian Press, 1977.

Glatzer, Nahum N., Ed. *I Am a Memory Come Alive: Autobiographical Writings of Franz Kafka*. New York: Schocken Books, 1976.

Heller, Erich and Juergen Born, Eds. *Letters to Felice*. Trans. James Stern and Elizabeth Duckworth. New York: Schocken Books, 1988.

Janouch, Gustav. *Conversations with Kafka.*Trans. Goronwy Rees. rev. ed. New York: New Directions, 1971.

Pawel, Ernst. *The Nightmare of Reason: A Life of Franz Kafka*. New York: Farrar, 1984.

Tauber, Herbert. *Franz Kafka: An Interpretation of His Works*. New York: Haskell House, 1969.

Jean-Paul Sartre

Kaufmann, Walter, Ed. *Existentialism from Dostoevsky to Sartre*. Magnolia, MA: Peter Smith, 1984.

Kern, Edith, Ed. *Sartre: A Collection of Critical Essays*. Englewood Cliffs: Prentice, 1962.

Suhl, Benjamin. *Jean-Paul Sartre: The Philosopher as Literary Critic*. New York: Columbia UP, 1973.

Albert Camus

Camus, Albert. *The Myth of Sisyphus and Other Essays*. New York: Knopf, 1955.

Bloom, Harold, Ed. *Albert Camus*. New York: Chelsea House, 1990. (Critical essays)

Cruickshank, John. *Albert Camus and the Literature of Revolt*. Westport, CT: Greenwood, 1978.

Thody, Philip. *Albert Camus: A Study of His Work*. New York: St. Martin, 1989.

Africa

General

Beier, Ulli, Ed. *Introduction to African Literature*. London: Longman, 1979.

Cook, David. *African Literature: A Critical View*. London: Longman, 1977.

Heywood, Christopher. *Aspects of South African Literature*. London: Heinemann, 1976.

——, Ed. *Perspectives on African Literature*. London: Heinemann/U of Ife P, 1971.

Kesteloot, Lilyan. *African Writers in French: A Literary History of Négritude*. Philadelphia: Temple UP, 1974. (Dadié, Diop, Senghor)

Willam, G.D. *The Writing of East and Central Africa*. London: Heinemann, 1985.

——, Ed. *African Writers on African Writing*. London: Heinemann, 1973. (Achebe and Gordimer)

Klein, Leonard S., Ed. *African Literatures in the 20th Century: A Guide*. New York: Ungar, 1986. (Achebe, Dadié, Gordimer, Paton, Senghor, Soyinka)

Lang, D.M., Ed. *The Penguin Companion to Literature: Vol. 4: Oriental and African*. Baltimore: Penguin, 1969.

Larson, Charles R. *The Emergence of African Fiction*. rev. ed. Bloomington: Indiana UP, 1972. (Achebe, Senghor, Soyinka)

Moore, Gerald. *Twelve African Writers*. Bloomington: Indiana UP, 1980. (Achebe, Senghor, Soyinka)

Morrel, Karan L., Ed. *In Person: Achebe, Awoonor & Soyinka*. Austin: U of Texas P, 1975.

Mphahlele, Ezekiel. *The African Image*. Salem, NH: Merrimack Book Service, 1972.

Olney, James. *Tell Me Africa: An Approach to African Literature*. Princeton: Princeton UP, 1973. (Achebe, Dadié, Soyinka)

Roscoe, Adrian. *Mother Is Gold: A Study in West African Literature*. Cambridge, Eng.: Cambridge UP, 1971. (Achebe, Diop, Senghor, Soyinka)

Seymour-Smith, Martin, Ed. *The New Guide to Modern World Literature*. New York: Peter Bedrick Books, 1985.

Dahomey (Traditional)

Courlander, Harold. *A Treasury of African Folklore*. New York: Crown, 1974.

Rothenberg, Jerome, Ed. *Technicians of the Sacred: A Range of Poetries from Africa, America, Asia, Europe & Oceania*. Berkeley: U of California P, 1985.

Trask, Willard R., Ed. *The Unwritten Song: Poetry of the Primitive and Traditional Peoples of the World*. Vol. 1. New York: Macmillan, 1966.

Alan Paton

Paton, Alan. *Towards the Mountain*. Magnolia, MA: Peter Smith, 1988. (Autobiography, Vol. 1)

Paton, Alan. *Journey Continued: An Autobiography*. New York: Macmillan, 1990. (Vol. 2)

Callan, Edward. *Alan Paton*. rev. ed. Boston: Hall, 1982.

Léopold Sédar Senghor

Vaillant, Janet C. *Black, French, and African: A Life of Léopold Sédar Senghor*. Cambridge: Harvard UP, 1990.

Doris Lessing

Lessing, Doris. Preface. *African Stories*. New York: Simon & Schuster, 1981.

——. *A Small Personal Voice: Essays, Reviews, Interviews*. New York: Random, 1975.

Bloom, Harold, Ed. *Doris Lessing*. New York: Chelsea House, 1986. (Critical essays)

Brewster, Dorothy. *Doris Lessing*. Boston: Twayne, 1965.

Pickering, Jean. *Understanding Doris Lessing*. Columbia: U of South Carolina P, 1990.

Sprague, Claire and Virginia Tiger. *Critical Essays on Doris Lessing*. Boston: Hall, 1986.

Nadine Gordimer

Gordimer, Nadine. Introduction. *Selected Stories*. New York: Viking, 1976.

Bazin, Nancy T. and Marilyn D. Seymour. *Conversations with Nadine Gordimer*. Jackson: UP of Mississippi, 1990.

Cooke, John. *The Novels of Nadine Gordimer: Private Lives—Public Landscapes*. Baton Rouge: Louisiana State UP, 1985.

Chinua Achebe

Achebe, Chinua. *Hopes and Impediments: Selected Essays*. New York: Doubleday, 1990.

Killam, Gordon D. *The Novels of Chinua Achebe*. London, Eng.: Heinemann, 1969.

Wole Soyinka

Soyinka, Wole. *Aké: The Years of Childhood*. New York: Random, 1989.

——. *Ìsarà: A Voyage Around "Essay."* New York: Random, 1989.

——. *Myth, Literature and the African World*. Cambridge, Eng.: Cambridge UP, 1976.

Jones, Eldred Durosimi. *The Writing of Wole Soyinka*. 3rd ed. Portsmouth, NH: Heinemann, 1988.

Maduakor, Obi. *Wole Soyinka: An Introduction to His Writing*. New York: Garland, 1987.

Moore, Gerald. *Wole Soyinka*. New York: Holmes and Meier, 1972.

Bessie Head

Barnett, Ursula A. *A Vision of Order: A Study of Black South African Literature in English (1914–1980)*. Amherst: U of Massachusetts P, 1983.

The Far East
General
Aston, W.G. *A History of Japanese Literature*. Rutland, VT: Charles E. Tuttle, 1972.

Giles, Herbert A. *A History of Chinese Literature*. Rutland, VT: Charles E. Tuttle, 1973.

——. *The Classical History of Chinese Literature*. 3 vols. Albuquerque: Gloucester Art, 1985.

Gowen, Herbert. *A History of Indian Literature*. New York: D. Appleton, 1931.

Keene, Donald. *Dawn to the West: Japanese Literature in the Modern Era. Fiction*. New York: Holt, 1984.

——. *Japanese Literature: An Introduction for Western Readers*. New York: Grove, 1955.

——. *The Pleasures of Japanese Literature*. New York: Columbia UP, 1988.

——, Ed. *Modern Japanese Literature from 1868 to Present Day*. New York: Grove, 1956.

Lang, D.M., Ed. *The Penguin Companion to Literature: Vol. 4: Oriental and African*. Baltimore: Penguin, 1969.

Lau, Joseph S.M. et al., Eds. *Modern Chinese Stories and Novellas: 1919–1949*. New York: Columbia UP, 1981. (Lu Hsün and Ting Ling)

Liu, James J. *Chinese Theories of Literature*. Chicago: U of Chicago P, 1979.

Rawlinson, Hugh G. *India: A Short Cultural History*. New York: Praeger, 1952.

Rimer, J. Thomas. *Modern Japanese Fiction and Its Traditions: An Introduction*. Princeton: Princeton UP, 1986.

Seymour-Smith, Martin, Ed. *The New Guide to Modern World Literature*. New York: Peter Bedrick Books, 1985.

Ueda, Makoto. *Modern Japanese Writers and the Nature of Literature*. Stanford: Stanford UP, 1976.

Wright, Arthur E. and Denis Twitchett. *Perspectives on the T'ang*. New Haven: Yale UP, 1973. (Li Po and Jiang Fang)

Yamanouchi, Hisaaki. *The Search for Authenticity in Modern Japanese Literature*. Cambridge, Eng.: Cambridge UP, 1978.

Li Po
Liu, James J. *The Art of Chinese Poetry*. Chicago: U of Chicago P, 1983.

Waley, Arthur. *The Poetry and Career of Li Po*. Winchester, MA: Unwin Hyman, 1951.

Yohannan, John D., Ed. *A Treasury of Asian Literature*. New York: New American Library, 1956.

Motokiyo Zeami
Mishima, Yukio. *Five Modern No Plays*. Trans. Donald Keene. New York: Knopf, 1957.

Pound, Ezra and Ernest Fenollosa. *The Classic Noh Theatre of Japan*. Westport, CT: Greenwood, 1977.

Rimer, J. Thomas and Yamazaki Masakazu, Trans. *On the Art of the No Drama: The Major Treatises of Zeami*. Princeton: Princeton UP, 1984.

Waley, Arthur. *The No Plays of Japan*. Rutland, VT: Charles E. Tuttle, 1976.

Rabindranath Tagore
Chakravarty, Amiya, Ed. *A Tagore Reader*. New York: Macmillan, 1961.

Kripalani, K. *Rabindranath Tagore: A Biography*. New York: Oxford UP, 1962.

Lu Hsün
Lu Hsün. *A Brief History of Chinese Fiction*. Trans. Hsien-yi Yang and Gladys Yang. Westport, CT: Hyperion, 1990.

Prušek, Jaroslav. *The Lyrical and the Epic: Studies of Modern Chinese Literature*. Bloomington: Indiana UP, 1980.

Sung-K'ang, Huang. *Lu Hsün and the New Culture Movement of Modern China*. Westport, CT: Hyperion, 1975.

Ryūnosuke Akutagawa
Yu, Beongcheon. *Akutagawa: An Introduction*. Detroit: Wayne State UP, 1972.

Yasunari Kawabata
Petersen, Gwen B. *The Moon in the Water: Understanding Tanizaki, Kawabata, and Mishima*. Honolulu: UP of Hawaii, 1979.

Ting Ling
Barlow, Tani E. with Gary J. Bjorge, Eds. *I Myself Am a Woman: Selected Writings of Ding Ling*. Boston: Beacon, 1989.
Feuerwerker, Yi-tsi M. *Ding Ling's Fiction: Ideology and Narrative in Modern Chinese Literature*. Cambridge: Harvard UP, 1982.
Kai-Yu, Hsu, Ed. *Literature of the Peoples' Republic of China*. Bloomington: Indiana UP, 1980.

Latin America
General
Anderson-Imbert, Enríque. *Spanish American Literature: A History*. 2 vols. Detroit: Wayne State UP, 1976.
Bassnett, Susan, Ed. *Knives and Angels: Women Writers in Latin America*. London: Jed Books, 1990.
Bloom, Harold, Ed. *Modern Latin American Fiction*. New York: Chelsea House, 1990. (Critical essays)
———. *Modern Spanish and Latin American Poetry*. New York: Chelsea House, 1990. (Critical essays)
Foster, David William and Virginia Ramos Foster, Eds. *Modern Latin American Literature*. 2 vols. New York: Ungar, 1975.
Franco, J. *An Introduction to Spanish American Literature*. Cambridge, Eng.: Cambridge UP, 1971.
Gallagher, David P. *Modern Latin American Literature*. New York: Oxford UP, 1973.
Garfield, E. Picon. *Women's Voices from Latin America: Interviews with Six Contemporary Authors*. Detroit: Wayne State UP, 1985.
Gonzáles Echevarría, Roberto. *The Voice of the Masters: Writing and Authority in Modern Latin American Literature*. Austin: U of Texas P, 1985.
Harss, Luis and Barbara Dohmann, Eds. *Into the Mainstream: Conversations with Latin American Writers*. New York: Harper, 1967.
King, John. *On Modern Latin American Fiction*. New York: Hill & Wang, 1989.
Martin, Gerald. *Journeys Through the Labyrinth: Latin American Fiction in the Twentieth Century*. New York: Verso, 1989.
Meyer, Doris, Ed. *Lives on the Line: The Testimony of Contemporary Latin American Authors*. Berkeley: U of California P, 1988.
Ortega, Julio. *Poetics of Change: The New Spanish-American Narrative*. Trans. Galen D. Greaser. Austin: U of Texas P, 1984.
Rodríguez Monegal, Emir, Ed. *The Borzoi Anthology of Latin American Literature: From the Time of Columbus to the Twentieth Century*. New York: Knopf, 1983.
———. *The Borzoi Anthology of Latin American Literature: The Twentieth Century—From Borges and Paz to Guimarães Rosa and Donoso*. New York: Knopf, 1977.
Seymour-Smith, Martin, Ed. *The New Guide to Modern World Literature*. New York: Peter Bedrick Books, 1985.
Solé, Carlos A., Ed. *Latin American Writers*. 3 vols. New York: Scribner's, 1989.
Torres-Rioseco, Arturo. *The Epic of Latin American Literature*. Berkeley: U of California P, 1964.
Ward, Philip, Ed. *The Oxford Companion to Spanish Literature*. Oxford, Eng.: Oxford UP, 1978.

Gabriela Mistral
Bates, Margaret. Introduction. *Selected Poems of Gabriela Mistral*. Ed. and Trans. Doris Dana. Baltimore: Johns Hopkins UP, 1971.

Castleman, William J. *Beauty and the Mission of the Teacher: The Life of Gabriela Mistral of Chile.* Smithtown, NY: Exposition Press, 1982.

Jorge Luis Borges

Agheana, Ion T. *The Meaning of Experience in the Prose of Jorge Luis Borges.* New York: Peter Lang, 1988.

——. *The Prose of Jorge Luis Borges: Existentialism and the Dynamics of Surprise.* New York: Peter Lang, 1984.

Alazraki, Jaime, Ed. *Borges and the Kabbalah and Other Essays on His Fiction and Poetry.* Cambridge, Eng.: Cambridge UP, 1988.

——. *Critical Essays on Jorge Luis Borges.* Boston: Hall, 1987.

Bell-Villada, Gene H. *Borges and His Fiction: A Guide to His Mind and Art.* Chapel Hill: U of North Carolina P, 1981.

Bloom, Harold, Ed. *Jorge Luis Borges.* New York: Chelsea House, 1986. (Critical essays)

Cortínez,Carlos, Ed. *Simply a Man of Letters: Papers of a Symposium on Jorge Luis Borges.* Orono: U of Maine P, 1982.

Friedman, Mary Lusky. *The Emperor's Kites: A Morphology of Borges' Tales.* Durham, NC: Duke UP, 1987.

Rodríguez Monegal, Emir. *Jorges Luis Borges: A Literary Biography.* New York: Dutton, 1978.

Sturrock, J. *Paper Tigers: The Ideal Fictions of Jorge Luis Borges.* Oxford: Oxford UP, 1978.

Wheelock, Carter. *The Mythmaker: A Study of Motif and Symbol in the Short Stories of Jorge Luis Borges.* Austin: U of Texas P, 1969.

Yates, Donald A. *Jorge Luis Borges: Life, Work, and Criticism.* Fredericton, New Brunswick, Canada: York Press, 1985.

Pablo Neruda

Neruda, Pablo. *Memoirs.* Trans. Hardie St. Martin. New York: Farrar, 1977.

——. *Passions and Impressions.* Trans. Margaret Sayers Peden. New York: Farrar, 1983.

Bloom, Harold, Ed. *Pablo Neruda.* New York: Chelsea House, 1989. (Critical essays)

de Costa, René. *The Poetry of Pablo Neruda.* Cambridge: Harvard UP, 1982.

Duran, Manuel and Margery Safir. *Earth Tones: The Poetry of Pablo Neruda.* Bloomington: Indiana UP, 1981.

Santí, Enrico Mario. *Pablo Neruda: The Poetics of Prophecy.* Ithaca, NY: Cornell UP, 1982.

Silvina Ocampo

Ocampo, Silvina. Preface. *Leopoldina's Dream.* Trans. Daniel Balderston. New York: Penguin, 1988.

João Guimarães Rosa

Vincent, Jon S. *João Guimarães Rosa.* Boston: Twayne, 1978.

María Luisa Bombal

Adams, M. Ian. *Three Authors of Alienation.* Austin: U of Texas P, 1975.

Octavio Paz

Paz, Octavio. *The Bow and the Lyre.* Trans. Ruth L.C. Simms. Austin: U of Texas P, 1973.

——. *Convergences: Essays on Art and Literature.* Trans. Helen Lane. San Diego: Harcourt, 1987.

Fein, John M. *Toward Octavio Paz: A Reading of His Major Poems, 1957–1976.* Lexington: UP of Kentucky, 1986.

Ivask, Ivar, Ed. *The Perpetual Present: The Poetry and Prose of Octavio Paz.* Norman: U of Oklahoma P, 1973.

Wilson, Jason. *Octavio Paz.* Boston: Hall, 1986.

——. *Octavio Paz: A Study of His Poetics.* Cambridge, Eng.: Cambridge UP, 1979.

José Donoso
Donoso, José. *The Boom in Spanish-American Literature: A Personal History.* Trans. Gregory Kolovakos. New York: Columbia UP/Center for Inter-American Relations, 1977.
Castillo-Feliú, Guillermo I., Ed. *The Creative Process in the Works of José Donoso.* York, SC: Spanish Literature Publications, 1982.
Foster, Merlin H., Ed. *Tradition and Renewal: Essays on Twentieth Century Latin American Literature and Culture.* Urbana: U of Illinois P, 1975.
MacAdam, Alfred J. *Modern Latin American Narratives: Dreams of Reason.* Chicago: U of Chicago P, 1977.

Rosario Castellanos
Ahern, Maureen, Ed. and Trans. *A Rosario Castellanos Reader: An Anthology of Her Poetry, Short Fiction, Essays, and Drama.* Austin: U of Texas P, 1988.
Dauster, Frank. *The Double Strand: Five Contemporary Mexican Poets.* Lexington: UP of Kentucky, 1987.
Meyer, Doris and Margarite Fernandez-Olmos. *Contemporary Women Authors of Latin America: Introductory Essays.* New York: Brooklyn College P, 1984.

Gabriel García Márquez
Bell-Villada, Gene H. *García Márquez: The Man and His Work.* Chapel Hill: U of North Carolina P, 1990.
Bloom, Harold, Ed. *Gabriel García Márquez.* New York: Chelsea House, 1989. (Critical essays)
Foster, David W. *Studies in the Contemporary Spanish-American Short Story.* Columbia: U of Missouri P, 1979.
Janes, Regina. *Gabriel García Márquez: Revolutions in Wonderland.* Columbia: U of Missouri P, 1981.
McGuirk, Bernard and Richard Cardwell. *Gabriel García Márquez: New Readings.* Cambridge, Eng.: Cambridge UP, 1987.
McMurray, George R., Ed. *Critical Essays on Gabriel García Márquez.* New York: Ungar, 1977.
McNerney, Kathleen. *Understanding Gabriel García Márquez.* Columbia: U of South Carolina P, 1989.
Minta, Stephen. *García Márquez: Writer of Colombia.* London, Eng.: Cape, 1987.
Ortega, Julio, Ed. *Gabriel García Márquez and the Powers of Fiction.* Austin: U of Texas P, 1988.
Williams, Raymond L. *Gabriel García Márquez.* Boston: Hall, 1984.

North America
General
Bloom, Harold, Ed. *The Critical Perspective: Vol. 9: Emily Dickinson to Lewis Carroll.* New York: Chelsea House, 1989. (Critical essays)
Ellmann, Richard and Robert O'Clair, Eds. *The Norton Anthology of Modern Poetry.* 2nd ed. New York: Norton, 1988.
Hart, James D., Ed. *The Oxford Companion to American Literature.* New York: Oxford UP, 1983.
Untermeyer, Louis, Ed. *Modern American Poetry.* New York: Harcourt, 1950.

Zuñi (Traditional)
Cushing, Frank Hamilton. *Zuñi Breadstuff.* New York: Museum of the American Indian/Heye Foundation, 1974.
Dutton, Bertha P. *American Indians of the Southwest.* rev. ed. Albuquerque: U of New Mexico P, 1983.
Green, Jesse, Ed. *Zuñi: Selected Writings of Frank Hamilton Cushing.* Lincoln: U of Nebraska P, 1979.
Scully, Vincent. *Pueblo: Mountain, Village, Dance.* Chicago: U of Chicago P, 1989.
Stevenson, Matilda Coxe. *The Zuñi Indians: Their Mythology, Esoteric Fraternities, and Ceremonies (1901–1902).* Glorieta, NM: Rio Grande Press, 1985.

Tedlock, Dennis and Barbara Tedlock. *Teachings from the American Earth: Indian Religion and Philosophy.* New York: Liveright, 1976.

Edgar Allan Poe
Bloom, Harold, Ed. *Edgar Allan Poe.* New York: Chelsea House, 1985. (Critical essays)
——. *Edgar Allan Poe's Tales of Poe.* New York: Chelsea House, 1987. (Critical essays)
Carlson, Eric W. *Edgar Allan Poe: Critical Essays.* Boston: Hall, 1987.
Levine, Stuart and Susan Levine, Eds. *The Short Fiction of Edgar Allan Poe: An Annotated Edition.* Urbana: U of Illinois P, 1990.
Peithman, Stephen, Ed. *The Annotated Tales of Edgar Allan Poe.* New York: Avenel Books, 1986.

Walt Whitman
Allen, Gay W. *The New Walt Whitman Handbook.* New York: New York UP, 1987.
——. *The Solitary Singer: A Critical Biography of Walt Whitman.* Chicago: U of Chicago P, 1985.
Bloom, Harold, Ed. *Walt Whitman.* New York: Chelsea House, 1985. (Critical essays)
Miller, Edwin H. *Walt Whitman's Poetry: A Psychological Journey.* New York: New York UP, 1968.
——. *Walt Whitman's "Song of Myself": A Mosaic of Interpretations.* Iowa City: U of Iowa P, 1989.
——, Ed. *Selected Letters of Walt Whitman.* Iowa City: U of Iowa P, 1990.

Emily Dickinson
Bloom, Harold, Ed. *American Women Poets.* New York: Chelsea House, 1986. (Critical essays)
——. *Emily Dickinson.* New York: Chelsea House, 1985. (Critical essays)
Budick, E. Miller. *Emily Dickinson and the Life of Language: A Study in Symbolic Poetics.* Baton Rouge: Louisiana State UP, 1985.
Diehl, Joanne F. *Dickinson and the Romantic Imagination.* Princeton: Princeton UP, 1981.
Franklin, R.W., Ed. *The Master Letters of Emily Dickinson.* Amherst: Amherst College P, 1986.
Johnson, Thomas J., Ed. *Emily Dickinson: Selected Letters.* Cambridge: Harvard UP, 1985.

Eugene O'Neill
Bloom, Harold, Ed. *Eugene O'Neill.* New York: Chelsea House, 1987. (Critical essays)
Bogard, Travis. *Contour in Time: The Plays of Eugene O'Neill.* New York: Oxford UP, 1988.
—— and Jackson R. Bryer, Eds. *Selected Letters of Eugene O'Neill.* New Haven: Yale UP, 1988.
Gelb, Arthur and Barbara Gelb. *O'Neill.* rev. ed. New York: Harper, 1974.
Griffin, Ernest. *O'Neill: A Collection of Criticism.* New Haven: Yale UP, 1976.
Törnqvist, Egil. *A Drama of Souls: Studies in O'Neill's Super-Naturalistic Techniques.* New Haven: Yale UP, 1969.

Ernest Hemingway
Baker, Carlos. *Ernest Hemingway: A Life Story.* New York: Macmillan, 1988.
——. *Hemingway: The Writer as Artist.* Princeton: Princeton UP, 1972.
——, Ed. *Ernest Hemingway: Selected Letters: 1917-1961.* New York: Macmillan, 1989.
Bloom, Harold, Ed. *Ernest Hemingway.* New York: Chelsea House, 1985. (Critical essays)
Brooks, Van Wyck. *Writers at Work: The* Paris Review *Interviews.* Second Series. New York: Viking, 1965.
Burgess, Anthony. *Hemingway and His World.* New York: Macmillan, 1985.
Meyers, Jeffrey. *Hemingway: A Biography.* New York: Harper, 1986.
——, Ed. *Hemingway: The Critical Heritage.* New York: Routledge, 1982.

Langston Hughes
Barksdale, Richard K. *Hughes: The Poet and His Critics.* Ann Arbor: UMI, 1977.
Bloom, Harold, Ed. *Langston Hughes.* New York: Chelsea House, 1990. (Critical essays)
Emanuel, James A. *Langston Hughes.* Boston: Hall, 1967.
Jemie, Onwuchekwa. *Hughes: An Introduction to the Poetry.* New York: Columbia UP, 1985.

Eudora Welty

Welty, Eudora. *The Eye of the Story: Selected Essays and Reviews*. New York: Random, 1990.
——. *One Writer's Beginnings*. Cambridge: Harvard UP, 1984.
Bloom, Harold, Ed. *Eudora Welty*. New York: Chelsea House, 1986. (Critical essays)
Brans, Jo. *Listen to the Voices: Conversations with Contemporary Writers*. Dallas: Southern Methodist UP, 1988.
Devlin, Albert J. *Eudora Welty: A Life in Literature*. Jackson: UP of Mississippi, 1987.
——. *Eudora Welty's Chronicle: A Story of Mississippi Life*. Jackson: UP of Mississippi, 1983.
Vande Kieft, Ruth M. *Eudora Welty*. rev. ed. Boston: Twayne, 1987.

Shirley Jackson

Friedman, Lenemaja. *Jackson*. New York: Macmillan, 1975.
Oppenheimer, Judy. *Private Demons: The Life of Shirley Jackson*. New York: Putnam, 1988.

Alice Munro

Martin, W.R. *Alice Munro: Paradox and Parallel*. Lincoln: U of Nebraska P, 1987.

Alice Walker

Walker, Alice. *In Search of Our Mother's Gardens: Womanist Prose*. San Diego: Harcourt, 1984.
——. *Living by the Word: Selected Writings: 1973–1987*. San Diego: Harcourt, 1989.
Bloom, Harold, Ed. *Alice Walker*. New York: Chelsea House, 1990. (Critical essays)

Great Britain
General
Allen, Walter. *The Short Story in English*. New York: Oxford UP, 1981.
Allison, Alexander W., et al., Eds. *The Norton Anthology of Poetry*. New York: Norton, 1975.
Drabble, Margaret, Ed. *The Oxford Companion to English Literature*. New York: Oxford UP, 1987.
Gilbert, Sandra M. and Susan Gubar. *The Madwoman in the Attic: A Study of Women and the Literary Imagination in the Nineteenth Century*. New Haven: Yale UP, 1979.
Leavis, F.R. *The Common Pursuit*. London: Hogarth, 1984. (Eliot and Milton)
Untermeyer, Louis, Ed. *Modern British Poetry*. San Diego: Harcourt, 1950.
——, Ed. *A Treasury of Great Poems: English and American*. New York: Simon & Schuster, 1955.

William Shakespeare

Adams, Robert M. *Shakespeare: The Four Romances*. New York: Norton, 1989.
Bamber, Linda. *Comic Women, Tragic Men*. Stanford: Stanford UP, 1982.
Bentley, Gerald E. *Shakespeare: A Biographical Handbook*. Westport, CT: Greenwood, 1986.
Bloom, Harold, Ed. *William Shakespeare's "The Tempest."* New York: Chelsea House, 1988. (Critical essays)
Frye, Northrop. *A Natural Perspective: The Development of Shakespearean Comedy and Romance*. San Diego: Harcourt, 1969.
Kernan, Alvin B. *The Playwright as Magician: Shakespeare's Image of the Poet in the English Public Theater*. New Haven: Yale UP, 1979.
Langbaum, Robert, Ed. "William Shakespeare." *The Tempest*. Critical Edition. New York: New American Library, 1987.
Levin, Harry. *Shakespeare and the Revolution of the Times: Perspectives and Commentaries*. Oxford: Oxford UP, 1976.
——, Herschel Baker, et al., Eds. *The Riverside Shakespeare*. Boston: Houghton, 1974.
Muir, Kenneth. *The Sources of Shakespeare's Plays*. New Haven: Yale UP, 1978.
Rowse, A.L. *Prefaces to Shakespeare's Plays*. London: Orbis, 1984.

Sandler, Robert, Ed. *Northrop Frye on Shakespeare*. New Haven: Yale UP, 1988.
Vickers, Brian. *Returning to Shakespeare*. New York: Routledge, 1989.

John Milton
Bloom, Harold, Ed. *John Milton*. New York: Chelsea House, 1986. (Critical essays)
Bush, Douglas. *The Early Seventeenth Century: 1600–1660*. New York: Oxford UP, 1990.
——. *John Milton*. New York: Macmillan, 1967.
Daiches, David. *Milton*. Chicago: Hutchinson House, 1957.
Tillyard, Eustace M. *The Metaphysicals and Milton*. Westport CT: Greenwood, 1976.

William Wordsworth
William Wordsworth and the Age of English Romanticism. New Brunswick, NJ: Rutgers UP, 1987.
Alan, G., Ed. *The Letters of William Wordsworth: A New Selection*. New York: Oxford UP,1985.
Bloom, Harold, Ed. *The English Romantic Poets*. New York: Chelsea House, 1986. (Critical essays)
——. *William Wordsworth.*New York: Chelsea House, 1985. (Critical essays)
Durrant, Geoffrey H. *William Wordsworth*. Cambridge, Eng.: Cambridge UP, 1969.
Frye, Northrop. *A Study of English Romanticism*. Chicago: U of Chicago P, 1983.
Hartman, Geoffrey H. *The Unremarkable Wordsworth*. Minneapolis: U of Minnesota P, 1987.
——. *Wordsworth's Poetry: 1787–1814.*Cambridge: Harvard UP, 1987.
Moorman, Mary, Ed. *The Journals of Dorothy Wordsworth*. Oxford: Oxford UP, 1971.

Elizabeth Barrett Browning
Forster, Margaret. *Elizabeth Barrett Browning: A Biography*. New York: Doubleday, 1989.
——. *The Life and Loves of a Poet*. New York: St. Martin, 1990.
Schuster, M. Lincoln, Ed. *A Treasury of the World's Great Letters: From Alexander the Great to Thomas Mann*. New York: Simon & Schuster, 1968.

Emily Brontë
Bloom, Harold, Ed. *The Brontës*. New York: Chelsea House, 1987. (Critical essays)
Frank, Katherine. *A Chainless Soul: The Life of Emily Brontë*. Boston: Houghton, 1990.
Gérin, Winifred. *Emily Brontë.*Oxford: Oxford UP, 1972.
Taylor, Irene. *Holy Ghosts: The Male Muses of Emily and Charlotte Brontë.*New York: Columbia UP, 1990.

Christina Rossetti
Bloom, Harold, Ed. *The Pre-Raphaelite Poets*. New York: Chelsea House, 1986. (Critical essays)
Rosenblum, Dolores. *Christina Rossetti: The Poetry of Endurance*. Carbondale: Southern Illinois UP, 1986.
Rossetti, William M., Ed. *Family Letters of Christina Georgina Rossetti, with Some Supplementary Letters and Appendices*. New York: Haskell House, 1969.

Joseph Conrad
Conrad, Joseph. "Heart of Darkness." Critical Edition. Ed. Robert Kimbrough. New York: Norton, 1971.
——. 1897 Preface. *The Nigger of the "Narcissus."* Critical Edition. Ed. Robert Kimbrough. New York: Norton, 1979.
Bloom, Harold, Ed. *Joseph Conrad*. New York: Chelsea House, 1986. (Critical essays)
Dowden, Wilfred S. *Joseph Conrad: The Imaged Style*. Nashville: Vanderbilt UP, 1970.
Guerard, Albert J. *Conrad the Novelist*. Cambridge: Harvard UP, 1958.
Karl, Frederick R. *Joseph Conrad: The Three Lives*. New York: Farrar, 1979.
—— and Laurence Davies, Eds. *The Collected Letters of Joseph Conrad*. 4 vols. Cambridge, Eng.: Cambridge UP, 1983–1990.

Meyers, Jeffrey. *Joseph Conrad: A Biography*. New York: Scribner's, 1991.
Watt, Ian. *Conrad in the Nineteenth Century*. Berkeley: U of California P, 1979.

William Butler Yeats
Yeats, William Butler. *Autobiography of William Butler Yeats: Consisting of Reveries over Childhood and Youth*. New York: Macmillan, 1988.
Bloom, Harold. *Yeats*. New York: Oxford UP, 1972.
———, Ed. *W.B. Yeats*. New York: Chelsea House, 1986. (Critical essays)
Domville, Eric and John Kelly, Eds. *The Collected Letters of W.B. Yeats. Vol. 1: 1856–1895*. New York: Oxford UP, 1986.
Ellmann, Richard. *a long the riverrun*. New York: Knopf, 1989.
———. *The Identity of Yeats*. Oxford: Oxford UP, 1964.
———. *Yeats, the Man and the Masks*. rev. ed. New York: Norton, 1978.

James Joyce
Joyce, James. *Dubliners*. Critical Edition. Ed. Robert Scholes and A. Walton Litz. New York: Penguin, 1985.
———. *Stephen Hero*. New York: New Directions, 1955.
Bloom, Harold, Ed. *James Joyce*. New York: Chelsea House, 1986. (Critical essays)
———. *James Joyce's* Dubliners. New York: Chelsea House, 1988. (Critical essays)
Ellmann, Richard. *James Joyce*. rev. ed. New York: Oxford UP, 1982.
———, Ed. *Selected Letters of James Joyce*. New York: Viking, 1975.
Gifford, Don. *Joyce Annotated: Notes for* Dubliners *and* A Portrait of the Artist as a Young Man. rev. ed. Berkeley: U of California P, 1982.
Torchiana, Donald T. *Backgrounds for Joyce's Dubliners*. Boston: Allen & Unwin, 1986.

T.S. Eliot
Bloom, Harold, Ed. *T.S. Eliot*. New York: Chelsea House, 1985. (Critical essays)
Frye, Northrop. *T.S. Eliot: An Introduction*. Chicago: U of Chicago P, 1981.
Headings, Philip R. *T.S. Eliot*. rev. ed. Boston: Hall, 1982.
Kenner, Hugh, Ed. *T.S. Eliot: A Collection of Critical Essays*. Englewood Cliffs: Prentice, 1962.
Kirk, Russell. *Eliot and His Age: T.S. Eliot's Moral Imagination in the Twentieth Century*. La Salle, IL: Sugden, 1984.
Olney, James, Ed. *T.S. Eliot: Essays from the* Southern Review. New York: Oxford UP, 1988.

Katherine Mansfield
Magalaner, Marvin. *The Fiction of Katherine Mansfield*. Carbondale: Southern Illinois UP, 1971.
Meyers, Jeffrey. *Katherine Mansfield: A Biography*. New York: New Directions, 1980.
Murry, John Middleton. Introduction. *The Short Stories of Katherine Mansfield*. New York: Ecco Press, 1983.
O'Sullivan, Vincent, Ed. *Katherine Mansfield: Selected Letters*. New York: Oxford UP, 1989.
——— and Margaret Scott, Eds. *The Collected Letters of Katherine Mansfield*. 2 vols. New York: Oxford UP, 1984, 1987.
Tomalin, Claire. *Katherine Mansfield: A Secret Life*. New York: Knopf, 1988.

NTC LANGUAGE ARTS BOOKS

Business Communication
Business Communication Today! *Thomas & Fryar*
Handbook for Business Writing, *Baugh, Fryar, & Thomas*
Meetings: Rules & Procedures, *Pohl*

Dictionaries
British/American Language Dictionary, *Moss*
NTC's Classical Dictionary, *Room*
NTC's Dictionary of Changes in Meaning, *Room*
NTC's Dictionary of Debate, *Hanson*
NTC's Dictionary of Literary Terms, *Morner & Rausch*
NTC's Dictionary of Theatre and Drama Terms, *Mobley*
NTC's Dictionary of Word Origins, *Room*
NTC's Spell It Right Dictionary, *Downing*
Robin Hyman's Dictionary of Quotations

Essential Skills
Building Real Life English Skills, *Starkey & Penn*
English Survival Series, *Maggs*
Essential Life Skills, *Starkey & Penn*
Essentials of English Grammar, *Baugh*
Essentials of Reading and Writing English Series
Grammar for Use, *Hall*
Grammar Step-by-Step, *Pratt*
Guide to Better English Spelling, *Furness*
How to be a Rapid Reader, *Redway*
How to Improve Your Study Skills, *Coman & Heavers*
NTC Skill Builders
Reading by Doing, *Simmons & Palmer*
Developing Creative & Critical Thinking, *Boostrom*
303 Dumb Spelling Mistakes, *Downing*
TIME: We the People, *ed. Schinke-Llano*
Vocabulary by Doing, *Beckert*

Genre Literature
The Detective Story, *Schwartz*
The Short Story & You, *Simmons & Stern*
Sports in Literature, *Emra*
You and Science Fiction, *Hollister*

Journalism
Getting Started in Journalism, *Harkrider*
Journalism Today! *Ferguson & Patten*
Publishing the Literary Magazine, *Klaiman*
UPI Stylebook, *United Press International*

Language, Literature, and Composition
An Anthology for Young Writers, *Meredith*
The Art of Composition, *Meredith*
Creative Writing, *Mueller & Reynolds*

Handbook for Practical Letter Writing, *Baugh*
How to Write Term Papers and Reports, *Baugh*
Literature by Doing, *Tchudi & Yesner*
Lively Writing, *Schrank*
Look, Think & Write, *Leavitt & Sohn*
Poetry by Doing, *Osborn*
World Literature, *Rosenberg*
Write to the Point! *Morgan*
The Writer's Handbook, *Karls & Szymanski*
Writing by Doing, *Sohn & Enger*
Writing in Action, *Meredith*

Media Communication
Getting Started in Mass Media, *Beckert*
Photography in Focus, *Jacobs & Kokrda*
Television Production Today! *Kirkham*
Understanding Mass Media, *Schrank*
Understanding the Film, *Bone & Johnson*

Mythology
The Ancient World, *Sawyer & Townsend*
Mythology and You, *Rosenberg & Baker*
Welcome to Ancient Greece, *Millard*
Welcome to Ancient Rome, *Millard*
World Mythology, *Rosenberg*

Speech
Activities for Effective Communication, *LiSacchi*
The Basics of Speech, *Galvin, Cooper, & Gordon*
Contemporary Speech, *HopKins & Whitaker*
Dynamics of Speech, *Myers & Herndon*
Getting Started in Public Speaking, *Prentice & Payne*
Listening by Doing, *Galvin*
Literature Alive! *Gamble & Gamble*
Person to Person, *Galvin & Book*
Public Speaking Today! *Prentice & Payne*
Speaking by Doing, *Buys, Sill, & Beck*

Theatre
Acting & Directing, *Grandstaff*
The Book of Cuttings for Acting & Directing, *Cassady*
The Book of Scenes for Acting Practice, *Cassady*
The Dynamics of Acting, *Snyder & Drumsta*
An Introduction to Modern One-Act Plays, *Cassady*
An Introduction to Theatre and Drama, *Cassady & Cassady*
Play Production Today! *Beck et al.*
Stagecraft, *Beck*

For a current catalog and information about our complete line
of language arts books, write:
National Textbook Company
a division of NTC Publishing Group
4255 West Touhy Avenue
Lincolnwood (Chicago), Illinois 60646-1975 U.S.A.